Venezuela

THE WORLD BIBLIOGRAPHICAL SERIES

This series, which is principally designed for the English speaker, will eventually cover every country in the world, each in a separate volume comprising annotated entries on works dealing with its history, geography, economy and politics; and with its people, their culture, customs, religion and social organization. Attention will also be paid to current living conditions – housing, education, newspapers, clothing, etc. – that are all too often ignored in standard bibliographies; and to those particular aspects relevant to individual countries. Each volume seeks to achieve, by use of careful selectivity and critical assessment of the literature, an expression of the country and an appreciation of its nature and national aspirations, to guide the reader towards an understanding of its importance. The keynote of the series is to provide, in a uniform format, an interpretation of each country that will express its culture, its place in the world, and the qualities and background that make it unique. The views expressed in individual volumes, however, are not necessarily those of the publisher.

VOLUMES IN THE SERIES

VOLUME 110

Venezuela

D. A. G. Waddell

Compiler

CLIO PRESS

OXFORD, ENGLAND · SANTA BARBARA, CALIFORNIA
DENVER, COLORADO

British Library Cataloguing in Publication Data

Waddell, D. A. G. (David Alan Gilmour) *1927*–
Venezuela. — (World bibliographical series, v. 110)
1. Venezuela. Bibliographies
I. Title   II. Series
016.987

ISBN 1-85109-106-8

Clio Press Ltd.,
55 St. Thomas' Street,
Oxford OX1 1JG, England.

ABC-CLIO,
130 Cremona Drive,
Santa Barbara,
CA 93117, USA.

Designed by Bernard Crossland.
Typeset by Columns Design and Production Services, Reading, England.
Printed and bound in Great Britain by
Billing and Sons Ltd., Worcester.

WORLD BIBLIOGRAPHICAL SERIES

General Editors:
Robert G. Neville (Executive Editor)
John J. Horton   Ian Wallace
Hans H. Wellisch   Ralph Lee Woodward, Jr.

John J. Horton is Deputy Librarian of the University of Bradford and currently Chairman of its Academic Board of Studies in Social Sciences. He has maintained a longstanding interest in the discipline of area studies and its associated bibliographical problems, with special reference to European Studies. In particular he has published in the field of Icelandic and of Yugoslav studies, including the two relevant volumes in the World Bibliographical Series.

Ian Wallace is Professor of Modern Languages at Loughborough University of Technology. A graduate of Oxford in French and German, he also studied in Tübingen, Heidelberg and Lausanne before taking teaching posts at universities in the USA, Scotland and England. He specializes in East German affairs, especially literature and culture, on which he has published numerous articles and books. In 1979 he founded the journal *GDR Monitor*, which he continues to edit.

Hans H. Wellisch is Professor emeritus at the College of Library and Information Services, University of Maryland. He was President of the American Society of Indexers and was a member of the International Federation for Documentation. He is the author of numerous articles and several books on indexing and abstracting, and has published *The Conversion of Scripts* and *Indexing and Abstracting: an International Bibliography*. He also contributes frequently to *Journal of the American Society for Information Science, The Indexer* and other professional journals.

Ralph Lee Woodward, Jr. is Chairman of the Department of History at Tulane University, New Orleans, where he has been Professor of History since 1970. He is the author of *Central America, a Nation Divided*, 2nd ed. (1985), as well as several monographs and more than sixty scholarly articles on modern Latin America. He has also compiled volumes in the World Bibliographical Series on *Belize* (1980), *Nicaragua* (1983), and *El Salvador* (1988). Dr. Woodward edited the Central American section of the *Research Guide to Central America and the Caribbean* (1985) and is currently editor of the Central American history section of the *Handbook of Latin American Studies*.

Contents

Contents

Introduction

Venezuela is in many ways typical of the Spanish-speaking Catholic countries of Latin America. It is a land of dramatic geographical contrasts, with a diverse society, made up of a blend of European, African and Amerindian strains. Great affluence co-exists with acute poverty, in conditions ranging from the primitive isolation of remote tribes in the interior to the international sophistication of the capital city, Caracas. However, like each of its neighbours, Venezuela has its own distinctive individuality. Most obviously, perhaps, its oil wealth has given it a comparatively high level of prosperity. This, in turn, has contributed to the maintenance of a representative two-party political system since 1958, when the last of the country's many dictators was overthrown. But every aspect of present-day Venezuela – be it wild life or the role of the church, the manufacturing industry or the electoral system, fine arts or foreign relations – derives in some way from its particular geographical location and historical evolution.

Venezuela is an entirely tropical country, situated between 1° and 12° N. and 60° and 73° W., and extending 924 miles from ESE to WNW, and 730 miles from NNE to SSW. It is bounded on the north by the Caribbean sea, on the west by Colombia, on the south by Brazil and on the east by Guyana. Its land area of 352,143 square miles (912,050 square kilometres) – roughly equivalent to France and Italy combined – comprises four major geographical regions. The dominating feature is the mountain chain, a branch of the Andes range, which stretches from the western border in a north-easterly arc, and continues as a coastal range running along the Caribbean shore to the eastern end of the country. Here, most of the population is concentrated. To the north-west of this backbone lies an area of lowland around Lake Maracaibo, which is the principal oil-producing region; and to the south are the vast plains (or *llanos*) of the Orinoco basin, alternately parched and flooded, which cover a third of the national territory with savanna and scrub woodland. The half of the country to the south of the Orinoco, the Guayana highlands, is a region of jungle and savanna, mostly populated only by small tribes of Indians, but with some important enclaves where mineral resources are exploited.

Pre-Columbian Venezuela did not produce anything comparable to the ancient civilizations of the Incas or the Aztecs, and seems rather to have been on the fringes of the Andean cultures in one direction and the Caribbean cultures in the other. Compared with the empires of Mexico and Peru, it offered few immediate attractions to the Spanish adventurers who first appeared on its shores around 1500. Its early development was slow, retarded rather than advanced by the lure of the mythical El Dorado; Caracas was not founded until 1567, and was the centre of a very modest colony producing a few plantation crops, principally cacao. In the seventeenth century, slave labour imported from Africa tended to replace the forced labour of the conquered Indians, who, in the settled area of the mountain chain, were gradually assimilated by miscegenation. In areas where the Spaniards did not settle – the Guayana highlands, the swampy delta of the Orinoco, and the sierras near the Guajira peninsula in the extreme north-west – Indian tribes survived and continue to survive in their traditional manner. One jungle group, the Yanomami, has remained so uncontaminated by contact with civilization that it has attracted intense interest from anthropologists.

Towards the end of the eighteenth century, Spanish imperial reforms began to stimulate the South American economy and to stir up change in the rather static colonial society. As a result, enhanced self-confidence and self-consciousness developed in some sectors of the population, which reacted in a revolutionary manner to the occupation of Spain and the usurpation of its monarchy by Napoleonic France in 1808–10. Venezuela was in the forefront of the independence movement, providing both its principal precursor and propagandist, Francisco de Miranda, and its greatest military and political figure, Simón Bolívar, and being the first colony both to repudiate imperial authority (19 April 1810) and to declare independence (5 July 1811). Spanish rule was twice restored before it was finally thrown off following the battle of Carabobo (24 June 1821). Independence was consummated within the context of the union of Gran Colombia, consisting of Venezuela, Colombia and Ecuador, which lasted from 1819 until 1830.

Venezuela entered on its career as a separate republic under the leadership of José Antonio Páez, a revolutionary general who ran the country, directly or indirectly, until 1848, in collaboration with the coffee planters, who had become the dominant economic interest group. The succeeding régime, that of the Monagas brothers (1848–58), degenerated into an unprincipled dictatorship, and was followed by a period of faction fights and civil wars, until the emergence of a new strong man in the person of Antonio Guzmán Blanco (1870–88). He called himself the 'civilizing autocrat' and was responsible for attracting foreign investment to build railways and to modernize the capital. A further period of instability supervened until 1899, when Cipriano Castro led a band of followers from the remote Andean state of Táchira to take over the capital and install a 'dynasty' of generals who ruled the country for most of the next sixty years. Of these, the most effective was the ruthless dictator, Juan Vicente Gómez (1908–35), whose rule saw the development of the oil industry, which was to dominate the economy thereafter. His successors gradually relaxed their grip, and mass political participation began with the formation of the *Acción Democrática* (AD) party in the 1940s. A brief experiment in democratic government was abruptly brought to a halt by a military coup in 1948, leading to the dictatorship of Marcos Pérez Jiménez which lasted until 1958.

Since then, a democratic constitutional two-party system has established itself, overcoming many difficult hurdles in the early years. The first milestone was the handing over of the presidency by the democratically elected Rómulo Betancourt (1959–63) to his democratically elected successor Raúl Leoni (1964–68); and the second, the handing over by AD's Leoni to a duly elected successor, Rafael Caldera (1969–73), from the opposing Christian democratic (COPEI) party. Power changed hands again in each of the next three elections, Carlos Andrés Pérez (AD, 1974–78) being followed by Luis Herrera Campins (COPEI, 1979–83) and Jaime Lusinchi (AD, 1984–88), but AD retained power in 1989, when Carlos Andrés Pérez embarked on a second term.

The democratic period has been marked by a growing independence in Venezuela's external relations. In the nineteenth century, the republic had little bargaining power against the developed European nations, and had to accept what little it was offered, over both commerce and its claims to part of the adjacent territory of British Guiana. In the early 1900s, Cipriano Castro, who tried to defy the powers, suffered humiliation and blockade; under Gómez the international oil companies began to 'call the tune'; and in the 1940s and 1950s the United States expected conformity to its hemispheric policies. In the 1960s, however, Venezuela joined with other oil producers to create in OPEC a body capable of defending their interests; in 1975, it nationalized its oil industry, and more recently it has increased its links with Caribbean and Central American countries and organizations. Its revived claim to the territory of its now independent neighbour, Guyana, however, remains unresolved.

The population of Venezuela at the last census in 1981 was 14,516,735; an official estimate in 1986 put it at 17,791,412; and the

United Nations projection for 1990 was 19,735,000. Two-thirds of Venezuelans are of mixed race, mainly *mestizo* (mixed European and Indian); some twenty per cent are of European origin, and are mostly to be found in the cities; around ten per cent are of African origin, and live, largely, along the Caribbean coast; and only about two per cent are pure Indian, these being mainly confined to the more remote areas.

Urbanization has been a significant factor in the social changes of the last half-century, which has seen a steady migration of the rural population to the cities. Now, over eighty per cent of Venezuelans live in urban areas, and of these over 3,000,000 are concentrated in Caracas. The capital city developed at the head of a fertile valley enclosed by steep mountains. All the farm land has long since been swallowed up in new developments, and the increasingly crowded *barrios* (urban districts) of the poor, perched precariously on the surrounding slopes, proliferate further and further from the centre. Other cities of the north-central highlands, such as Valencia (ca. 1,000,000), Maracay (over 800,000) and Barquisimeto (ca. 700,000) have also grown, as well as Maracaibo (over 1,250,000) in the west and Barcelona/Puerto La Cruz (ca. 400,000) in the east; and particularly notable has been the development, since the 1960s, of the new city of Ciudad Guayana (nearly 500,000) on the Orinoco, based on the mineral wealth and hydroelectric power of the Caroní river area.

A birth rate of 33 per 1,000, against a death rate of less than 6 per 1,000, has meant an annual increase of almost three per cent and a population over half of which is under twenty years of age. This has posed problems for the democratic régimes, which have been committed to the promotion of welfare and the expansion of educational opportunity, but on the whole the social achievements of the last thirty years have been quite impressive. For example, eighty-seven per cent of the adult population is now literate; life expectancy is sixty-eight years; and the proportion of the national budget devoted to education rose from 6.3 per cent in 1958 to 15.7 per cent in 1981.

Since the time of Gómez, the Venezuelan economy has been dominated by oil. Venezuelan leaders have long realized that they cannot permanently rely on a finite resource such as petroleum, and have sought to diversify through industrial development and agrarian reform. As a result, the industrial sector, including construction, now accounts for twenty-three per cent of the work force. The country can now produce many of its own requirements in manufactures, and is developing the metallurgical base for heavy industry in the Guayana interior. On the other hand, agrarian reform, originally undertaken to satisfy the land hunger of the *campesinos* (peasants) and to retard the drift to the cities, did no more than scratch the surface of both problems before giving way in the face of the pressures of profit-oriented agribusiness. Only fourteen per cent of the labour force is now on the land, compared with forty-five per cent in the 1950s. In spite of efforts to develop other sectors, the country remains heavily dependent on oil and petroleum products, which still account for over ninety per cent of exports, although the industry employs only about 50,000 people directly. This dependence was reflected in lavish spending during the bonanza of high international oil prices in the 1970s, and in austerity measures during the traumatic debt crisis in the 1980s. Riots in early 1989 in response to price rises, in which hundreds of lives were lost, were a sharp reminder that the social peace and political stability of the previous quarter-century had owed much to the maintenance of a high standard of living (at least in Latin American terms), and that the gross disparities between rich and poor, blatantly obvious in everyday life in Caracas, might not be endured indefinitely.

In the cultural sphere, Venezuela's achievements are less marked, in comparison with the rest of Latin America, than in the political and economic. It has produced neither a Neruda, an Orozco, nor a Villa-Lobos. To some extent this reflects the values of the society, which tend toward the materialistic, the practical and the immediate, rather than the spiritual, the reflective and the transcendental. It is true that the most famous of all Latin American novels is Rómulo Gallegos's *Doña Bárbara*. But Gallegos's works, for all their literary merit, may be said to have a significance which is as much socio-political as artistic – as might be expected from an author who became President of the Republic. Similarly, it is not surprising that Villanueva's architecture, combining utilitarian and aesthetic considerations, should be Venezuela's most striking contribution in the realm of modern art. It might, however, be fanciful to suggest that the extreme rapidity of Venezuelan speech is a manifestation of a certain temperamental impatience.

These are, however, characteristics that have produced a vibrant 'go-getting' society, which in few respects conforms to the Anglo-Saxon stereotype of the Latin American way of life. Venezuela has come a long way in the short time since the ending of authoritarian rule released the creative energies of its people, and it has demonstrated that it has the human and material resources to make an ever greater impact in the Caribbean, in South America, and in the world at large.

The bibliography

This book, in accordance with the norms of the series of which it forms a part, is designed as a selective annotated bibliography for English-language readers. The literature in English on Venezuela is not vast, and it has proved possible to include virtually all the English-language publications, on every aspect of Venezuela, that appeared to be of real importance or enduring usefulness. This has been the main criterion for selection. It has meant, on the one hand, a certain amount of duplication of coverage. No attempt has been made to pick only the best book on a particular subject: rather, wherever possible, several alternatives have been included, since many items are available in some libraries but not in others. On the other hand, it has involved the omission of many items that have seemed of only ephemeral significance, or of interest only to specialists. Also excluded, of course, is the great bulk of what has been written about Venezuela in the language of the country. In view of the intended readership, works in Spanish have generally been included only where there is a substantial amount of material which is intelligible with a very limited knowledge of the language – for example, in the form of illustrations, tables, diagrams, statistics or lists. In a few sections, however, such as science, sport and media, where there is little or no published work in English, some more solid Spanish-language items will be found. The inevitable result is a degree of subject imbalance, reflecting the fact that some topics, such as travel, history and anthropology, have generated much more writing in English than others.

The arrangement is analytical, but the allocation of a particular item to one subject section rather than another (for example, a study of agricultural education to agriculture rather than education) has necessarily been arbitrary. In view of the high proportion of works with relevance to two or more subject sections, no cross-referencing has been made between sections. Thus it is essential to use the subject index as well as the table of contents to find all the material on any topic. It is also important to note that the items in each section have been arranged alphabetically by author and *not* in order of importance or preference. Works in the same section by the same author have been arranged alphabetically by title, with those of sole authorship preceding those of joint. Bibliographies on particular subjects have been included in the appropriate subject sections, only more general bibliographical works appearing in the bibliography section. In view of the availability of a recent list of dissertations (no. 814), no section on unpublished theses has been included.

Acknowledgements

It is a pleasure to express my gratitude to those institutions and individuals who helped in the preparation of this book.

These are: the Carnegie Trust for the Universities of Scotland for two research grants, which contributed towards travel and maintenance on visits to libraries in London; the British Academy for an award which assisted with travel to Spain and maintenance both there and in the United States and Venezuela; the British Council for funding a lecturing visit to Venezuela, which enabled me to extend my research to the libraries there; and the University of Stirling for a contribution to subsistence expenses in Caracas.

The staff in the libraries where I worked – in London, the British Library, London University Senate House and Institute for Latin American Studies, University College London, the Hispanic and Luso-Brazilian Council, and the Venezuelan Embassy; in Spain, the Biblioteca Nacional, the Instituto de Cooperación Iberoamericana, and the Escuela de Estudios Hispanoamericanos; in Venezuela, the Biblioteca Nacional and Hemeroteca Nacional, the Universidad Central, the Instituto Venezolano de Investigaciones Científicas, the British Embassy, and the Fundación John Boulton; in the United States, the Boston Public Library and the Widener and other libraries of Harvard University; and the Library of my own University of Stirling – who met the many demands made on them promptly and courteously.

My friends Fernando Murillo and Pedro J. Grases, who smoothed my way in Madrid and Caracas respectively; Giles Fitzherbert, British Ambassador to Venezuela and Stephen Garner-Winship of the British Council there, whose assistance went far beyond the call of duty; Luis Castro Leiva, Hermán González Oropeza, Francine Jacome, Ildefonso Leal, Angelina Pollak-Eltz, Oscar Sambrano Urdaneta, and Andrés Serbín, who assisted me in various ways in Caracas; fellow series authors Alan Biggins, Harold Blakemore, and Henry Finch, for valuable advice; Robert Neville and Rachel Houghton of Clio Press for considerate editorship; and my wife Barbara, for her support throughout the enterprise, and in particular for undertaking much tedious catalogue work in Spain and Massachusetts.

D. A. G. Waddell
University of Stirling
November 1989.

The Country and its People

1 **Area handbook for Venezuela.**
Howard I. Blutstein (et al.). Washington, DC: US Government
Printing Office, 1977. 3rd ed. 354p. bibliog. (American University,
Foreign Area Studies Handbook).

A comprehensive general survey of the country in 1976, which has chapters on
geography, history, society, culture, the economy, government, politics and external
relations, internal security and the armed forces, and numerous tables.

2 **Venezuela in pictures.**
Prepared by Lincoln A. Boehm. Minneapolis, Minnesota: Lerner, 1987.
64p. (Visual Geography Series).

A well-illustrated introduction to the country, designed for older children, covering
land, history, people, economy and government.

3 **Venezuela.**
Charles Brewer-Carías. Caracas: Editorial Arte for Oficina Central de
Información, 1975.

A collection of 138 magnificent colour photographs illustrating the different regions of
the country, its people, and its flora and fauna, by a distinguished explorer and
naturalist.

4 **Cocks and bulls in Caracas. How we live in Venezuela.**
Olga Briceño, illustrated by Kay Peterson Parker. Boston,
Massachusetts: Houghton, Mifflin, 1945. 161p.

Offers a charming commentary on traditional home and family life in upper-class
circles in the 1940s.

1

5 **Impresiones de Venezuela.** (Impressions of Venezuela.)
   Wenzel Fischer. Caracas: Santiago, 1977. [n.p.].

One hundred and seventy-four colour photographs, illustrating the landscape, flora and fauna, people and places, give a vivid cross-sectional view of the country and the various lifestyles of its people.

6 **Venezuela: land of opportunity.**
   Alfred P. Jankus, Neil M. Malloy. New York: Pageant, 1956. 259p.
   bibliog.

Sketches history, geography, customs, and the economy, and gives information regarding living conditions and business opportunities during the Pérez Jiménez régime of the 1950s.

7 **Caracas everyday.**
   Dorothy Kamen-Kaye. Caracas: Editorial Elite, 1947. 256p.

Reprints articles originally published in a column entitled 'A Woman's Angle' in an English-language newspaper, *Caracas Journal*, between February 1945 and September 1947. Together, they provide a valuable and charming record by a sensitive observer of day-to-day life in Venezuela.

8 **Speaking of Venezuela.**
   Edited by Dorothy Kamen-Kaye. Caracas: Editorial Elite, 1947. 248p.
   bibliog.

A collection of pieces by various authors, originally published in the English-language newspaper, *Caracas Journal*, which are classified under the headings: 'Caracas', 'Historic and Cultural', 'All over Venezuela' and 'Matters of Fact'.

9 **Venezuela.**
   Herbert Kirchoff. Buenos Aires: Kraft, 1956. 131p.

A collection of black-and-white photographs, with captions in Spanish and English, illustrating Caracas (where the main emphasis is on the new architecture of the 1950s), the various regions of the country, and the petroleum industry.

10 **Venezuela.**
   Edwin Lieuwen. London: Oxford University Press, for Royal Institute of International Affairs, 1965. 2nd ed. 211p. bibliog. 3 maps.

This was an excellent introductory survey in its day; it is now, inevitably, somewhat out of date, though not yet superseded. It covers geography, history, economics, politics and international relations, and concludes with an assessment of the Betancourt government of 1959 to 1964.

11 **Bellermann y el paisaje venezolano, 1842-1845.** (Bellermann and the Venezuelan countryside, 1842-45.)
   Renate Löschner. Caracas: Editorial Arte, 1977. 119p. bibliog.

Fine reproductions of eighty-two striking drawings and paintings by the German artist Ferdinand Bellermann, who visited Venezuela in 1842-45, illustrating the appearance of the country, its architecture and its vegetation in the mid-nineteenth century.

Löschner's introduction gives an account, in German and Spanish, of the painter, his travels and his works.

12 **Venezuela.**
Marion Morrison. New York: Chelsea House, 1987. 96p.

A brief illustrated introduction to the country for younger children, covering geography, history, economic and social conditions and prospects. It may be said to supersede *Let's visit Venezuela*, by John C. Caldwell (New York: John Day, 1962), which covered much the same ground on a similar scale.

13 **Caracas: una quimera urbana.** (Caracas: an urban chimera.)
Ramón Paolini. Caracas: Editorial Arte, 1985. 101p.

A sequence of black-and-white photographs which display remarkable images of Caracas and its architecture.

14 **In search of the jaguar.**
Stan Steiner. New York: Times Books, 1979. 187p.

In quest of the 'soul' of Venezuela, a perceptive American journalist made a circuit of the country at the height of the petroleum boom of the 1970s. He reports his conversations with, for example, oilmen in Maracaibo, planners in Guayana, a bishop, a feminist, and a playwright, and gives his impressions of the people of the coast, the cities, the delta, the *llanos*, and the mountains, in a series of vivid vignettes.

15 **Pueblos: Venezuela 1979-1984.** (Towns: Venezuela 1979-84.)
Martín Vegas, Ramón Paolini, Federico Vegas. Caracas: Fundación Polar, 1984. 152p.

A collection of fine colour photographs of small towns, mainly in the north-east and north-west of the country, illustrating their streets, buildings, houses and people.

16 **Fascinating Venezuela.**
Karl Weidmann. Caracas: Oscar Todtmann, 1987. 166p.

This collection of colour photographs, with an introduction and captions in English, Spanish and German, is divided into sections covering Caracas, the east, the south and the west of the country. It gives a contemporary picture of architecture, landscape, flora and fauna, and people and places.

17 **The Caribbean: Venezuelan development, a case history.**
Edited by A. Curtis Wilgus. Gainesville, Florida: University of Florida Press, 1963. 301p. bibliog. (The Caribbean Conference Series, vol. 13).

Now perhaps primarily of historical interest, at the time of publication this represented a convenient English-language distillation of the wisdom of the leading Venezuelan experts in various fields. It comprises an introduction by the editor, and papers on: background, by Guillermo Zuloaga, Irving Rouse, and Arturo Uslar Pietri; education, by Lorenzo Monroy, Francisco de Venanzi, and Santiago Vera Izquierdo; the public sector, by Alejandro Oropeza Castillo, Benito Raúl Losada, Enrique Tejera París, Eugenio Mendoza, and Teodoro Moscoso; the private sector of the economy, by Peter R. Nehemkis, Jr., Armando Branger, Gustavo J. Vollmer, John F. Gallagher, Harry A. Jarvis, and Harry W. Jones; and on agrarian reform, by Eduardo Mendoza G.,

Víctor Manuel Giménez Landínez, Armando González, and Gastón Vivas Berthier. There is a bibliography by Nettie Lee Benson.

18 **The land and people of Venezuela.**
Raymond A. Wohlrabe, Werner E. Krausch. Philadelphia; New York: Lippincott, 1959. 124p. (Portraits of the Nations Series).

Sketches the history and geography of the country, and its political and economic state in 1959.

Geography

General

19 **Central America, the West Indies and South America.**
Edited and extended by Henry Walter Bates, translated by A.H.
Keane. London: Edward Stanford, 1878. 571p. (Stanford's
Compendium of Geography and Travel).
An adaptation of the work of the German geographer Von Hellwald, with an
ethnological appendix by Keane. Chapter IV (p. 220-24) describes the mountain
systems of Venezuela; Chapter V (p. 225-35) deals with the *llanos* and the Orinoco
area; and Chapter XII (p. 303-16) discusses climate and vegetation, and economic,
cultural and political matters.

20 **Geologic structure and orogenic history of Venezuela.**
Walter Herman Bucher. New York: Geological Society of America,
1952. 113p. bibliog. (Memoir Series, no. 49).
Bucher provides text, to accompany his geologic tectonic map of Venezuela, consisting
of a region-by-region description of the country's geology.

21 **Latin America: an economic and social geography.**
J.P. Cole. London: Butterworths, 1975. 2nd ed. 470p.
In addition to numerous references to the country in the ten analytical chapters, there
is a chapter devoted to Venezuela (p. 339-58), which includes ten tables and seven
figures.

22 **Venezuela: search for a middle ground.**
Raymond E. Crist, Edward P. Leahy. New York; Toronto; London:
Van Nostrand Reinhold, 1969. 128p. bibliog. (Van Nostrand Searchlight
Books).
Briefly outlines the physical, social and economic geography of the country, and its
geopolitical significance in the Western hemisphere.

23 **Resources and territories in the possible Venezuela.**
Pedro Cunill Grau, translated by Iraida Rodríguez Roussú, Emilia
Jiménez G. Caracas: Lagoven, 1987. 110p. bibliog.
This well-illustrated study of the advantages of the country's tropical location, and of
the possibilities of sustained self-sufficient development offered by the diversity of its
regions, is a work of popularization by a professor of geography. One of the major
themes is set out more fully in the author's *The territorial diversity, base of the
Venezuelan development* (Caracas: Lagoven, 1984. 125p.).

24 **Latin America.**
Preston Everett James, C.W. Minkel. New York; Chichester,
England; Toronto: John Wiley, 1986. 5th ed. 578p. 7 maps. bibliog.
Chapter twenty (p. 272-92) of this standard geographical text covers Venezuela, both
generally and by region.

25 **The geology of Venezuela and Trinidad.**
Ralph Alexander Liddle. Fort Worth, Texas: MacGowan, 1928. 552p.
bibliog.
Based on extensive field work in the 1920s, this work describes the physiographic
regions of the country, its geological history and structure, and its economic geology.

26 **Colombia and Venezuela.**
David James Robinson, Alan Gilbert. In: *Latin America: geographical
perspectives*. Edited by Harold Blakemore, Clifford T. Smith. London;
New York: Methuen, 1983, 2nd ed., p. 187-240. 10 maps.
A succinct analysis of the physical, historical and economic geography of the two
countries, which treats them both individually and in comparative terms.

27 **Stratigraphical lexicon of Venezuela.**
Venezuela. Ministerio de Minas e Hidrocarburos, Dirección de
Geología. Caracas: Editorial Sucre, 1956. 664p. bibliog. (Boletín de
Geología. Special Publication, no. 1).
Consists of 400 articles on different stratigraphic units, with chronological and
alphabetical lists, prepared by thirty-three contributors, and edited by a board headed
by Armando Schwarck Anglade.

28 **Diccionario de tierras y aguas de Venezuela.** (Dictionary of the lands and waters of Venezuela.)
Marco Aurelio Vila. Caracas: Ministerio de Obras Públicas, Dirección de Cartografía Nacional, 1976. 290p.
Gives an alphabetically arranged list of short descriptive entries relating to rivers, mountains, lakes, islands, valleys, waterfalls etc.

29 **Vocabulario geográfico de Venezuela.** (Geographical vocabulary of Venezuela.)
Marco Aurelio Vila. Caracas: Corporación Venezolana de Fomento, 1971. 400p.
A dictionary of the specialised terms which are used in Venezuelan geographical description.

Regional

30 **The geography of Margarita and adjacent islands, Venezuela.**
Charles S. Alexander. Berkeley, California; Los Angeles: University of California Press, 1958. 193p. bibliog. (University of California Publications in Geography, vol. 12, no. 2).
A systematic scholarly study of Venezuela's largest island, covering physiography, climate, vegetation, population and occupations, with an appendix listing cultivated plants.

31 **Los páramos se van quedando solos.** (The mountains: a region neglected.)
Bárbara Brändli. Caracas: Editorial Arte, 1981. 2nd ed. 220p.
A collection of excellent photographs, illustrating how the 'march of progress' has tended to by-pass the bleak high plateau land of the Andean mountain area and its inhabitants. There is a commentary in Spanish, taking the form of interviews with local people.

32 **The lost world of Venezuela and its vegetation.**
Charles Brewer-Carías. Caracas: Cromotip, 1987. 225p.
A magnificent collection of colour photographs illustrating the topography and vegetation of southern Venezuela.

33 **Along the *llanos*-Andes border in Venezuela: then and now.**
Raymond E. Crist. *Geographical Review*, vol. 46, no. 2 (1956), p. 187-208.
Discusses the geology, climate, population and economic activities of the region around Barinas, making interesting comparisons between the situation in the 1950s and

7

that at the time of his earlier exploration of the area, reported in his 'Along the *llanos*-Andes border in Zamora, Venezuela', *Geographical Review*, vol. 22 (1932), p. 411-22.

34 **Westward thrusts the pioneer zone in Venezuela: a half-century of economic development along the *llanos*-Andes border.**
Raymond E. Crist. *American Journal of Economics and Sociology*, vol. 42, no. 3 (1983), p. 451-62.

Shows how highway construction, public education and health services, farm credits and subsidies, and improvements in land titles and agricultural techniques have transformed the Barinas area.

35 **Changing patterns of land use in the Valencia lake basin of Venezuela.**
Raymond E. Crist, Carlos E. Chardon. *Geographical Review*, vol. 31, no. 3 (1941), p. 430-43.

Discusses the physical setting, climate, historic land use, and planning opportunities of the basin, and the fluctuating level of the lake itself.

36 **Technology and tradition: regional and urban development in Guayana.**
John R. Dinkelspiel. *Inter-American Economic Affairs*, vol. 23, no. 4 (1970), 47-79.

Argues that the preference for high-technology and capital-intensive projects over considerations of social welfare, which characterised the development programme for the Guayana area, owed more to Venezuelan political, social and institutional traditions than to the influence of foreign investors and technical experts.

37 **Geographical Review.**
Vol. 21, no. 3 (1931).

Includes 'The Pacaraima-Venezuela expedition', by H.E. Anthony (et al.) (p. 353-62); 'Problems of the Roraima-Duida region as presented by the bird life', by Frank M. Chapman (p. 363-72); and 'Notes on an exploratory journey in southeastern Venezuela' by Desmond Holdridge (p. 373-78). All three papers deal with the extreme south-east of the country.

38 **The Orinoco-Ventauri region, Venezuela.**
Charles B. Hitchcock. *Geographical Review*, vol. 37, no. 4 (1947), p. 525-66.

Presents the report of an expedition in 1947, describing the country traversed, vegetation, wildlife, inhabitants, natural resources, and transportation, with appendices on ornithology, geology and climate.

39 **The Sierra de Perijá, Venezuela.**
Charles B. Hitchcock. *Geographical Review*, vol. 44, no. 1 (1954), p. 1-28.

Reports on the changes to the region between 1918, when it was described in Theodoor De Booy's 'An exploration of the Sierra de Perijá, Venezuela' and 'The western Maracaibo lowland, Venezuela', *Geographical Review*, vol. 6, no. 5, 6 (1918), p. 385-410, 481-500, and the author's expedition in 1953. Twenty-six photographs are included.

40 **Bailadores: an agro-social study of a rural Venezuelan region.**
Earl Jones, Luis Ocando, Juan Guevara. Caracas: Fundación La Salle
de Ciencias Naturales, Instituto Caribe de Antropología y Sociología,
1964. 192p. bibliog. (*Antropológica* Supplement, no. 3).
A general survey of the administrative area of Bailadores, in the Andean state of
Mérida, which is based on field and library research carried out by a large team in
1964. It covers physiography, agriculture, family composition and housing, customs
and beliefs, and social organization.

41 **Cerro de la Neblina, Amazonas, Venezuela: a newly discovered sandstone
mountain.**
Bassett Maguire. *Geographical Review*, vol. 45, no. 1 (1955), p. 27-51.
This account of the discovery and ascent of the mountain close to the Brazilian border,
in 1953-54, also offers thirteen illustrations, and appendices on nomenclature, ecology,
geology and climate.

42 **The peasant farmhouse: continuity and change in the Venezuelan Andes.**
Luise Margolies. *Boletín del Centro de Investigaciones Históricas y
Estéticas* [Caracas], no. 22 (1977), p. 82-124.
Traces the history of Andean rural dwellings from pre-colonial times to the twentieth
century, and notes the gradual disappearance of the traditional farmhouse, a result of
outward migration. It is illustrated by sixteen pages of photographs.

43 **Stratigraphy and structure of the Goajira peninsula, northwestern
Venezuela and northeastern Colombia.**
John F. Rollins. Lincoln, Nebraska: University of Nebraska Press,
1965. 102p. bibliog. (University of Nebraska Studies: New Series,
no. 30).
Describes the geology of the peninsula, a small coastal strip of which is Venezuelan.
Seventeen detailed stratigraphic sections illustrate the piece.

44 **The ecology of neotropical savannas.**
Guillermo Sarmiento, translated by Otto Solbrig. Cambridge,
Massachusetts; London: Harvard University Press, 1984. 235p. bibliog.
The *llanos* area of Venezuela is the source of much of the data for this ecological
analysis of the savanna, defined as a type of ecosystem of warm tropical lowlands,
dominated by bunch grasses and sedges with clear seasonal variations.

45 **The Cerro Duida region of Venezuela.**
G.H.H. Tate, Charles B. Hitchcock. *Geographical Review*, vol. 20,
no. 1 (1930), p. 32-52.
An account of the geography of the region is offered by members of the first
expedition to reach the summit of Mount Duida and to study its ecology.

46 **Economic backwardness in the Venezuelan Andes. A study of the traditional sector of the dual economy.**
R.F. Watters. *Pacific Viewpoint* [Wellington, New Zealand], vol. 8, no. 1 (1967), p. 17-67.

This interesting analysis of the problems of very low productivity and standards of living in Andean rural areas is based on detailed case studies of sample communities. It concludes that the major causes – archaic technology, inadequate land tenure, and the peasant's stubborn attachment to his little plot of land – require remedies encompassing sociological, cultural and institutional factors, rather than purely economic ones.

47 **An exploration of the Río de Oro, Colombia-Venezuela.**
H. Case Willcox. *Geographical Review*, vol. 11, no. 3 (1921), p. 372-83.

Describes a journey between the Río Magdalena in Colombia and Lake Maracaibo in 1920, and the mapping of the Río de Oro, the course of which was followed for most of the way.

Atlases

48 **Latin American history. A teaching atlas.**
Cathryn L. Lombardi, John V. Lombardi. Madison, Wisconsin; London: University of Wisconsin Press, 1983. 104p. bibliog.

Includes: analytical maps of the whole of Latin America, and of its constituent parts; maps illustrating boundary disputes; and comparative figures on various aspects of populations, economies and societies in recent times.

49 **Atlas geográfico y económico (Venezuela visualizada).** (Geographic and economic atlas [Venezuela pictorialized].)
Leví Marrero. Caracas: Editorial Cultural Venezolana, 1978. 243p.

A collection of pictorial maps of Venezuela and of each individual state, with numerous diagrams, charts, statistics and photographs covering all aspects of activity. A nine-page supplement, *Venezuela en cifras* (Venezuela in figures), gives a summary of geographical, demographic and economic statistics for the mid 1970s.

50 **Atlas de Venezuela y del mundo.** (Atlas of Venezuela and the world.)
Prepared by Técnicas Educativas. Caracas: Teduca, 1981. 214p.

Intended both for schools and for the general public, this atlas devotes p. 25-56 to Venezuela. In addition to a series of maps covering the various regions of the country, there are climatic and economic tables relating to each area, and maps of the national geology, climate, vegetation, population, minerals, energy sources, agriculture, industry and ethnology.

Description and Travel

Nineteenth century

51 **Notes on Colombia, taken in the years 1822-3. With an itinerary of the route from Caracas to Bogotá and an appendix. By an officer of the United States' army.**
Richard Bache.   Philadelphia: Carey & Lea, 1827. 303p.
A record, presented in diary form, of the journey on which the writer accompanied William Duane, author of *A visit to Colombia* (q.v.). It contains well-observed details of places and people. The appendix gives information on the republic's commercial relations, its products and its exports.

52 **The voyage of the U.S. schooner *Nonsuch* up the Orinoco: journal of the Perry mission of 1819 to South America.**
Edited by Maury Baker.   *Hispanic American Historical Review*, vol. 30, no. 4 (1950), p. 480-98.
The diary reproduced here was kept by the American warship's chaplain, and describes the journey up the Orinoco, the city of Angostura, and many of the personalities of the revolutionary government based there in 1819. There is a brief introduction by the editor.

53 **Venezuela: a visit to the gold mines of Guyana, and a voyage up the river Orinoco during 1886, with a brief sketch of the mineral wealth and resources of Venezuela, and its history to the present time. With a map of the mines; and appendices containing the mining laws of Venezuela, report on the mines by the minister of war, extract from British consular reports, and an outline of the clauses of treaties under which Great Britain claims certain territories on the Essequibo.**
William Barry. London: Marshall, 1886. 159p.

Records a visit undertaken as the representative of British investors in a failed Venezuelan gold mine, and describes the journey from England via Trinidad and the Orinoco to Ciudad Bolívar and the mining area of El Callao, with digressions on geography, history, topography, the customs of the country, and the boundary dispute. The appendices comprise seventy-eight pages.

54 **Venezuela: a land where it's always summer.**
William Eleroy Curtis. London: Osgood, McIlvaine, 1896. 315p.

Offers descriptions by a late-nineteenth century American traveller, covering geography, history, politics, society, and agriculture. The main focus is on Caracas, but La Guayra, Puerto Cabello and Ciudad Bolívar are also taken in. Curtis concludes with a discussion of the Guiana boundary dispute, and an appendix of diplomatic correspondence on the subject.

55 **Recollections of four years in Venezuela.**
Charles Daniel Dance. London: Henry S. King, 1876. 303p.

Describes life in and around Maturín, and a journey to Ciudad Bolívar, in the 1850s.

56 **A statistical, commercial and political description of Venezuela, Trinidad, Margarita and Tobago: containing various anecdotes and observations, illustrative of the past and present state of these interesting countries; from the French of M. Lavaysse, with an introduction and explanatory notes by the editor.**
Jean François Dauxion Lavaysse, edited by Edward Blaquière.
London: Whittaker, 1820; Reprinted, Westport, Connecticut: Negro Universities Press, Greenwood, 1969. 479p.

First published in Paris in 1813, this is based on travels in the first decade of the nineteenth century. Half of the volume focuses on Venezuela, and consists of: a historical sketch and geographical description of the various provinces of Venezuela; a discussion of the customs of the inhabitants; an account of animal and plant life; and comments on its trade, both legal and contraband, at the end of the colonial period. There is a modern Spanish edition of the original French text, entitled *Viaje a las islas de Trinidad, Tobago, Margarita y a diversas partes de Venezuela en la América meridional*, translated and introduced by Angelina Lemmo, (Caracas: Universidad Central de Venezuela, Instituto de Antropología e Historia, 1967. 400p.).

57 **Three gringos in Venezuela and Central America.**
Richard Harding Davis.   New York: Harper, 1896. 282p.
Only the last chapter, 'The Paris of South America', deals with Venezuela, but the description of Caracas, its inhabitants, and its relations with the United States, by an American novelist and travel writer, is elegant and penetrating.

58 **A voyage to the eastern part of Terra Firma, or the Spanish Main, in South America, during the years 1801, 1802, 1803 and 1804. Containing a description of the territory under the jurisdiction of the Captain-General of Caraccas, composed of the provinces of Venezuela, Maracaibo, Varinas, Spanish Guiana, Cumana, and the island of Margaretta; and embracing every thing relative to the discovery, conquest, topography, legislation, commerce, finance, inhabitants and productions of the provinces, together with a view of the manners and customs of the Spaniards, and the savage as well as civilized Indians.**
François Depons.   New York: Riley, 1806. 3 vols.
A translation of the Paris edition of 1806, this represents the first complete study of the country ever published. It includes chapters on discovery and settlement; geography; population, manners and customs; indigenous Indians; civil, military and religious organization; agriculture; commerce; taxation; and descriptions of the towns, of Guayana and of the Orinoco. A good Spanish edition of the original French text is *Viaje a la parte oriental de Tierra Firme en la América meridional*, translated by Enrique Planchart, and introduced by Pedro Grases (Caracas: Banco Central de Venezuela, 1960. 2 vols. [Colección histórico-económico venezolana, vol. IV]).

59 **A visit to Colombia, in the years 1822 & 1823, by Laguayra and Caracas, over the cordillera to Bogota, and thence by the Magdalena to Cartagena.**
William Duane.   Philadelphia: Thomas Palmer, 1826. 632p.
A 'conversational narrative', by an early American supporter of Spanish American independence, of a journey undertaken in pursuit of the settlement of claims by parties in the United States against the government of the Colombian republic, of which Venezuela then formed part. It includes many details about the countryside, and anecdotes about the revolutionary wars.

60 **Venezuela: or sketches of life in a South American republic; with the history of the loan of 1864.**
Edward B. Eastwick.   London: Chapman & Hall, 1868. 2nd ed. 418p.
The author visited Venezuela in 1864, as financial commissioner for the London finance company responsible for the loan of that year; chapter six gives an account of his negotiations. The final two chapters and several appendices deal with the resources of the country and its international indebtedness. The rest of the book is self-confessed 'chit-chat' about the places he visited, including Caracas, La Guaira, Puerto Cabello and Valencia, and the persons he encountered, including President Falcón. Some of these chapters were first published in *All the Year Round*, a weekly journal edited by Charles Dickens.

61　**Venezuela, el más bello país tropical.** (Venezuela, the most beautiful tropical land.)
Anton Goering, translated by María Luisa G. de Blay.　Mérida, Venezuela: Universidad de los Andes, 1962. 172p.

The author was a German painter and naturalist, who spent the years 1864-74 in Venezuela collecting specimens of birds and animals for the Zoological Society of London. This account of his travels was originally published in Leipzig in 1893, with the title, *Vom tropischen tieflande zum ewisen schnee*, lavishly illustrated with twelve charming watercolours (all reproduced here) and sixty-four drawings (twenty-eight reproduced here).

62　**Reminiscences of South America: from two and a half years' residence in Venezuela.**
John Hawkshaw.　London: Jackson & Walford, 1838. 260p.

The author was in Venezuela from 1832 to 1834, as an engineer at the copper mines of Aroa. He describes Aroa, La Guaira, Caracas, Puerto Cabello, Tucacas, Valencia, Maracay and Barquisimeto, and comments on people, customs, plants, animals, climate, native products, and the potential of the country.

63　**Personal narrative of travels to the equinoctial regions of the new continent, during the years 1799-1804, by Alexander de Humboldt and Aimé Bonpland.**
Alexander de Humboldt, translated by Helen Maria Williams.
London: Longman, 1814-29. Reprinted, Amsterdam: Theatrum Orbis Terrarum; New York: Da Capo, 1971. 7 vols.

The great bulk of this classic geographical work (which was originally published in French) concerns Venezuela. It gives a detailed description of all parts of the country in 1799-1800, including information on climate, population, native peoples, and flora and fauna, and an appendix on geological structure.

64　**Letters written from Colombia, during a journey from Caracas to Bogotá and thence to Santa Martha in 1823.**
London: G. Cowie, 1824. 208p.

An account in journal form, of which the first four sections, or 'letters', relate to Venezuela (p. 1-105). It is a record of impressions of the country, its geography, its people, its products and its potential as a location for European enterprise. Authorship has been attributed both to John Hankshaw and to F. Hall.

65　**With the trade winds. A jaunt in Venezuela and the West Indies.**
Ira Nelson Morris.　New York; London: G.P. Putman's Sons, 1897. 157p.

The latter part of the book (p. 90-157) is an engaging account of travels by train from La Guayra to Macuto, Caracas, Valencia, and Puerto Cabello, and by steamboat to Maracaibo and up the Orinoco to Ciudad Bolívar, with some acute observations of people and manners.

66 **Life and nature under the tropics; or sketches of travel among the Andes, and on the Orinoco, Rio Negro, Amazons, and in Central America.**
Henry Morris Myers, Philip Van Ness Myers. New York:
D. Appleton, 1871. 358p.

Presents the report of a natural history expedition, organized by Williams College, Massachusetts, in 1867. The first thirteen chapters (p. 1-193) deal with travel to Caracas, Valencia, Puerto Cabello, then via the Pao, Apure and Orinoco rivers to the Río Negro and the Amazon. A quite detailed description is given of the journey, the places visited, the inhabitants, the wildlife, and, especially, the flora.

67 **Accounts of nineteenth-century South America. An annotated checklist of works by British and United States observers.**
Bernard Naylor. London: Athlone, 1969. 80p. (University of London Institute of Latin American Studies Monographs, no. 2).

Brief descriptions of books in English by travellers, divided into three chronological parts (1800-30, 1830-70 and 1870-1900) each of which has a section on northern South America, and lists several works on Venezuela.

68 **Wild scenes in South America; or life in the llanos of Venezuela.**
Ramón Páez. New York: Charles Scribner, 1862. 502p.

The memoirs of the son of President José Antonio Páez, of which over half is devoted to a visit to his father's estates in the *llanos* of Apure in 1846-47. He records his impressions of the country, its people and its wildlife, and includes accounts of hunting and of the rounding-up and branding of cattle. Two chapters describe his father's rôle in the wars of independence, and the last eight deal with the downfall of his presidential régime, his attempts to regain power, and his imprisonment and exile. A revised version, entitled *Travels and adventures in South and Central America. First Series. Life in the llanos of Venezuela* (London: Sampson, Low, Son & Marston, 1868. 473p.), omits the concluding political chapters, and adds an introduction and a few further descriptive chapters, based largely on Humboldt's *Personal narrative* . . . (q.v.).

69 **Down the Orinoco in a canoe.**
Santiago Pérez Triana, introduced by R.B. Cunninghame Graham.
London: Heinemann, 1902. 253p.

This narrative, by a refugee from political troubles in Colombia in the 1890s, describes his journey down the Orinoco through Venezuela to the Atlantic, comments on scenery and wildlife, and gives anecdotes of persons and places.

70 **The Colombian and Venezuelan republics, with notes on other parts of Central and South America.**
William Lindsay Scruggs. Boston, Massachusetts: Little, Brown, 1905. 2nd ed. 380p.

Based on the author's personal observations during his time in South America between 1872 and 1899, and on his experiences as United States minister to Colombia and Venezuela, this work includes descriptive chapters on: the coastal area and Caracas; the geography and the agricultural and mineral resources of the country; and the Anglo-Venezuelan boundary dispute and the arbitration award.

71 **Sketch of the present state of Caracas: including a journey from Caracas through La Victoria and Valencia to Puerto Cabello.**
Robert Semple. London: C. Baldwin, 1812. 176p.

This is one of the earliest first-hand accounts of a British visitor to independent Venezuela; the author arrived in November 1810 and stayed until 1811. He describes a journey from Caracas overland to Valencia and Puerto Cabello, commenting on the topography and the character of the inhabitants, and gives a rather critical view of the independent government, its declaration of independence, and Miranda's influence on it.

72 **The land of Bolivar, or war, peace and adventure in the republic of Venezuela.**
James Mudie Spence. London: Sampson Low, Marston, Searle & Rivington, 1878. 2 vols. bibliog.

Although primarily an account of travels, with descriptions of various parts of the country in 1871-72, this also includes chapters on geography, history, the author's dealings with the Guzmán Blanco régime over mining concessions, and Venezuela's prospects for economic development. The work is lavishly illustrated, and there are twenty appendices on various subjects, including archaeology, minerals, flora and fauna, literature, arts and religion.

73 **Notes of a botanist on the Amazon and Andes.**
Richard Spruce, edited by Alfred Russel Wallace. London: Macmillan, 1908. Reprinted, New York; London: Johnson Reprint, 1970. 2 vols.

This work was edited from Spruce's journals of his travels on the Amazon and its tributaries, on the Orinoco, and in Peru, Ecuador and the Pacific Coast, 1847-64. Four chapters of the first volume deal with botanical explorations of the extreme south of Venezuela, 1852-54. The reprint has a new foreword by Richard Evans Schultes.

74 **Rambles and scrambles in North and South America.**
Edward Sullivan. London: Richard Bentley, 1852. 424p.

In this narrative of a journey to the United States and the Caribbean in 1850-51, four chapters (p. 375-416) are devoted to Venezuela. The country made a very favourable impression on the author, who comments on Margarita, Barcelona, La Guaira, Caracas, Maracay, Valencia and Puerto Cabello, and on persons he met and anecdotes he was told.

75 **Narrative of travels on the Amazon and Rio Negro, with an account of the native tribes and observations on the climate, geology, and natural history of the Amazon valley.**
Alfred Russel Wallace. London: Reeve, 1853. 541p.

Although he travelled mainly in Brazil, the author spent the early months of 1851 on the Venezuelan side of the border, and recorded his impressions of the area and its wildlife.

76 **Present state of the Spanish colonies; including a particular report of Hispañola, or the Spanish part of Santo Domingo; with a general survey of the settlements on the south continent of America, as relates to history, trade, population, customs, manners &c. with a concise statement of the sentiments of the people on their relative situation to the mother country &c.**
William Walton.   London: Longman, Hurst, Rees, Orme & Brown, 1810. 2 vols.

An appendix containing a geographical description of Venezuela in the early-nineteenth century, entitled 'Survey of the East Coast of South America from Cape Vela to the Oronoko, from actual observation and the best authority, intended to assist the trader in his access to this part of the coast' appears in volume one (p. 245-87). Though less specifically, much of the general description in the main body of the work applies to Venezuela.

77 **Venezuela; or two years on the Spanish Main.**
Walter E. Wood.   Middlesborough, England: Jordison; London: Simpkin, Marshall, Hamilton, Kent, 1896. 196p.

An engineer involved in an abortive railway construction project in the Barcelona/Narical area of eastern Venezuela, in 1888-89, wrote this description of places and customs.

Twentieth century

78 **Venezuela: a democracy.**
Henry Justin Allen.   New York: Doubleday, Doran, 1940. 289p.

An informal account of a tour of the country in 1939, which praises the achievements of the López Contreras régime.

79 **The path of the conquistadores. Trinidad and Venezuelan Guiana.**
Lindon Bates, Jr.   Boston, Massachusetts; New York: Houghton Mifflin, 1912. 308p.

Gives an anecdotal account of a journey from Trinidad up the Orinoco to Ciudad Bolívar and the *llanos* in the early years of the Gómez régime.

80 **Our search for a wilderness. An account of two ornithological expeditions to Venezuela and to British Guiana.**
Mary Blair Beebe, Charles William Beebe.   New York: Henry Holt, 1910. 408p.

The first two chapters deal with the wildlife of the area around Guanoco and La Brea near the Gulf of Paria in north-east Venezuela. The third, 'A woman's experiences in Venezuela', gives Mary Beebe's impressions of people and places on an expedition in 1908.

81 **Venezuela. A commercial and industrial handbook, with a chapter on the Dutch West Indies.**
P.L. Bell. Washington, DC: US Department of Commerce, Bureau of Foreign and Domestic Commerce, 1922. 472p. (Special Agents Series, no. 212).
A detailed factual survey of geography, population, social conditions, the economy, regions, trade and finance, and commercial practices, which is of interest as a description of the situation in 1921.

82 **The journal of an expedition across Venezuela and Colombia, 1906-1907. An exploration of the route of Bolívar's celebrated march of 1819 and of the battlefields of Boyacá and Carabobo.**
Hiram Bingham. New Haven, Connecticut: Yale; London: Fisher Unwin, 1909. 287p.
Records in diary form the first expedition of the celebrated discoverer of Macchu Pichu, which was undertaken in an attempt to arrive at a just evaluation of Bolívar's military achievements. It concludes that the Liberator's feat in the Boyacá campaign of 1819 has few equals in military history. The work is illustrated by numerous photographs.

83 **Indians on horseback.**
Gustaf Bolinder. London: Dennis Dobson, 1957. 189p.
An anecdotal account of travels among the mounted nomads of the Guajira peninsula on the Venezuelan/Colombian border in 1920, which includes comments on some of the changes noted on returning in 1955.

84 **We dared the Andes. Three journeys into the unknown.**
Gustaf Bolinder, translated by Elsa Krause. London; New York: Abelard-Schuman, 1958. 240p.
The story of expeditions made in 1915, 1920 and 1936, by a Swedish ethnologist and his wife, into the Sierra de Perijá on the Colombian-Venezuelan border. They encountered the feared Motilon Indians and the pygmy Maraca tribe.

85 **The sons of El Dorado: Venezuelan adventure.**
Donald Cameron. London: Longmans, 1968. 216p.
A Scottish seaman's reminiscences of a visit to Caracas and Ciudad Bolívar in the 1950s make up this volume.

86 **Venezuela.**
Leonard V. Dalton. London; Leipzig: Fisher Unwin, 1912. 320p.
bibliog. (The South American Series).
A systematic survey, which includes chapters on geography, geology, flora and fauna, history, administration, native peoples, the various regions, the economy, transport, and future prospects. There are appendices on population, trade, climate, and finance, and thirty-five photographic illustrations.

87 **Devil mountain.**
Leonidas Richardson Dennison. New York: Hastings House, 1942.
271p.
A record of the exploration of the Auyan-Tepui and the Angel Falls in Venezuelan Guayana, undertaken by an American mining engineer in the 1930s.

88 **My jungle book.**
Herbert Spencer Dickey. Boston, Massachusetts: Little, Brown, 1932.
298p.; London: Hutchinson, 1932. 286p.
An informal account of exploration on the upper Orinoco around 1930, written by an American medical doctor.

89 **Scientific exploration in Venezuelan Amazonas.**
M.J. Eden. *Geographical Journal*, vol. 137, no. 2 (1971), p. 149-56.
Gives a summary of the hydrological, ecological, agricultural and ethno-botanical research undertaken in an expedition, by hovercraft, to the Río Negro, the Casiquiare canal and the Orinoco, in 1968.

90 **Venezuela.**
Erna Fergusson. New York: Knopf, 1939. 346p.
This is a traveller's account of a journey around the various regions of the country in the aftermath of the Gómez régime.

91 **To the source of the Orinoco.**
Joseph Grelier, translated by H.A.G. Schmuckler. London: Herbert Jenkins, 1957. 190p.
A first-hand account of the 1951 Franco-Venezuelan expedition to locate the source of the river, which includes a summary of previous explorations, and a brief description of the terrain and its inhabitants.

92 **Inside Latin America.**
John Gunther. London: Hamish Hamilton, 1942. 388p. bibliog.
Chapter XII, 'The high cost of Venezuela' (p. 147-54), gives a brief impression of the country in 1941, by a popular political journalist and travel writer of the time.

93 **Venezuela: impressions of the country and its people, gathered during recent months of travel and observation.**
Thomas F. Lee. *Mentor* [Springfield, Ohio; New York], vol. 13, no. 10 (1925), p. 1-36.
This article features the author's photographs. The accompanying text outlines the discovery and history of the country, and the regions and their inhabitants; gives a sketch of Bolívar; records an interview with President Gómez; and illustrates life in Caracas in the 1920s. In the same issue there is a comment on the Venezuelan painter Tito Salas (p. 53), and a brief article on Venezuelan writers and literature by Antonio Reyes (p. 54).

94 **Men of Maracaibo.**
Jonathan Norton Leonard. New York: G.P. Putnam's Sons, 1933.
287p.

Records racy impressions of relations between American expatriates and Venezuelans in the Maracaibo area in the 1930s.

95 **Up the Orinoco to the land of the Maquiritares.**
Leo E. Miller. *Geographical Review*, vol. 3, no. 4 (1917), p. 261-77.

A narrative of a zoological expedition in 1912-13 to the Mount Duida area and the river Cunucunuma, which includes comments on the navigation of the Orinoco, its peoples and its wildlife. Another pertinent article by Miller appeared in the same journal, vol. 3, no. 5 (1917), p. 356–74, entitled 'The land of the Maquiritares'.

96 **Up the Orinoco and down the Magdalena.**
H.J. Mozans. New York; London: D. Appleton, 1910. 439p. bibliog.

To his own impressions of the country, derived from his journey in 1907, the American author adds those of previous travellers, drawn from their published accounts.

97 **Desolate marches; travels in the Orinoco llanos of Venezuela.**
Ludovico M. Nesbitt. London: Cape, 1935; New York: Harcourt,
Brace, 1936. 320p.

Presents an account of a journey from Caracas through the eastern *llanos* to Barcelona, and of an expedition to survey part of the state of Anzoátegui, in 1927.

98 **Into the lost world.**
David Nott. Englewood Cliffs, New Jersey: Prentice-Hall, 1975. 186p.

This is a popular account of the exploration of the Sarisariñama plateau and encounters with the Makiritare Indians in south-east Venezuela.

99 **In trouble again. A journey between the Orinoco and the Amazon.**
Redmond O'Hanlon. Harmondsworth, England: Penguin, 1989. 347p.
bibliog.

This entertaining account by a British ornithologist of travels in the Amazonas territory on the southern border of Venezuela, tells of his encounters with various kinds of wildlife, and with the Yanomami Indians.

100 **The Rio Negro, the Casiquiare canal, and the upper Orinoco, September**
1919-April 1920.
A. Hamilton Rice. *Geographical Journal*, vol. 58, no. 5 (1921),
p. 321-44.

Comprises the report of an expedition to explore the upper Orinoco and to map the area.

101 **Venezuela's place in the sun. Modernizing a pioneering country.**
Nicholas Roosevelt. New York: Round Table, 1940. 88p.

A brief illustrated survey, which incorporates tourist information, a general description, and an assessment of economic prospects, in 1940.

102 **The Bolivar countries: Colombia, Ecuador, Venezuela.**
William R. Russell. New York: Coward, McCann, 1949. 308p.
bibliog. (Invitation to Travel Series).

An informal account of travels, giving contemporary visitors an idea of what they could expect. Venezuela is dealt with on p. 217-71.

103 **Red cloth and green forest.**
Alfonso Vinci, translated by James Campbell. London: Hutchinson, 1959. 274p.

An account of explorations to the country of the Shirian and Guayaca peoples in southern Venezuela in 1954-55, written by a geologist, prospector and mountaineer.

104 **The new El Dorado: Venezuela.**
Edward Ward. London: Robert Hale, 1957. 189p.

This informal and optimistic portrait of the country during the boom years of Pérez Jiménez takes in Caracas, the Maracaibo oilfields, agricultural areas, the Andes, the Caroní project, and the *llanos*.

105 **The flowing road: adventures on the great rivers of South America.**
Caspar Whitney. London: Heinemann, 1912. 319p.

Describes the journeys of an American explorer, from the Río Negro in Brazil to Ciudad Bolívar, and on the Orinoco, Apure, Atabapo, Casiquiare and Portuguesa rivers, in the early 1900s. The travels were mostly undertaken by canoe.

Tourist guides

106 **Guide to Venezuela.**
Janice Bauman, Leni Young. Caracas: Ernesto Armitano, 1987. 3rd ed. 925p.

A comprehensive tourist guide to all parts of the country, which includes general description and notes on tourist attractions, as well as information on hotels, restaurants, transportation, shopping and entertainment.

107 **The South American handbook.**
Edited by Ben Box, Joyce Candy. Bath, England: Trade & Travel Publications, 1924- . annual.

The sixty-sixth annual edition of this outstanding guide (1989. 1440p.) devotes p. 880-932 to Venezuela, and contains basic information for tourists.

108 **Backpacking in Venezuela, Colombia and Ecuador. Treks in the northern Andes.**
Hilary Bradt, George Bradt. Boston, Massachusetts; Chalfont St. Peter, England: Bradt Enterprises, 1979. 126p. bibliog.
The section on Venezuela (p. 40-51) is mainly concerned with the El Avila national park (above Caracas), and the hiking area of the Sierra Nevada de Mérida, which includes the country's highest mountain, Pico Bolívar (5,007 metres).

109 **South America on a shoestring.**
Geoff Crowther. South Yarra, Victoria: Lonely Planet, 1980. 442p.
Venezuela is dealt with on p. 422-36, with the emphasis being on cheap accommodation and transport.

110 **Indextur. A tourist's directory to Venezuela.**
Edited by J. Rafael Márquez, translated by Jaime Tello. Caracas: Cromotip/Lagoven, 1985. 209p.
An illustrated Baedeker-type guide, containing, in addition to the usual information about what to see and where to stay, an introduction to each part of the country by a native 'man of letters'.

111 **Caracas and environs.**
Gene Ryder, Mary Ryder. Caracas: Librería Galax, 1976. 166p. (Galax Pocket Guide).
Gives basic tourist information, and a guide to the capital, for sightseers.

112 **Venezuela. Guía turística.** (Venezuela. Tourist's guidebook.)
VIASA (Venezuelan National Airline). Caracas: Editorial Binev, [1987]. 188p.
With text in Spanish and English, this includes general tourist information, region-by-region descriptions, and lists of hotels, restaurants and places of interest, embellished by thirty-three plates of colour photographs. There is also a 'handy-format' edition by the same publisher (120p.), in English only, compiled by Mario Rugiadi Battini.

113 **Central and South America and the Caribbean.**
Edited by Jane Walker, Mark Ambrose. London: Michael Joseph, 1981. 448p. (The Business Traveller's Handbook, vol. 2).
Practical information for the business visitor to Venezuela is set out on p. 194-208.

114 **Cities of the world. Volume 2. The Western hemisphere (exclusive of the United States).**
Edited by Margaret Walsh Young, Susan L. Stetler. Detroit, Michigan: Gale Research, 1985. 2nd ed. 734p.
Contains (p. 694-715) descriptions of Caracas and Maracaibo, and a profile of the country in general, for tourists or intending residents.

Flora and Fauna

115 Studies of birds and mammals of South America.
Axel Amuchástegui.   London: Tryon Gallery; Princeton, New Jersey: Van Nostrand, 1967. 63p.

This collection of outstanding illustrations includes five of birds and four of mammals whose habitats include Venezuela.

116 High jungle.
William Beebe.   London: Bodley Head, 1950. 379p.

A popular account of scientific studies of wildlife in tropical cloud jungle which were undertaken in the national park of Aragua in 1945, 1946 and 1948, by the director of tropical research of the New York Zoological Society.

117 Poisonous plants of Venezuela.
Henrik Blohm.   Cambridge, Massachusetts: Harvard University Press, 1962. 136p. bibliog.

Includes over 100 species, many with illustrations, arranged by botanical classifications. Each is described in terms of the conditions, symptoms and treatment of the poisoning.

118 Mycological explorations of Venezuela.
Carlos E. Chardon, Rafael A. Toro.   Río Piedras, Puerto Rico: University of Puerto Rico, 1934. 353p. (Monographs of the University of Puerto Rico, Series B Physical and Biological Sciences, no. 2).

Consists of a review of earlier descriptions of Venezuelan fungi, an account of collecting expeditions undertaken in 1930-32, and descriptions of the species encountered.

119   **A guide to the birds of Venezuela.**
Rodolphe Meyer De Schauensee, William H. Phelps, Jr.   Princeton,
New Jersey: Princeton University Press, 1978. 424p. bibliog.

Describes all species known to inhabit Venezuela and its adjacent islands. Almost all
are illustrated on forty colour and thirteen black-and-white plates or line drawings.
There are short notes on habits, habitats and bird calls. Latin, English and Spanish
names are given and separately indexed.

120   **South America and Central America: a natural history.**
Jean Dorst.   London: Hamish Hamilton, 1967. 298p. (The Continents
We Live On).

Chapter six 'Grassy plains under the sierras' (p. 42-57) gives a brief account of the flora
and fauna of the various regions of Venezuela. They are illustrated by magnificent
photographs.

121   **Orchids of Venezuela. An illustrated field guide.**
Galfrid Clement Keyworth Dunsterville, Leslie A. Garay.
Cambridge, Massachusetts: Harvard University, Botanical Museum,
1979. 3 vols.

In handy paperback form, this work consists of black-and-white drawings of over 1,000
species of orchid, and gives references to where detailed descriptions may be found. It
revises and enlarges the six volumes of the authors' *Venezuelan orchids illustrated*
(q.v.) published between 1959 and 1976.

122   **Venezuelan orchids illustrated.**
Galfrid Clement Keyworth Dunsterville, Leslie A. Garay.   London:
André Deutsch, 1959-76. 6 vols.

Based on extensive field work, these handsome volumes consist of detailed line
drawings and descriptions of 1,000 species of orchids, from all parts of the country.

123   **The pearl fishery of Venezuela.**
Paul J. Galtsoff.   Washington, DC: United States Department of the
Interior, Fish and Wild Life Service, 1950. 26p. (Special Scientific
Report: Fisheries, no. 26).

A brief review of the history of pearl fishing around Margarita island, and of the
condition of the fishery in 1948.

124   **Plantas ornamentales de Venezuela.** (Ornamental plants of Venezuela.)
Jesús Hoyos F.   Caracas: Sociedad de Ciencias Naturales La Salle,
1982. 550p. bibliog. (Monografía, no. 31).

Descriptions of 538 types of plant are accompanied by fine colour photographs.

125 **History of botanical exploration in Territorio Federal Amazonas, Venezuela.**
Otto Huber, John J. Wurdack.   Washington, DC: Smithsonian Institution, 1984. 83p. 10 maps. bibliog. (Smithsonian Contributions to Botany, no. 56).

Contains detailed information on botanical activities in Amazonas territory, in the south of the country, from 1800 to 1982, arranged both chronologically and alphabetically by collectors. Shows itineraries, places of deposit of specimens collected, and resulting publications.

126 **Aquatic biota of tropical South America.**
Edited by Stuart H. Hurlbert, Gilberto Rodríguez, Newton Dias Dos Santos.   San Diego, California: San Diego State University, 1981. 2 vols.

A bibliography relating to the flora and fauna of the inland waters of the northern part of South America, and including many titles relating to Venezuela. Part one covers Arthropoda (mainly shell-fish and insects), and part two covers Anarthropoda (including aquatic bacteria, parasites, amphibia, water-birds and freshwater mammals).

127 **Tropical botany.**
Edited by Kai Larsen, Lauritz B. Holm-Nielsen.   London; New York; San Francisco: Academic Press, 1979. 453p.

These proceedings of a symposium held in Aarhus, Denmark in 1978 include Julian A. Steyermark's 'Plant refuge and dispersal centres in Venezuela: their relict and endemic effect' (p. 185-221); and Bassett Maguire's 'Guayana, region of the Roraima sandstone formation' (p. 223-38).

128 **The orchid hunters: a jungle adventure.**
Norman MacDonald.   London: Hale, 1940. 282p.

An informal account of an orchid-collecting expedition, conducted largely in Colombia, but also extending into Venezuela, undertaken by two young Americans in the 1930s.

129 **The botany of the Guayana highland. Parts 1-12.**
Bassett Maguire (et al.).   *Memoirs of the New York Botanical Garden*, vol. 8, no. 2 (1953), p. 87-160; vol. 9, no. 3 (1957), p. 235-392; vol. 10, no. 1 (1958), p. 1-156; no. 2 (1960), p. 1-37; no. 4 (1961), p. 1-87; no. 5 (1964), p. 1-278; vol. 12, no. 3 (1965), p. 1-285; vol. 17, no. 1 (1965), p. 1-439; vol. 18, no. 2 (1969), p. 1-290; vol. 23, no. 1 (1972), p. 1-382; vol. 29, no. 1 (1978), p. 1-288; vol. 32, no. 1 (1981), p. 1-391; vol. 38 (1984).

This massive long-term project reports on a series of expeditions, undertaken from 1948 to 1979, and gives data on locations, collectors and the plants found. Further parts may still be published.

130 **The origin of the bird fauna of the south Venezuelan highlands.**
Ernst Mayr, William H. Phelps, Jr. *Bulletin of the American Museum of Natural History*, vol. 136, no. 5 (1967), p. 269-328. maps.

A description, illustrated by photographs, of the bird life of the *tepuis* (isolated, perpendicular, table-top sandstone mountains, that rise for some 2,000 metres from the surrounding forest or savanna, in the state of Bolívar and the territory of Amazonas).

131 **Ornithological gazetteer of Venezuela.**
Raymond A. Paynter Jr. Cambridge, Massachusetts: Harvard University, Museum of Comparative Zoology, Bird Department, 1982. 245p. bibliog. (Ornithological Gazetteer of the Neotropics).

This alphabetical list of geographical locations gives references to publications describing the bird life of each, and has a very full bibliography.

132 **Hundred of the best known birds of Venezuela.**
Kathleen Deery Phelps. Caracas: Editorial Lectura, 1963. 3rd. ed. 107p.

Consists of vivid colour illustrations and brief descriptions of 100 species of Venezuelan birds. They are classified systematically and indexed under their scientific and popular names, both English and Spanish.

133 **Biological diversification in the tropics.**
Edited by Ghillean T. Prance. New York: Columbia University Press, 1982. 714p.

These proceedings of the fifth International Symposium of the Association for Tropical Botany, held in Venezuela in February 1979, include Julian A. Steyermark's 'Relationships of some Venezuelan forest refuges with lowland tropical floras' (p. 182-220) and Otto Huber's 'Significance of savanna vegetation in the Amazon territory of Venezuela' (p. 221-44).

134 **Contribution to the flora of Venezuela. Botanical exploration of Venezuela. Parts 1-4.**
Julian A. Steyermark (et al.). *Fieldiana: Botany* [Chicago], vol. 28, nos. 1-4 (1951-57). 1225p.

Records the identification of collections of specimens which were made in various parts of the country by the author, in 1943-45. Part one deals with Musci to Sarraceniaceae; part two with Droseraceae to Umbelliferae; part three with Ericaceae to Compositae; and part four with Algae to Spermatophyta.

135 **Flora del Avila. Flora y vegetación de las montañas del Avila, de la Silla y del Naiguatá.** (Flora of the Avila. Flora and vegetation of the Avila, Silla and Naiguatá mountains.)
Julián A. Steyermark, Otto Huber. Caracas: Sociedad Venezolana de Ciencias Naturales, 1978. 971p. bibliog.

A brief introductory account of the ecological features of the range of mountains that separates Caracas from the sea is followed by detailed descriptions of its plant life, arranged by families, genera and species, and copiously illustrated with black-and-white drawings and sixteen colour plates.

136 **Mamíferos de Venezuela.** (Mammals of Venezuela.)
Jaime Tello.   Caracas: Fundación La Salle de Ciencias Naturales,
1979. 192p. bibliog.

Gives scientific names and non-technical descriptions of the various species of Venezuelan mammals, and illustrates them with over eighty colour plates.

137 **High altitude tropical biogeography.**
Edited by François Vuilleumier, Maximina Monasterio.   New York;
Oxford: Oxford University Press and American Museum of Natural
History, 1986. 649p.

Includes María Léa Salgado-Labouriau's 'Late quaternary paleoecology of Venezuelan high mountains' (p. 202-17); Julian A. Steyermark's 'Speciation and endemism in the flora of Venezuelan tepuis' (p. 317-73); and other articles with some references to Venezuela.

Prehistory and Archaeology

138 **Excavations at La Mata, Maracay, Venezuela.**
Wendell C. Bennett. *Anthropological Papers of the American Museum of Natural History*, vol. 36, pt. 2 (1937), p. 69-137.
Gives a detailed account of one of the early investigations in the Lake Valencia area.

139 **An archaeological chronology of Venezuela.**
José María Cruxent, Irving Rouse. Washington, DC: Pan-American Union, General Secretariat, Organization of American States, 1958-59. 2 vols. maps. bibliog. (Social Science Monographs, no. 6).
Volume I is a region-by-region survey of the available knowledge of Venezuelan archaeology in the 1950s, updating the 1943 work of Osgood and Howard (q.v.), followed by a detailed chronology, analysing the findings in terms of six chronological periods and five geographical divisions. Volume II is a collection of chronological charts and maps, and illustrations of the styles of artefacts, in presumed chronological order for each region and area of the country. The drawings are followed by 104 plates of photographic illustrations.

140 **La Pitía: an archaeological series in northwestern Venezuela.**
Patrick Gallagher. New Haven, Connecticut: Yale University, Department of Anthropology, 1976. 249p. bibliog. (Yale University Publications in Anthropology, no. 76).
This report of the excavation of pottery at a site on the Guajira peninsula coast of the Gulf of Venezuela throws some light on the relationship of the prehistoric culture of the area to those of Colombia and of other parts of Venezuela. It contains numerous illustrations.

141 **Archaeology of northwestern Venezuela.**
Alfred Kidder II. Cambridge, Massachusetts: Harvard University,
1944. 178p. bibliog. (Papers of the Peabody Museum, Archaeology and
Ethnology, vol. 26/1).
Gives details of excavations undertaken in 1933-34 at La Cabrera, near Maracay, and
at Carache, in the state of Trujillo; reviews previous archaeological work; records
reconnaissances undertaken; and attempts to establish relationships between the
various Venezuelan prehistoric cultures. It is illustrated by eighteen photographic
plates of artefacts discovered.

142 **New archaeological sites from the state of Falcón, Venezuela.**
Gladys Ayer Nomland. Berkeley, California: University of California
Press, 1935. 114p. bibliog. (Ibero-Americana, no. 11).
Reports the excavations at three coastal sites – Coro, El Mamón and La Maravilla –
which indicated long occupancy, probably by people of Arawak stock.

143 **An archaeological survey of Venezuela.**
Cornelius Osgood, George D. Howard. New Haven, Connecticut:
Yale University Press; London: Oxford University Press, 1943. 153p.
bibliog. (Yale University Publications in Archaeology, no. 27).
The report of a survey carried out in 1941, summarizing the available archaeological
information for each of the administrative divisions of the country, and describing
work done on a number of particular sites. Fuller details of an excavation by each of
the authors, one in the state of Guárico and the other near Lake Valencia, are given in
Howard's, *Excavations at Ronquín, Venezuela*, and Osgood's, *Excavations at Tocorón,
Venezuela* (New Haven, Connecticut; London: Yale University Press, 1943. 90p., 60p.
bibliogs. [Yale University Publications in Archaeology, nos. 28, 29]).

144 **Parmana: prehistoric maize and manioc subsistence along the Amazon
and Orinoco.**
Anna Curtenius Roosevelt. New York: Academic Press, 1980. 320p.
bibliog. (Studies in Archaeology).
A discussion of archaeological investigations in the Parmana area of Guárico state,
suggesting that a phase of maize cultivation was associated with higher population
density.

145 **Venezuelan archaeology.**
Irving Rouse, José M. Cruxent. New Haven, Connecticut; London:
Yale University Press, 1963. 179p. bibliog. (Caribbean Series, no. 6).
Designed for the non-specialist and illustrated by numerous plates and figures, this
concise volume summarizes the findings of sixteen years' study, and suggests that
Venezuela, a neglected field in New World archaeology, is worthy of more attention
than it has received. The authors identify and describe four chronological epochs, and
twelve distinct cultural ethnic groups, concluding that west and central Venezuela
reached a significantly higher level of culture before the Spanish conquest than did the
eastern parts of the country.

146 **Aboriginal cultural development in Venezuela.**
Mario Sanoja. In: *Aboriginal cultural development in Latin America.*
Edited by Betty Meggers, Clifford Evans. Washington, DC:
Smithsonian Institution, Publication 4517, 1963, p. 67-76. (Smithsonian
Miscellaneous Collections, vol. 146, no. 1).

A succinct summary of prehistoric Venezuela, showing a distinct pre-ceramic epoch
from ca. 5000 BC to ca. 1000 BC, and thereafter a ceramic epoch during which different
traditions established themselves in the eastern and western zones of the country.

147 **Native peoples of South America.**
Julian Haynes Steward, Louis C. Faron. New York; Toronto;
London: McGraw Hill, 1959. 481p.

This widely available standard work summarizing knowledge about pre-hispanic
cultures, as of 1959, gives a concise survey of Venezuela (p. 239-46) within the context
of the South American continent as a whole.

148 **The prehistory and ethnohistory of the Carache area in western
Venezuela.**
Erika Wagner. New Haven, Connecticut: Yale University,
Department of Anthropology, 1967. 137p. bibliog. (Yale University
Publications in Anthropology, no. 71).

A report on archaeological investigations at Carache in Trujillo state, revealing
evidence that the culture patterns of the Andean and sub-Andean areas met and co-
existed there. The text is followed by twenty plates of sites and artefacts.

Native Peoples

Anthropology

149 **Development programmes among indigenous populations of Venezuela: background, consequences and a critique.**
Nelly Arvelo-Jiménez. In: *Land, people and planning in contemporary Amazonia.* Edited by Françoise Barbira-Scazzocchio. Cambridge, England: Cambridge University Centre of Latin American Studies, 1980, p. 210-21. (Occasional Publication, no. 3).
A highly critical examination of the *Empresa Indígena* (native enterprise) development programme, which attempted to re-organize indigenous Indian communities into peasant co-operatives.

150 **The politics of cultural survival in Venezuela: beyond *indigenismo*.**
Nelly Arvelo-Jiménez. In: *Frontier expansion in Amazonia.* Edited by Marianne Schmink, Charles H. Wood. Gainesville, Florida: University of Florida Press, 1984, p. 105-26.
Argues that government policy towards the Indians in Amazonas territory is leading to the destruction of indigenous cultures in the name of progress. The policy is known as *indigenismo*.

151 **Carib-speaking Indians: culture, society and language.**
Edited by Ellen B. Basso. Tucson, Arizona: University of Arizona Press, 1977. 122p. (Anthropological Papers of the University of Arizona, no. 28).
Includes general surveys of the Carib family of languages, by Marshall Durbin, and of the status of Carib ethnography by the editor, as well as two studies on particular groups of Venezuelan Caribs, on naming among the Panare, by Jean-Paul Dumont, and on village formation among the Ye'cuana, by Nelly Arvelo-Jiménez.

152 **Yanoáma. The narrative of a white girl kidnapped by Amazonian Indians.**
Ettore Biocca, translated from the Italian by Dennis Rhodes. New York: Dutton, 1970. 382p. bibliog.

Helena Valero was captured as a little girl and lived among the Yanoáma for some twenty years before escaping. Her unique story, as told to Biocca, throws much light on the way of life of this most isolated of Indian tribes. The text is illustrated by fifty-seven photographs, taken by missionary Luigi Cocco and the author.

153 **Studying the Yanomamo.**
Napoleon A. Chagnon. New York; London; Sydney: Holt, Reinhart, Winston, 1974. 270p. (Studies in Anthropological Method).

Relates the author's experiences of collecting anthropological information in the Yanomamo land on the Venezuelan/Brazilian border.

154 **Yanomamö: the fierce people.**
Napoleon A. Chagnon. New York: Holt, Reinhart, Winston, 1983. 3rd ed. 224p. bibliog. (Case Studies in Cultural Anthropology).

Presents a systematic anthropological study of an Indian tribe living in the tropical forest in the headwaters of the Orinoco; the tribe is largely unaffected by the outside world.

155 **The anatomy of a land invasion scheme in Yecuana territory, Venezuela.**
Walter Coppens. Copenhagen: International Work Group for Indigenous Affairs, 1972. 23p. (IWGIA Document, no. 9).

Gives a brief account of an attempt by foreign entrepreneurs to create a private estate in an area traditionally used by the Makiritare Indians.

156 **Shabono.**
Florinda Donner. New York: Delacorte, 1982. 305p.

An anthropologist's account, cast in first-person story form, of her stay in one of the *shabonos* (palm-thatched communal dwellings) of the Yanomama Indians of the Brazilian-Venezuelan border.

157 **The headman and I. Ambiguity and ambivalence in the fieldworking experience.**
Jean-Paul Dumont. Austin, Texas: University of Texas Press, 1978. 211p. bibliog.

An anthropologist reflects on his experiences in researching among the Panare Indians of the Orinoco, and on their attitude towards him.

158 **Under the rainbow: nature and supernature among the Panare Indians.**
Jean-Paul Dumont. Austin, Texas; London: University of Texas Press, 1976. 178p. bibliog. (Texas Pan-American Series).

An anthropological investigation of the culture and thought of the Panare Indians of the Orinoco region, which is based on field work conducted in 1967 and 1969.

159 **Bibliografía básica de etnología de Venezuela.** (Basic bibliography of
Venezuelan ethnology.)
Helmuth Fuchs.   Seville, Spain: Universidad de Sevilla, Facultad de
Filosofía y Letras, 1964. [n.p.]. (Publicaciones del Seminario de
Antropología Americana, vol. 5).
Lists 2,413 items arranged alphabetically by authors; there is a subject index.

160 **Adaptive responses of native Amazonians.**
Edited by Raymond B. Hames, William T. Vickers.   New York;
London; Paris: Academic Press, 1983. 516p.
Includes studies of two Venezuelan groups: Jonathan Hill and Emilio F. Moran's
'Adaptive strategies of Wakuénai peoples to the oligotrophic rain forest of the Río
Negro basin' (p. 113-35); and Hames' 'The settlement pattern of a Yanomamo
population bloc: a behavioral ecological interpretation' (p. 393-427).

161 **The Panare: tradition and change on the Amazonian frontier.**
Paul Henley.   New Haven, Connecticut; London: Yale University
Press, 1982. 263p. bibliog.
This history of the Panare Indians of the Orinoco considers their ecomomic and social
organization, and the impact on them of recent contacts with the outside world.

162 **The Piaroa: a people of the Orinoco basin. A study in kinship and
marriage.**
Joanna Overing Kaplan.   Oxford: Clarendon, 1975. 236p.
A detailed technical report, based on field work carried out in 1968, which underlines
the problem of applying conventional anthropological concepts to a tiny and widely-
dispersed population, living in communal dwellings housing sixteen to fifty persons and
separated from each other by a half-day's journey.

163 **Indian societies of Venezuela: their blood group types.**
Miguel Layrisse, Johannes Wilbert.   Caracas: Fundación La Salle de
Ciencias Naturales, Instituto Caribe de Antropología y Sociología,
1966. 318p. bibliog. (Monografía, no. 13).
Brings together the results of twenty-eight expeditions surveying the distribution of
blood types within sixteen contemporary indigenous societies in Venezuela, and relates
them to ecological and cultural data.

164 **Ecological determinants of chieftainship among the Yaruro Indians of
Venezuela.**
A. Leeds.   In: *Environment and cultural behaviour. Ecological studies
in cultural anthropology.* Edited by Andrew P. Vayda. Austin, Texas;
London: University of Texas Press, 1969, p. 377-94.
Explains the weakness of the institution of chieftainship among the Yaruro in terms of
the individualist nature of their subsistence activities, and of the need for community
decision-making, rather than authoritarian direction, on important policy matters, such
as when to move villages, and where to.

165 **The ideology of the Yaruro Indians in relation to socio-economic organization.**
Anthony Leeds. *Antropológica* [Caracas], no. 9 (1960), p. 1-10.
Makes an attempt to explain the way in which the Yaruro organize their social and economic activities, in terms of their view of the universe and of good and evil.

166 **Tales of the Yanomami: daily life in the Venezuelan forest.**
Jacques Lizot, translated by Ernest Simon.   Cambridge, England: Cambridge University Press; Paris: Editions de la Maison des Sciences de l'Homme, 1985. 201p. bibliog. (Cambridge Studies in Social Anthropology, no. 55).
Describes the daily material, social and religious life of the Yanomami Indians of Amazonia, as told by themselves to an ethnographer who lived among them for many years.

167 **The Yanomami in the face of ethnocide.**
Jacques Lizot.   Copenhagen: International Work Group for Indigenous Affairs, 1976. 36p. bibliog. (IWGIA Document, no. 22).
Argues that the economic and social effects of missionary activity between 1968 and 1975 were thoroughly detrimental to the Yanomami Indians.

168 **Fajardo's people: cultural adjustment in Venezuela; and the little community in Latin American and North American contexts.**
Thomas McCorkle.   Los Angeles: University of California at Los Angeles, Latin American Center; Caracas: Editorial Sucre, 1965. 164p. bibliog.
An ethnographic study, based on field work carried out in 1952-53, of the small communities of the indigenous Guayquerí people in Fajardo and in adjacent settlements around the town of Porlamar on the island of Margarita.

169 **The Guahibo: people of the savanna.**
Robert V. Morey, Donald J. Metzger.   Vienna: Stiglmayr, 1974. 147p. bibliog. (Acta Ethnologica et Linguistica, no. 31; Series Americana, no. 7).
An anthropological description of the Guahibo Indians of the Orinoco *llano* on the Venezuelan-Colombian border, which covers their means of subsistence, kinship and family patterns, community relations, and belief systems. It seeks to account for the survival of their culture in the face of centuries of European contact.

170 **Ethnographic bibliography of South America.**
Timothy O'Leary.   New Haven, Connecticut: Human Relations Area Files, 1963. 387p.
Includes titles relating to Venezuela (p. 351-72), sub-divided by ethnic groups.

171 **Bibliografía antropológica venezolana.** (Bibliography of Venezuelan anthropology).
Angelina Pollak-Eltz. Caracas: Universidad Católica Andrés Bello, Instituto de Lenguas Indígenas y Centro de Estudios Comparativos de Religión, 1985. 75p.

Lists 630 books, arranged alphabetically by name of author. They are indexed under fifteen subject headings and eighteen ethnic headings (Afrovenezuelans, *mestizos*, Indians in general, and fifteen sub-groups of different Indian cultures). Although no articles are included, there is a list of the relevant journals and reviews published in Venezuela.

172 **Oil and steel. Processes of Karinya culture change in response to industrial development.**
Karl H. Schwerin. Los Angeles: University of California at Los Angeles, Latin American Center, 1966. 287p. bibliog. (Latin American Studies, vol. 4).

An anthropological study, based on field work carried out in 1961-62, of the differing impact of the petroleum and steel industries on two communities of Karinya Carib Indians in the state of Anzoátegui.

173 **The Yanoama Indians: a cultural geography.**
William J. Smole. Austin, Texas; London: University of Texas Press, 1976. 272p. bibliog.

A systematic discussion, focusing on the Yanoama tribe in the Parima highlands near the border of Venezuela and Brazil, embracing their distribution patterns, their means of livelihood, and their effects on the landscape.

174 **Uriji jami! Life and belief of the forest Waika in the upper Orinoco.**
Inga Steinvorth Goetz, translated by Peter T. Furst. Caracas: Asociación Cultural Humboldt, 1969. 207p.

Presents a non-technical description of the habitat, beliefs and free-roaming lifestyle (*uriji jami*, in their language) of the Waika group of Yanoama Indians of the forests at the headwaters of the Orinoco. It is lavishly illustrated with magnificent colour photographs, and provides an ideal introduction for the general reader.

175 **Handbook of South American Indians. Vol.4. The circum-Caribbean tribes.**
Edited by Julian Haynes Steward. Washington, DC: Smithsonian Institution, 1948. (Bureau of American Ethnology, Bulletin 143).
Reprinted, New York: Cooper Square, 1963. 609p. bibliog.

Includes 'The Otomac', 'Food-gathering tribes of the Venezuelan *llanos*' and 'The tribes north of the Orinoco river', by Paul Kirchhoff (p. 439-68, 481-93); and 'The tribes of northwestern Venezuela' and 'The tribes of north central Venezuela', by Gregorio Hernández de Alba (p. 469-79).

176 **Terminology, alliance and change in Warao society.**
María Matilde Suárez. *Nieuwe West-Indische Gids* [The Hague],
vol. 48, no. 1 (April 1971), p. 56-122.

Attempts to explain the society of the Warao Indians of the Orinoco delta by means of
a systematic study of their relationship terminology and marriage practices.

177 **Order without government. The society of the Pemon Indians of
Venezuela.**
David John Thomas. Urbana, Illinois; Chicago; London: University
of Illinois Press, 1982. 265p. bibliog. (Illinois Studies in Anthropology,
no. 13).

An anthropological study of the Carib-speaking Pemon group of Indians of south-east
Venezuela, based on extensive field work in the 1970s. It lays particular stress on the
egalitarian nature of their society, and the way in which it emphasizes personal
autonomy and the dispersal of power.

178 **Guajiro personality and urbanization.**
Lawrence Craig Watson. Los Angeles: University of California at Los
Angeles, Latin American Center, 1968. 209p. bibliog. (Latin American
Studies, vol. 10).

An anthropological study comparing the personality traits of Guajiro Indians in their
traditional rural environment with those of urbanized members of the tribe in Barrio
Ziruma, a suburb of Maracaibo.

179 **Now you are a woman./Ahora eres una mujer.**
Maria-Barbara Watson-Franke. Mexico, DF: Ediciones
Euroamericanos, 1984. 127p. bibliog. (Biblioteca Interamericana
Bilingüe, no. 6).

An 'anthropological novel' relating the transition from childhood to adulthood of a
Guajiro girl living with her Indian tribe in the Guajira peninsula in northwestern
Venezuela. It is, in fact, a composite picture drawn from the experiences of many
informants. The text is in English and Spanish, and is illustrated by sixteen colour
photographs.

180 **Enculturation in Latin America: an anthology.**
Edited by Johannes Wilbert. Los Angeles: University of California at
Los Angeles, Latin American Center, 1976. 421p. (Latin American
Studies, vol. 37).

This collection of essays on informal and non-formal education among selected Indian
societies includes Maria-Barbara Watson-Franke's 'To learn for tomorrow: enculturation of girls and its social importance among the Guajiro of Venezuela'; Johannes
Wilbert's 'To become a maker of canoes: an essay in Warao enculturation'; and
Lawrence C. Watson's 'The education of the cacique in Guajiro society and its
functional implications' and 'Urbanization, cognition and socialization of educational
values: the case of the Guajiro Indians of Venezuela'.

181 **Survivors of El Dorado. Four Indian cultures of South America.**
Johannes Wilbert. New York; Washington, DC; London: Praeger,
1972. 212p. bibliog.
A good introduction to the anthropology of the surviving Indian societies of
Venezuela, this makes a study of four tribal cultures, based on different types of food
procurement. It considers: the Yanoama hunters of the headwaters of the Orinoco on
the Brazilian border; the Warao fishermen of the Orinoco delta; the Makiritare
horticulturalists of the Amazonas territory; and the Goajiro cattle-herders of the
Guajira peninsula. Each is described in terms of habitat, language, material culture
and technology, food-quest, social organization, life cycle and religious beliefs. It is
illustrated by photographs and line drawings.

182 **Tobacco and shamanism in South America.**
Johannes Wilbert. New Haven, Connecticut; London: Yale
University Press, 1987. 294p. bibliog.
Venezuela figures prominently in this continent-wide study of the use of tobacco for
magico-ritualistic purposes, which developed out of the author's interest in its cultural
significance among the Warao Indians of the Orinoco delta. The book also deals with
the various types of wild and cultivated *nicotiana* plants; the various recorded methods
of tobacco ingestion; and the pharmacological effects of nicotine administration.

183 **Demographic and biological studies of the Warao Indians.**
Edited by Johannes Wilbert, Miguel Layrisse. Los Angeles:
University of California at Los Angeles, Latin American Center, 1980.
252p. bibliog. (Latin American Studies, vol. 45).
Includes studies by various authors on topics such as demography, migration, vital
statistics, blood grouping, anthropometrics and biomedical characteristics.

Folk literature

184 **Bibliografía de la literatura indígena venezolana.** (Bibliography of the
literature of Venezuelan Indians.)
Lubio Cardozo. Mérida, Venezuela: Universidad de los Andes,
Facultad de Humanidades y Educación, Escuela de Letras, Centro de
Investigaciones Literarias, 1970. 122p.
Lists printed versions of Venezuelan Indian literature, classified by type (e.g. songs,
stories, legends, myths, poems) and by tribal group. It includes an alphabetical list of
collectors, researchers, editors etc.

185 **Watunna. An Orinoco creation cycle.**
Marc de Civrieux, translated by David M. Guss. San Francisco: North
Point, 1980. 195p.
A compendium of the oral traditions of the Makiritare Indians of the upper Orinoco,
based on the author's twenty years of repeated visits to listen to fragments and

episodes of the stories. It incorporates their myths about their heavenly ancestors, which serve as tribal law and models for earthly behaviour.

186 **Folk-literature of the Warao Indians. Narrative material and motif content.**
Johannes Wilbert. Los Angeles: University of California at Los Angeles, Latin American Center, 1970. 614p. bibliog. (Latin American Studies Series, vol. 15).
Over 200 narratives of the Warao ('boat-people') Indians of the Orinoco delta are preceded by a brief ethnographic introduction, and followed by an analysis of motifs. This incorporates much of the material previously published in the author's *Warao oral literature* (Caracas: Editorial Sucre, 1964. 199p. Instituto Caribe de Antropología y Sociología. Fundación La Salle de Ciencias Naturales. Monograph, no. 9).

187 **Geography and telluric lore of the Orinoco delta.**
Johannes Wilbert. *Journal of Latin American Lore*, vol. 5, no. 1 (1979), p. 129-50.
A fascinating exploration of the relationship between the mythic cosmology of the Warao Indians and the ecological imperatives of their homeland in the Orinoco delta.

188 **Yupa folktales.**
Johannes Wilbert. Los Angeles: University of California at Los Angeles, Latin American Center, 1974. 191p. bibliog. (Latin American Studies Series, vol. 24).
Stories told by members of the Yupa tribe of Indians of the Sierra de Perijá, on the mountainous Colombian border west of Lake Maracaibo, are preceded by an ethnographic description of the culture, and followed by an analysis of motif content.

History

General

189 Venezuela and Colombia.
Harry Bernstein.   Englewood Cliffs, New Jersey: Prentice-Hall, 1964.
152p. bibliog. (Modern Nations in Historical Perspective).
The first half of the book provides an intelligible sketch of the main themes in the history of Venezuela from the first European settlements to 1964. The remainder is a separate treatment of Colombia.

190 Genealogical historical guide to Latin America.
Lyman De Platt.   Detroit, Michigan: Gale Research, 1978. 273p.
(Gale Genealogy and Local History Series, no. 4).
The first half of the book discusses available sources, categories of civil and ecclesiastical records, palaeography, abbreviations etc. for the whole of Latin America. The second half deals with each country in turn. Chapter 30 (p. 265-68) lists the specific sources extant in Venezuela.

191 Caracas: la ciudad colonial y guzmancista. (Caracas: the city from colonial times to the era of Guzmán Blanco.)
Graziano Gasparini.   Caracas: Ernesto Armitano, 1978. 351p.
This discussion of the development of the city and its architecture, from its foundations to the late-nineteenth century, is profusely illustrated with plans and photographs.

192 **Banditry and social conflict on the Venezuelan *llanos*.**
Miguel Izard, Richard W. Slatta. In: *Bandidos: the varieties of Latin American banditry.* Edited by Richard W. Slatta. New York; Westport, Connecticut; London: Greenwood, 1987, p. 33-47. (Contributions in Criminology and Penology, no. 14).
Gives an outline of the conflict between the *llaneros* and the authorities, as expressed in various forms of criminal activity, from the Spanish settlement in the sixteenth century until the permanent establishment of governmental authority in the 1920s.

193 **The rise of Caracas as a primate city.**
John V. Lombardi. In: *Social fabric and spatial structure in colonial Latin America.* Edited by David James Robinson. Ann Arbor, Michigan: University Microfilms International, 1979, p. 433-72. (Dellplain Latin American Studies, no. 1).
Reviews the development of the capital and its relationship to the rest of the country from its foundation in 1560. Stresses the importance of the accumulation of bureaucratic functions as a result of Spanish colonial policy in the late-eighteenth century, and notes challenges to its supremacy during the independence period and the Federalist wars, eventually overcome by its consolidation under Guzmán Blanco and Gómez.

194 **Venezuela: the search for order, the dream of progress.**
John V. Lombardi. New York; Oxford: Oxford University Press, 1982. 348p. 9 maps. bibliog.
An excellent short history covering the whole period from the Spanish conquest to 1980, and giving considerable attention to social and economic, as well as to political history. It also includes: a chronology, prepared by Mary B. Floyd, (p. 269-87); a substantial and discursive bibliographic essay (p. 288-314); and a statistical supplement containing thirty tables (p. 315-33).

195 **Venezuelan history: a comprehensive working bibliography.**
John V. Lombardi, Germán Carrera Damas, Roberta E. Adams (et al.). Boston, Massachusetts: G.K. Hall, 1977. 530p.
Lists 4,647 publications under headings 'General', 'History', 'Bolívar', 'Church', 'Civilization', 'Education', 'Geography', 'Petroleum', 'Population', and 'Urbanization', and includes an author index.

196 **Venezuela through its history.**
William D. Marsland, Amy L. Marsland. New York: Crowell, 1954. 277p. bibliog.
An eminently readable survey of Venezuelan history from earliest times to 1952.

197 **A history of Venezuela.**
Guillermo Morón, translated by John Street. London: Allen & Unwin, 1964. 268p. bibliog.
An adaptation and abridgement of the third edition of the author's popular text-book, *Historia de Venezuela* (Caracas, 1961) which is fuller on the colonial and independence

periods than on the post-1830 period. This book concludes with two chapters specially written for the English edition, one by the author on the years 1936-62, and the other by Manuel Rodríguez Mena on the contemporary economic scene in Venezuela in the early 1960s.

198 **Historical dictionary of Venezuela.**
Donna Keyse Rudolph, G.A. Rudolph. Metuchen, New Jersey: Scarecrow, 1971. 142p. bibliog. (Latin American Historical Dictionaries, no. 3).
Short entries, alphabetically arranged, identify the historical significance of over 600 events, personalities, places and institutions.

Colonial period (ca. 1500-ca. 1800)

199 **Venezuelan "libranzas", 1788-1807: from economic nostrum to fiscal imperative.**
Jacques A. Barbier. *Americas. A Quarterly Review of Inter-American Cultural History*, vol. 37, no. 4 (1981), p. 457-78.
Analyses the fiscal and economic causes and consequences of the introduction of bills of exchange in dealings between Spain and Venezuela in the late colonial period.

200 **Patrons, brokers and clients in the families of the elite in colonial Caracas, 1595-1627.**
Stephanie Blank. *Americas. A Quarterly Review of Inter-American Cultural History*, vol. 36, no. 1 (1979), p. 90-115.
A study of the rôles and relationships of different groups within the Caracas élite, with a series of charts showing family connections.

201 **Patrons, clients, and kin in seventeenth-century Caracas: a methodological essay in colonial Spanish American history.**
Stephanie Blank. *Hispanic American Historical Review*, vol. 54, no. 2 (1974), p. 260-83.
Outlines the methodology used to establish that almost half of the adult male Europeans in the city in the period 1595-1627 were involved in a single kinship network, and that the élite was related to the lower strata of society by a patron-clientele system.

202 **Biographical dictionary of audiencia ministers in the Americas, 1687-1821.**
Mark A. Burkholder, D.S. Chandler. Westview, Connecticut; London: Greenwood, 1982. 491p. bibliog.
The thirty-seven persons who served in the *audiencia* of Caracas from its establishment in 1786 are listed in an appendix (p. 380-81), and the biography of each can be found in the alphabetically-arranged main body of the work.

203 **The colonial elite of early Caracas. Formation and crisis, 1567-1767.**
Robert J. Ferry.   Berkeley, California; Los Angeles; London:
University of California Press, 1989. 342p. bibliog.

This study, which is based largely on local archival records, is a major contribution to the social and economic history of the colonial period. In addition to establishing the close-knit nature of the élite by the use of family reconstitution techniques, it throws much light on the replacement of Indian labour by African slavery, and on the development of cacao production.

204 **The search for El Dorado.**
John Hemming.   London: Michael Joseph, 1978. 223p. bibliog.

Offers an illustrated account of the early explorations of Venezuela and adjacent territories in the sixteenth century, and of their relationship to the El Dorado legend.

205 **The Caracas Company, 1728-1784. A study in the history of Spanish monopolistic trade.**
Roland Dennis Hussey.   Cambridge, Massachusetts: Harvard
University Press; London: Oxford University Press, 1934. 358p.
bibliog. (Harvard Historical Studies, no. 37).

Gives a scholarly account of the history of the commercial organization that dominated the Venezuelan economy in the mid-eighteenth century.

206 **Petty capitalism in Spanish America. The *pulperos* of Puebla, Mexico City, Caracas, and Buenos Aires.**
Jay Kinsbruner.   Boulder, Colorado; London: Westview, 1987. 159p.
bibliog. (Dellplain Latin American Series, no. 21).

A comparative study of small retail grocers and their stores in several Spanish American cities, including Caracas, which covers the period 1750-1850.

207 **Pre-revolutionary Caracas: politics, economy and society, 1777-1811.**
Peter Michael McKinley.   Cambridge, England; London; New York:
Cambridge University Press, 1985. 245p. bibliog. (Cambridge Latin
American Studies, no. 56).

This revisionist work attempts to argue, on the basis of some new material (in particular a collection of 800 wills), that the province of Caracas on the eve of revolution was economically prosperous, socially harmonious, and content with its place in the imperial structure, rather than in the throes of economic crisis and social tension, as traditional views have suggested.

208 **Status and loyalty of regular army officers in late colonial Venezuela.**
Gary M. Miller.   *Hispanic American Historical Review*, vol. 66, no. 4
(1986), p. 667-96.

Analyses Spanish regular army officers in Venezuela in terms of birthplace, social origins, promotion experience, political power, and wealth and economic status, and correlates these variables with attitudes of loyalty to the Crown or alignment with the patriot forces in the period 1810-12.

209 **Spanish pearl-fishing operations on the Pearl Coast in the sixteenth century.**
Sanford A. Mosk. *Hispanic American Historical Review*, vol. 18, no. 3 (1938), p. 392-400.
A brief account of one of the main attractions, for the Spaniards, of Venezuela, and in particular of Cumaná and the island of Cubagua, this discusses the use of Indian and Negro divers, and the quantities and values of the pearls extracted.

210 **The British attacks on the Caracas coast, 1743.**
J.C.M. Ogelsby. *Mariner's Mirror: the Journal of the Society for Nautical Research*, vol. 58, no. 1 (1972), p. 27-40.
Describes the failure of British attacks on La Guaira and Puerto Cabello during the War of Jenkins' Ear, from the point of view of British naval history.

211 **The conquest and settlement of Venezuela.**
José Oviedo y Baños, translated by Jeannette Johnson Varner. Berkeley, California; Los Angeles; London: University of California Press, 1987. 305p. bibliog.
This is the first English translation of the classic account, originally published in Madrid in 1723, of the exploration and colonization of the country; there are vivid descriptions of encounters with the Indians and of internal disputes among the Spaniards. The author was born in Bogotá, son of a colonial official, brought up in Lima, and educated in Caracas under the supervision of his uncle, who was its bishop. He settled in the city, obtained wealth and office, and in his fifties produced what is regarded as the first notable literary work by an American-born resident of Venezuela. His account ends in 1600. No trace has survived of a projected second volume covering the seventeenth century.

212 **The cacao economy in the eighteenth-century province of Caracas and the Spanish cacao market.**
Eugenio Piñero. *Hispanic American Historical Review*, vol. 68. no. 1 (1988), p. 75-100.
Argues that the Caracas Company operated profitably as a link between Venezuelan producers and the Spanish market without coming into conflict with the interests of local merchants, but that its operations did little to stimulate other branches of the colonial economy.

213 **Public land policy and use in colonial Caracas.**
Kathy Waldron. *Hispanic American Historical Review*, vol. 61, no. 2 (1981), p. 258-77.
Analyses the public land policy of the Caracas municipality in the second half of the eighteenth century, using city council archives, ecclesiatical censuses, and legal records of property transactions.

Independence period (ca. 1800-ca. 1830)

214 **Journal of voyages to Marguaritta, Trinidad and Maturin, with the author's travels across the plains of the llaneros to Angustura, and subsequent descent of the Orinoco in the years 1819 and 1820, comprising his several interviews with Bolivar, the supreme chief, sketches of the various native and European generals and a variety of characteristic anecdotes hitherto unpublished.**
William Jackson Adam. Dublin: R.M. Tims, 1824. 160p.

An unvarnished and impartial account of his experiences, with comments on persons and places, by a captain in the Irish Legion of volunteers that supported the cause of independence.

215 **South American emancipation. Documents historical and explanatory, shewing the designs which have been in progress, and the exertions made by General Miranda, for South American emancipation, during the last twenty-five years.**
José María Antepara. London: Juigné, 1810. 299p.

This compilation, published by a native of Guayaquil who was an associate of Miranda's in London, includes a number of documents relating to the Precursor's expedition to Venezuela in 1806, and some subsequent letters to correspondents in Caracas.

216 **The history of Don Francisco de Miranda's attempt to affect a revolution in South America. In a series of letters to which are annexed, sketches of the life of Miranda and geographical notices of Caraccas.**
James Biggs. London: T. Gilbert, 1809. 312p.

An eye-witness account by an officer who took part in the expedition, this is a slightly enlarged revision of the first edition (Boston, Massachusetts: Oliver & Munroe, 1808).

217 **Narrative of the expedition to South America, which sailed from England at the close of 1817, for the service of the Spanish patriots: including the military and naval transactions, and the ultimate fate of that expedition: also the arrival of Colonels Blosset and English, with British troops for that service, their reception and subsequent proceedings, with other interesting occurrences.**
Charles C. Brown. London: John Booth, 1819. 194p.

The author served as an artillery captain in the Venezuelan forces. After his return to England in 1819, he wrote this book to discourage other Britons from following his example. A Spanish translation was published in *Narraciones de dos expedicionarios británicos de la independencia: James Hackett, Charles Brown*, translated by M.A. Osorio Jiménez (Caracas: Instituto Nacional de Hipódromos, 1966. Colección Venezolanista, Serie Viajeros, 1).

218 **The Santander regime in Gran Colombia.**
David Bushnell. Newark, Delaware: University of Delaware Press,
1954; Westport, Connecticut: Greenwood, 1970. 381p. bibliog.
A detailed study of the domestic history of Colombia, Venezuela and Ecuador during
the period 1821-27, when Vice-President Francisco de Paula Santander was chief
executive of the united republic. A series of analytical chapters deal with political and
judicial reforms, financial and economic problems, and social, educational and
religious policies; the closing chapters discuss the increasing difficulties over the
relationship between Venezuela and the central government in Bogotá, which were
ultimately to lead to the break-up of the Gran Colombian union in 1830.

219 **Campaigns and cruises in Venezuela and New Granada, and in the
Pacific Ocean; from 1817 to 1830: with the narrative of a march from
the river Orinoco to San Buenaventura on the coast of Chocó; and
sketches of the west coast of South America from the Gulf of California
to the archipeligo of Chiloë. Also tales of Venezuela: illustrative of
revolutionary men, manners and incidents.**
London: Longmans, 1831. 3 vols.
The author (variously identified as Richard Longueville Vowell, William D. Mahoney
and Lieutenant Wise) left England in 1817, joined Bolívar's forces at Angostura, and
served in the Boyacá campaign. This is dealt with in the first half of volume 1, the
remainder of which deals with New Granada and the Pacific coast. Volumes 2 and 3
consist of tales of Venezuela: volume 2 *The earthquake of Caracas* is a story based on
the incident of 1812; and volume 3 *The savannas of Varinas* is a story based on the
campaigns of Bolívar and Páez in the interior of the country in 1818.

220 **A narrative of proceedings in Venezuela in South America in the years
1819 and 1820; with general observations on the country and its people;
the character of the republican government, and its leading members
&c. Also a description of the country of Caraccas; of the force of
General Morillo; the state of the royalists; and the spirit of the people
under their jurisdiction.**
George Laval Chesterton. London: John & Arthur Arch, 1820. 257p.
The author served as a captain in the British Legion with the independence forces, and
was captured by the Spanish royalists.

221 **Renato Beluche: smuggler, privateer and patriot, 1780-1860.**
Jane Lucas De Grummond. Baton Rouge, Louisiana; London:
Louisiana State University Press, 1983. 300p. bibliog.
This biographical study, of a minor figure who was a patriot privateer in the wars of
independence and a Venezuelan sea captain thereafter, gives revealing glimpses of war
and trade in the Caribbean in the first half of the nineteenth century.

222 **History of the revolution of Caracas; comprising an impartial narrative of the atrocities committed by the contending parties, illustrating the real state of the contest, both in a commercial and political point of view, together with a description of the llaneros, or people of the plains of South America.**
George Dawson Flinter.   London: W. Glindon, 1819. 212p.
A pro-royalist account of the independence struggle by an Irish officer, who attempted to dissuade his fellow countrymen from volunteering for service with the patriot forces, and to advance his own interests in the service of the King of Spain.

223 **Foreign legionaries in the liberation of Spanish South America.**
Alfred Hasbrouck.   New York: Columbia University Press, 1928.
Reprinted, Octagon, 1969. 470p. bibliog.
Although somewhat outdated, and based in part on unreliable sources, this remains the fullest account in English of the activities of the British Legion in Venezuela in the wars for independence. There are thirteen appendices containing names and other details of volunteers taken from contemporary documents.

224 **Narrative of the expedition to the rivers Orinoco and Apure in South America, which sailed from England in November 1817, and joined the patriotic forces in Venezuela and Caraccas.**
Gustavus Hippisley.   London: Murray, 1819. 653p.
This detailed account of the conditions experienced by the first group of British legionaries to reach Venezuela is highly critical of the patriot leadership. It was allegedly used as a soporific by Byron, on his voyage to join the Greek revolutionaries.

225 **Carabobo, 24 June 1821. Some accounts written in English./Carabobo, 24 junio 1821. Algunas relaciones escritas en inglés.**
Edited by Eric T.D. Lambert, translated by Simón Crespo, Jeffrey Stann.   Caracas: Fundación John Boulton, 1974. 103p.
Comprises ten contemporary accounts, originally published in Dublin newspapers, taken from letters received from British participants in the decisive battle of the war of independence. Also includes a list of the names of some 500 British, Irish and German soldiers who took part, and the reminiscences of one of the wounded, given forty years later to a British traveller. There is a Spanish translation (p. 55-103).

226 **The Spanish American Revolutions, 1808-1826.**
John Lynch.   London: Weidenfeld & Nicolson, 1973. 433p. bibliog.
(Revolutions in the Modern World).
The book as a whole provides an admirable account of the historical context in which Venezuelan independence took place. Chapter six, 'Venezuela, the violent revolution' (p. 189-226) is an excellent survey of the Venezuelan phase of the liberation movements, making full use of modern scholarship.

227 **The liberators. A study of independence movements in Spanish America.**
Irene Nicholson.   London: Faber & Faber, 1969. 336p.
This book, which concentrates more on motives and trends of thought than on
campaigns and battles, contains substantial sections on Miranda and Bolívar.

228 **Outline of the revolution in Spanish America; or an account of the
origin, progress, and actual state of the war carried on between Spain
and Spanish America; containing the principal facts which have marked
the struggle.**
[Manuel Palacio Fajardo.]   London: Longman, Hurst, Rees, Orme &
Brown, 1817. 362p.
A substantial part of the work, written 'By a South American', is devoted to events in
Venezuela between 1810 and 1816.

229 **Memoirs of Gregor McGregor; comprising a sketch of the revolution in
New Grenada and Venezuela, with biographical notices of Generals
Miranda, Bolivar, Morillo and Horé, and a narrative of the expeditions
to Amelia Island, Porto Bello, and Rio de la Hache, interspersed with
revolutionary anecdotes.**
M. Rafter.   London: Stockdale, 1820. 426p.
A hostile account of the career of the Scottish adventurer, who played a distinguished
part on the patriot side in the 1816 campaign, but was subsequently involved in some
rather discreditable incidents. Written to discourage potential volunteers, by an officer
who joined McGregor's forces only in order to attempt to obtain the release of his
brother, who had been captured by the Spaniards in an earlier expedition, it includes a
number of incidental comments on persons and events of the period 1816-19.

230 **Recollections of a service of three years during the war of extermination
in the republics of Venezuela and Colombia. By an officer of the
Colombian navy.**
London: Hunt & Clarke, 1828. 2 vols.
These reminiscences of a British volunteer, who travelled widely through the country,
are attributed to Captain Cowie.

231 **The life of Miranda.**
William Spence Robertson.   Chapel Hill, North Carolina: University
of North Carolina Press, 1929. Reprinted, New York: Cooper Square,
1969. 2 vols. bibliog.
This excellent work remains the standard biography of Francisco de Miranda (1750-
1816), Precursor of Spanish American independence. It draws heavily on Miranda's
own papers, which were not available to the author when he prepared the dissertation
on which his earlier study, *Francisco de Miranda and the revolutionizing of Spanish
America* (Washington, DC: Government Printing Office, 1909. American Historical
Association Report, 1907, vol. 1, p. 189-540), was based.

232 **The rise of the Spanish American republics as told in the lives of their liberators.**
William Spence Robertson. New York: Collier, 1961. 348p. bibliog.
Originally published in 1918, this remained for over half a century the best general introduction to the revolutionary period, until the publication of Lynch's *Spanish American Revolutions* (q.v.). Three of its seven biographical chapters are on the Venezuelans Francisco de Miranda, Simón Bolívar and Antonio José de Sucre.

233 **Journal of an expedition of 1400 miles up the Orinoco and 300 up the Arauca; with an account of the country, the manners of the people, military operations, &c.**
J.H. Robinson. London: Black, Young & Young, 1822. 397p.
A first-hand account of travel by a surgeon who served with the patriot forces, which makes highly critical comments on the people and their government.

234 **A general account of Miranda's expedition, including the trial and execution of ten of his officers, and an account of the imprisonment and sufferings of the remainder of his officers and men who were taken prisoners. Upon the authority of a person who was an officer under Miranda, who was taken and condemned to ten years imprisonment, and who after suffering nearly two years, effected his return home.**
John H. Sherman. New York: McFarlane & Long, 1808. 120p.
Includes interesting details of the first phase of Miranda's 1806 expedition, and of the interrogation, condemnation, imprisonment and execution of prisoners.

235 **Antonio José de Sucre (Gran Mariscal de Ayacucho). Hero and martyr of American independence. A sketch of his life.**
Guillermo A. Sherwell. Washington, DC: The Author, 1924. 236p. bibliog.
A work of popularization rather than scholarship, this was published to mark the centenary of Sucre's victory at Ayacucho, which ended the independence wars, by the one-time secretary-general of the Inter-American High Commission. Sherwell's similar book, *Simón Bolívar (El Libertador). Patriot, warrior, statesman, father of five nations. A sketch of his life and work*, originally published in 1921, was reprinted for the centenary of Bolívar's death (Baltimore, Maryland, 1930. 233p.).

236 **History of the adventures and suffering of Moses Smith, during five years of his life; from the beginning of the year 1806, when he was betrayed into the Miranda expedition, until June 1811, when he was nonsuited in an action at law, which lasted three years and a half, to which is added a biographical sketch of Gen. Miranda.**
Moses Smith. Albany, New York: Packard & Van Benthuysen, 1814. 146p.
A first-hand account by a young American, who was deceived into sailing to Venezuela with Miranda's expedition, of his journey, capture and imprisonment, and his impressions of the Precursor.

237 **Pablo Morillo and Venezuela, 1815-1820.**
Stephen K. Stoan.   Columbus, Ohio: Ohio State University Press.
1974. 249p. bibliog.
A sympathetic analysis, based largely on manuscripts in Spanish archives, of the
royalist administration during the Bolivarian campaigns for independence.

238 **Miranda: world citizen.**
Joseph Francis Thorning.   Gainesville, Florida: University of Florida
Press, 1952. 324p. bibliog.
A biography which stresses its subject's world-wide vision, and makes use of various
contributions to Miranda scholarship subsequent to Robertson's standard *Life of
Miranda* (q.v.).

239 **Morillo's attempt to pacify Venezuela.**
Laura F. Ullrick.   *Hispanic American Historical Review*, vol. 3, no. 4
(1920), p. 535-65.
Gives a brief narrative account of the Spanish expedition, led by General Pablo
Morillo, which attempted to restore Venezuela and New Granada to royalist rule
between 1815 and 1820.

240 **An exposé on the dissensions of Spanish America . . . intended as a
means to induce the mediatory influence of Great Britain, in order to put
an end to a destructive civil war, and to establish permanent quiet and
prosperity, on a basis consistent with the dignity of Spain, and the
interests of the world.**
William Walton.   London: Glindon, 1814. 480p.
This was sub-titled 'Respectfully addressed to HRH the Regent of the United
Kingdom'. Includes many references and two appendices relating to events in
Venezuela between 1810 and 1814.

Simón Bolívar (1783-1830)

241 **Simón Bolívar: South American liberator.**
Hildegarde Angell.   New York: Norton, 1930. 296p. bibliog.
A lively, though now somewhat dated, biography.

242 **Bolivar and the political thought of the Spanish American revolution.**
Víctor Andrés Belaunde.   Baltimore, Maryland: Johns Hopkins, 1938.
Reprinted, New York: Octagon, 1967. 451p. bibliog.
A detailed critical analysis of Bolívar's political thought within the ideological context
of the revolution, showing how its complexities and contradictions reflected contrasts
in the American reality, and development in the light of experience. It is still of value
to the English reader despite half a century of subsequent Bolivarian scholarship.

243 **Memoirs of Simón Bolívar, president liberator of the republic of Colombia; and of his principal generals; comprising a secret history of the revolution, and the events which preceded it, from 1807 to the present time.**
H. Lafayette Villaume Ducoudray-Holstein. London: Colburn & Bentley, 1830. 2 vols.
A highly disparaging account of the career and character of the Liberator, written by his one-time chief-of-staff.

244 **Birth of a world. Bolivar in terms of his peoples.**
Waldo Frank. Boston, Massachusetts: Houghton Mifflin, 1951. 432p. bibliog.
One of the best-known biographies, concentrating rather more on the political than the military side, and emphasizing the relevance of Bolívar's continental vision to the world rôle of the United States in the mid-twentieth century.

245 **Hispanic American Historical Review.**
Special Issue, vol. 63, no. 1 (1983). 232p.
This number, commemorating the bicentenary of the birth of the Liberator, contains John Lynch's 'Bolívar and the caudillos' (p. 3-35); Simon Collier's 'Nationality, nationalism, and supranationalism in the writings of Simón Bolívar' (p. 37-64); David Bushnell's 'The last dictatorship: betrayal or consummation?' (p. 65-105); and Germán Carrera Damas's 'Simón Bolívar, el culto heroico y la nación' (p. 107-45).

246 **Simón Bolívar and Spanish American independence: 1783-1830.**
John J. Johnson, Doris M. Ladd. Princeton, New Jersey; Toronto; London: Van Nostrand, 1968. 223p. bibliog.
Part I sketches the independence movement and Bolívar's rôle in it. Part II is a selection of 'readings', which includes extracts both from Bolívar's own writings and from works about him and the Spanish American revolutions.

247 **Selected writings of Bolivar.**
Compiled by Vicente Lecuna, edited by Harold A. Bierck, translated by Lewis Bertrand. New York: Colonial, 1951. 2nd ed. 2 vols.
This valuable collection of 327 documents contains translations of all of the Liberator's important political writings, as well as numerous examples of letters, proclamations, and public addresses. There is a useful introduction by the editor. Nineteen of the political documents are reproduced, with brief introductory remarks, in *The political thought of Bolívar. Selected writings*, edited by Gerald E. Fitzgerald (The Hague: Martinus Nijhoff, 1971. 143p.); and six of the best known are printed in *Simón Bolívar: his basic thoughts*, edited by Manuel Pérez Vila (Caracas: Presidency of the Republic, 1981. 166p.).

248 **Bolívar. The life of an idealist.**
Emil Ludwig, translated by Mary B. Lindsay. New York: Alliance
Book Corporation, 1942. 362p.
Written, at the request of the Venezuelan government, by a biographer of Napoleon
and Lincoln, this interesting biography concentrates on the Liberator's character,
idealism and inner conflicts, rather than on his campaigns.

249 **Bolivar.**
Salvador de Madariaga. London; Sydney; Toronto: Hollis & Carter,
1952. bibliog. Reprinted, Westport, Connecticut: Greenwood, 1979.
711p.
This full-scale biography, though based on much detailed research, is an anti-
Bolivarian polemic rather than an objective work of scholarship.

250 **Simon Bolivar.**
Gerhard Masur. Albuquerque, New Mexico: University of New
Mexico Press, 1969. 2nd ed. 572p. bibliog.
A comprehensive account of the life of the Liberator, based on a wide range of source
materials. Though first published in 1948, it is still the best full-scale biography in
English.

251 **Bolívar and the war of independence. Memorias del General Daniel
Florencio O'Leary. Narración.** (Memoirs of General Daniel Florence
O'Leary. Narrative.)
Daniel Florencio O'Leary, abridged, translated and edited by Robert
F. McNerney, Jr. Austin, Texas; London: University of Texas Press,
1970. 386p.
An English abridgement of the major part of the *Narración* – the 'official' biography of
the Liberator, covering the period to the end of 1826, written soon after Bolívar's
death by the Irish volunteer who had become his chief aide-de-camp and close friend.
The *Narración* constituted the first three volumes of the *Memorias*, eventually
published in thirty-one volumes (Caracas: 1879-88), the remaining volumes consisting
of printed texts of the main body of Bolívar's papers, which he had entrusted to
O'Leary for preservation and arrangement.

252 **Bolívar the liberator.**
Lauran Paine. London: Hale, 1970. 207p. bibliog.
A short 'broad-brush' account of its subject, based on secondary authorities.

253 **Bibliography of the Liberator Simón Bolívar.**
Pan American Union. Washington, DC: Pan American Union, 1933.
107p. (Bibliographic Series, no. 1).
Compiled in the Columbus Memorial Library of the Pan American Union to
commemorate the 150th anniversary of Bolívar's birth (24 July 1783), this is a revision
and enlargement of the bibliography compiled for the centenary of his death (17
Dec. 1830), and includes many items published in connection with that centennial.
Listed by author's name are 1,424 titles. There is a brief biography of Bolívar, in
English and Spanish, by Enrique Coronado Suárez.

254 **Simón Bolívar, "El Libertador". A life of the chief leader in the revolt against Spain in Venezuela, New Granada and Peru.**
F. Loraine Petre. London; New York: Lane, 1910. 459p. bibliog.

An attempt by a military historian to 'revive interest' in Europe in a figure who had fallen into 'undeserved oblivion'. A solid work, it is based on a limited range of printed sources, and attempts to steer a course between the traditional polarized attitudes of adulation and denigration, but ends with its own strongly opinionated conclusion.

255 **Bolívar as viewed by contemporary diplomats of the United States.**
J. Fred Rippy. *Hispanic American Historical Review*, vol. 15, no. 3 (1935), p. 287-97.

Quotes, and discusses, the comments on the Liberator by various American representatives between 1818 and 1830.

256 **Bolívar. A continent and its destiny.**
J.L. Salcedo-Bastardo, translated by Annella McDermott. Richmond, England: Richmond, 1977. 191p. bibliog.

A concise introduction, by a distinguished Venezuelan scholar, politican and diplomat, to the central figure in Venezuelan history, outlining the historical context in which Simón Bolívar came to prominence; his character, ideas and achievements; and his significance in the evolution of modern Latin America.

257 **Bolivar and the independence of Spanish America.**
John Brande Trend. London: Hodder & Stoughton for English Universities Press, 1946. 287p. bibliog. (Teach Yourself History Series).

Offers a short biography in chronological form, which is still a useful introduction, despite its date.

258 **The four seasons of Manuela. A biography. The love story of Manuela Sáenz and Simón Bolívar.**
Victor W. Von Hagen. New York: Duell, Sloan & Pearce; Boston, Massachusetts: Little, Brown, 1952. 320p. bibliog.

This biography of the most significant woman in Bolívar's later life throws much light on the Liberator and his associates.

259 **Simon Bolivar.**
Elizabeth Dey Jenkinson Waugh. London; Glasgow, Scotland: Collins, 1944. 364p.

A simply presented account, presumably intended for high-school students.

260 **Simon Bolivar.**
Dennis Wepman. London; Toronto; New York: Burke, 1988. 111p. bibliog. (World Leaders Past and Present).

A brief illustrated life for teenage readers.

261 **Bolívar.**
   Donald E. Worcester.   London: Hutchinson, 1978. 243p. (The Library
   of World Biography).
A straightforward concise life of the Liberator, which provides a useful study of its
subject.

National period (ca. 1830- .)

262 **Rómulo Betancourt and the transformation of Venezuela.**
   Robert Jackson Alexander.   New Brunswick, New Jersey; London:
   Transaction, 1982. 737p. bibliog.
A full-scale biography of the major figure in the development of Venezuela's first
popularly-based political party, and leader of the country, 1945-48 and 1959-63, who is
described by the author as 'the greatest Venezuelan since Simón Bolívar'.

263 **The Venezuelan democratic revolution. A profile of the regime of
   Rómulo Betancourt.**
   Robert J. Alexander.   New Brunswick, New Jersey: Rutgers
   University Press, 1964. 345p.
A sympathetic view of the aims and achievements that characterized the period
1959-63, in political, economic and social terms.

264 **The Democratic left in exile: the antidictatorial struggle in the
   Caribbean, 1945-1959.**
   Charles D. Ameringer.   Coral Gables, Florida: University of Miami
   Press, 1974. 352p. bibliog.
Venezuela's *Acción Democrática* figures prominently in this scholarly study of the
history of reformist movements throughout the Caribbean and Central American area.
Its activities, both underground and in exile, between its overthrow in the military
coup of 1948 and its return to power in 1959 are fully explored, as are its relationships
with like-minded parties in other countries.

265 **The Gómez regime in Venezuela and its background,**
   Pedro Manuel Arcaya.   Washington, DC: Sun Printing Office, 1936.
   238p.
Gómez's minister in Washington justifies the dictatorship, on the grounds of
Venezuela's previously turbulent history, the country's desire for strong leadership,
and the benefits conferred by the régime.

266 **Venezuela: oil and politics.**
   Rómulo Betancourt, translated by Everett Bauman.   Boston,
   Massachusetts: Houghton, Mifflin, 1979. 408p.
Originally written in exile, and published in Mexico in 1955, Betancourt's vigorous
account of the achievements of his period as provisional president between 1945 and

1948, and its aftermath in the dictatorship of Pérez Jiménez, is a work of fundamental importance. Also included is an epilogue, prepared in 1967 for the second Spanish edition, summarizing the oil policy of the *Acción Democrática* government under the author's presidency, 1959-64.

267 **The Venezuelan armed forces in politics, 1935-1959.**
Winfield J. Burggraaff.   Columbia, Missouri: University of Missouri Press, 1972. 241p.

Analyses the political behaviour of the officer corps between the death of Gómez and the presidency of Betancourt, in an attempt to explain why the military intervened in this period and not thereafter.

268 **Venezuelan regionalism and the rise of Táchira.**
Winfield J. Burggraaff.   *Americas. A Quarterly Review of Inter-American Cultural History*, vol. 25 (1968), p. 160-73.

Outlines the development of the Táchira region in the nineteenth century, and explains the origins and success of Cipriano Castro's revolution of 1899.

269 **The creation of the Venezuelan naval squadron, 1848-1860.**
Francis James Dallett.   *American Neptune*, vol. 30 (1970), p. 260-78.

A sketch of the early history of the Venezuelan navy, giving details of national vessels, and discussing its origins in the mid-century civil wars and in the need to control smuggling.

270 **Colombia, Ecuador and Venezuela, c.1880-1930.**
Malcolm Deas.   In: *The Cambridge History of Latin America. Volume V – c.1870-1930*. Edited by Leslie Bethell. Cambridge, England; London; New York: Cambridge University Press, 1986, p. 641-82.

There is a brief survey of Venezuelan history from Guzmán Blanco to Gómez (p. 670-82).

271 **Venezuela, Colombia and Ecuador: the first half-century of independence.**
Malcolm Deas.   In: *The Cambridge History of Latin America. Volume III – From Independence to c.1870*. Edited by Leslie Bethell.   ·
Cambridge, England; London; New York: Cambridge University Press, 1985, p. 507-38.

A co-ordinated analytical study of economic, social and political developments in the three countries, covering the years c.1820-70.

272 **Populism in Venezuela, 1935-48: Betancourt and *Acción Democrática*.**
Steven Ellner.   In: *Latin American populism in comparative perspective*. Edited by Michael L. Conniff. Albuquerque, New Mexico: University of New Mexico Press, 1982, p. 135-49.

Makes an interesting analysis of the reasons for Betancourt's early adoption and eventual abandonment of populist techniques and policies.

273 **The indictment of a dictator: the extradition and trial of Marcos Pérez Jiménez.**
Judith Ewell. College Station, Texas: Texas A & M University Press, 1981. 203p. bibliog.
Discusses the legal proceedings against Pérez Jiménez brought by the Betancourt government in an attempt to eradicate caudillism from Venezuelan politics.

274 **Venezuela: a century of change.**
Judith Ewell. London: Hurst; Stanford, California: Stanford University Press, 1984. 258p. bibliog.
A well-presented survey of the period from the 1890s to the 1980s, covering political, socio-economic and cultural developments, incorporating the findings of much recent research, and appending a few tables of basic statistics.

275 **A city comes of age: Caracas in the era of Antonio Guzmán Blanco (1870-1888).**
John H. Galey. *Boletín del Centro de Investigaciones Históricas y Estéticas* (Caracas), no. 15 (1973), p. 77-113.
Offers an interesting discussion of the economic, social and architectural development of the capital and its communications in the late-nineteenth century.

276 **Venezuela and its ruler.**
Nemesio García Naranjo, translated by Calla Wheaton Esteva. New York: Carranza, 1927. 174p.
A collection of newspaper articles, based on a visit to Venezuela in 1926, about President Juan Vicente Gómez and the achievements of his régime, by a Mexican journalist with a marked preference for dictatorship.

277 **Caudillism and militarism in Venezuela, 1810-1910.**
Robert L. Gilmore. Athens, Ohio: Ohio University Press, 1964. 211p. bibliog.
Argues that, before the professionalization of the Venezuelan army under the dictatorship of Juan Vicente Gómez between 1908 and 1935, the country was subject to caudillism – the union of personalism and violence for the conquest of power – rather than militarism – undue military interference, over the state. The caudillism which characterized nineteenth-century Venezuela is attributed to the social background, the legacy of the wars of independence, political discontents, and the availability of ambitious local leaders and irregular militia forces.

278 **José Antonio Páez.**
Robert Bontine Cunninghame Graham. London: Heinemann, 1929. 328p. bibliog.
A lively and sympathetic, but somewhat unscholarly, biography of the leading figure in Venezuelan history from the mid 1820s to the mid 1840s. The author (1852-1936), a Scottish landowner and radical politician, was a prolific writer on South America, where he had lived among the gauchos in the 1870s and was known as 'Don Roberto'. A visit to Venezuela in 1925 gave rise to this biography, and also to some evocative

short sketches, two of which 'Los niños toreros' (The boy bull-fighters) and 'Los llanos del Apure' (The plains of the Río Apure) were reprinted in *The South American sketches of R.B. Cunninghame Graham*, edited by John Walker (Norman, Oklahoma: University of Olkahoma Press, 1978, p. 265-80).

279 **Democracy and dictatorship in Venezuela, 1945-1958.**
Glen L. Kolb. Hamden, Connecticut: Archon. 1974. 228p. bibliog.
(Connecticut College Monograph, no. 10).

An interpretative account of the first *Acción Democrática* administration and of the dictatorship of Pérez Jiménez, which stresses the struggle between liberal-democratic and conservative-personalist forces, and the influence of United States policy on events.

280 **A halo for Gómez.**
John Lavin. New York: Pageant, 1954. 471p. bibliog.

An informal biography, which acknowledges the achievements of Gómez's despotism without dismissing its excesses.

281 **Venezuela's "generation of '28": the genesis of political democracy.**
John D. Martz. *Journal of Inter-American Studies*, vol. 6, no. 1 (1964), p. 17-32.

A discussion of the emergence of a group of students in opposition to the Gómez dictatorship in 1928, and of its subsequent evolution into an embryonic democratic political movement in 1936-37.

282 **Venezuela. Siglo XIX en fotografía.** (Venezuela. The nineteenth century in photographs.)
Carlos Eduardo Misle. Caracas: Compañía Anónima Nacional Teléfonos de Venezuela (CANTV), 1981. 200p. bibliog.

A collection of daguerrotypes and photographs from the 1840s to the 1890s, mainly of people and places, with a commentary on technical and historical aspects.

283 **The illustrious American: the development of nationalism in Venezuela under Antonio Guzmán Blanco.**
Julian Nava. *Hispanic American Historical Review*, vol. 45, no. 4 (1965), p. 527-43.

Discusses various social and cultural aspects of the Guzmán Blanco period, including attitudes to race, the family and women; education and learned societies; literature and the arts; and the development of national self-awareness.

284 **Memoirs of a soldier of fortune.**
Rafael de Nogales, with a preface by R.B. Cunninghame Graham.
London: Wright & Brown, [n.d.]. 334p.

Includes five chapters telling of adventures in the author's native Venezuela between 1909 and 1913, when he was opposing the Gómez dictatorship.

285   **Foreign influences on Venezuelan political thought, 1830-1930.**
William Whately Pierson, Jr.   *Hispanic American Historical Review*,
vol. 15, no. 1 (1935), p. 3-42.
Reviews the works of Venezuelan political and constitutional writers, and concludes
that the country absorbed many different foreign influences, that of France being most
significant on the philosophical side, and that of the United States on the institutional
side.

286   **Gómez: the shame of America. Fragments from the *Memoirs of a citizen
of the republic of Venezuela in the days of her decadence*.**
José Rafael Pocaterra.   Paris: Delpeuch, 1929. 255p.
A translation of some chapters from the middle two volumes of the author's *Memorias
de un venezolano de la decadencia* (Caracas; Madrid: Ediciones Edime, 1966. 4 vols.),
parts of which had been previously published in Mexico and Colombia in the 1920s. It
records Pocaterra's experiences in Gómez' prisons.

287   **The dictators of Venezuela.**
J. Fred Rippy.   In: *South American dictators during the first century of
independence*. Edited by Alva Curtis Wilgus. Washington, DC: George
Washington University Press, 1937. Reprinted, New York: Russell &
Russell, 1963, p. 391-426.
Includes brief sketches of José Antonio Páez, Antonio Guzmán Blanco, Cipriano
Castro, and Juan Vicente Gómez.

288   **Coffee and capitalism in the Venezuelan Andes.**
William Roseberry.   Austin, Texas: University of Texas Press, 1984.
256p. bibliog. (Institute of Latin American Studies, University of
Texas. Latin American Monographs, no. 59).
A study of the social and economic history of the coffee-producing district of Bonocó
in Trujillo state, which utilizes Marxist analysis to discuss the changing relationships of
its peasant farmers to the national economy, as coffee gave way to petroleum as its
dominant driving force.

289   **Gómez, tyrant of the Andes.**
Thomas Rourke (pseudonym of Daniel Joseph Clinton).   New York:
William Morrow, 1936. 320p. bibliog.
A lively journalistic biography that paints a highly critical portrait of the dictator, by an
author who later published *Simón Bolívar* (London: Michael Joseph, 1940. 385p.), a
largely factual biography of the Liberator.

290   **Oil politics in Venezuela during the López Contreras administration
(1936-41).**
Kelvin Singh. *Journal of Latin American Studies*, vol. 21, no. 1
(1989), p. 89-104.
This analysis of the relations between the international oil companies and the
Venezuelan government, based on the records of the United States Department of
State, suggests that President López may have been pursuing personal advantage as
much as national interests.

291 **The harassed exile: General Cipriano Castro, 1908-1924.**
William M. Sullivan. *Americas. A Quarterly Review of Inter-American Cultural History*, vol. 33, no. 2 (1976), p. 282-97.
An account of the ex-president's travels in exile, and of the extraordinary efforts made by his successor Gómez and by foreign governments to prevent his return to Venezuela.

292 **The Venezuelan *golpe de estado* of 1958: the fall of Marcos Pérez Jiménez.**
Philip B. Taylor, Jr. Washington, DC: Institute for the Comparative Study of Political Systems, 1968. 96p. (Political Studies Series, no. 4).
A brief analysis of the overthrow of Pérez Jiménez which places it in its historical context.

293 **Caudillo; a portrait of Antonio Guzmán Blanco.**
George S. Wise. New York: Columbia University Press; London, Toronto, Bombay: Oxford University Press, 1951. 190p. bibliog.
Two chapters on the colonial background, two on Venezuela from independence to 1870, and two on the dictatorship of Guzmán Blanco (1870-88), are followed by four chapters analysing the régime as a case study in caudillism, each of which focuses on a different aspect: 'ideological irresponsibility', 'the unqualified use of force', 'financial chicanery', and 'personalism'.

294 **Young man of Caracas.**
Thomas Russell Ybarra. New York: Washburn, 1941. 324p.; London: Hall, 1943. 271p.
The reminiscences of military and political affairs in the 1890s, written by the son of a Venezuelan general married to the daughter of the United States Minister. The author was born in 1880, lived much of his adult life in New York and Boston, and published *Bolívar, the passionate warrior* (New York: Washburn, 1929. 375p.), a colourfully-written, but essentially derivative biography, designed for a North American audience, to mark the centenary of the Liberator's death.

Politics and Government

General

295 **A problem of political integration in Latin America. The *barrios* of Venezuela.**
Michael Bamberger. *International Affairs*, vol. 44, no. 4 (1968), p. 709-19.
This analysis of the causes and consequences of the comparatively low level of political participation by those in the urban squatter settlements in the 1960s is still of interest to the student of the evolution of democratic politics in Venezuela.

296 **Venezuela: politics in a petroleum republic.**
David Eugene Blank. New York; London: Praeger; Stanford, California: Hoover Institution Press, 1984. 225p. bibliog. (Politics in Latin America: a Hoover Institution Series).
A new synthesis of Venezuelan politics, which places the political culture and the party system in their historical and socio-economic settings. Blank is also author of a textbook for this field, *Politics in Venezuela: a country study* (Boston, Massachusetts: Little, Brown, 1973. 293p.)

297 **The challenge of Venezuelan democracy.**
José Antonio Gil Yepes, translated by Evelyn Harrison I., Loló Gil de Yenes, Danielle Salti. New Brunswick, New Jersey; London: Transaction, 1981. 280p.
Considers how relationships between the business and governmental élites could be improved, so as to enhance economic, social and political development, and so contribute to the consolidation of Venezuelan democracy.

298 **Guerrilla movements in Latin America.**
Richard Gott. London: Nelson, 1970. 452p. bibliog.
Part two, 'Revolutionary failure in Venezuela' (p. 93-165), is a study of guerrilla activity and of the political proponents of armed struggle in the 1960s. The remainder of the book provides a continental context within which the Venezuelan experience should be seen.

299 **Venezuela.**
William L. Hamilton. In: *Students and politics in developing nations.*
Edited by Donald Kenneth Emmerson. London: Pall Mall, 1968,
p. 350-89.
Discusses the extent of student participation in politics, the characteristics of student leaders, and the rôle of political students, under the Gómez and Pérez Jiménez dictatorships, in the periods of transition in 1936 and 1958, and in the representative democracy of the 1960s.

300 **Democracy in Latin America: Colombia and Venezuela.**
Edited by Donald L. Herman. New York; Westport, Connecticut;
London: Praeger, 1988. 342p. bibliog.
A collection of fourteen essays by various authors on the politics of the 1980s. Four deal specifically with Venezuela and five compare the two countries. Among the topics discussed are political parties and elections, economic development, the state, the church, public opinion, public order, and external relations.

301 **Petroleum and political pacts: the transition to democracy in Venezuela.**
Terry Lynn Karl. *Latin American Research Review*, vol. 22, no. 1
(1987), p. 63-94.
A largely theoretical discussion, arguing that the establishment of a democratic political system in 1958 resulted from changes in the socio-economic structure. These arose from the development of the oil industry, and from a series of 'pacts' among different sections of the élite, which defined the parameters within which reforms could take place, and excluded certain broad economic questions from the party political arena.

302 **Latin American politics: a historical bibliography.**
Santa Barbara, California; Denver, Colorado; Oxford: ABC-Clio,
1984. 290p. (Clio Bibliographical Series, no. 16).
Includes sixty-seven annotated entries relating to periodical articles on Venezuelan politics published between 1973 and 1982.

303 **Conflict and political change in Venezuela.**
Daniel H. Levine. Princeton, New Jersey: Princeton University Press,
1973. 285p. bibliog.
A theoretical study in conflict resolution, illustrated by two case-studies, rather than a descriptive survey of Venezuelan politics. The book contains material based on interviews, conducted in the late 1960s, with leaders concerned in many fields of activity in Venezuela, regarding their views on the rôle of the church and of secular authorities in educational reform, and on the place of students in politics.

304 **The transition to democracy: are there lessons from Venezuela?**
Daniel H. Levine. *Bulletin of Latin American Research*, vol. 4, no. 2 (1985), p. 47-61.
Accounts for the survival of democratic government since 1958 in terms of the emphasis placed by successive political leaders on caution, conciliation, and compromise, rather than on specific programmes, and on the growing legitimization of the political system through the alternation of political power between broad-based political parties as a result of elections, details of which are illustrated by four statistical tables. Concludes with a brief discussion of how far the Venezuelan model might be applied to other Latin American countries.

305 **Venezuela and Paraguay: political modernity and tradition in conflict.**
Leo B. Lott. New York: Holt, Rinehart & Winston, 1972. 395p. bibliog. (Modern Comparative Politics Series).
A text-book which compares the political systems of the two countries in 1968.

306 **Policy-making and the quest for consensus: nationalizing Venezuelan petroleum.**
John D. Martz. *Journal of Inter-American Studies and World Affairs*, vol. 19, no. 4 (1977), p. 483-509.
Discusses the way in which the Pérez régime in 1974-75 tried unsuccessfully to achieve a political consensus over the detailed implementation of the nationally agreed policy of nationalizing the oil industry.

307 **Venezuela: democratic politics of petroleum.**
John D. Martz. In: *Politics, policies, and economic development in Latin America.* Edited by Robert Wesson. Stanford, California: Hoover Institution Press, Stanford University, 1984, p. 161-87.
Makes a survey of the background to the fiscal crisis of 1983, which is attributed to lax management and consensus politics. Concludes that, although the country has not reduced its dependence on oil, its oil wealth has enabled it to become modernized, educated and healthy, and given it the capacity to surmount the crisis.

308 **Venezuela: the democratic experience.**
Edited by John D. Martz, David J. Myers. New York; Toronto; Tokyo, etc.: Praeger, 1986. rev. ed. 489p. bibliog.
A complete rewriting of the first edition of 1977, placing emphasis on subsequent developments, this collection of essays adds up to an impressive analysis of Venezuela's political institutions and policy-making in the 1980s. It comprises John V. Lombardi's 'The patterns of Venezuela's past'; R. Lynn Kelley's 'Venezuelan constitutional forms and realities'; Enrique A. Baloyra's 'Public opinion and support for the regime: 1973-1983'; the editors' 'The politics of economic development'; Myers's 'The Venezuelan party system: regime maintenance under stress'; José Antonio Gil Yepes's 'Political articulation of the military sector in Venezuelan democracy'; Gene E. Bigler and Enrique Viloria V.'s 'State enterprises and the decentralized public administration'; William S. Stewart's 'Public administration'; Martz' 'Petroleum: the national and international perspectives'; David E. Blank's 'Petroleum: the community and regional perspectives'; Steven Ellner's 'Educational

policy'; Donald L. Herman's 'Agriculture'; H. Dieter Heinen and Walter Coppens's 'Indian affairs'; Ildemaro Jesús Martínez's 'Venezuelan local government'; Charles D. Ameringer's 'Foreign policy of democratic Venezuela'; and the editors' 'Venezuelan democracy: performance and prospects'. The first edition, a similar volume of essays. many by the same authors, is still well worth consulting as an authoritative account of the politics of the 1960s and early 1970s.

309 **Tutelary pluralism: a critical approach to Venezuelan democracy.**
Luis J. Oropeza.   Cambridge, Massachusetts: Harvard University Center for International Affairs, 1983. 127p. bibliog. (Harvard Studies in International Affairs, no. 46).
Argues that the main dichotomy in Venezuelan politics is between the military authoritarian and the liberal democratic traditions, and that it is reconciled by 'tutelary pluralism', whereby élite-dominated political parties control popular participation to a sufficient extent to ensure consensus, but without allowing power to be concentrated so far as to encourage despotism.

310 **Latin American democracies: Colombia, Costa Rica, Venezuela.**
John A. Peeler.   Chapel Hill, North Carolina; London: University of North Carolina Press, 1985. 193p. bibliog.
Compares and contrasts the factors influencing the emergence of liberal democracy in the three republics, its maintenance throughout the 1960s and 1970s, and its future prospects.

311 **Urbanization and politics.**
John A. Peeler.   Beverly Hills, California; London: Sage, 1977. 56p. bibliog. (Sage Professional Papers in Comparative Politics, vol. 6).
Argues, on the basis of a comparative study of Caracas and Bogotá, against a simplistic relationship between urbanization and political instability, and stresses the significance of a full understanding of the development of the political culture of the country.

312 **Political mobilization of the Venezuelan peasant.**
John Duncan Powell.   Cambridge, Massachusetts: Harvard University Press, 1971. 259p.
Describes the process by which the peasants were incorporated into politics, largely by the *Acción Democrática* (AD – 'Democratic action') party. Considers how the party retained their support by means of the agrarian reforms of the 1960s.

313 **The politics of the barrios in Venezuela.**
Talton F. Ray.   Berkeley, California; Los Angeles: University of California Press, 1969. 211p. bibliog.
Makes an analysis of the political behaviour and attitudes of the inhabitants of the shanty towns in and around Venezuelan cities and of their rôle in national politics. It is based on the author's work experience in an urban community development organization in the early 1960s.

Parties and elections

314 The Communist Party of Venezuela.
Robert Jackson Alexander. Stanford, California: Hoover Institution Press, 1969. 246p. bibliog. (Comparative Communist Party Politics, Hoover Institution Studies, no. 24).

Describes the history of the *Partido Comunista de Venezuela* (PCV), its structure and organization, its relation to the Venezuelan political environment, its international connections and the determinants of its behaviour.

315 Political parties in the Americas. Canada, Latin America and the West Indies.
Edited by Robert Jackson Alexander. Westport, Connecticut; London: Greenwood, 1982. 2 vols. (The Greenwood Historical Encyclopaedia of the World's Political Parties).

Venezuela is covered in volume 2 (p. 690-742). A brief historical summary is followed by an alphabetical listing of parties, with notes on each, varying from a few lines to several pages, depending on the significance of its rôle.

316 Leonardo Ruiz Pineda: leader of the Venezuelan resistance, 1949-1952.
Charles D. Ameringer. *Journal of Interamerican Studies and World Affairs*, vol. 21, no. 2 (1979), p. 209-32.

Compares the historical reality of the rôle of Ruiz (who led the underground remnants of the AD until he was killed by the dictatorial régime) with the 'democratic martyr' myth created by the party on its return to power. A comment by Steven Ellner, 'Leonardo Ruiz Pineda: Acción Democrática's *guerrillero* for liberty', *Journal of Interamerican Studies and World Affairs*, vol. 22, no. 3 (1980), p. 389-92, adds further information and suggests some modifications to Ameringer's conclusions.

317 Elections and negotiation. The limits of democracy in Venezuela, 1958-1981.
Eduardo Arroyo Talavera. New York: Garland, 1986. 450p. bibliog.

Presented as a doctoral dissertation, this is a sophisticated and critical analysis of Venezuela's democratic political system, and its dependence on negotiations and compromises between the political parties on the one hand and the business élite and the military on the other.

318 Dimensions of campaign participation: Venezuela, 1973.
Enrique A. Baloyra, John D. Martz. In: *Political participation in Latin America: vol. I Citizen and state.* Edited by John A. Booth, Mitchell A. Seligson. New York; London: Holmes & Meier, 1978, p. 61-84.

Argues, on the basis of survey evidence, that political partisanship was a more important determinant of campaign participation than social class.

319 **Political attitudes in Venezuela: societal cleavages and political opinion.**
Enrique A. Baloyra, John D. Martz. Austin, Texas: University of
Texas Press, 1979. 300p.

An analysis of the political beliefs, attitudes and orientations of the Venezuelan public,
at the time of the elections of 1973, which is based on a sample survey of 1,500
respondents. The conclusions show a strong commitment to elections, developmental
policies and anti-communism, and opposition to one-party rule and military coups.
Ideology emerges as quite as important as social class in influencing affiliations, and
regional analysis reveals a higher rate of active political participation in the periphery
than at the urban centre.

320 **Factionalism in the Venezuelan communist movement, 1937-48.**
Steve Ellner. *Science and Society*, vol. 45, no. 1 (1981), p. 52-70.

Discusses the split in the communist movement over attitudes towards the national
bourgeoisie, and its effects on left-wing politics.

321 **Inter-party agreement and rivalry in Venezuela: a comparative
perspective.**
Steven Ellner. *Studies in Comparative International Development*,
vol. 19, no. 4 (1984-85), p. 38-66.

A study based on an analysis of newspaper reportage and of internal party
organizations, which suggests that rivalry between the two major parties, AD and
the *Comité de Organización Política Electoral Independiente* (Christian democratic
party – COPEI) was genuine and acute, rather than contrived in order to give
legitimacy to the two-party system.

322 **Political party dynamics and the outbreak of guerilla warfare in
Venezuela.**
Steve Ellner. *Inter-American Economic Affairs*, vol. 34, no. 2 (1980),
p. 3-24.

Attempts to explain why leftist groups opted for armed struggle in 1962, and how this
contributed to their failure to unite party political opposition against the AD régimes
of Betancourt and Leoni.

323 **The Venezuelan left in the era of the Popular Front, 1936-45.**
Steven Ellner. *Journal of Latin American Studies*, vol. 11, no. 1
(1979), p. 169-184.

Examines the relationship between the communist left, as represented by the PCV,
and the non-communist left, as represented by AD and its antecedents, in the period
before and during World War II.

324 **The Venezuelan political party system and its influence on economic
decision making at local level.**
Steve Ellner. *Inter-American Economic Affairs*, vol. 36, no. 3 (1982),
p. 79-103.

Uses a case study of a government-sponsored tourism development project at
Barcelona-Puerto La Cruz to illustrate the extent of party polarization and national
centralization in the Venezuelan political system.

325 **Venezuela's *Movimiento al Socialismo*: from guerrilla defeat to innovative politics.**
Steve Ellner, foreword by Michael L. Conniff. Durham, North Carolina; London: Duke University Press, 1988. 262p. bibliog.
A detailed study of the political party *Movimiento al Socialismo* (MAS – 'Movement towards Socialism'), from its beginnings in 1971 as a dissident left-wing communist group, through its swing towards the centre in the 1970s, and on to its return to its original orientation in 1985. It covers ideology; relationships with other parties; electoral performance; and party organization and structure, and argues that MAS played a more significant rôle in the Venezuelan party system than its poor electoral showing (usually about six per cent of total votes) would suggest.

326 **Christian democracy in Venezuela.**
Donald L. Herman. Chapel Hill, North Carolina: University of North Carolina Press, 1980. 289p. bibliog.
Part I deals with the evolution, history, ideological development and internal structure of COPEI, and part II with the policies and performance of its first president of the republic, Rafael Caldera (1969-73).

327 **The development of Acción Democrática de Venezuela.**
Harry Kantor. *Journal of Inter-American Studies*, vol. 1, no. 2 (1959), p. 237-55.
Traces the history of AD and its leader down to the election of Betancourt as president in December 1958, and outlines its programme.

328 **Acción Democrática: evolution of a modern political party in Venezuela.**
John D. Martz. Princeton, New Jersey: Princeton University Press, 1966. 443p. bibliog.
A comprehensive study of the development of Venezuela's first popularly based political party, from its origins to 1964; of its organization and structure; and of its relationships with peasants, organized labour, the military and other parties.

329 **The Venezuelan elections of December 1, 1963.**
John D. Martz. Washington, DC: Institute for the Comparative Study of Political Systems, 1964. 3 parts. (Election Analysis Series, no. 2).
Part I (64p.) is an analysis of the participants, the campaign and the results. Part II (64p.) is a compendium of candidate biographies and party platforms. Part III (26p.) is a detailed tabular presentation of the election statistics.

330 **Electoral mobilization and public opinion: the Venezuelan campaign of 1973.**
John D. Martz, Enrique A. Baloyra. Chapel Hill, North Carolina: University of North Carolina Press, 1976. 339p. bibliog.
Offers a detailed analysis of the campaigns of the main parties in the 1973 presidential and congressional elections.

331 **Urban electoral behavior in Latin America. The case of metropolitan Caracas, 1958-68.**
John D. Martz, Peter B. Harkins. *Comparative Politics*, vol. 5, no. 3 (1973), p. 523-49.
A detailed analysis of voting patterns, both in Caracas generally, and in the urban slum areas, revealing significant differences between classes in the city, and between Caracas and the rest of the country.

332 **Democratic campaigning in Venezuela: Caldera's victory.**
David J. Myers. Caracas: Fundación La Salle de Ciencias Naturales, Instituto Caribe de Antropología y Sociología, 1973. 251p. (Monografía no. 17).
A detailed discussion of the 1968 presidential and congressional election campaigns, which utilizes thirty-seven tables.

333 **Urban voting, structural changes, and party system evolution: the case of Venezuela.**
David J. Myers. *Comparative Politics*, vol. 8, no. 1 (1975), p. 119-51.
Reinterprets party performances in the elections of 1958, 1963, 1968 and 1973 in terms of structural cleavages between 'modern' and 'traditional' sectors, and between 'centre' and 'periphery' interests.

334 **Populism and political development in Latin America.**
A.E. van Niekerk. Rotterdam, Netherlands: Rotterdam University Press, 1974. 230p. bibliog.
Chapter 4, 'Venezuela: populism and democratic socialism' (p.61-76), criticizes the use of the term 'populist' as a description of the AD in the period up to 1968, in the context of usage elsewhere on the continent.

335 **Venezuela at the polls: the national elections of 1978.**
Edited by Howard R. Penniman. Washington, DC: American Enterprise Institute for Public Policy Research, 1980. 287p.
Comprises John D. Martz' 'The evolution of democratic politics in Venezuela'; Henry Wells' 'The conduct of Venezuelan elections: rules and practice'; Robert E. O'Connor's 'The electorate'; David J. Myers' 'The Acción Democrática campaign'; Donald L. Herman's 'The Christian Democratic party'; John D. Martz' 'The minor parties'; Robert E. O'Connor's 'The media and the campaign'; David Blank's 'The regional dimension of Venezuelan politics'; David J. Myers' 'The election and the evolution of Venezuela's party system'; and an appendix of election returns.

336 **The Christian democrats of Venezuela.**
Franklin Tugwell. *Journal of Inter-American Studies*, vol. 7, no. 2 (1965), p. 245-67.
Analyses the evolution and growth of COPEI, to the point of its refusal to enter into a coalition with President Leoni of AD in 1964.

Constitution and legal system

337 **The congress of Venezuela. A legal analysis.**
José Guillermo Andueza. *Constitutional and Parliamentary Information* [Geneva], 3rd series, no. 121 (1980), p. 11-53.
A detailed description of the Venezuelan legislature, covering its composition, prerogatives and functioning; its legislative procedures; its control over the executive; and its internal regulations.

338 **A guide to the law and legal literature of Venezuela.**
Helen L. Clagett. Washington, DC: Library of Congress, 1947. 128p.
Gives information on writings concerned with all aspects of law – civil, commercial, criminal, constitutional, administrative, military and international.

339 **The constitutions of Colombia.**
William Marion Gibson. Durham, North Carolina: Duke University Press, 1948. 478p. bibliog.
Includes (p.41-66) an English translation of the text of the Colombian constitution of 1821, which applied to Venezuela until 1830, with a brief historical introduction.

340 **The evolution of law in the barrios of Caracas.**
Kenneth L. Karst, Murray L. Schwartz, Audrey J. Schwartz. Los Angeles: University of California at Los Angeles, Latin American Center, 1973. 125p. (Latin American Studies, vol. 20).
A study, based on a survey carried out in 1967, of the development of a customary legal order in the urban squatter settlements around Caracas, and of its eventual merging into the wider systems of national law and government. It covers property ownership, family relations, commercial dealings, security of persons and property, and community organization.

341 **The role of the Venezuelan senate.**
R. Lynn Kelley. In: *Latin American legislatures: their role and influence.* Edited by Weston H. Agor. New York; Washington, DC; London: Praeger, Pall Mall, 1971, p. 461-511. (Praeger Special Studies in International Politics and Public Affairs).
Describes the part played by the upper house of the Venezuelan legislature in the constitutional process, based on interviews with a majority of its members in 1968-69, and on an analysis of its proceedings.

342 **American-Venezuelan private international law.**
Richard S. Lombard. Dobbs Ferry, New York: Oceana, 1965. 125p. (Parker School of Foreign and Comparative Law, Bilateral Studies in Private International Law, no. 14).
This study of those Venezuelan rules of private international law that are of special relevance to Americans has not yet been superseded. The topics discussed include

nationality, the status of aliens, marriage and divorce, estates and wills, contracts and torts, law relating to corporations, and judicial procedures.

343 **Venezuela.**
Juan Manuel Mayorca. In: *Criminology. A cross-cultural perspective.*
Edited by Dae H. Chang. Durham, North Carolina: Carolina
Academic Press, 1976, vol. 2, p. 980-1039.

A wide-ranging article by a Venezuelan scholar, covering the evolution of criminal law, views on causality and penal philosophy, the rôle of the courts, the police and the penitentiary system, parole, preventive policy, and the study of criminology. It includes ten tables of criminal statistics for the 1960s.

344 **A statement of the laws of Venezuela in matters affecting business.**
Organization of American States, prepared by Pedro Silveira Barrios.
Washington, DC: Pan American Union, 1977. 4th ed. 333p. bibliog.

A summary of basic legislation, with emphasis on commercial, industrial and labour law. There is a more detailed study of the situation regarding foreign investment, price control, unfair competition and 'antitrust' provision in *Venezuelan law governing restrictive business practices*, by Gustavo Brillembourg (Washington, DC: International Law Institute, 1985. 383p.).

345 **Constitution of the republic of Venezuela, 1961.**
Pan American Union. Washington, DC: Pan American Union,
General Secretariat, Organization of American States, 1961. 48p.

The text of the country's fundamental law, which defines the rights and duties of citizens, and the composition and functions of organs of government.

346 **National anthems of the world.**
Edited by W.L. Reed, M.J. Bristow. London; New York; Sydney:
Blandford, 1987. 7th ed. 513p.

The words by Vicente Salias (1786-1816) and music by Juan José Landaeta (1780-1814) of the Venezuelan national anthem, 'Gloria al bravo pueblo', are on p. 486-88, with an English translation by T.M. Cartledge.

Administration and local government

347 **Latin American military aviation.**
John M. Andrade. Leicester, England: Midland Counties
Publications, 1982. 288p.

The section on Venezuela (p. 266-84) consists of a brief historical review; a table showing the current organization of the Venezuelan air force; a list of the strengths and serial numbers of each type of aircraft, with photographs of twenty of them; and details of the aircraft used by the Venezuelan army, national guard, national police, navy, and by the school of civil aviation for armed forces training.

348 **Professional soldiers and restrained politics in Venezuela.**
Gene E. Bigler. In: *New military politics in Latin America.* Edited by
Robert Wesson. New York: Praeger; Stanford, California: Hoover
Institution Press, 1982, p. 175-96.

Analyses the system of civilian control of the military which has been developed since
1959, examines the increasing professionalization of the military, and assesses the
possible threats to the stability of civil-military relationships.

349 **The administrative reform experience in Venezuela, 1969-1975:**
strategies, tactics and perspectives.
Allan-Randolph Brewer-Carias. In: *The management of change in*
government. Edited by Arne F. Leemans. The Hague: Martinus Nijhoff
for the Institute of Social Studies, 1976, p. 213-37.

An account of the difficulties that obstructed planning and the implementing of change
in government institutions, by the then president of Venezuela's Public Administration
Commission.

350 **Urban government for Valencia, Venezuela.**
Mark W. Cannon, R. Scott Fosler, Robert Witherspoon. New York;
Washington, DC; London: Praeger, 1973. 152p. bibliog. (Praeger
Special Studies in International Politics and Government. The
International Urban Studies of the Institute of Public Administration,
New York, no. 9).

Discusses the rôles of national, state and local organs of government, with particular
reference to transportation, education, sanitation and housing, in a city whose
population grew from under 100,000 to over 300,000 in the 1950s and 1960s.

351 **The challenge of urban development in Valencia. Administrative aspects**
of rapid growth.
Mark W. Cannon, Carlos M. Morán. Caracas: Fundacomun, 1966.
[n.p.].

A compendium of information on the Valencia area, covering its governmental
organization, planning and land use policies, water supply, public housing, transportation, and education, and concluding with an evaluative summary of administrative
problems. It is still of interest for its analysis, though inevitably outdated in respect of
detail.

352 **Armed forces in Latin America. Their histories, development, present**
strength and military potential.
Adrian J. English. London: Jane, 1984. 490p. bibliog.

A useful comparative study, which includes (p. 441-67) a succinct survey of the
development and current strength in personnel and weapons of the army, navy, air
force and national guard.

353 **Regional planning in Venezuela. Recent directions.**
Jonathan Charles Greenwood. *Third World Planning Review*, vol. 6,
no. 1 (1984), p. 239-53.
Makes an analysis of the significance of the changes in regional planning administration
and practice since 1980.

354 **Power structure in a Venezuelan town: the case of San Cristóbal.**
Gary Hoskin. In: *Case studies in social power.* Edited by Hans-Dieter
Evers. Leiden, Netherlands: Brill, 1969, p. 28-47. (International
Studies in Sociology and Social Anthropology, vol. 7).
This report of a survey of the main leaders of the community of the principal city of the
state of Táchira considers their relationships to political parties, to business, to the
church, and to labour organizations, and their involvement in certain specific
community issues.

355 **Estado y gasto público en Venezuela, 1936-1980.** (The state and public
expenditure in Venezuela, 1936-1980.)
Miriam Kornblith, Thais Maingon. Caracas: Universidad Central de
Venezuela, 1985. 295p.
A discussion, illustrated by numerous tables, of the changing distribution of public
expenditure between ministries, and between central and local government.

356 **The political economy of Latin American defense expenditures. Case
studies of Venezuela and Argentina.**
Robert E. Looney. Lexington, Massachusetts; Toronto: Heath, 1986.
325p. bibliog. (Lexington Books).
Shows that in the period 1950-83, Venezuela's military budgets remained fairly stable.
They were subject to less severe cutbacks in periods of austerity than other types of
social and economic expenditure, but also were subject to less rapid expansion in times
of increased government resources.

357 **A guide to the official publications of the other American republics. XIX:
Venezuela.**
Compiled by Otto Neuberger. Washington, DC: Library of Congress,
1948. 59p. (Latin American Series, no. 34).
This list of government publications of all kinds, arranged by the originating
departments of government, and indexed by title and subject, is a useful guide to
sources of information on the first half of the twentieth century.

358 **Revenue sharing in practice: national-state-local subventions in Venezuela.**
Charles J. Savio. In: *Latin American urban research. Vol. 3. National-local linkages: the interrelationships of urban and national politics in Latin America.* Edited by Francine F. Rabinovitz, Felicity M. Trueblood. Beverly Hills, California; London: Sage, 1973, p. 79-93.
An analysis, with nine tables, of subventions from the Venezuelan national government to state and local governments around 1970, showing how they were influenced by party political considerations.

359 **Latin America: a naval history, 1810-1987.**
Robert L. Scheina. Annapolis, Maryland: Naval Institute Press, 1987. 442p. bibliog.
Contains a number of scattered references to Venezuela, as well as a discussion of the rôle of the navy in the overthrow of Pérez Jiménez in 1958, and in a series of unsuccessful coups against Betancourt in 1962.

360 **Change and bureaucracy: public administration in Venezuela.**
Bill Stewart. Chapel Hill, North Carolina: University of North Carolina Press, 1978. 140p. bibliog. (James Sprunt Studies in History and Political Science, vol. 56).
A discussion of the nature of the Venezuelan bureaucracy is followed by the report of the results of a survey taken in 1971 of the attitudes of a sample of Venezuelan public administrators, in relation to efficiency, innovation and personal priorities.

361 **Development administration in Latin America.**
Edited by Clarence E. Thurber, Lawrence S. Graham. Durham, North Carolina: Duke University Press, 1973. 453p.
This collection of papers, prepared for seminars organized by the Latin American Development Administration Committee of the Comparative Administration Group, includes Roderick T. Groves' 'The Venezuelan administrative reform movement, 1958-1963', which discusses the work of the Public Administration Commission; Fred D. Levy Jr.'s 'Economic planning in Venezuela', which considers the rôle of the Venezuelan Planning Commission; and chapters by John Shearer and Mark W. Cannon on mobilizing human resources, which contain references to Venezuela.

362 **The Latin American military institution.**
Edited by Robert Wesson. New York; Westport, Connecticut; London: Praeger, 1986. 234p.
There are sections on Venezuela, by Gene E. Bigler, in each of the chapters dealing with the ranks, officers, foreign influences, inter-service relations, ideologies and doctrines, and political rôles of military institutions throughout Latin America.

Diplomatic History and International Relations

General

363 **Venezuela: politics of oil.**
David Eugene Blank. In: *United States influence in Latin America in the 1980s*. Edited by Robert Wesson. New York: Praeger; Stanford, California: Hoover Institution Press, 1982, p. 73-101.
Considers the prospects for the continuance of the dominating position of the United States in Venezuela's political and economic external relations, in the light of increasing European and Japanese penetration of Venezuelan markets, and of the possibilities of greater Brazilian, Cuban and Soviet influence.

364 **Contemporary Venezuela and its role in international affairs.**
Edited by Robert D. Bond. New York: New York University Press, 1977. 267p. (Council on Foreign Relations Books).
A valuable collection of penetrating essays, comprising Daniel H. Levine's 'Venezuelan politics: past and future'; Pedro-Pablo Kuczynski's 'The economic development of Venezuela: a summary view as of 1975-76'; Franklin Tugwell's 'Venezuela's oil nationalization: the politics of aftermath'; Kim Fuad's 'Venezuela's role in OPEC: past, present and future'; John D. Martz' 'Venezuelan foreign policy toward Latin America'; Franklin Tugwell's 'The United States and Venezuela: prospects for accommodation'; and Bond's 'Venezuela's role in international affairs'.

365 **Venezuelan foreign policy: its organization and beginning.**
Douglas H. Carlisle. Washington, DC: University Presses of America, 1979. 208p. bibliog.
Essentially an analysis of the foreign policy of the Gómez régime (1908-35), particularly of its organizational aspects, this gives background information on the earlier development of the ministry of foreign affairs and on the diplomatic problems of Gómez's predecessor, President Castro.

366 **The development of Venezuelan geopolitical analysis since World War II.**
Judith Ewell. *Journal of Interamerican Studies and World Affairs*, vol. 24, no. 3 (1982), p. 295-320.
Discusses the views of several Venezuelan writers on geo-political topics, and considers the ways in which they have influenced the country's foreign policy.

367 **The foreign policies of Venezuela and Colombia: collaboration, competition and conflict.**
William A. Hazleton. In: *The dynamics of Latin American foreign policies: challenges of the 1980s.* Edited by Jennie K. Lincoln, Elizabeth G. Ferris. Boulder, Colorado; London: Westview, 1984, p. 151-70. (Westview Special Studies on Latin America and the Caribbean).
Analyses: the capacity of Venezuela, and Colombia, to exercise international influence; their foreign policy objectives and strategies; and their regional rôle in the Caribbean and circum-Caribbean.

368 **Ideology, economic power and regional imperialism: the determinants of foreign policy under Venezuela's Christian Democrats.**
Donald L. Herman. *Caribbean Studies*, vol. 18, no. 1-2 (1978), p. 43-83.
Discusses various aspects of the foreign policy of the Caldera administration (1969-73) and concludes that, although the COPEI was committed to international social justice, ideological motives were much less important in determining policy than the desire to increase Venezuela's economic power, so as to enable the country to compete effectively for influence in the Caribbean, Central America and the Andean community.

369 **Boundaries, possessions and conflicts in South America.**
Gordon Ireland. Cambridge, Massachusetts: Harvard University Press, 1938. 345p.
Includes sections on boundary disputes and adjustments between Venezuela and Colombia, Brazil and Great Britain (over Guyana), and outlines treaty relations between Venezuela and other Latin American nations.

370 **Diplomacy and dependency: Venezuela, the United States, and the Americas.**
Sheldon B. Liss. Salisbury, North Carolina: Documentary Publications, 1978. 356p. bibliog.
This compilation of information on Venezuela's inter-American relations and policies from the 1900s to the 1970s is based on official publications and newspaper comments.

371 **Venezuelan foreign policy and the role of political parties.**
John D. Martz. In: *Latin American nations in world politics*. Edited
by Heraldo Muñoz, Joseph S. Tulchin. Boulder, Colorado; London:
Westview, 1984, p. 133-89. (Foreign Relations of the Third World,
no. 3).

Discusses the relationship of foreign policy attitudes with party ideologies, and the
weakening, during the régime of President Herrera Campins (1979-83), of the
bipartisan consensus that had prevailed for the previous twenty years.

372 **Venezuela's contribution to the contemporary law of the sea.**
Kaldone G. Nweihed. *San Diego Law Review*, vol. 11, no. 3 (1974),
p. 603-32.

Discusses two specific contributions: the Anglo-Venezuelan Gulf of Paria treaty of
1942, which, as the earliest treaty between two states to delimit, explore and exploit a
submerged area, had a significant influence on continental shelf doctrine; and the
important rôle Venezuela played in the international discussions of 1971-72 in the
clarification of the distinction between the 'territorial sea' (territorial waters of up to
twelve miles) and the 'patrimonial sea' (up to 200 miles) exploitable for economic
purposes, but subject to freedom of navigation.

The Guyana boundary

373 **The Venezuela-Guyana border dispute: Britain's colonial legacy in Latin
America.**
Jacqueline Anne Braveboy-Wagner. Boulder, Colorado; London:
Westview, 1984. 349p. maps. bibliog.

Describes the territory in question and the history of the dispute, with emphasis on the
events of the 1960s both before and after the independence of Guyana in 1966.
Analyses developments during the twelve-year moratorium inaugurated by the
protocol of Port-of-Spain in 1970; the subsequent re-opening of the question; and
possible solutions.

374 **The Venezuela-British Guiana boundary arbitration of 1899.**
Clifton J. Child. *American Journal of International Law*, vol. 44,
no. 4 (1950), p. 682-93.

A detailed discussion of the allegations (presented in Otto Schoenrich's 'The
Venezuela-British Guiana boundary dispute', *American Journal of International Law*,
vol. 43, no. 3 (1949), p. 523-30) that the arbitration decision was the result of a 'deal'
between the British and Russian governments.

375 **The Venezuelan boundary controversy.**
Grover Cleveland. Princeton, New Jersey: Princeton University Press; London: Oxford University Press, 1913. 122p.
An account, by the ex-President of the United States, of the origins of the dispute and of the rôle of his administration in settling it.

376 **The Anglo-Venezuelan boundary controversy.**
Paul R. Fossum. *Hispanic American Historical Review*, vol. 8, no. 3 (1928), p. 299-329. map.
Reviews Venezuela's attempts to involve the United States in its controversy with Great Britain over the boundary with British Guiana, in the period 1876-96.

377 **Report on the boundary question with British Guiana submitted to the national government by Venezuelan experts.**
Hermann González Oropeza, Pablo Ojer Celigueta. Caracas: Ministerio de Relaciones Exteriores, 1967. 50p. maps.
Brief summary of the Venezuelan claims, when the issue was revived at the United Nations in the 1960s, with an appendix of documentary extracts.

378 **The Guyana-Venezuela territorial issue.**
Georgetown, Guyana: National Library, 1982. 46p.
This select list of articles, mainly from Guyanese newspapers, on the boundary dispute, is available in the National Library of Guyana. The pieces cover the period April 1966 to May 1982 and are arranged by year, and within each year by author and title.

379 **Anglo-American rivalries and the Venezuela crisis of 1895.**
Robert Arthur Humphreys. *Transactions of the Royal Historical Society*, Fifth Series, vol. 17 (1967), p. 131-64.
A masterly survey of the Guyana boundary dispute and arbitration, which brings out the extent to which Venezuelan interests were subordinated to those of Britain and the United States in the settlement of the crisis.

380 **The Venezuela-Guyana boundary dispute in the United Nations.**
Basil A. Ince. *Caribbean Studies*, vol. 9, no. 4 (1970), p. 5-26.
Reviews the controversy to the end of 1968, with special reference to Venezuelan action before the United Nations in the 1960s, particularly during the twenty-third session of the General Assembly (Sept.-Dec. 1968).

381 **Which way out? A study of the Guyana-Venezuela boundary dispute.**
Leslie B. Rout, Jr. East Lansing, Michigan: Michigan State University, 1971. 130p. map. bibliog.
A lucid summary of the dispute down to 1970, this is still of some interest for the author's account of his own impressions, formed on visits to Caracas and Georgetown at that time.

382   **The Venezuelan question: British aggressions in Venezuela, or the Monroe Doctrine on trial; Lord Salisbury's mistakes; fallacies of the British 'Blue Book' on the disputed boundary.**
William Lindsay Scruggs.   Atlanta, Georgia: Franklin, 1896. 91p.

A revised and enlarged form of the author's famous pamphlet *British aggressions in Venezuela, or the Monroe Doctrine on trial* (Atlanta, 1894), which stimulated American interest in the boundary question and precipitated an international crisis.

383   **Diplomacy or war. The Guyana-Venezuela border controversy.**
Jai Narine Singh.   Georgetown, Guyana: The Author, 1982. 170p.

Essentially a collection of the basic documents bearing on the dispute, with a commentary.

Caribbean and Central America

384   **Cuba and Venezuela: liberal and conservative possibilities.**
Demetrio Boersner.   In: *The new Cuban presence in the Caribbean.* Edited by Barry B. Levine. Boulder, Colorado: Westview; Epping, England: Bowker, 1983, p. 91-105. (Westview Special Studies on Latin America and the Caribbean).

Reviews the fluctuations in Venezuela's relations with Cuba between 1958 and 1982.

385   **Venezuelan policies toward Central America.**
Demetrio Boersner.   In: *Political change in Central America: internal and external dimensions.* Edited by Wolf Grabendorff, Heinrich-W. Krumwieder, Jörg Todt. Boulder, Colorado; London: Westview, 1984, p. 245-60. (Westview Special Studies on Latin America and the Caribbean).

Makes a useful analysis of Venezuela's interests in the Central American situation, and its policy changes from 1958 to 1983.

386   **Venezuelan policy in the Caribbean basin.**
Robert D. Bond.   In: *Central America: international dimensions of the crisis.* Edited by Richard E. Feinberg. New York; London: Holmes & Meier, 1982, p. 187-200.

Surveys Venezuela's increasing involvement in Caribbean and Central American issues in the 1970s, and indicates some of the problems it faces in these areas in the 1980s.

Diplomatic History and International Relations. Caribbean and Central
America

387   **Oil and Caribbean influence: the role of Venezuela.**
      Winfield J. Burggraaff.   In: *The restless Caribbean: changing patterns
      of international relations.* Edited by Richard Millett, W. Marvin Will.
      New York; London; Toronto etc.: Praeger, 1979, p. 193-203.
A brief article assessing the significance of Venezuela's increased involvement in
Caribbean development under President Carlos Andrés Pérez (1974-79), following the
rise of world oil prices.

388   **Curaçao and Guzmán Blanco. A case study of small power politics in the
      Caribbean.**
      Cornelis Ch. Goslinga.   The Hague: Martinus Nijhoff, 1975. 143p.
      bibliog. (Verhandlingen van het Koninklijk Instituut voor Taal-, Land-
      en Volkenkunde, no. 76).
A monograph on political relations between Venezuela and the Dutch colony of
Curaçao in the period 1870-88, based on the records of the Dutch and Venezuelan
foreign offices.

389   **Venezuela and the Puerto Ordaz agreement.**
      George W. Grayson.   *Inter-American Economic Affairs*, vol. 38, no. 3
      (1984), p. 49-73.
Discusses the beginnings of closer relations between Venezuela and its Central
American and Caribbean neighbours under President Caldera (1969-73), and the
development under his successor Pérez (1974-79), of a regional aid programme, the
Puerto Ordaz agreement, as a mechanism to assist the area to adjust to the rise in
world oil prices. Argues that the failure of Venezuela to manage its own economy
effectively limited the possibility of maintaining and developing the scheme without
assistance, and led to an agreement with Mexico in 1980 to share the burden.

390   **Castro, the Kremlin, and communism in Latin America.**
      D. Bruce Jackson.   Baltimore, Maryland: Johns Hopkins Press, 1969.
      163p. (Washington Center of Foreign Policy Research, School of
      Advanced Studies, Johns Hopkins University, Studies in International
      Affairs, no. 9).
A study of Cuban-Soviet relations between 1964 and 1967, which throws some light on
the conflict, within the Venezuelan left, over the question of the alternative policies of
armed struggle or constitutional participation.

391   **Ideology and oil: Venezuela in the circum-Caribbean.**
      John D. Martz.   In: *Colossus challenged: the struggle for Caribbean
      influence.* Edited by H. Michael Erisman, John D. Martz. Boulder,
      Colorado: Westview, 1982, p. 121-48. (Westview Special Studies on
      Latin America and the Caribbean).
Reviews Venezuela's policy towards the Caribbean and Central America in the 1970s
and early 1980s, and analyses the ideological, geo-political, economic and domestic
political factors that have influenced it.

392 **Venezuela's pursuit of Caribbean basin interests. Implications for United States national security.**
David J. Myers.   Santa Monica, California: Rand, 1985. 45p. (A Project Air Force Report Prepared for the United States Air Force, no. R-2994-AF).
Venezuela's political, economic, territorial and military interests in the Caribbean basin; its capabilities and limitations as an important regional power; and the areas of probable conflict and co-operation with the United States as a result of its Caribbean policy are all analysed.

393 **The role of Venezuela in the Caribbean since 1958.**
Carlos Antonio Romero.   In: *Confrontation in the Caribbean basin. International perspectives on security, sovereignty and survival.* Edited by Alan Adelman, Reid Reading. Pittsburgh, Pennsylvania: University of Pittsburgh, University Center for International Studies, Center for Latin American Studies, 1984, p. 147-64. (Latin American Monograph and Document Series, no. 8).
This paper, delivered at an international conference in Pittsburgh in 1982, focuses on the Caribbean policies of successive Venezuelan governments since 1958; examines the formulation of the 'diplomacy of projection' policy of the régime of President Herrera Campins (1979-83); and discusses the relationship of foreign policy to domestic party politics. The paper is followed by a comment by J.D. Martz.

United States

394 **United States economic penetration of Venezuela and its effects on diplomacy, 1895-1906.**
Charles Carreras.   New York; London: Garland, 1987. 252p. bibliog. (Foreign Economic Policy of the United States).
Presented as a doctoral dissertation, this is a detailed study, based on archival sources, of the operations in Venezuela of American firms engaged in the extraction of asphalt and other products. It considers the marketing of American manufactures, and of the relations of the firms with their own government and with that of Venezuela at the turn of the century.

395 **Envoy to Caracas. The story of John G.A. Williamson, nineteenth-century diplomat.**
Jane Lucas De Grummond.   Baton Rouge, Louisiana: Louisiana State University Press, 1951. 228p.
Describes Williamson's stay in Caracas as United States consul and chargé d'affaires from 1826 to 1840. It is based largely on his own account, subsequently edited by the author and published as *Caracas diary, 1835-40. The journal of John G.A. Williamson, first diplomatic representative of the United States to Venezuela* (Baton Rouge, Louisiana: Camellia, 1954. 444p.), which contains much information on personalities and events, and on early United States-Venezuelan relations.

396 **The Jacob Idler claim against Venezuela, 1817-1890.**
Jane Lucas De Grummond. *Hispanic American Historical Review,*
vol. 34, no. 2 (1954), p. 131-57.
Discusses the lengthy legal history of a claim by an American supplier of war material
to the revolutionary forces in 1820-21, which figured in United States-Venezuelan
diplomatic relations for much of the nineteenth century.

397 **Venezuelan foreign economic policy and the United States.**
Janet Kelly Escobar. In: *Economic issues and political conflict: US –
Latin American relations.* Edited by Jorge I. Domínguez. London;
Boston, Massachusetts; Toronto: Butterworth, 1982, p. 107-41.
Considers the causes of the development of economic nationalism in Venezuela since
1958, and its effects on United States-Venezuelan economic relations in the areas of
trade, investment, finance and oil.

398 **The extradition of Marcos Pérez Jiménez, 1959-1963: practical
precedent for enforcement of administrative honesty?**
Judith Ewell. *Journal of Latin American Studies,* vol. 9, no. 2 (1977),
p. 291-313.
Suggests that the success of the legal proceedings by the Venezuelan government to
have the ex-dictator extradited from the United States may have owed as much to
political expediency as to judicial merit.

399 **Diplomatic relations of the United States and Venezuela, 1880-1915.**
P.F. Fenton. *Hispanic American Historical Review,* vol. 8, no. 3
(1928), p. 330-56.
A review of various issues in Venezuelan-American relations, including United States
involvement in the settlement of debts to European creditors; claims by American
citizens; problems over recognition of revolutionary régimes; and difficulties over the
navigation of the Orinoco.

400 **American diplomacy in Venezuela, 1835-1865.**
William H. Gray. *Hispanic American Historical Review,* vol. 20, no. 4
(1940), p. 551-74.
Shows that the interests of the United States and Venezuela in the mid-nineteenth
century were compatible and their relations essentially amicable. America refrained
from intervening in Venezuelan affairs, and claims by American citizens were handled
by diplomacy rather than coercion.

401 **Venezuela, Uncle Sam and OPEC. A story for all Americans.**
William H. Gray. Austin, Texas: O.E.G. Foundation, 1982. 181p.
bibliog.
A 'popular' history of Venezuela and its relations with the United States, in which two
concluding chapters by Rómulo Quintero and Katherine Raup de Quintero add a
Venezuelan viewpoint.

402 **Roosevelt's second Venezuelan controversy.**
Embert J. Hendrickson. *Hispanic American Historical Review*,
vol. 50, no. 3 (1970), p. 482-98.

Reviews United States relations with Venezuela, mainly over claims by American
companies against the government of President Castro, from the ending of the
blockade crisis of 1902-03 to the settlement of outstanding issues with President Gómez
in 1909. The same author's 'Root's watchful waiting and the Venezuelan controversy',
Americas, vol. 23 (1966), p. 115-29, is a detailed discussion of the breaking of
diplomatic relations with Castro and their resumption after his supersession.

403 **Roosevelt and the Caribbean.**
Howard C. Hill.   Chicago: University of Chicago Press, 1927. 233p.

This scholarly study of the Caribbean policy of President Theodore Roosevelt includes
a substantial chapter on the Venezuelan crisis of 1902-04.

404 **U.S. assistance to Venezuela and Chile in combatting insurgency 1963-64
– two cases.**
Immanuel J. Klette.   *Conflict: All Warfare Short of War. An
International Journal*, vol. 3, no. 4 (1982), p. 227-44.

The author, a retired colonel of the US Air Force, was the head of a US special action
team (consisting on average of eight US military personnel) that visited Venezuela for
eight months from September 1963 to advise on counter-insurgency measures in the
context of the threat to the constitutional government from the *Fuerzas Armadas de
Liberación Nacional* (FALN – 'Armed forces for national liberation').

405 **The road to OPEC: United States relations with Venezuela, 1919-1976.**
Stephen G. Rabe.   Austin, Texas: University of Texas Press, 1982.
262p. bibliog. (Texas Pan American Series).

United States policies and Venezuelan reactions, from the arrival of American oil
companies to the nationalization of the petroleum industry, are analysed on the basis
of US State Department records and a variety of other sources.

406 **Bolívar and the United States.**
William R. Shepherd. *Hispanic American Historical Review*, vol. 1,
no. 3 (1918), p. 270-98.

This attempt to refute allegations by various Spanish-American historians, that Bolívar
was unfriendly towards the United States in his attitudes and policies does not seem to
have had much affect. The Liberator's own writings were used as a source.

407 **The Venezuelan question. Castro and the Asphalt Trust from official
records.**
Orray E. Thurber.   New York: [n.p.], 1907. 170p.

A reprint of numerous documents regarding the dispute between the Venezuelan
government and the New York and Bermudez Company (part of the Asphalt Trust),
and the attempt by the American organization to overthrow the régime of President
Castro, and to involve the United States government in its support.

408 **A bibliography of United States-Latin American relations since 1810.**
Compiled by David F. Trask, Michael C. Meyer, Roger R. Trask.
Lincoln, Nebraska: University of Nebraska Press, 1968. 441p.
Chapter XVI 'The United States and Venezuela' (p. 317-24) contains about 180 items
on US-Venezuelan relations. A *Supplement to a bibliography of United States-Latin
American relations since 1810*, compiled by Michael C. Meyer (Lincoln, Nebraska;
London: University of Nebraska Press, 1979. 193p.) contains in chapter XVI a further
sixty-five items on Venezuela.

409 **Alliance for progress. President Kennedy's visit to Venezuela.**
Venezuela. Presidency of the Republic, General Secretariat. Caracas:
Imprenta Nacional, 1962. 78p.
A collection of speeches and photographs relating to President Kennedy's visit in
December 1961 (the first to Venezuela by a US President), with an appendix setting
out the principles of Kennedy's 'Alliance for Progress' policy.

Other countries

410 **Oil, politics, and economic policy making: Venezuela and the Andean
Common Market.**
William P. Avery. *International Organization*, vol. 30, no. 4 (1976),
p. 541-71.
A detailed review of the factors leading to Venezuela's initial rejection and ultimate
acceptance of membership of the Andean Common Market in 1973, and of the likely
consequences of participation, both for Venezuela and for the other members.

411 **Venezuela, Brazil and the Amazon basin.**
Robert D. Bond. In: *Latin American foreign policies: global and
regional dimensions.* Edited by Elizabeth G. Ferris, Jennie K. Lincoln.
Boulder, Colorado: Westview, 1981, p. 153-64.
Discusses the background to, and prospects for, closer Venezuelan-Brazilian relations,
following the signing in 1978 of the Amazon Pact, providing for the co-ordinated
development of their respective Amazon territories by these two countries plus
Bolivia, Colombia, Ecuador, Guyana, Peru and Surinam.

412 **First among equals: Great Britain and Venezuela, 1810-1910.**
George E. Carl. Ann Arbor, Michigan: University Microfilms
International, 1980. 171p. bibliog. (Dellplain Latin American Series,
no. 5).
This admirable study of Anglo-Venezuelan economic relations in the nineteenth
century outlines the origins of British trading connections during the late colonial and
independence periods; analyses the 'reciprocity' agreement of 1835; discusses the
volume, value and commodity composition of Anglo-Venezuelan trade, the mercantile
institutions through which it was organized, and the ships and routes by which it was

carried; and examines the efforts of British diplomatic and consular officials to advance their country's commercial interests.

413 **Sir Robert Ker Porter's Caracas diary, 1825-1842: a British diplomat in a newborn nation.**
Edited by Walter Dupouy. Caracas: Editorial Arte, 1966. 1305p. bibliog.

A valuable source of detailed information, with an introduction (100p.) and numerous notes by the editor.

414 **The Japanese and Venezuela.**
C. Harvey Gardiner. *Revista Interamericana* [Puerto Rico], vol. 5, no. 3 (1975), p. 359-77.

Reviews Japanese-Venezuelan connections down to 1974, showing that they were virtually non-existent until World War II, but that economic relations developed rapidly from the mid 1950s.

415 **Germany's vision of empire in Venezuela, 1871-1914.**
Holger H. Herwig. Princeton, New Jersey: Princeton University Press, 1986. 285p. bibliog.

A case study of 'imperialism', analysing the rôle of German trade, investment, migration, and military and naval activities. Concludes that German designs in South America, and in Venezuela in particular, were inspired by naval officers and politicians, and bore little relation to economic or strategic realities. The author has also published (with J. Leon Helguera) a bilingual study on the most dramatic incident in German-Venezuelan relations, *Krupp salvos at Fort Libertador: Germany and the international blockade of Venezuela, 1902-03. A study in gunboat diplomacy./Alemania y el bloqueo internacional de Venezuela, 1902-1903* (Caracas: Editorial Arte for Ministerio de Relaciones Exteriores, 1977. 139p.).

416 **Gunboat diplomacy, 1895-1905: great power pressure in Venezuela.**
Miriam Hood. London: Allen & Unwin, 1983. 2nd ed. 210p. bibliog.

Written by a member of the distinguished Blanco-Fombona family, who was for many years Counsellor for Cultural Affairs at the Venezuelan Embassy in London, this work seeks to explain why the blockade of 1902, a minor incident from the British point of view, assumes much more significance in its Venezuelan context. The first half of the book is an extensive background discussion of Anglo-Venezuela relations in the second half of the nineteenth century, and a foreword, preface and appendix to the second edition link the past to the contemporary disputes over the Guyana boundary and the Falklands War.

417 **Great Britain and the Caribbean, 1901-1913: a study in Anglo-American relations.**
Warren G. Kneer. East Lansing, Michigan: Michigan State University Press, 1975. 242p. bibliog.

The Venezuelan intervention of 1902-03 figures prominently in this study, which is based on the records of the British Foreign Office and the US State Department.

418   **The allied coercion of Venezuela, 1902-03 – a reassessment.**
Desmond Christopher St.Martin Platt.   *Inter-American Economic Affairs*, vol. 15, no. 4 (1962), p. 3-28.
Argues, on the basis of British Foreign Office records, that the notorious blockade of 1902 was a legitimate response to the persistent violation by Venezuela of international law regarding the rights of aliens, rather than an intervention on behalf of foreign bondholders, as it has frequently been represented.

Population

General

419 **Some aspects of family composition in Venezuela.**
Eduardo E. Arriaga. *Eugenics Quarterly*, vol. 15, no. 3 (1968), p. 177-91.

Uses census material and vital statistics from the period 1950-63 to discuss family sizes, nuclear and extended families, differences betwen rural and urban areas, legal marriages and consensual unions and their dissolution, and fertility rates.

420 **The existence of a Latin American mortality pattern: an analysis of the Colombia and Venezuela cases.**
Carmen Elisa Florez. Bogotá: Universidad de los Andes, Facultad de Economía, Centro de Estudios sobre Desarrollo Económico (CEDE), 1985. 153p. (Documento CEDE, no. 081).

A technical analysis of adult mortality data in the periods between censuses, 1951-61 and 1961-71, with graphs and tables. Concludes that the pattern of age at death for Venezuela and Colombia differs from the United Nations Latin American pattern.

421 **The handbook of national population censuses. Latin America and the Caribbean, North America, and Oceania.**
Doreen S. Goyer, Eliane Domschke. Westport, Connecticut; London: Greenwood, 1983. 711p.

The Venezuelan section (p. 342-50) gives dates of censuses to 1971, and details of the topics covered, procedures followed, and resulting publications.

422 **People and places in colonial Venezuela.**
John V. Lombardi. Bloomington, Indiana; London: Indiana
University Press, 1976. 484p. maps.

Part I uses ecclesiastical records to reconstruct the population history of Venezuela in the late-eighteenth and early-nineteenth centuries. In addition to analysing the overall picture, it includes a detailed case study of the city of San Carlos in the state of Cojedes. It also incorporates excellent maps and figures (by Cathryn L. Lombardi), showing the location of each parish, and population distribution by region, urban category, race and marital status. Part II, which constitutes two-thirds of the volume, consists of tables of population data for each of the 206 parishes. There is an average of about ten returns for each parish within the period 1771-1838.

423 **Fertility decline during rapid urbanization: the influence of class and kinship.**
John Stuart MacDonald, Leatrice D. MacDonald. *Habitat International*, vol. 6, no. 3 (1982), p. 301-21.

A discussion of the results of a sample survey of over 1,000 women in Ciudad Guayana in 1975, correlating fertility with a range of other factors, conducted to throw some light on the effects of 'modernization' and the patterns of family composition.

424 **Geografía de la población de Venezuela.** (Geography of the population of Venezuela.)
Emilio A. Osorio Alvarez. Caracas: Ariel-Seix Barral, 1985. 233p. bibliog. (Colección Geografía de Venezuela Nueva, no. 4).

A useful survey, illustrated by seventy-five tables, which outlines the origins and development of the population from earliest times to 1981 and analyses the results of the 1981 census in terms of: geographical distribution; age, sex, family and household structure; vital statistics; migration; and trends and future prospects.

425 **Ensayo sobre demografía económica de Venezuela.** (An essay on the economic demography of Venezuela.)
Julio Páez Celis. Caracas: Ministerio de Fomento, Dirección General de Estadística y Censos Nacionales, 1974. 111p.

A discursive essay, illustrated by sixty-four tables, covering population growth, migration, birth- and death-rates, age structure, urbanization, labour supply, unemployment and underemployment, standard of living, national income distribution, and human resource management.

426 **Guide to Latin American and West Indian census material: a bibliography and union list. 1. Venezuela.**
Compiled by Ann E. Wade. London: Institute of Latin American Studies, University of London, 1981. 30p.

Records the holdings of libraries in Britain of the reports of nine major censuses of population, and eight agricultural, industrial or economic censuses, taken between 1869 and 1971.

Migration

427 Margarita island, exporter of people.
Charles S. Alexander. *Journal of Inter-American Studies*, vol. 3, no. 4 (1961), p. 548-57.
Offers a brief historical survey of migration from the island to mainland Venezuela.

428 Migrations and occupations in Venezuela.
Chi-Yi Chen. In: *Human resources in Latin America: an interdisciplinary focus.* Edited by Frank T. Bachmura. Bloomington, Indiana: Indiana University, Graduate School of Business Research, 1968, p. 36-48. (Indiana Business Paper, no. 16).
An assessment of the significance of both internal and international migration for Venezuela, based on the 1961 census. Concludes that migrants, internal and foreign, play a significant economic rôle in their new abodes, which are mainly in urban areas; but that the movement of internal migrants adversely affects the rural areas of the country which they leave. Chen's contribution is followed (p. 49-52) by a comment by Dale W. Adams.

429 Circular migration in Venezuelan frontier areas.
Mary Ellen Conaway. *International Migration*, vol. 15, no. 1 (1977), p. 35-42.
Discusses various patterns of migration, involving the combination of rural subsistence and wage-earning activities, as a concomitant of the industrial development of the Orinoco river area.

430 Migration studies in Venezuela.
Mary Ellen Conaway. *Antropológica* [Caracas], no. 50 (1978), p. 93-127.
A review of the literature on Venezuelan migration published between 1939 and 1976, divided into studies of immigration and of internal migration, and of those with a statistical and those with a cultural emphasis.

431 History, patterns and migration: a case study in the Venezuelan Andes.
Mario DiPolo, María Matilde Suárez. *Human Organization. Journal of the Society for Applied Anthropology*, vol. 33, no. 2 (1974), p. 183-95.
A detailed study of the history and patterns of migration in the municipality of El Morro, near the city of Mérida, concluding that effective migration from rural conditions to an urban centre is generally a process involving two successive generations.

432 **Observations on the relationship between intra-rural migration and achievement motivation in Mérida State, Venezuela.**
David A. Eastwood. *Journal of Latin American Studies*, vol. 7, no. 2 (1975), p. 305-27.
Reports on a series of comparative surveys carried out in 1969-70 in Andean and lowland villages in Mérida state. Concludes that those who migrated from highlands to lowlands had higher achievement motivation, and made some improvements in their conditions, but remained at a low level of technology and income, and dissatisfied with their situation. Lacking the capacity to initiate change themselves, they looked to government for assistance, but with negligible results.

433 **Reality or delusion: migrant perceptions of levels of living and opportunity in Venezuela, 1961-1971.**
David A. Eastwood. *Journal of Developing Areas*, vol. 17, no. 4 (1983), p. 491-99.
An attempt to establish how far the expectations, of internal migrants, of better standards of living in their new abodes actually corresponded to the reality.

434 **Illegal aliens in the western hemisphere: political and economic factors.**
Kenneth F. Johnson, Miles W. Williams. New York: Praeger, 1981. 207p. bibliog.
Chapter four 'Clandestine migration between Colombia and Venezuela' (p. 110-39) is a study, based on the evidence of various surveys, of the inflow of 'undocumented' Colombians, estimated at 1.5 million, or ten per cent of the Venezuelan labour force in the late 1970s. It concludes that it has suited the convenience of both governments to connive at illegal movements, and to perpetuate the insecurity of the individual migrants involved.

435 **Myth maps and migration in Venezuela.**
R.C. Jones. *Economic Geography*, vol. 54, no. 1 (1978), p. 75-91.
On the basis of interviews in five zones of rural out-migration, this article compares potential migrants' perceptions of economic opportunities and quality of life in urban areas with objective measurements of these variables, and concludes that misconceptions about actual conditions are an important factor in urban in-migration rates.

436 **The impact of international migration on Venezuelan demographic and social structure.**
Mary Monica Kritz. *International Migration Review*, vol. 9, no. 4 (1975), p. 513-43.
A study, based on the census reports of 1950 and 1961, of the flow of immigrants into Venezuela in the 1940s and 1950s; their ethnic origins, demographic composition, location and occupational patterns; and the social policy implications of the phenomenon. There are twelve illustrative tables.

437 **Motives and objectives of migration: selective migration and preferences toward rural and urban life.**
Leatrice D. MacDonald, John Stuart MacDonald. *Social and Economic Studies* [Jamaica], vol. 17, no. 4 (1968), p. 417-34.

This is the report of a survey, conducted in 1965-66, into the motivations of both migrants and non-migrants in Ciudad Guayana and its rural hinterland, which concludes that the salient factor was the individual respondent's perception of employment opportunities.

438 **White collar migrants in the Americas and the Caribbean.**
Edited by Arnaud F. Marks, Hebe M.C. Vessuri. Leiden, Netherlands: Royal Institute of Linguistics and Anthropology, Department of Caribbean Studies, 1983. 254p.

Includes Vessuri's 'Scientific immigrants in Venezuela; national identity and international science' (p. 171-98); and Maryluz Schloeter, María Matilde Suárez and Ricardo Torrealba's 'Selective Latin American migration in Venezuela: the case of SIDOR (Siderúrgica del Orinoco)' (p. 199-234).

439 **Agricultural colonization and immigration in Venezuela, 1810-1860.**
Wayne D. Rasmussen. *Agricultural History*, vol. 21, no. 3 (1947), p. 155-62.

Outlines the largely unsuccessful attempts by the Venezuelan government, between independence and 1860, to encourage European immigration into the country.

440 **Economic growth and immigration in Venezuela.**
Saskia Sassen-Koob. *International Migration Review*, vol. 13, no. 3 (1979), p. 455-74.

Reviews immigration flows and policies between the 1940s and 1970s, and analyses the effects of the oil price rise of 1973 on Venezuela's demand for and supply of immigrant labour. Five tables illustrate the text.

441 **Internal migration in Venezuela.**
María Matilde Suárez, Ricardo Torrealba. *Urban Anthropology*, vol. 8, nos. 3-4 (1979), p. 291-311.

Includes tables showing net migratory flows between states in each intercensal period from 1926 to 1971, and identifies two migratory cycles – one prior to the early 1950s, towards the petroleum-producing regions and the central industrialized areas, and a subsequent second cycle, in which the oil-producing zones began to lose population, and inflow was concentrated in the central area and the new industrial centre of Ciudad Guayana.

442 **Venezuelan migration. An analysis of problems migration creates in developing countries. Arguments and proposals for an active migration policy. Postulating a migration policy-making model.**
Chris Tanner. Diessenhofen, Switzerland: Verlag Ruegger, 1980. 270p. bibliog. (Institut für Lateinamerikaforschung und Entwicklungsammerarbeit en der Hochschule St.Gallen für Wirtschaft- und Sozialwissenschaften. Buchreihe Band 22).
Discusses theories of migration; reviews the population history of Venezuela to 1900; analyses the impact on the geographical distribution of population of twentieth-century developments, such as petroleum exploitation, the rise of manufacturing, and agrarian reform schemes; attempts to quantify internal migration and to forecast its future consequences; and argues in favour of coherent migration policy making.

Ethnic minorities

443 **The struggle for abolition in Gran Colombia.**
Harold A. Bierck, Jr. *Hispanic American Historical Review*, vol. 33, no. 3 (1953), p. 365-86.
Discusses the laws passed between 1816 and 1830 relating to the emancipation of black slaves, and considers the extent to which they were implemented.

444 **Venezuela's national colonization program: the Tovar colony, a German agricultural settlement.**
Oscar Olinto Camacho. *Journal of Historical Geography*, vol. 10, no. 3 (1984), p. 279-89.
Gives a brief account of the origins and early history of the importation of German settlers to work on the lands of the Tovar family, and of the survival of a distinctive enclave to the present day.

445 **Jews of the Latin American republics.**
Judith Laikin Elkin. Chapel Hill, North Carolina: University of North Carolina Press, 1980. 298p. bibliog.
Includes references to Jewish migration from Curaçao to Venezuela in the nineteenth century, and to the Jewish population of 15,000-17,000 in 1972, eighty per cent of which was urban.

446 **The Jews of Coro, Venezuela.**
Isaac S. Emmanuel. Cincinatti, Ohio: American Jewish Archives, 1973. 63p. (Monographs of the American Jewish Archives, no. 8).
A brief account of the small community of Curaçao Jews who established themselves in the town of Coro in the 1820s and 1830s. It considers the contribution they made, the difficulties they encountered, and their eventual dispersal (largely to Caracas) in the early twentieth century, and gives detailed lists of circumcisions, marriages and burials.

447 Confederate exiles in Venezuela.

Alfred Jackson Hanna, Kathryn Abbey Hanna. Tuscaloosa, Alabama: Confederate, 1960. 149p. bibliog. (Confederate Centennial Studies, no. 15).

A documented account of an unsuccessful attempt in the late 1860s to establish settlers from the southern United States in Venezuelan Guayana after their defeat in the American Civil War.

448 The decline and abolition of Negro slavery in Venezuela, 1820-1854.

John V. Lombardi. Westport, Connecticut: Greenwood, 1971. 217p. bibliog. (Contributions to Afro-American Studies, no. 7).

Describes the policies of manumission and apprenticeship, and the rôle of slaves in the economy and society, from the wars of independence until the final abolition of slavery in 1854.

449 The faceless enemy. A true story of injustice.

Pir Nasir. Pompano Beach, Florida: Universidad de Oriente and Exposition Press of Florida, 1985. 207p.

An account, by a Pakistani professor of parasitology at the Universidad de Oriente, of the attitude of the police and other authorities towards a campaign of harassment by stone-throwing and fire-raising at his home in Cumaná, by unknown tormentors, presumed to be racially motivated against immigrant families.

450 Bibliografía afrovenezolana. (Afrovenezuelan bibliography.)

Angelina Pollak-Eltz. *Montalbán* [Caracas], no. 5 (1976), p. 1023-47.

Lists 357 items, in each case indicating which of fourteen topical categories is dealt with. The author's supplement containing a further 208 items entitled *Nuevos aportes a la bibliografía afro-venezolana* was produced in typescript form (Caracas: Centro de Religiones Comparadas, Universidad Católica Andrés Bello, 1983. 16p.).

451 The black family in Venezuela.

Angelina Pollak-Eltz. Vienna (Horn-Wien): Berger, 1974. 179p. (Wiener Beiträge zur Kulturgeschichte und Linguistik, no. 18).

An anthropological study of the structure and functioning of the lower-class Negro family in Venezuela, which is based largely on field work involving a sample of 200 households in the Barlovento region of the state of Miranda. Some comparative data are offered from smaller samples of various ethnic groups in other regions of the country, and in the lower-class *barrios* of Caracas.

452 The devil dances in Venezuela.

Angelina Pollak-Eltz. *Caribbean Studies*, vol. 8, no. 2 (1968), p. 65-73.

Discusses the custom among Afrovenezuelans of performing Devil Dances annually on Corpus Christi Day, and describes the differences between the practices in San Francisco de Yare, Naiguatá and Patameno, noting the combination of Spanish and West African elements in them.

453 **Socialization of schoolchildren among Afro-Venezuelans.**
Angelina Pollak-Eltz. *International Social Science Journal* [Paris],
vol. 31, no. 3 (1979), p. 470-76.

A brief summary of child-rearing practices, based on field work in black peasant
communities in coastal areas of Venezuela.

454 **El negro en Venezuela: aporte bibliográfico.** (The Negro in Venezuela:
bibliographical materials.)
José Marcial Ramos Guédez. Caracas: Instituto Autónomo Biblioteca
Nacional y de Servicios de Bibliografía, 1985. 279p.

Enlarges the author's *Bibliografía afrovenezolana* (Caracas, 1980), adding 564 titles to
the 936 in the first edition, to total 1,500 items about the Negro in Venezuela, divided
into bibliographies, books and pamphlets, articles, and Afrovenezuelan literature.

455 **Topo. The story of a Scottish colony near Caracas 1825-1827.**
Hans P. Rheinheimer. Edinburgh: Scottish Academic Press, 1988.
168p. bibliog.

This handsome volume gives a detailed history of the short-lived Scottish settlement,
based on both documentary and archaeological evidence, and is illustrated by fine
reproductions of fourteen contemporary water-colours by Meinhard Retemeyer.

456 **The African experience in Spanish America, 1502 to the present day.**
Leslie B. Rout, Jr. Cambridge, England; London; New York etc.:
Cambridge University Press, 1976. 404p. bibliog. (Cambridge Latin
American Studies, no. 23).

In addition to many references to Venezuela throughout the book, there are specific
sections on colonial slave rebellions in the country, and on the conditions of blacks
since emancipation.

457 **Slavery and race relations in Latin America.**
Edited by Robert Brent Toplin. Westport, Connecticut; London:
Greenwood, 1974. 450p. (Contributions in Afro-American and African
Studies, no. 17).

Includes John V. Lombardi's 'The abolition of slavery in Venezuela: a non-event'
(p. 228-52); and Winthrop R. Wright's 'Elitist attitudes toward race in twentieth-
century Venezuela' (p. 325-47).

458 **The Guayrians at Guelph in Upper Canada. Scottish settlers for Canada
from Venezuela: a bureaucratic problem in 1827.**
Edgar Vaughan. Guelph, Ontario: Guelph Historical Society, 1979.
112p. (Historic Guelph. The Royal City. Vol. XVIII).

Describes the brief residence of a Scottish colony at Topo, between Caracas and La
Guaira in 1825-26; the background of the settlers; and their subsequent fortunes after
they were re-settled in Canada in 1827.

Languages

Indigenous

459 **Gramática y diccionario de la lengua pemón.** (Grammar and dictionary of the Pemón language.)
Cesáreo de Armellada.   Caracas: Artes Gráficas, 1943-44. 2 vols. bibliog.

A study of the language of the Pemón group of Carib Indians (including the Arekuma, Taurepan and Kamarakoto tribes) inhabiting the basin of the Caroní river, written by a Capuchin missionary who lived there for eight years. The first volume deals with grammar, and the second is a Pemón/Spanish dictionary and a Spanish/Pemón vocabulary.

460 **Diccionario guarao-español, español-guarao.** (Warao-Spanish, Spanish-Warao dictionary).
Basilio Marío de Barral.   Caracas: Editorial Sucre, 1957. 276p. (Sociedad de Ciencias Naturales La Salle, Monografía, no. 3).

Presents a detailed vocabulary of the language spoken by some 8,000 Warao Indians, mainly in the Orinoco delta, and a briefer table of Warao equivalents of Spanish words.

461 **Manual glotológico del idioma Wo'tiheh.** (Wo'tiheh language manual).
Pedro J. Krislogo B.   Caracas: Universidad Católico Andrés Bello, Centro de Lenguas Indígenas, Instituto de Investigaciones Históricas, 1976. 170p. bibliog.

Describes the language of the Piaróa Indians of the Orinoco region on the Colombian border, with a discussion of its grammar, and a Spanish/Wo'tiheh vocabulary.

462 **Diccionario yanomami-español.** (Yanomami-Spanish dictionary.)
Jacques Lizot, translated by Roberto Lizarralde. Caracas:
Universidad Central de Venezuela, Facultad de Ciencias Económicas y
Sociales, 1975. 103p. bibliog.
Based on anthropologist Lizot's field work, and originally published as a Yanomami-
French vocabulary, the dictionary contains some 7,000 entries of expressions used by
the tribe, which numbers about 12,000-15,000 persons, and is located on the
Venezuelan-Brazilian border.

463 **Diccionario guajiro-español.** (Guajiro-Spanish dictionary.)
Antonio J. López Epieyú. Maracaibo, Venezuela: Corpozulia, 1981.
104p.
A concise vocabulary of the language of the 30,000 Colombian and Venezuelan
inhabitants of the Guajira peninsula, which draws attention to some basic errors in the
earlier pioneering work of Martha Hildebrandt, *Diccionario guajiro-español* (Caracas:
Ministerio de Justicia, Comisión Indigenista, 1963. 273p.).

464 **Léxico yaruro-español, español-yaruro.** (Yaruro-Spanish,
Spanish-Yaruro vocabulary.)
Hugo Obregón Muñoz, Jorge Díaz Pozo, Luis Jesús Pérez. San
Fernando de Apure, Venezuela: Gobernación del Estado Apure,
Corporación de Desarrollo de la Región de los Llanos, 1984. 293p.
bibliog.
Gives a vocabulary of the language of the Yaruro (Pumé) Indians of the state of
Apure.

465 **Gramática de la lengua guajira.** (Grammar of the Guajiro language.)
Jesús Olza Zubiri, Miguel Angel Jusayú. Caracas: Universidad
Católica Andrés Bello, Centro de Lenguas Indígenas, 1978. 455p.
A systematic description of the grammatical structure of the language of the Indians of
the Guajira peninsula. The same team (Jusayú, Olza and the Centre for Indigenous
Languages of the Catholic University) has also produced dictionaries of the language:
Diccionario sistemático de la lengua guajira (1988, 299p.), a new edition of *Diccionario
de la lengua guajira. Guarijo-Español* (1977), and *Diccionario de la lengua guajira. II
Castellano-Guajiro* (1981, 228p.).

466 **Diccionario ilustrado yupa-español/español-yupa.** (Illustrated Yupa-
Spanish/Spanish-Yupa dictionary.)
Félix María de Vegamián. Caracas: Formateca, 1978. 383p.
A dictionary of the language of the Yupa Indians of the Sierra de Perijá on the
Colombian border of the state of Zulia, with an introductory section about the tribe,
and a discussion of the grammatical structure of the language. The illustrations are
mainly of local artefacts and their nomenclature.

Venezuelan Spanish

467 **Sobre el español que se escribe en Venezuela.** (On the Spanish written in
Venezuela.)
María Rosa Alonso. Mérida, Venezuela: Universidad de Los Andes,
Facultad de Humanidades y Educación, 1967. 125p. bibliog.

A thematic discussion of various aspects of the differences between Venezuelan and
peninsular Spanish, including the use of native Indian words and loan words from
other languages, the formation of suffixes and adjectives, and neologisms and
archaisms.

468 **The *criollo* way. A brief guide to the slang and idioms of Venezuela.**
Clive Bashleigh. Caracas: Las Mercedes Bookstore, [n.d.] 80p.

A collection of Spanish words, phrases, proverbs and similes in common usage in
Venezuela in the 1960s, arranged alphabetically and explained in English.

469 **El castellano en Venezuela: estudio crítico.** (The Spanish language in
Venezuela: a critical study.)
Julio Calcaño. Caracas: Ministerio de Educación, Dirección de
Cultura, 1950. 571p. (Biblioteca Venezolana de Cultura. Colección
Andrés Bello).

A reprint of the classic work on the Spanish language in Venezuela, originally
published in 1897, which remains of some value for the study of nineteenth-century
writings.

470 **Spanish pronounciation in the Americas.**
D. Lincoln Canfield. Chicago; London: University of Chicago Press,
1981. 118p. bibliog.

A brief survey of the origin of American variants of Spanish, is followed by a country-
by-country analysis, which includes brief comments on Venezuela.

471 **Lenguaje coloquial venezolano.** (Venezuelan colloquial language.)
Aura Gómez de Ivashevsky. Caracas: Universidad Central de
Venezuela, Facultad de Humanidades y Educación, Instituto de
Filología 'Andrés Bello', 1969. 502p. bibliog.

A discussion of Venezuelan popular usage, which is arranged analytically under modes
of address, conversational forms, and euphemisms.

472   **El habla de Caracas. Estudio lingüístico sobre el español hablado en la capital venezolana.** (The speech of Caracas. A linguistic study of the Spanish spoken in the Venezuelan capital.)
Edited by Esteban Emilio Mosonyi.   Caracas: Universidad Central de Venezuela, Ediciones de la Biblioteca, 1971. 286p. bibliog. (Estudio de Caracas. Volumen VI Personalidad, Educación, Lenguaje, Tomo V).
A detailed study of the phonology, morphology and syntax of the spoken Spanish of Caracas. with a discussion of a number of the factors affecting it.

473   **Venezolanismos y otras palabras muy usadas.** (Venezuelan expressions and other frequently used words.)
Inés de Muller.   Caracas: [n.p.], 1961. 70p.
Presents a typescript alphabetical list of special Venezuelan words or usages, with Spanish and English equivalents. Lists of: names of places, flora and fauna, and old Indian chieftains; idiomatic expressions; and words for commercial establishments.

474   **Buenas y malas palabras en el castellano de Venezuela.** (Good and bad words in Venezuelan Spanish.)
Angel Rosenblat.   Madrid: Editoral Edime, 1974. 1st Series, 4th ed. 2 vols; 1969. 2nd series, 3rd ed. 2 vols.
A learned but captivating discussion of the divergences of Venezuelan from standard Spanish, which gives 100 such cases in each series, and offers a vigorous defence of the Venezuelan manner of speaking as an index of national identity.

475   **Léxico popular venezolano.** (Dictionary of Venezuelan popular usage.)
Francisco Tamayo.   Caracas: Universidad Central de Venezuela, Dirección de Cultura, 1977. 330p. bibliog.
Lists terms used in popular Venezuelan Spanish, many of which are concerned with plants and with cookery.

476   **Diccionario de venezolanismos. Tomo I A-I.** (Dictionary of Venezuelan words and usages. Vol. I A-I.)
Edited by María Josefina Tejera.   Caracas: Academia de la Lengua, Universidad Central de Venezuela, Facultad de Humanidades y Educación, Instituto de Filología 'Andrés Bello', 1983. 549p. bibliog.
This alphabetical list of Venezuelan words, or of special Venezuelan meanings of Spanish words, gives documented examples of actual usages.

Society and Social Conditions

General

477 **Las clases sociales y el estado en Venezuela.** (The social classes and the state in Venezuela.)
Sergio Aranda. Caracas: Editorial Pomaire, 1983. 172p. bibliog.
This monograph includes an analysis, illustrated by numerous detailed tables, of changes that took place in the make-up of the social classes and in the distribution of the population among occupations, between the census of 1950 and that of 1971.

478 **El traje de Venezuela.** (Venezuelan costume.)
Isabel Aretz. Caracas: Monte Avila, 1977. 287p. bibliog.
A study, with numerous illustrations, of the history of costume in Venezuela, which includes both the dress of the indigenous Indians, past and present, and the traditional folk costume and ceremonial wear of the creole communities.

479 **The politics of change in Venezuela.**
Frank Bonilla, José A. Silva Michelena. Cambridge, Massachusetts; London: M.I.T., 1967-71. 3 vols. bibliog.
These are the reports of a major project of social research, undertaken jointly by the Centro de Estudios del Desarrollo of the Universidad Central de Venezuela (CENDES) and the Center for International Studies of the Massachusetts Institute of Technology. The first volume, *A strategy for research in social policy*, includes contributions by José Ahumada, John R. Mathiason, Gabriela de Bronfenmajer, Allan Kessler, Walter H. Slote and Daniel Lerner as well as by the editors. The second volume, *The failure of elites*, is the work of Bonilla, and the third, *The illusion of democracy in dependent nations*, of Michelena. Each volume contains numerous tables setting out the results of various surveys, and the whole work constitutes a most revealing discussion of Venezuelan society in the 1960s.

480 **The Venezuelan peasant in country and city.**
Edited by Luise Margolies.   Caracas: Ediciones Venezolanas de
Antropología, 1979. 126p.

A collection of research papers presented at a symposium of anthropologists held in
San Francisco in 1975, which, taken together, constitute a valuable conspectus of the
changing condition of the peasantry. It consists of Karl H. Schwerin's 'The role of
migratory labor in Kariña culture change'; Angelina Pollak-Eltz's 'Migration from
Barlovento to Caracas'; María Matilde Suárez and Mario Dipolo's 'An historical
approach to the study of rural-urban migration'; the editor's 'Urbanization and the
family farm: structural antagonism in the Venezuelan Andes'; William Roseberry's 'On
the economic formation of Bonocó'; and Yvan Breton's 'The role of petty commodity
production among Venezuelan fishermen'.

481 **Family and kinship in Middle America and the Caribbean.**
Edited by Arnaud F. Marks, Rene A. Römer.   Leiden, Netherlands:
Royal Institute of Linguistics and Anthropology, Department of
Caribbean Studies; Curaçao, Netherlands Antilles: Institute of High
Studies, [1975]. 672p.

These proceedings of the fourteenth seminar of the Committee of Family Research of
the International Sociological Association, held in Curaçao in September 1975, include
Luise Margolies and María Matilde Suárez's 'The peasant family in the Venezuelan
Andes' (p. 382-404) and Angelina Pollak-Eltz's 'The black family in Venezuela'
(p. 417-30).

482 **The structural parameters of emerging life styles in Venezuela.**
Lisa Redfield Peattie.   In: *The culture of poverty: a critique.* Edited by
Eleanor Burke Leacock. New York: Simon & Schuster, 1971,
p. 285-98.

Offers reflections on the social situation of a lower-class community in Ciudad
Guayana.

483 **The family in Venezuela.**
Angelina Pollak-Eltz.   In: *The family in Latin America.* Edited by
Man Singh Das, Clinton J. Jesser. New Delhi: Vikas, 1980, p. 12-45.

A very useful survey, based on field work conducted in 1969-72, analysing the family
systems of different classes and groups. There are sections on: the upper-class
patriarchal family; the egalitarian middle-class family; varying family and household
compositions among four geographically and ethnically distinct groups of the rural
lower-classes; and family patterns among the urban lower-class formed by migration
from the rural areas.

484 **A further look at the culture of poverty: ten Caracas *barrios*.**
Audrey James Schwartz.   *Sociology and Social Research*, vol. 59,
no. 4 (1975), p. 362-86.

Concludes, on the basis of interviews with over 600 inhabitants of ten squatter
settlements in Caracas in 1967, that the concept of a self-perpetuating 'culture of
poverty' was not applicable to the Caracas *barrios*, where there were marked

differences in levels of education and economic security, and where surprisingly 'middle class' outlooks and behaviour were in evidence.

485 **The historical development of urban anthropology in Venezuela.**
María Matilde Suárez, Ricardo Torrealba. In: *Town-talk. The dynamics of urban anthropology.* Edited by Ghaus Ansari, Peter J.M. Das. Leiden, Netherlands: E.J. Brill, 1983, p. 132-39.
Discusses the shift in emphasis of Venezuelan anthropology from tribal to peasant societies, and thence through the study of rural-urban migration to urban anthropology.

486 **Café con leche: a brief look at race relations in twentieth century Venezuela.**
Winthrop R. Wright. *Maryland Historian*, vol. 1, no. 1 (1970), p. 13-22.
An objective study which compares and contrasts relations between black and white in Venezuela and the United States. The author is an American historian.

Urbanization

487 **Planning a pluralist city: conflicting realities in Ciudad Guayana.**
Donald Appleyard. Cambridge, Massachusetts; London: MIT, 1976. 312p. bibliog. (Publications of the Joint Center for Urban Studies).
Compares the ideas of the planners of the new city with the perceptions of the inhabitants, on the basis of survey evidence.

488 **Pirates and invaders: land acquisition in urban Colombia and Venezuela.**
Alan Gilbert. *World Development*, vol. 9, no. 7 (1981), p. 657-78.
The techniques by which the poor acquire housing land in Bogotá and Valencia are juxtaposed. Although these methods are illegal, they are covertly permitted by the authorities in the interests of social and political stability.

489 **Planning, invasions and land speculation.**
Alan Gilbert. *Third World Planning Review*, vol. 6, no. 1 (1984), p. 225-38.
An examination of the rôle of the state in the process of land allocation, and its influence on urban planning and housing, based on a case study of the city of Valencia.

490 **The political economy of land. Urban development in an oil economy.**
Alan Gilbert, Patsy Healey.   Aldershot, England; Brookfield,
Vermont: Gower, 1985. 163p. bibliog.
Examines urban development, with particular reference to the influence of the
government on land use, using the city of Valencia as an illustrative example.

491 **Urban planning in a Venezuelan city. Five plans for Valencia: content,
concepts and context.**
Patsy Healey.   *Town Planning Review*, vol. 46, no. 1 (1975), p. 63-82.
Presents a discussion of five plans produced for the rapidly-growing city of Valencia
between 1953 and 1968. It explains some of their technical shortcomings, and questions
how far planning may be appropriate in a situation, where there is constant change, no
general consensus on the public interest, and no disposition on anyone's part to give it
primacy.

492 **Social urbanization and Caracas: a historical anthropological analysis.**
Robert H. Lavenda.   *Urban Anthropology*, vol. 8, no. 3-4 (1979),
p. 365-81.
A study of urbanization and social change in Caracas in the period 1870-1908, which
discusses its relation to internal and external migration.

493 **Propositions for planning new towns in Venezuela.**
Edward Lynch.   *Journal of Developing Areas*, vol. 7, no. 4 (1973),
p. 549-70.
Analyses the planning process used in the creation of Ciudad Guayana, and in the
projected new towns of Tuy (south of Caracas) and El Tablazo (near Maracaibo).
Stresses that the development of poor *barrios* is unavoidable; that they must be
integrated into the new towns; and that local interests should be consulted.

494 **Planning implementation and social policy. An evaluation of Ciudad
Guayana, 1965 and 1975.**
John Stuart MacDonald.   Oxford: Pergamon, [1979]. 211p. (Planning
in Progress, vol. 11, parts 1/2).
A dynamic view of the development of the city based on two surveys, separated by ten
years, covering employment, health, housing, migration, public opinion and social
structure. It concludes that the planning processes used had serious unanticipated
consequences, such as the concentration of the working population in unplanned
shanty dwellings at the opposite end of the city from the factories.

495 **Jobs and housing: alternative developments in the Venezuelan Guayana.**
John Stuart MacDonald, Leatrice D. MacDonald.   *Journal of Inter-
American Studies and World Affairs*, vol. 13, no. 3-4 (1971), p. 342-66.
A report on a survey of attitudes to housing in Guayana, concluding that the provision
of better rural housing did not restrain migration to higher paid jobs in Ciudad
Guayana, and that the failure of the authorities to consult the populace resulted in
policy errors in housing provision in the new city.

496 **Caracas: the politics of intensifying primacy.**
David J. Myers. In: *Latin American urban research. Vol. 6. Metropolitan Latin America: the challenge and the response.* Edited by Wayne A. Cornelius, Robert V. Kemper. Beverly Hills, California; London: Sage, 1978, p. 227-58.

Analyses the dominant position of the capital, and governmental attempts in the 1960s and early 1970s to solve the problems it generated – in public services, housing and planning, and through overspill from the Federal District into other administrative entities.

497 **Planning: rethinking Ciudad Guayana.**
Lisa Redfield Peattie. Ann Arbor, Michigan; University of Michigan Press, 1987. 174p.

An anthropologist involved in the Guayana project in the 1960s looks back on why things did not ultimately happen as planned. She throws a fascinating light on Venezuelan social, political and economic realities.

498 **The view from the barrio.**
Lisa Redfield Peattie. Ann Arbor, Michigan: University of Michigan Press, 1968. 147p.

A study, based on two years' field work in the early 1960s, of the process of economic development, as reflected in the lives of the inhabitants of the *barrio* of La Laja, in the new city of Ciudad Guayana.

499 **The city as centre of change in modern Venezuela.**
David James Robinson. In: *Cities in a changing Latin America: two studies in urban growth in the development of Mexico and Venezuela.* David J. Fox, David James Robinson. London: Latin American Publications Fund, 1969, p. 23-48.

A brief discussion of the causes and effects of urban development, which includes diagrams and tables.

500 **Planning urban growth and regional development: the experience of the Guayana project of Venezuela.**
Edited by Lloyd Rodwin. Cambridge, Massachusetts; London: MIT, 1969. 524p.

Published for the Joint Center for Urban Studies of the Massachusetts Institute of Technology and Harvard University, this comprises twenty-five essays by various authors on different aspects of the planning of the new city of Ciudad Guayana, under the broad headings of 'General perspectives, diagnosis and policies', 'Implementation issues' and 'Commentary on methods and goals'.

501 **Urbanization in the Americas from its beginnings to the present.**
Edited by Richard P. Schaedel, Jorge E. Hardoy, Nora Scott Kinzer. The Hague; Paris: Mouton, 1978. 676p.

Includes Angelina Pollak-Eltz's 'Household composition and mating patterns among lower-class Venezuelans' and María-Pilar García and Rae Lesser Blumberg's 'The unplanned ecology of a planned industrial city: the case of Ciudad Guayana, Venezuela'.

502 **New cities in Venezuela.**
Alan Turner, Jonathan Smulian. In: *The city in the Third World.* Edited by D.J. Dwyer. London: Macmillan; New York: Barnes & Noble, 1974, p. 237-53.
Discusses the plans for new cities near Maracaibo and south of Caracas, which are designed to reduce the pressure of urbanization on the capital. The article was originally published in *Town Planning Review*, vol. 42 (1971), p. 3-18.

503 **Caracas: focus of the new Venezuela.**
Francis Violich. In: *World capitals: toward guided urbanization.* Edited by H. Wentworth Eldredge. Garden City, New York: Anchor/Doubleday, 1975, p. 246-92.
A wide-ranging survey by an urban planner, which outlines: the context of urban primacy in Latin America; the historical development of Caracas; the social, economic and physical problems of the growth of the capital; and the process and policy of urban planning. Eight illustrations are included.

Health

504 **Epidemics in a tribal population.**
Napoleon A. Chagnon, Thomas F. Melancon. In: *The impact of contact. Two Yanomamo case studies.* John Saffirio (et al.). Cambridge, Massachusetts: Cultural Survival, 1983, p. 53-78. (Occasional Paper, no. 11).
An analysis of the direct demographic effects and likely social consequences of the 1973 epidemic of an upper respiratory infection, which caused the deaths of twenty-five per cent of the population of the three affected villages.

505 **The health and survival of the Venezuelan Yanoama.**
Edited by Marcus Colchester. Copenhagen: International Work Group for Indigenous Affairs, 1985. 104p. bibliog. (IWGIA Documentation Series, no. 53).
Comprises essays on health and medical services among the Venezuelan groups of this relatively uncontacted people.

506 **"Simplified medicine" in the Venezuelan health services.**
C.L. González. In: *Health by the people.* Edited by Kenneth W. Newell. Geneva: World Health Organization, 1975, p. 169-90.
Describes the development from 1962 of a branch of the health service designed to deliver some elements of basic health care to remote and dispersed populations. This

was to be achieved through the use of trained medical auxiliaries, as part of a system involving continuous availability, adequate supervision, and facilities for referral within the structure. The achievements of its first decade of operation are appraised.

507 **Trypanosomiasis and leishmaniasis with special reference to Chagas' disease.**
B.A. Newton (et al.). Amsterdam; London; New York: Elsevier, 1974. 353p. (Ciba Foundation Symposium, New Series, 20).

Gives the proceedings of an international symposium, held in Caracas in 1973, on certain parasitical diseases experienced in Venezuela and other tropical countries.

508 **Folk-medicine in Venezuela.**
Angelina Pollak-Eltz. Vienna (Wien-Föhrenau): Stiglmayr, 1982. 231p. bibliog. (Acta Ethnologica et Linguistica, no. 53. Series Americana, no. 9).

Discusses spiritual healing and herbal curing, as practised in Venezuela, and analyses their Amerindian, African and Spanish roots.

509 **La ciencia en Venezuela. IV ciclo de conferencias.** (Science in Venezuela. 4th series of lectures.)
Jesús Romero (et al.). Valencia, Venezuela: Universidad de Carabobo, Dirección de Cultura, 1976. 306p.

A series of lectures by medical specialists, indicating the state of medical research in the country.

510 **Etiology, hunger and folk disease in the Venezuelan Andes.**
María Matilde Suárez. *Journal of Anthropological Research*, vol. 30, no. 1 (1974), p. 41-54.

Reports the conclusions of a field survey, conducted in 1971-72, of folk perceptions of the causes, symptoms and treatment of diseases in the peasant community of El Morro in the state of Mérida.

511 **Infectious diseases and health services in Delta Amacuro, Venezuela.**
Werner Wilbert. Vienna (Wien-Föhrenau): Stiglmayr, 1984. 117p. bibliog. (Acta Ethnologica et Linguistica, no. 58. Series Americana, no. 10).

Collates data from health ministry records on the principal infectious diseases and main causes of death in the Orinoco delta area in the period 1950-80, and compares these with those from other regions, throwing considerable light on rural health care provision.

Religion

512 **Directorio de la iglesia católica en Venezuela.** (Directory of the Catholic Church in Venezuela.)
Centro de Investigaciones en Ciencias Sociales (CISOR). Caracas: Secretariado Permanente del Episcopado (SPEV), 1975. [n.p.].

Contains sections on: the universal Church; the organization and central services of the Church in Venezuela; lay organizations; the clergy, listed by diocese and parish; the religious orders and their officials; and gives an alphabetical list of the clergy. All are based on data relating to the end of 1974.

513 **Religiosidad popular en Venezuela: estudio preliminar.** (Popular attitudes towards religion and religious observances in Venezuela. A preliminary study.)
Centro de Investigaciones en Ciencias Sociales (CISOR). Caracas: CISOR, 1970. 263p. bibliog.

The report of a survey into religious observances and their significance, which formed part of an international investigation into popular religiosity in Latin America. It is based on interviews with a sample of 351 persons, evenly distributed between the states of Mérida and Monagas, between rural and urban dwellers, and between males and females. It includes numerous tables, and concludes that, while religious attitudes were predominantly Catholic, they were, in the great majority of cases, reliant on habit or convention.

514 **Attendance at Mass and fertility in Caracas.**
Ronald Cosper. *Sociological Analysis. A Journal in the Sociology of Religion*, vol. 36, no. 1 (1975), p. 43-56.

Reports the results of a survey which show that in Caracas, in contrast to other Roman Catholic communities, church attendance bears little relation to views on ideal family size, to knowledge or use of contraception, or to fertility levels.

515 **Democracy and the Church in Venezuela.**
Daniel H. Levine. *Journal of Interamerican Studies and World Affairs*, vol. 18, no. 1 (1976), p. 3-22.

Shows that, contrary to expectations, the Church prospered under the democratic régime which was inaugurated in 1958, and changed internally to accommodate itself to new circumstances.

516 **Religion and politics in Latin America: the Catholic Church in Venezuela and Colombia.**
Daniel Levine. Princeton, New Jersey: Princeton University Press, 1981. 342p. bibliog.

Compares the institutionally poor and weak Church in Venezuela with its powerful and influential neighbour in Colombia, concentrating on the changing rôle of religion in political and social life. It gives a collective view of the Catholic leaders, and their views on the Church's place in politics and society, based on interviews with the bishops, undertaken in 1971-73; discusses the importance of various lay institutions; and analyses trends at local level through the study of six sample dioceses, including San Cristóbal, Valencia and Cumaná in Venezuela.

517 **Gather together in my name: reflections on Christianity and community.**
Arturo Paoli, translated from the Italian by Robert R. Barr. Maryknoll, New York: Orbis, 1987. 192p.

Records an Italian priest's attempt to interpret Christianity in a manner relevant to the circumstances of a small rural settlement in western Venezuela.

518 **A history of the Church in Venezuela, 1810-1930.**
Mary Watters. Chapel Hill, North Carolina: University of North Carolina Press, 1933. Reprinted, New York: AMS, 1971, 260p. bibliog.

Seeks to explain why the Church lost the power and influence it had enjoyed, in colonial times, earlier and more completely in Venezuela than in other Latin American countries. There is a substantial introductory chapter on the colonial period, and the study effectively ends around 1890, with only a few concluding pages indicating that little material change in the relations between Church and State took place between the régime of Guzmán Blanco and the time of writing.

Education

519 **Student alienation: a Venezuela study.**
Robert F. Arnove.   New York; Washington, DC; London: Praeger,
1971. 209p. bibliog. (Praeger Special Studies in International
Economics and Development).
The report on a field study into the ways in which a university's institutional features
(such as patterns of student-faculty interaction, reward systems, and connections to
sources of employment) influence the eventual integration of the student into society.
It was conducted in 1967-68 in the Universidad de Oriente, an experimental institution
with a technical bias, which then catered largely for students from lower-middle- and
lower-class backgrounds from a rather backward area of the country.

520 **Investments in education under dictatorial and democratic regimes: the
case of Venezuela.**
Kenneth W. Beasley.   In: *Human resources in Latin America: an
interdisciplinary focus.* Edited by Frank T. Bachmura. Bloomington,
Indiana: Indiana University, Graduate School of Business Research,
1968, p. 157-81. (Indiana Business Paper, no. 16).
Compares government investment in primary education in the periods 1948-58 and
1958-66, and concludes that the record of the democratic régime is much better in
terms of increased enrolments and school construction, and reduced illiteracy, as well
as with regard to the percentage of the national budget devoted to the field. Beasley's
contribution is followed (p. 182-85) by a comment by Ian T. Ball.

521 **Education in Venezuela.**
G.E.R. Burroughs.   Newton Abbot, England; London: David &
Charles; Hamden, Connecticut: Archon, 1974. 121p. (World Education
Series).
A succinct survey, covering the historical background, the rôle of the government, the
general educational structure, teachers and their training, primary and secondary
schools and universities, and the special problems of education in rural areas.

522 **Bibliografía educativa venezolana.** (Bibliography of Venezuelan education.)
Aura Franchi Molina.   Maracaibo, Venezuela: Universidad del Zulia, Facultad de Humanidades y Educación, 1974. 135p.

Lists, predominantly, articles from Venezuelan periodicals, and groups them according to a detailed subject classification.

523 **A case study in distance learning systems. The Universidad Nacional Abierta of Venezuela (UNA).**
H.Z. Friedman.   Milton Keynes, England: Open University, Centre for International Cooperation and Services, 1978. 29p. bibliog.

A brief factual account of the Venezuelan 'open university' and the context of the educational system in which it operates. There are six appendices.

524 **Education in Venezuela.**
Delia Goetz.   Washington, DC: Federal Security Agency, Office of Education, 1948. 104p. bibliog. (Bulletin 1948, no. 14).

A descriptive account of Venezuelan education, based on a visit in 1946. Discusses the organization of educational administration; the provision of elementary, secondary and vocational education; the training of teachers; and the university sector.

525 **Educational reform and administrative development: the cases of Colombia and Venezuela.**
E. Mark Hanson.   Stanford, California: Hoover Institution Press, 1986. 246p. bibliog. (Education and Society Series, no. 3).

Makes a comparative study of changes in the administrative organization of education in the two countries in the period 1968-80. Chapters ten to thirteen (p. 143-208) deal with Venezuela, and describe both the pre-existing education system and the administrative structure of the ministry of education, and the separate unsuccessful attempts at decentralization under the successive Caldera and Pérez régimes. The author concludes that expensive sweeping changes in Venezuela were much less effective than the cumulative minor improvements carried out within the Colombian political consensus.

526 **Venezuela. A study of the educational system of Venezuela and a guide to the academic placement of students from Venezuela in educational institutions in the United States.**
Gary Hoover.   Washington, DC: American Association of Collegiate Registrars and Admissions Officers, 1978. 129p. bibliog. (World Education Series).

A brief review of curricula at institutions of intermediate and higher education in Venezuela, which gives detailed information on both grading systems and suggested parallels with grades at United States institutions.

527 **The new professional in Venezuelan secondary education.**
Thomas J. LaBelle. Los Angeles: University of California at Los
Angeles, Latin American Center, 1973. 195p. bibliog. (Latin American
Studies, no. 23).

Presents the report of a survey, conducted in 1971, of the background and attitudes of
a sample of 638 students undergoing training for secondary school teaching or
administration. Concludes that the teaching profession is an important means of social
mobility; that students in training are highly committed to their profession; that they
rank educational development very high among national priorities; and that they
believe the school system has a decisive rôle to play, but that it should be more
vocationally oriented.

528 **Build a mill, build a city, build a school: industrialization, urbanization**
and education in Ciudad Guayana.
Noel F. McGinn, Russell G. Davies. Cambridge, Massachusetts;
London: MIT, 1969. 334p. (Publications of the Joint Center for Urban
Studies).

Describes the school system developed in Guayana, analyses its effectiveness, and
offers the design for an appropriate educational system for the new city.

529 **The right to be intelligent.**
Luis Alberto Machado, translated by Mark C. Wheeler. Oxford;
New York; Toronto etc.: Pergamon, 1980. 63p.

An impassioned plea for the right to full educational development, based on the view
that intelligence is culturally not genetically determined, by the Venezuelan minister of
state for the development of human intelligence. The author was the first such minister
to be appointed in the world.

530 **Mass higher education in Venezuela.**
Ivan Olaizola. London: London Association of Comparative
Educationists, 1984. 24p. (LACE Occasional Papers, no. 12).

This prints a lecture given by the vice-minister of education, which contains a useful
collection of facts and figures on educational expansion since 1958, and comments on
the way in which quality in higher education was sacrificed in favour of quantity, to
meet the demands of the rising expectations of an increasing population.

531 **Simón Bolívar: educator.**
Luis B. Prieto, translated by James D. Parsons. Garden City, New
York: Doubleday, 1970. 159p.

Refutes the traditional view of Rousseau as a major influence on Bolívar's educational
thought, and discusses how the Liberator contributed to the development of Latin
American education. The example of his own life, his views on the relationship of
education to politics, and his ideas on methods and content of instruction are seen as
part of his legacy.

532 **Individual decisions and educational planning: occupational choices of Venezuelan secondary students.**

Gordon C. Ruscoe. *International Development Review*, vol. 10, no. 2 (1968), p. 20-25.

Reports on a survey of students' occupational and educational decisions, and stresses that any professional workforce planning must attempt to influence their choices at the secondary rather than at the university level.

533 **The development of education in Venezuela.**

George I. Sánchez. Washington, DC: United States Department of Health, Education and Welfare, Office of Education, 1963. 114p. bibliog. (Office of Education Bulletin 1963, no. 7).

An American professor of education, with previous experience of Venezuela, visited the country in 1961; this is his report on the state of the nation's education. The first half reviews the history of education to the end of the Pérez Jiménez dictatorship in 1958. The second describes the education system in operation under the democratic régime, covering: administrative organization; school provision; enrolment; and curricula, at elementary, secondary and higher levels, and for vocational education and teacher training. There is an interesting conclusion on the educational problems still facing Venezuela in the early years of constitutional rule.

534 **Education, class, and nation: the experiences of Chile and Venezuela.**

Kalman H. Silvert, Leonard Reissman. New York; Oxford; Amsterdam: Elsevier, 1976. 242p.

Reports on the results of a survey of attitudes, towards such topics as family, religion, society, and politics, administered to samples of students, parents and teachers at different types of primary and secondary schools and universities in various locations in each country. Concludes that the formal educational institutions of Chile and Venezuela are effective in changing the world views of their pupils, so that they value universal national interests more highly than particular class interests.

535 **The education–work transition of Venezuelan university students.**

Dieter K. Zschock (et al.). *Journal of Interamerican Studies and World Affairs*, vol. 16, no. 1 (1974), p. 96-118.

An exploratory survey of student and élite attitudes towards higher education and professional employment, based on small samples of leaders in the public and private sectors and of engineering and administration students from two Caracas universities, is here described and analysed.

Sport and Recreation

536 **Nowhere to play.**
Judith Elkin, illustrated by Monika Doppert. London: Adam &
Charles Black, 1982. 46p.
This picture book for young children is an English version of Kurusa's *La calle es libre*
(Venezuela, 1981). It is based on the true story of the efforts of the children of the
shanty town of San José de la Urbana in Caracas to get a playground.

537 **The festival of progress: the globalizing world-system and the
transformation of the Caracas carnival.**
Robert H. Lavenda. *Journal of Popular Culture*, vol. 14, no. 3
(1980), p. 465-75.
Discusses the transformation of the Caracas carnival, during the régime of Guzmán
Blanco in the 1870s, from a wild and rowdy 'rite of reversal', to an occasion that was
officially organized and sponsored by the new élite.

538 **The book of Latin American cooking.**
Elisabeth Lambert Ortiz. London: Hale, 1984. 335p.
The recipes in this volume are arranged in sections according to the type of food. The
country of origin is indicated for each recipe, twenty-two of which are from Venezuela.

539 **Monedas venezolanas.** (Venezuelan coins.)
Mercedes Carlota de Pardo. Caracas: Banco Central de Venezuela,
1973. 2nd ed. 2 vols. bibliog. (Colección histórico-económico
venezolana, vol. VI).
Volume I of this authoritative work, by a former head of the numismatics section of
the central bank, includes a history of the coinage from the start of production in 1802
to 1973, followed by descriptions and photographs of the coins, and tables of quantities
circulated. Volume II is a compendium of the texts of laws and decrees relating to the
coinage.

540 **La pelea de gallos en Venezuela.** (Cock-fighting in Venezuela.)
Omar Alberto Pérez. Caracas: Ediciones Espada Rota, 1984. 267p.
bibliog.

Comprises an alphabetical lexicon of the specialized vocabulary used in the sport; an account of its history; and an anthology of literature relating to it, including Venezuelan laws and regulations, poems and verses, and stories and articles.

541 **El deporte en Venezuela.** (Sport in Venezuela.)
Luis Felipe Rodríguez (et al.). Caracas: Universidad Central de
Venezuela, Dirección de Cultura, 1968. 580p. (Colección Foros y
Seminarios, Serie Foros).

Presents the proceedings of a forum organized by the sports administration of the Central University and the Association of Sporting Journalists in 1968. Among the topics covered are: an outline of the origins of the organization of baseball, football and cycling, of the formation of an Olympic committee in 1938, and of a national sports institute in 1949; a review of the organization of sport in 1968, including the participation of the state, of private bodies, of educational establishments, and of the military; a sketch of possible future developments; a discussion of the international dimension; and an account of sports reporting.

542 **La fiesta brava en Caracas. Cuatro siglos de historia.** (Bull-fighting in
Caracas. Four centuries of history.)
Carlos Salas. Caracas: Concejo Municipal del Distrito Federal, 1978.
360p. bibliog.

Much of this compilation chronicles the principal bull-fighting events of the twentieth century. There is also information on the early history of the sport, on the bull-rings, and on the biographies of the leading bull-fighters.

543 **Sinopsis de las monedas venezolanas y nociones de numismática.**
(Synopsis of Venezuelan coins and rudiments of numismatics.)
Alberto Sívoli G. Caracas: Banco Industrial de Venezuela, 1966.
283p. bibliog.

The first part is a description, with illustrations, of coins issued in Venezuela from the establishment of the first mint in 1802 until 1960.

544 **Venezuela: a study of the international travel market.**
United States Travel Service, Research and Analysis Division.
Washington, DC: United States, Department of Commerce, 1977. 63p.

Comprises the results of a sample survey among residents of Caracas and Maracaibo, into their international travel habits, patterns, attitudes, destinations and purposes, with special reference to recreational travel to the United States.

545 **Catálogo especializado de estampillas de Venezuela.** (Specialized
catalogue of Venezuelan postage stamps.)
Juan José Valera. Caracas: Litojet, 1985. 9th ed. 536p.

This chronological list of stamps issued gives information on the current market prices. There are numerous illustrations.

Economics

General

546 **Venezuelan economic development. A politico-economic analysis.**
Loring Allen. Greenwich, Connecticut: JAI, 1977. 310p. bibliog.
(Contemporary Studies in Economic and Financial Analysis, vol. 7).
An analysis of the Venezuelan economy in 1975, reviewing changes since 1935 in
economic policy, growth and structure, public sector, human resources, financial
sector, trade, agriculture, and the petroleum and manufacturing industries. The
generally highly favourable view of Venezuela's progress, in both the political and
economic fields, is only marginally qualified by the concluding remark that the country
remains uncomfortably dependent on oil for the maintenance of its much increased
prosperity.

547 **La economía venezolana: una interpretación de su modo de**
funcionamiento. (The Venezuelan economy: an interpretation of how it
works.)
Sergio Aranda. Caracas: Editorial Pomaire, 1984. 2nd ed. 328p.
bibliog.
Originally published in 1974, this is an analysis, by a Chilean economist and former
planning official, of the development of the Venezuelan economy in its world context
since 1920. It is illustrated by over 100 tables. This second edition includes an
additional chapter (with a further eight tables) on the period 1975-84.

548 **Banking on oil in Venezuela.**
Gene Bigler, Franklin Tugwell. In: *Bordering on trouble. Resources*
and politics in Latin America. Edited by Andrew Maguire, Janet Welsh
Brown. Bethesda, Maryland: Adler & Adler, 1986, p. 152-89.
An acute analysis of the shortcomings of Venezuela's management of its rich resources
in the 1960s and 1970s, of the nature and extent of the economic crisis of the 1980s,
and of the country's response to the situation.

549 **South American economic handbook.**
Edited by Harold Blakemore. London: Euromonitor Publications, 1986. 274p.
Chapter thirteen (p. 207-33) contains a brief survey of the Venezuelan economy, designed for the businessperson.

550 **A reappraisal of the economic record of Venezuela, 1939-1959.**
Thomasine Cusack. *Journal of Inter-American Studies*, vol. 3, no. 4 (1961), p. 477-96.
Analyses the country's economic growth in terms both of factors affecting Latin America generally, and of those peculiar to Venezuela; and assesses the economic prospects of the Betancourt régime.

551 **La economía venezolana, 1944-1984.** (The Venezuelan economy, 1944-1984.)
Oscar A. Echevarría. Caracas: Fedecámaras, 1984. 148p. bibliog.
A survey of the development and growth of the economy, and of the economic crisis of the 1980s, illustrated by eighty-five statistical tables.

552 **Venezuela: the oil boom and the debt crisis.**
Ramón Escovar Salom. In: *Latin America and the world recession.* Edited by Esperanza Durán. Cambridge, England; London; New York, etc.: Cambridge University Press, 1985, p. 120-29.
Analyses the ways in which the pattern of political and economic development pursued in the 1960s was upset, first by the sudden increase in oil prices in 1973, and then by their fall in 1982, which massively increased the burden of international debts contracted in the boom years.

553 **Oil and development: Venezuela.**
Klaus Esser. Berlin, GFR: German Development Institute, 1977. 2nd ed. 90p.
An incisive critique of the development plans of the Pérez régime of the 1970s, suggesting why the high oil revenues were not likely to produce a sustainable dynamic economy.

554 **Regional development policy: a case study of Venezuela.**
John Friedmann. Cambridge, Massachusetts; London: MIT, 1966. 279p.
Part I deals with the general issues of the structure and process of regional development. Part II discusses Venezuela, and includes chapters on urbanization, on the Guayana region, and on the design and implementation of appropriate policies. Two maps illustrate particular features.

555 **Venezuela: from doctrine to dialogue.**
John Friedmann. Syracuse, New York: Syracuse University Press, 1965. 87p. bibliog. (National Planning Series, no. 1).
Traces the evolution of national planning procedures under the Betancourt government, 1958-63, and is now mainly of historic interest.

556 **The second four-year plan of Venezuela.**
Mostafa Fathy Hassan. *Journal of Inter-American Studies*, vol. 9, no. 2 (1967), p. 296-320.
Discusses the targets of the 1963-66 economic plan for growth, employment and diversification, and explains the failure to realise them in terms of the absence of economic policies designed to improve the investment climate.

557 **Inter-American Economic Affairs.**
Vol. 7, no. 4 (1954).
This issue, devoted to various aspects of the Venezuelan economy in the 1950s, remains of some interest from a historical point of view. It comprises J.I. González Gorrondona's 'Monetary considerations in Venezuela'; Bernardo Ferrán's 'Venezuelan agriculture'; John Hickey's 'The Venezuelan food supply'; Juan Sardá's 'Industrial development in Venezuela'; Virgil Salera's 'On investment in basic services: with some applications to the Venezuela case'; J. Fred Rippy's 'The Venezuelan claims settlement of 1903-05: a case study in the cost of disorder, despotism and deficient capital and technology'; and Hernán Avendaño's 'Some aspects of petroleum trade and production in Venezuela'.

558 **The economic development of Venezuela.**
International Bank for Reconstruction and Development. Baltimore, Maryland: Johns Hopkins University Press, 1961. 494p.
Gives the conclusions of an economic survey mission, undertaken by the International Bank in 1959, to analyse the various sectors of the Venezuelan economy.

559 **A bibliography on South American economic affairs. Articles in nineteenth-century periodicals.**
Tom B. Jones, Elizabeth Ann Warburton, Anne Kingsley.
Minneapolis, Minnesota: University of Minnesota Press, 1955. 146p.
The bibliography is based on an analysis of over 200 nineteenth-century periodicals published in Europe and the Americas. There is a short general section, and a specifically Venezuelan section. The latter lists around 200 items, classified under agriculture, commerce, communications, finance, immigration, industry, labour, mining and transportation.

560 **External debt and development strategy in Latin America.**
Edited by Antonio Jorge, Jorge Salazar-Carillo, Frank Diaz-Pou.
New York; Oxford; Toronto: Pergamon, 1985. 269p.
Includes two brief articles on this major issue of the 1980s: Henry Gómez-Samper's 'The management of Venezuela's external debt' (p. 57-63); and Mostafa F. Hassan's 'Venezuela's external debt problem' (p. 65-69).

113

561 **Economic planning in Venezuela.**
Fred D. Levy, Jr. New York; Washington, DC; London: Praeger,
1968. 204p. bibliog.
Discusses the evolution of a mechanism for economic planning during the Betancourt
régime, and attempts to assess its effectiveness. There are thirty-seven statistical tables.

562 **Venezuela's economic crisis: origins and successes in stabilization.**
Robert E. Looney. *Journal of Social, Political and Economic Studies*,
vol. 11, no. 3 (1986), p. 327-37.
An incisive analysis of the origins of the economic crisis of 1983, which also considers
the steps taken to deal with it by the Herrera and Lusinchi administrations.

563 **Venezuela: business and finances.**
Rodolfo Luzardo. Englewood Cliffs, New Jersey: Prentice-Hall, 1957.
167p.
A description, supported by twenty-seven tables and seventeen charts, of the various
industries of Venezuela, and of the state of the country's finances. It was designed as a
guide for potential American investors during the dictatorship of Pérez Jiménez, and is
still of some interest for comparison with current conditions.

564 **Venezuela: economic and commercial conditions.**
Alfred Cedric Maby. London: HMSO, 1951. 254p. (Overseas
Economic Surveys).
A compilation by the First Secretary (Commercial) at the British Embassy in Caracas,
made in early 1951, describing government departments, commercial laws, banking,
mining, energy, agriculture, industry, transport, public works, and trade, with twenty-
two statistical appendices. A similar but briefer study with the same title, compiled by
R.S. Scrivener, was published by HMSO in 1954 (95p.).

565 **The renegotiation of Venezuela's foreign debt during 1982 and 1983.**
Eduardo Mayobre. In: *Politics and economics of external debt crisis:
the Latin American experience*. Edited by Miguel S. Wionczek.
Boulder, Colorado: Westview, 1985, p. 325-47. (Westview Special
Studies on Latin America and the Caribbean).
Explains why Venezuela, with smaller foreign debts and a stronger economy than most
other Latin American countries, experienced extreme difficulty in meeting and re-
scheduling its international financial obligations in 1982-83.

566 **The oil price increase and the alleviation of poverty. Income distribution
in Caracas, Venezuela in 1966 and 1975.**
Philip Musgrove. *Journal of Development Economics*, vol. 9, no. 2
(1981), p. 229-50.
Compares two Caracas household budget surveys, and finds that mean real incomes
rose substantially, especially among the rich, and that the proportion of the population
classified as poor decreased, though their mean income did not rise.

567 **Petrodollars and the state: the failure of state capitalist development in Venezuela.**
James F. Petras, Morris H. Morley. *Third World Quarterly*, vol. 5, no. 1 (1983), p. 7-27.

Argues that the policies of the Pérez and Herrera régimes, from 1974 onwards, tended to encourage private accumulation rather than socio-economic redistribution; did not produce economic independence out of oil wealth; and left the country dependent on foreign finance capital.

568 **VII plan de la nación, 1984-1988. Lineamientos generales.** (7th national plan, 1984-1988. General outlines.)
Venezuela. Presidencia de la República. Oficina Central de Coordinación y Planificación. Caracas: CORDIPLAN, 1985. 120p.

Summarizes the critical economic situation at the outset of the plan, which was due to the arresting of the growth pattern by the debt crisis, and outlines a new strategy for development towards national objectives.

Finance and commerce

569 **Business yearbook for Brazil, Mexico and Venezuela, 1981.**
Edited by S.J. Andrade, S.M.A. Barrow. London: Graham & Trotman, 1980. 329p.

Part I consists of general discussions of the economies, transport, banking, taxation, investment, oil, and trade, most of which have a separate section on Venezuela. Part II contains a section on each of the three countries, that on Venezuela (p. 277-329) containing details on governmental institutions, business travel, economic and financial conditions, consumer demand, import regulations and duties, and development plans.

570 **Oil policies and budgets in Venezuela, 1938-1968.**
Enrique A. Baloyra. *Latin American Research Review*, vol. 9, no. 2 (1974), p. 28-72.

Compares the budget expenditures of the 'authoritarian' régimes of 1938-45 and 1948-58 with those of the 'democratic' régimes of 1945-48 and 1958-68, and the extent to which each type of system managed relations with the oil companies to maximise the national benefit. Concludes that there was a clear contrast between the 'fearful permissiveness' of the military régimes and the 'determined bluff-calling' of the AD; and that the latter was more effective in increasing Venezuela's share of oil profits, and gave higher priority to education and health and lower priority to communications than the former.

571 **Capital markets in Latin America. A general survey and six country studies.**
Antonín Basch, Milic Kybal.   New York; Washington, DC; London: Praeger, for Inter-American Devlopment Bank, 1970. 163p. bibliog. (Praeger Special Studies in International Economics and Development).
Offers a survey of investment and financial institutions in Latin American in the period 1960-68, and a detailed study of the capital market in Venezuela (p. 147-56).

572 **Mercantile credit and financing in Venezuela, 1830-1870.**
Susan Berglund.   *Journal of Latin American Studies*, vol. 17, no. 2 (1985), p. 371-96.
Uses the records of the commercial house of Boulton to illustrate the structure of mercantile credit and the rôle of mercantile houses in public finance in nineteenth-century Venezuela.

573 **Reform of the Venezuelan fiscal system.**
Edited by Tomás Enrique Carrillo Batalla.   Ames, Iowa: Iowa State University Press, 1989. 411p.
This is the English translation of the important report of the Venezuelan Commission on Fiscal Study and Reform, submitted to the government in 1983. It embodies the results of the Commission's extensive investigations into, and recommendations for the reform of, government revenue and expenditure; public credit; planning and budget; fiscal administration, accounting and control; and personnel administration.

574 **Venezuela: business opportunities in the 1980s.**
Paul Clifford.   London: Metra Consulting Group, 1980. 223p. (Business Opportunity Reports on Latin America).
A compendium of data, incorporating numerous tables, covering development plans, energy, infrastructure, mining, agriculture, trading and investment conditions, and the commercial environment.

575 **Venezuela – now!**
Confederation of British Industry.   London: CBI, 1975. 48p.
This report of a Confederation of British Industry (CBI) mission to Venezuela in March 1975 outlines business opportunities in eleven different sectors of the economy, and gives twelve appendices of facts and figures.

576 **Stock exchanges of Latin America.**
David K. Eiteman.   Ann Arbor, Michigan: University of Michigan Graduate School of Business Administration, 1966. 83p. (Michigan International Business Studies, no. 7).
Chapter IV 'Venezuelan stock exchanges' (p. 54-65) describes the formation of the 'Bolsa de Caracas' in 1947 and the 'Bolsa de Miranda' in 1958, and considers their mode of operation; the nature of Venezuelan shares; membership and procedure of the exchanges; and the volume of transactions in the period 1963-65.

577 **The Manoa Company.**
Charles G. Jackson. *Inter-American Economic Affairs*, vol. 13, no. 4 (1960), p. 12-45.
Recounts the history of an American company set up to exploit land, transport and mineral concessions in the Orinoco delta area in the 1880s and 1890s.

578 **Major companies of Brazil, Mexico and Venezuela, 1979-80.**
Edited by S.J. Longrigg. London: Graham & Trotman, 1979. 405p.
The Venezuelan section (p. 301-61) lists details of around 700 companies, arranged alphabetically, with a classified index under seventy-four categories of business activity.

579 **Co-operation among developing countries: some Venezuelan experiences.**
Eduardo López Pérez. *Development and Peace* [Budapest], vol. 1, no. 1 (1980), p. 92-105.
Makes a study of Venezuela's experience of financial co-operation with other less developed countries, especially since the establishment of the Venezuelan Investment Fund in 1974; and of its dealings with organizations such as the Caribbean Development Bank, the Central American Economic Integration Bank, and the Andean Development Corporation.

580 **Las inversiones extranjeras en Venezuela.** (Foreign investment in Venezuela.)
José Antonio Mayobre. Caracas: Editorial Monte Avila, 1970. 103p.
This essay by an ex-minister of finance analyses foreign investment in Venezuela, and stresses the need to adopt a policy towards it which is designed to further the national interest. It includes a number of tables illustrating the level and distribution of external capital.

581 **Determinants of the demand for imports of Venezuela.**
Oscar Melo, Michael G. Vogt. *Journal of Development Economics*, vol. 14, no. 3 (1984), p. 351-58.
Estimates real income and relative price elasticities of demand for imports in the period 1967-79, and concludes that Venezuela made much progress in import substitution, but that the oil price rise led to an increase in all categories of imports in 1974-79.

582 **Venezuela: tax and investment profile.**
Cano Pérez & Asociados. London; New York; Caracas: Touche Ross International, 1988. 55p.
A compendium of practical information for foreigners doing business with Venezuela, discussing investment factors, exchange controls, establishing a business, and taxation.

583 **A market for U.S. products: Venezuela.**
Reynaldo Rodriguez. Washington, DC: United States Department of Commerce, 1964. 65p. (A supplement to *International Commerce*).
A handbook of basic information for American exporters, which analyses demand for commodities and explains Venezuelan trade practices and regulations.

584 **Economic pressure groups and policy-making in Venezuela: the case of FEDECAMARAS reconsidered.**
René Salgado. *Latin American Research Review*, vol. 22, no. 3 (1987), p. 91-121.

Discusses the extent to which the Venezuelan federation of chambers of commerce (FEDECAMARAS) was able to influence government policy following the devaluation of the *bolívar* in 1983. The article is followed by comments by Robert Bond, Janet Kelly de Escobar and Diego Abente, and a rejoinder by the author.

585 **The fiscal system of Venezuela.**
Carl S. Shoup. Baltimore, Maryland: Johns Hopkins University Press, 1959. 491p.

This report of a commission on the fiscal system, set up by the provisional government which followed the overthrow of Pérez Jiménez, describes and analyses the tax system as of 1958, and suggests a number of reforms.

586 **Economía y finanzas de Venezuela, 1830-1944.** (The economy and finances of Venezuela, 1830-1944.)
Ramón Veloz. Caracas: Academia Nacional de la Historia, 1984. 478p. (Biblioteca de la Academia Nacional de la Historia, Serie Economía y Finanzas, no. 7).

Gives a year-by-year summary of public income and expenditure; details the produce of various taxes, exports (identifying principal products) and imports, and exchange rates etc.; and makes general comments on economic conditions.

587 **The Venezuelan capital markets law.**
Christopher Wiles. *International Lawyer*, vol. 8, no. 2 (1974), p. 303-15.

Describes the provisions and significance of the law enacted in January 1973 to encourage the formation of private capital. In particular, it considers the setting up of a National Securities Commission to superintend the workings of a securities market and safeguard the interests of participants, and the offering of incentives to companies to raise capital by public offer.

588 **Venezuelan investment in Florida, 1979.**
Mira Wilkins. *Latin American Research Review*, vol. 16, no. 1 (1981), p. 156-65.

Gives some facts and figures about investments by Venezuelans in Florida real estate and banks, with comments on the possible causes and effects of the flight of capital from the country.

Statistics

589 **Socio-economic data and parameters of Venezuela, 1950-1965.**
Co-ordinated by Oscar A. Echevarría. Washington, DC: Inter-American Development Bank, Socio-Economic Development Division, 1967. [n.p.].
A collection of series of economic statistics for the period 1950-65, including: chain indexes; indexes with 1950 base; chronological trends; and values per capita and per worker, together with analytical and predictive models and graphs.

590 **Statistical yearbook for Latin America and the Caribbean, 1988 edition.**
Economic Commission for Latin America. Santiago: United Nations, 1989. 782p.
This is a bilingual official edition of a selection of the main statistical series available on the social and economic data of both the region and the individual countries, covering social development and welfare; economic growth, prices, trade and finance; population, national accounts, natural resources and production, employment and social conditions.

591 **Series estadísticas para la historia de Venezuela.** (Statistical series for the history of Venezuela).
Miguel Izard. Mérida, Venezuela: Universidad de los Andes, Consejo de Desarrollo Científico y Humanístico, Facultad de Humanidades, Escuela de Historia, 1970. 251p. bibliog.
Comprises four sections of tables, covering: population, production, prices and trade. Most of the material relates to the period from independence to around 1940, but some of the series date back to the colonial period.

592 **Anuario del comercio exterior de Venezuela, 1987.** (Venezuelan foreign trade annual, 1987.)
Venezuela. Presidencia de la República. Caracas: Oficina Central de Estadística e Información, 1988. 755p.
Gives detailed tables of imports and exports, by quantity and value, type of goods, and source or destination.

593 **Anuario estadístico de Venezuela, 1987.** (Statistical annual of Venezuela, 1987.)
Venezuela. Presidencia de la República. Caracas: Oficina Central de Estadística e Información, 1988. 956p.
Contains hundreds of tables of official statistics under the headings: 'Physical (geography and climate)'; 'Demographic (population distribution, birth, marriage and death rates, migration)'; 'Economic (agriculture, industry, production, construction, foreign trade, services, transport, communications, tourism, balance of payments, national accounts, public finance, banking, insurance, foreign investment, prices and wages)'; 'Social (housing, urban development, social security, medicine and health, co-

operatives, labour)'; 'Cultural (education, science and technology)'; and 'Political, administrative and judicial (elections, public administration, justice, traffic accidents, property registers)'.

594 **Statistical abstract of Latin America. Vol. 26.**
Edited by James W. Wilkie, David E. Lorey. Enrique Ochoa. Los Angeles: University of California at Los Angeles, Latin American Center, 1988. 942p.

An annual publication of over 1,000 tables, displaying a wide variety of social and economic statistics both for Latin America as a whole and for individual countries, including Venezuela.

Industry

General

595 **Nationalization of oil in Venezuela. Re-defined dependence and legitimization of imperialism.**
Vegard Bye. *Journal of Peace Research*, vol. 16, no. 1 (1979), p. 57-78.
Analyses the extent of foreign dominance of the Venezuelan economy before and after the nationalization of the oil industry in 1976, and finds little significant change.

596 **Reproducing dependency: auto industry policy and petrodollar circulation in Venezuela.**
Fernando Coronil, Julie Skurski. *International Organization*, vol. 36, no. 1 (1982), p. 61-94.
An examination of the unsuccessful attempt by the first administration of President Carlos Andrés Pérez (1974-78) to develop the local production of vehicle engines, and of the resulting tension between import-substitution and export-promotion strategies for national development.

597 **The Venezuelan Petroleum Corporation and the debate over government policy in basic industry, 1960-76.**
Steve Ellner. Glasgow, Scotland: University of Glasgow, Institute of Latin American Studies, 1987. 46p. (Occasional Paper, no. 47).
Presents a detailed examination of debates over industrial policy, both within and between parties, and between government and the national oil company, up to the nationalization of 1976.

598 **The changing marketing structure in the industrial development of Venezuela.**
Phillip D. Grub, Arthur R. Miele. *Journal of Developing Areas*, vol. 3, no. 4 (1969), p. 513-26; vol. 4, no. 1 (1969), p. 69-80.
Part one discusses marketing in the pharmaceutical industry, and part two examines the marketing of cosmetic products and toiletry preparations. They note that both markets and marketing techniques changed significantly in the course of the 1960s.

599 **Venezuelan industrialization, dependent or autonomous? A study of national and foreign participation in the industrial development of a Latin American OPEC country.**
Fred Jongkind. Amsterdam: Centre for Latin American Research and Documentation, 1981. 229p. bibliog. (CEDLA Incidentele Publikaties, no. 21).
The basis for this volume was provided by interviews, undertaken in 1976-77, of a ten per cent sample of industrialists from firms employing more than fifty workers. It argues that Venezuelan industrialization since the end of the 1950s can be attributed more to national than to foreign efforts, and that the rôle of foreign capital and transnational corporations was much smaller than 'dependency' theories would suggest.

600 **Manufacturing in Venezuela: studies on development and location.**
Weine Karlsson. Stockholm: Almquist & Wiksell International, 1975. 240p. maps. bibliog. (Publications of the Institute of Latin American Studies, Stockholm. Series A Monographs, no. 2).
An analysis, which is illustrated by numerous tables, diagrams and maps, of the geography of manufacturing developments, with particular reference to oil refining, cotton textiles, and food products. It shows an increasing concentration in Caracas and the north-central region of the country.

601 **Energy policies of the world: Venezuela.**
Aníbal R. Martínez. Newark, Delaware: University of Delaware, College of Marine Studies, Center for the Study of American Policy, 1975. 100p. bibliog.
Reviews Venezuela's energy resources, production and consumption, and urges the formulation and enforcement of a long-term energy policy, designed to lessen wasteful use of petroleum and natural gas, and to expand the development of 'renewable' resources, such as hydroelectric power and solar energy.

602 **Foreign investment in the petroleum and mineral industries. Case studies of investor-host country relations.**
Raymond F. Mikesell (et al.). Baltimore, Maryland; London: Johns Hopkins University Press, 1971. 459p.
Includes Gertrude G. Edwards' 'Foreign petroleum companies and the state in Venezuela' (p. 101-28); William G. Harris' 'The impact of the petroleum export industry on the pattern of Venezuelan economic development' (p. 129-56); and Henry Gomez' 'Venezuela's iron-ore industry' (p. 312-44).

603 **Accumulation and the state in Venezuelan industrialization.**
Juan Pablo Pérez Sáinz, Paul Zarembka. *Latin American
Perspectives*, vol. 6, no. 3 (1979), p. 205-29.
Analyses the emergence of the industrial sector in Venezuela, and how it was
influenced by the oil-producing sector as a basis for capital accumulation; and reviews
the developments of the period 1958-73, with special attention paid to the use of
labour, and to the rôle of the state.

604 **Multinationals in Latin America. The politics of nationalization.**
Paul E. Sigmund. Madison, Wisconsin; London: University of
Wisconsin Press, 1980. 426p. bibliog.
Chapter seven (p. 225-55) 'Venezuela – a new pattern of nationalization?' examines
why Venezuela achieved the nationalization of petroleum and other foreign-exploited
resources with much less conflict and controversy than other Latin American countries,
and suggests that its example shows that it was possible to bargain with multinational
companies so as to receive the benefits of technology and marketing skills after
nationalization.

605 **The state and industrialization in Venezuela.**
Heinz Sonntag, Rafael de la Cruz. *Latin American Perspectives*,
vol. 12, no. 4 (1985), p. 75-104.
Traces the development of industry since the 1920s, and analyses the importance of the
rôle of the state in the process of capitalist industrialization.

Petroleum

606 **The first big oil hunt: Venezuela, 1911-1916.**
Ralph Arnold, George A. Macready, Thomas W. Barrington. New
York; Washington, DC; Hollywood, California: Vantage, 1960. 353p.
This story of pioneering petroleum explorations in Venezuela, told by the American
geologists who undertook them, is illustrated by numerous photographs.

607 **A golden adventure. The first 50 years of Ultramar.**
Paul Atterbury, Julia MacKenzie. London: Hurtwood, 1985. 287p.
An official history of the evolution of a small exploration company, formed in 1935 to
develop oilfields in Venezuela, into an organization producing oil and gas on four
continents.

608 **Venezuela's oil.**
Rómulo Betancourt, translated by Donald Peck. London: Allen &
Unwin, 1978. 275p.
Comprises essays and speeches by the ex-president and others on oil policy in the 1960s
and the nationalization of the industry in 1975.

609 **The nationalization of the Venezuelan oil industry: from technocratic success to political failure.**
Gustavo Coronel. Lexington, Massachusetts: D.C. Heath, 1983. 292p. bibliog.

A critical account of the performance of the Venezuelan oil industry after its nationalization in 1975, by an experienced petroleum engineer and manager who was a member of the board of Petróleos de Venezuela, the holding company of the nationalized industry, from 1975 to 1979. He argues that the industry suffered from political interference and 'cronyism'.

610 **Petroleum in Venezuela: a history.**
Edwin Lieuwen. Berkeley, California: University of California Press, 1954. Reprinted, New York: Russell & Russell, 1967. 160p. map. bibliog. (University of California Publications in History).

Makes a pioneering survey of the development of the Venezuelan oil industry and its domestic and international implications from its beginnings to 1952. It incorporates an oil-field map and a table of annual production as compared with other leading producers.

611 **Chronology of Venezuelan oil.**
Anibal R. Martinez. London: Allen & Unwin, 1969. 207p. bibliog.

A chronologically arranged list of facts about Venezuelan oil, from earliest times to 1967, drawn from various published sources. These are not identified for each entry, but are indicated in a general way in the bibliography. There is an appendix of fourteen tables, listing oil-fields, refineries, pipelines, reserves, production and exports.

612 **Gumersindo Torres: the pioneer of Venezuelan petroleum policy.**
Aníbal R. Martínez, translated by Patricia Pernalete. Caracas: Petróleos de Venezuela, 1980. 138p.

This brief biography of the man who, as minister of development (1917-22 and 1929-31), was responsible for the establishment of the legal and administrative organization within which the oil industry operated, was the winning entry in a prize competition held on the centenary of the subject's birth in 1875.

613 **The journey from Petrolia.**
Aníbal R. Martínez, translated by Patricia Pernalete. Caracas: Petróleos de Venezuela, 1986. 123p. bibliog.

An account of the history of the Compañía Petrolia del Táchira, which operated Venezuela's first oil-field, La Alquitrana in the state of Táchira, from 1878 to the 1930s.

614 **Our gift, our oil.**
Anibal R. Martinez. Vienna: The Author, 1966. 199p.

A personal plea by the author, who was at the time an official of the Organization of Petroleum Exporting Countries (OPEC), and Venezuelan delegate to the World Petroleum Congress, for rational development of the oil resources of his country and other producing nations, which throws light on the Venezuelan industry and government policy in the 1960s.

615 **Juan Vicente Gómez and the oil companies in Venezuela, 1908-1935.**
Brian S. McBeth.   Cambridge, England; London; New York etc.:
Cambridge University Press, 1983. 275p. bibliog. (Cambridge Latin
American Studies, no. 43).

This study revises the traditional view of Gómez as an instrument of the international
oil companies. Making use of new material from various Venezuelan archival sources,
it concludes that the dictator and his government took a close interest in maximizing
the country's benefit from the industry, and in protecting its workers.

616 **The symbiotic relationship of Creole and Venezuela.**
Robert G. Mogull.   *Journal of Human Relations*, vol. 20, no. 4 (1972),
p. 459-67.

Outlines the way in which the Creole Petroleum Corporation, Venezuela's largest oil
producer prior to nationalization, contributed to the country's development through
investment in other sectors of the economy and through the employment, education
and training of Venezuelan personnel. It also indicates how Creole could have done
more in developing community initiative and democratic awareness.

617 **The nationalization of Venezuelan oil.**
James Petras, Morris Morley, Steven Smith.   New York: Praeger,
1977. 173p. (Praeger Special Studies in International Economics and
Development).

Interprets the nationalization of the Venezuelan oil industry in 1975-76 as a move by
the developing national capitalist bourgeoisie to strengthen its own position in the
economy and the society, which was made in conjunction with, rather than in
opposition to, United States economic interests.

618 **Oil and politics in Latin America. Nationalist movements and state
companies.**
George Philip.   Cambridge, England; London; New York etc.:
Cambridge University Press, 1982. 577p. bibliog. (Cambridge Latin
American Studies, no. 40).

Part I discusses the rôle of Latin America in the world oil environment. Part II
considers the expropriation of foreign oil companies, and devotes a chapter to the
nationalization of Venezuelan oil. Part III focuses on state oil companies and has a
chapter on Petrovén. The book includes a number of statistical tables.

619 **The political economy of Venezuelan oil.**
Laura Randall.   New York; Westport, Connecticut; London:
Greenwood, 1987. 247p. bibliog.

Examines: the effects of the development of the oil industry on Venezuelan society;
governmental attempts at its regulation; the functioning of the nationalized industry;
labour relations in the petroleum business; and the impact of oil development on the
industrial and service sectors, and on the rest of the economy.

620 **The Venezuelan state oil reports to the people.**
Rubén Sáder Pérez.   Caracas: Corporación Venezolana del Petróleo,
1969. 366p.
A collection of writings, speeches and broadcasts about the Venezuelan national oil
company in the 1960s, by its Director General.

621 **Oil in the economic development of Venezuela.**
Jorge Salazar-Carillo.   New York; Washington, DC; London: Praeger,
1976. 215p. (Praeger Special Studies in International Economics and
Development).
Investigates the extent to which the Venezuelan oil industry contributed as a 'leading
sector' to the general development of the country's economy between 1946 and 1973.
The text is supplemented by numerous tables and a statistical appendix.

622 **Petroleum in Venezuela: a bibliography.**
William M.Sullivan, Brian S. McBeth.   Boston, Massachusetts: G.K.
Hall, 1985. 538p.
Lists over 5,000 items, about one-third of which are annotated.

623 **The Creole Petroleum Corporation in Venezuela.**
Wayne C. Taylor, John Lindeman.   Washington, DC: National
Planning Association, 1955. 103p. (United States Business Performance
Abroad, Fourth Case Study).
Reviews the social and economic impact of the largest foreign oil company operating in
Venezuela, and its relations with the government in the period 1935-55.

624 **The politics of oil in Venezuela.**
Franklin Tugwell.   Stanford, California: Stanford University Press,
1975. 210p. bibliog.
Surveys the strategies of successive Venezuelan governments in their relations with
foreign oil companies, concentrating on the period 1958-73. Tugwell includes
consideration of the patterns of bargaining and conflict with the international oil
companies, and the interdependence of domestic politics, petroleum policy and rapid
social change, up to the eve of the nationalization of the industry.

625 **Oil: the making of a new economic order. Venezuelan oil and OPEC.**
Luis Vallenilla.   New York; London; Paris etc.: McGraw Hill, 1975.
302p.
Reviews the history of the petroleum industry in Venezuela, up to the point
immediately prior to nationalization, and suggests a strategy for the reduction of its
dependence on the developed world, through action over oil prices, investments and
international terms of trade.

Mining

626 **Mining in the Caribbean.**
Edited by Stanley H. Dayton. *Engineering and Mining Journal*,
vol. 178, no. 11 (1977), p. 49-198.
Includes (p. 63-69) 'Venezuela: a mining scene of booming activity', which gives facts
and figures on the production and planned development of iron and steel, and of
bauxite and aluminium.

627 **Caroni gold.**
Leonidas Richardson Dennison. New York: Hastings House, 1943.
274p.
This informal account of the gold rush of 1926 was written by an American mining
engineer who became mayor of the mining village of Paviche on the Caroní river.

628 **Diamonds in Venezuela.**
W.C. Fairbairn. *Mining Magazine*, vol. 125, no. 4 (1971), p. 349-53.
Sketches the history of diamond mining in Venezuela, the locations of past and present
workings, methods used, the labour force, laws, taxes, and levels of production.

629 **Development of Venezuela's iron-ore deposits.**
John C. Rayburn. *Inter-American Economic Affairs*, vol. 6, no. 1
(1952), p. 52-70.
Reviews various abortive iron-mining projects, from the 1880s to the 1930s, and
describes Bethlehem Steel's developments at El Pao in the 1940s and the beginnings of
the much larger Cerro Bolívar undertaking of US Steel.

630 **United States investments in Venezuelan asphalt.**
John C. Rayburn. *Inter-American Economic Affairs*, vol. 7, no. 1
(1953), p. 20-36.
A brief history of the mining of natural asphalt by American companies in various
parts of Venezuela from the 1890s to the 1930s, and of their embroilments with the
Venezuelan government and law courts.

631 **Venezuela y sus riquezas minerales.** (Venezuela and its mineral
resources.)
Alberto Sívoli G. Caracas: Ediciones del Cuatricentenario de
Caracas, 1967. 145p. maps.
An alphabetical list of minerals, noting the distribution and production levels of each,
with eighteen maps.

632 **The prospects of gold mining in Venezuela, and a guide to the Guayana gold fields.**
William Greville Wears.   London: Head & Mark, 1888. rev. ed. 69p.
A description of the locations, geological characteristics, and living and working conditions in the Guayana gold field, with details of the prospects of the main mines, and advice to potential investors, now, of course, only of historical interest.

633 **Venezuela: the iron and steel industry.**
Peter J. West.   *Bank of London and South America Review*, vol. 13, no. 3 (1979), p. 138-48.
Outlines the development of the industry in the 1970s and its prospects for the 1980s.

Agriculture and Food Supply

634 To sow or not to sow: a historiographical essay on the Venezuelan agrarian question, 1973-1980.
Rafael R. Bilbao. *Revista de Historia de América*, no. 94 (1982), p. 133-50.
Identifies many obstacles in the way of Venezuelan agricultural development, explains the failure of agrarian reform, and advocates remedies. The latter include: raising the educational level among the rural population; providing credit, health, cultural and recreational facilities in rural areas to retard urban migration; improving transport; regulating of land use more effectively; and giving agricultural self-sufficiency a higher priority than industrialization.

635 Traditional agricultural skill training among peasant farmers in Venezuela.
Ray Chesterfield, Kenneth Ruddle. *Anthropos. International Review of Ethnology and Linguistics*, vol. 74, no. 3-4 (1979), p. 549-65.
Based on field research undertaken in 1972, this article analyses the procedures by which children are taught subsistence agricultural techniques in the communities of the Isla de Guara, in the Orinoco delta.

636 Venezuela: agrarian reform at mid-1977.
Paul Cox.   Madison, Wisconsin: University of Wisconsin Land Tenure Center, 1978. 66p. bibliog. (Research Paper, no. 71).
This judicious assessment of agrarian reform since 1959, based on statistical data, concludes that its achievements were considerably less than anticipated, in that the majority of the agricultural population remained very poor, and the traditional agrarian structure was replaced by an agro-industrial one, rather than one benefiting the small farmer.

Agriculture and Food Supply

637 **The agriculture of Brazil and Venezuela: business opportunities.**
Dennis E. Frith. London: Graham & Trotman, 1978. 148p.

The opportunities and needs of Venezuela in agriculture and agro-industry are discussed (p. 80-132). A general section (p. 80-97) covers geography, the political and economic background, population, labour, laws and taxation. An agriculture section (p. 99-114) discusses the main products, agricultural methods, financing, irrigation and infrastructure; and an agro-industry section (p. 115-29) includes comments on food processing, fertilizers and machinery. A final section explains how to approach the market. There are sixteen tables.

638 **Races of maize in Venezuela.**
Ulysses J. Grant (et al.). Washington, DC: National Academy of Sciences, National Research Council, 1963. 92p. bibliog. (Publication no. 1136).

Identifies and describes nineteen different types of maize growing in Venezuela, many of them mixtures of recently introduced varieties with older indigenous ones.

639 **Scarcity amidst plenty: food problems in oil-rich Venezuela.**
Howard Handelman. Hanover, New Hampshire: American Universities Field Staff, 1978. 19p. (AUFS Reports, 1978, no. 42, South America).

A brief survey of the relationship between agricultural development and food supplies, which makes special reference to the policies of the 1970s. Six tables are included.

640 **The ecology of swidden cultivation in the upper Orinoco rain forest, Venezuela.**
David R. Harris. *Geographical Review*, vol. 61, no. 4 (1971), p. 475-95.

Reports on a survey of shifting agriculture at ten locations on the Casiquiare and upper Orinoco rivers in 1968. Both areas of active cultivation and fallow plots in the course of forest regeneration were examined, and the crops and soil nutrients noted. Findings suggest that the traditional manioc may be ecologically better suited to the rain forest than the introduced maize.

641 **The agricultural development of Venezuela.**
Louis E. Heaton. New York; Washington, DC; London: Praeger, 1969. 321p. (Praeger Special Studies in International Economics and Development. Bench Mark Studies on Agricultural Development in Latin America, no. 5).

A study of Venezuelan agriculture in the period 1961-65, which analyses changes in levels of production, productivity, consumption and nutrition, and in the extent of the sector's contribution to the national economy, and considers the impact of the Agricultural Reform Law of 1960.

642 **Patterns of land tenancy and their social repercussions.**
George W. Hill, José A. Silva Michelena, Ruth Oliver de Hill. In: *Contemporary cultures and societies of Latin America.* Edited by Dwight B. Heath, Richard N. Adams. New York: Random House, 1965, p. 211-35.

This report of a survey of a sample of small farmers, taken from five different agricultural regions of the country, presents material on land tenure, the size of holdings, principal products, methods of work, incomes and the use of credit. This information is preceded by a discussion of the historical origins of the system of land tenancy and of the patterns shown in the census of 1950.

643 **Social welfare and tenure problems in the agrarian reform program of Venezuela.**
George W. Hill, Gregorio Beltrán, Cristina Mariño. In: *Land tenure.* Edited by Kenneth H. Parsons, Raymond J. Penn, Philip M. Raup. Madison, Wisconsin : University of Wisconsin Press, 1956, p. 293-304.

Reviews the evolution of the land tenure system in the country, and is still interesting for its analysis of the inter-relationships between social welfare and land reform.

644 **An implicit food policy. Wheat consumption changes in Venezuela.**
W. Jaffé Carbonell, Harry Rothman. *Food Policy*, vol. 2, no. 4 (1977), p. 305-17.

Examines the progressive substitution of maize by wheat as the dietary staple since the 1940s, and attributes it to growing urbanization and a number of government measures which, although not explicitly intended to bring about this change, amounted in effect to an implicit food policy.

645 **Venezuela's land reform: progress and change.**
John Kirby. *Journal of Inter-American Studies and World Affairs*, vol. 15, no. 2 (1973), p. 205-20.

Considers the progress made in the decade following the passing of the Agrarian Reform Law of 1960. Kirby notes that although the law permitted large-scale expropriation, this did not take place. Rather an attempt was made to slow down the drift of population to the cities by opening up marginal land to subsistence farmers, without interfering with commercial agriculture. Many of the 117,000 families settled operated at very low levels of technology and remained too poor to provide much of a market for the industrial sector.

646 **The first Venezuelan coffee cycle, 1830-1855.**
John V. Lombardi, James A. Hanson. *Agricultural History*, vol. 44, no. 4 (1970), p. 355-67.

Discusses the political and economic factors which explain the rapid rise of coffee production in the 1830s, and the difficulties it encountered from the early 1840s.

Agriculture and Food Supply

647 **Approaches to agricultural policy in Venezuela.**
John D. Martz. *Inter-American Economic Affairs*, vol. 34, no. 3 (1980), p. 25-53.

Surveys political attitudes to agricultural reforms throughout the 1960s and 1970s, and notes the gradual, and perhaps subconscious, shift in emphasis from social justice for the peasant to the promotion of large-scale entrepreneurial farming, as the increasing urbanization of the population reduced the political significance of the rural electorate.

648 **The Yupka cultivation system. A study of shifting cultivation in Colombia and Venezuela.**
Kenneth B. Ruddle. Berkeley, California; Los Angeles; London: University of California Press, 1974. 197p. bibliog. (Ibero-America, no. 52).

A detailed study, based on field work carried out in the Sierra de Perijá area in 1969-71, which concludes that the traditional patterns of shifting cultivation among the Yupka tribal group were undergoing rapid change towards conformity with the occupational practices of other Venezuelan peasant communities.

649 **Education for traditional food procurement in the Orinoco delta.**
Kenneth Ruddle, Ray Chesterfield. Berkeley, California; Los Angeles; London: University of California Press, 1977. 172p. bibliog. (Ibero-Americana, no. 53).

Fieldwork, conducted in 1972 and 1973, by a geographer and an educationalist, forms the basis of this study of the training of children in food procurement on the island of Guara in the Orinoco delta.

650 **Hunger in a land of plenty.**
George Schuyler. Cambridge, Massachusetts: Schenkman, 1980. 262p. bibliog.

This journalistic account of Venezuelan agriculture, based on conversations with farmers around the country, is highly critical of the development of large-scale high-technology 'agribusiness' and its implications for nutrition, health, employment, urban conditions, and political democracy.

651 **The population of Venezuela and its natural resources.**
William Vogt. Washington, DC: Pan American Union, 1946. 52p.

Prepared by the chief of the conservation section of the division of agricultural co-operation of the Pan American Union, this is largely a discussion of the causes and consequences of land erosion in Venezuela, with numerous photographic illustrations.

652 **Agrarian reform in Latin America. An annotated bibliography.**
Compiled by the staff of the Land Tenure Center Library of the University of Wisconsin. Madison, Wisconsin: University of Wisconsin Press, 1974. 2 vols.

Includes 229 annotated entries on items relating to Venezuela (vol. II, p. 491-530).

653 **Rural development in Venezuela: a bibliography.**
Compiled by the staff of the Land Tenure Center Library of the
University of Wisconsin. Madison, Wisconsin: University of
Wisconsin Press, 1972. 67p. (Training and Methods Series, no. 20).
Includes references to a number of ephemeral items, not readily traceable elsewhere.

654 **Food dependency and malnutrition in Venezuela, 1958-1974.**
Eleanor Witte Wright. In: *Food, politics and society in Latin America.*
Edited by John C. Super, Thomas C. Wright. Lincoln, Nebraska;
London: University of Nebraska Press, 1985, p. 150-73. (Latin
American Studies Series).
Argues that the goals of the successive governments of Betancourt, Leoni and Caldera
– to reduce dependence on imported foodstuffs by increasing domestic production, and
to reduce malnutrition through income redistribution – were not achieved, because of
the increasing concentration of the market by large national and multinational
concerns.

Transport and Communications

655 **Civil aircraft registers of Venezuela.**
Edited by Ian P.Burnett.   Tonbridge, England: Air-Britain, 1984.
154p.
Lists registration symbols and aircraft types, and also in many cases gives details of
ownership and bases, of all Venezuelan civil aircraft for which details could be found,
from the 1930s to the 1980s.

656 **Airlines of Latin America since 1919.**
Ronald Edward George Davies.   London: Putnam, 1984. 698p.
bibliog.
Chapter nine (p. 190-201) sketches the history of civil aviation in Venezuela. An
appendix (p. 656-59) lists the composition of the Venezuelan airline fleets.

657 **Steamboat transportation on the Orinoco.**
William H. Gray.   *Hispanic American Historical Review*, vol. 25, no. 4
(1945), p. 455-69.
Describes the characteristics of the waterway, and comments on the concessions
granted by the government, the volume of traffic, the vessels used and the cargoes
carried from 1815 to 1940.

658 **Historia de la aviación civil en Venezuela.** (History of civil aviation in
Venezuela).
David R. Iriarte.   Caracas: Oficina Central de Información, 1971.
2nd ed. 630p.
The first chapter, which forms more than a quarter of the book, is a chronological
compilation of facts about Venezuelan civil aviation in general. Chapter two gives
details of the history of flying clubs, and chapter three is an extensive account of the
school of civil aviation, including lists of graduates and outlines of syllabuses and
examinations. Other chapters deal with accidents and their investigation, crop-

spraying, aerial photography, aviation law, Venezuelan airlines, and foreign airlines operating in Venezuela.

659   **Railways of South America. Part II: Bolivia, Colombia, Ecuador, Guianas, Paraguay, Peru, Uruguay and Venezuela.**
William Rodney Long.   Washington, DC: United States Department of Commerce, Bureau of Foreign and Domestic Commerce, 1927. 420p. maps. (Trade Promotion Series, no. 39).
The section on Venezuela (p. 340-420) brings out very clearly the fact that the country's railways were originally a series of separate lines to carry freight from various sources to different points of shipment on the Caribbean coast. Each of the three government-owned, nine privately-owned, and eleven industrial railways, and four street-car lines is described, in most cases with maps and traffic and financial statistics up to 1926. An appendix prints the railroad law of 1918.

660   **Communications and information technologies: freedom of choice for Latin America?**
Armand Mattelart, Hector Schmucler, translated from the French by David Buxton.   Norwood, New Jersey: Ablex, 1985. 186p. bibliog.
Venezuela is one of the countries discussed in this study of the evolution of the Latin American electronics industry. The state of development of audiovisual media, computers and telecommunications; attitudes of the state, private firms and the public to information technology; and the rôle of the transnational information industry all come under consideration.

661   **Caracas: urban growth and transportation.**
Anthony Penfold.   *Town Planning Review*, vol. 41, no. 2 (1970), p. 103-20.
An analysis of the need for and discussion of the plans for the Caracas Metro system, eventually implemented in the 1980s.

662   **Investments in Venezuelan telephones.**
John C. Rayburn.   *Inter-American Economic Affairs*, vol. 9, no. 2 (1955), p. 55-66.
Describes the involvement of various foreign and national companies in the Venezuelan telephone business between 1883 and 1953.

663   **Rail transportation in Venezuela, 1835-1955.**
John C. Rayburn.   *Inter-American Economic Affairs*, vol. 10, no. 4 (1957), p. 23-46.
Offers an account of the construction and investment history of the country's eleven major railway lines.

664   **Transport technology for developing regions: a study of road transportation in Venezuela.**
Richard M. Soberman.   Cambridge, Massachusetts; London: MIT, 1966. 177p. bibliog.

Largely a technical and theoretical report, but including much detailed information on the planned development of the Guayana region and the anticipated demands on transportation, and on the local costs of alternative forms of transport.

665   **Transportation and urbanization in Caracas, 1891-1936.**
E. Jeffrey Stann.   *Journal of Interamerican Studies and World Affairs*, vol. 17, no. 1 (1975), p. 82-100.

Describes the development of the facets of the transport system – street-cars, railroads, buses and private cars – and their relationship to the growth of the urban area in the late-nineteenth and early-twentieth centuries.

666   **Transportation and economic development in Latin America.**
Charles J. Stokes.   New York; Washington, DC; London: Praeger, 1968. 203p. (Praeger Special Studies in International Economics and Development).

Chapter two (p. 11-72) is a case study which analyses the causes and consequences of the decision to construct the *autopista* between Las Tejerías and Valencia. It was completed in 1958, and this piece concludes that it brought significant cost benefits, as well as stimulating economic development in Aragua and Carabobo states.

Labour and Unions

667 **Labor in Latin America: comparative essays on Chile, Argentina, Venezuela and Colombia.**
Charles Bergquist. Stanford, California: Stanford University Press, 1986. 397p.
Chapter four (p. 191-273) deals specifically with Venezuela, in this cross-country study. It is mainly concerned with the development of a labour force for the oil industry and the evolution of its organization. The comparative absence of class-based militancy is explained in terms of the substantial benefits that organized labour was able to obtain from the prosperous industry.

668 **Migrant female labour in the Venezuelan garment industry.**
Margalit Berlin. In: *Women and change in Latin America.* Edited by June Nash, Helen Safa. South Hadley, Massachusetts: Bergin & Garvey, 1986, p. 260-72.
A revealing study based on the author's observations, made when working as a seamstress in a Venezuelan factory. She stresses the differences in management/worker and worker/worker relations between Colombian immigrants and Venezuelans, and explains these in terms of varying pressures with regard to their legal status, housing situation and the location of their families.

669 **Working-class mobilization and political control: Venezuela and Mexico.**
Charles L. Davis. Lexington, Kentucky: University Press of Kentucky, 1989. 211p.
A comparative study, based on interviews with some 500 workers in each country in 1979-80, of the extent to which participation in the political process by organized labour is controlled by the ruling régimes.

670 **Venezuela.**
Steve Ellner. In: *Latin American labor organizations.* Edited by
Gerald Michael Greenfield, Sheldon L. Maram. New York; Westport,
Connecticut; London: Greenwood, 1987, p. 727-60.

A brief introduction and a bibliography are followed by an alphabetical list of labour
organizations, with an account of the history of each. Included in the appendices to the
volume are a chronology of Venezuelan labour activity from 1928 to 1985 (p. 802-03),
and identifications of eight of the major figures involved (p. 829).

671 **Economic growth and employment problems in Venezuela: an analysis of
an oil based economy.**
Mostafa Fathy Hassan. New York; Washington, DC; London:
Praeger, 1975. 185p. bibliog. (Praeger Special Studies in International
Economics and Development).

Notes that rapid economic growth was accompanied by substantial unemployment, and
proposes policies designed to maximize employment, by reducing urban-rural
differentials, by limiting the importation of capital-intensive technology, and by
improving industrial training.

672 **Political and economic determinants of collective bargaining in
Venezuela.**
Oscar Hernández Alvarez, Héctor Lucena. *International Labour
Review,* vol. 124, no. 3 (1985), p. 363-76.

A concise review of collective bargaining since the establishment of favourable political
conditions in the 1960s, which illustrates the influence of fluctuating economic
conditions on agreements, disputes, strikes and stoppages.

673 **The Federación Campesina de Venezuela.**
International Labour Office. Geneva: International Labour Office,
1982. 23p.

A study, conducted in 1977, of the federation of peasant unions, which were founded
in 1947 and affiliated with the Venezuelan workers' confederation. An account of its
organization and of the services it offers, and suggestions as to how it might develop
are given.

674 **Freedom of association and conditions of work in Venezuela.**
International Labour Office. Geneva: International Labour Office,
1950. 185p. (Studies and Reports. New Series, no. 21).

The report of a mission which was sent to Venezuela by ILO in 1949, at the invitation
of the government. It concludes that, in the circumstances following the military coup
of the preceding year, trade unions were not enjoying freedom of action and
organization comparable to that in other countries. The mission found that Venezuelan
social legislation was very progressive, but that it was not effectively applied in many
parts of the country; that health cover was not sufficiently extensive; that political
conditions hampered collective agreements; and that certain of the guarantees in the
United Nations declaration of human rights were not operative.

675 **Labor and change in a party-mediated democracy: institutional change in Venezuela.**
Jennifer L. McCoy. *Latin American Research Review*, vol. 24, no. 2 (1989), p. 35-67.

Traces the relationships between labour, political parties and the state, from the emergence of the labour movement in the 1930s, through its close involvement with the ruling party in the 1960s, to the evolution of a shared party- and state-mediated form of representation of labour interests in the period 1974-83.

676 **The politics of adjustment: labor and the Venezuelan debt crisis.**
Jennifer L. McCoy. *Journal of Interamerican Studies and World Affairs*, vol. 28, no. 4 (1986-7), p. 103-38.

Analyses the differences in the reactions of organized labour to the austerity measures imposed by the régimes of Presidents Herrera and Lusinchi in response to the debt crisis of the 1980s. A revised version of the article, entitled 'Venezuela: austerity and the working class in a democratic regime', appeared in *Paying the costs of austerity in Latin America*, edited by Howard Handelman, Werner Baer (Boulder, Colorado; San Francisco; London: Westview, 1989, p. 195-223).

677 **Limitations of legislation in improving working conditions: the Venezuelan experience.**
Enrique Marín Quijada. *International Labour Review*, vol. 118, no. 1 (1979), p. 113-22.

Offers a review of labour legislation and of actual working conditions, and the outline of a strategy for improvement.

678 **The growth and democratization of the Venezuelan labor movement.**
John D. Martz. *Inter-American Economic Affairs*, vol. 17, no. 2 (1963), p. 3-18.

A brief review of developments, from the origins of labour organization in 1919, through alternating periods of suppression and comparative freedom to 1963, when a modern institutional structure, with an accepted rôle in society, was in place.

679 **Venezuela: the peasant union movement.**
John Duncan Powell. In: *Latin American peasant movements*. Edited by Henry A. Landsberger. Ithaca, New York; London: Cornell University Press, 1969. p. 62-100.

An account of the organization of the peasant union movement, its historical background, its objectives and its link with the political system; it is partly based on survey evidence obtained in 1966. It concludes that the peasant movement was a significant influence on the establishment and maintenance of representative democracy.

680 **Income distribution, technology and employment in the Venezuelan industrial sector.**
Víctor Tokman. In: *Income distribution in Latin America.* Edited by Alejandro Foxley. Cambridge, England: Cambridge University Press, 1976, p. 201-22.

Argues that a technological policy designed to promote labour-intensive techniques would both improve the utilization of available factors of production, and facilitate an improvement in the distribution of income.

681 **The political, economic and labor climate in Venezuela.**
Cecilia M. Valente. Philadelphia: University of Pennsylvania, The Wharton School, Industrial Research Unit, 1979. 280p. (Multinational Industrial Relations Series, no. 4. Latin American Studies, 4d. Venezuela).

A discussion of labour organization in Venezuela, and an analysis of the nation's labour law and practice, placed in their political and economic contexts. Highlights the gap between well-paid organized labour and the poor, and the danger of high-wage labour encouraging the substitution of capital-intensive production techniques.

682 **New agricultural cooperatives on the basis of sexual polarisation induced by the state. The 'model' collective cooperative 'Cumparipa', Venezuela.**
Claudia von Werlhof. *Boletín de Estudios Latinoamericanos y del Caribe,* no. 35 (1983), p. 39-50.

Presents a discussion of labour conditions, particularly as they affect the wives of members of the co-operative, in a collective in the state of Yaracuy.

Science and Technology

683 **Primer plan nacional de ciencia y tecnología período 1976-1980.** (The first national plan for science and technology for the period 1976-1980.) Consejo Nacional de Investigaciones Científicas y Tecnológicas. Caracas: CONICIT, 1977. 7 vols.

Comprises a series of pamphlets covering different sectors: agriculture, ecology, electronics and telecommunications, food technology, health, hydrocarbons, and metallurgy.

684 **La investigación en Venezuela. Condiciones de su desarrollo.** (Research in Venezuela. Conditions for its development.) Olga Gasparini. Caracas: Instituto Venezolano de Investigaciones Científicas, 1969. 262p. bibliog.

Presents the report of a sample survey of individuals and groups, concerned with scientific research in Venezuela. It shows the level and nature of research activity, and recommends the formulation of a national policy for research.

685 **La ciencia en Venezuela, 1970.** (Science in Venezuela, 1970.) Marcos Ghigliore (et al.). Valencia, Venezuela: Universidad de Carabobo, Dirección de Cultura, 1970. 558p.

A series of lectures on a wide variety of scientific topics, which illustrate the range of activities of Venezuelan researchers in 1970.

686 **Research on research in Venezuela.** Charles V. Kidd. *Science*, vol. 149, no. 3685 (1965), p. 727-29.

A brief summary of the main findings and recommendations of the report arising from a meeting of scientists, educators and business executives. Aiming to promote economic development, it resulted in the establishment of a national research council. The report was published in full as *La ciencia: base de nuestro progreso. Bases para la*

141

creación de un consejo nacional de investigaciones científicas y tecnológicas en Venezuela (Science: the foundation for our progress. Bases for the creation of a national scientific and technological council in Venezuela), edited by Marcel Roche (et al.) (Caracas: Ediciones IVIC, 1965. 291p.), and contained brief surveys of the history of the various scientific disciplines in Venezuela to 1940, covering mathematical and physical sciences, geology, chemistry, botany, zoology, medicine, pharmacy and agricultural science.

687 **Fuentes energéticas: una perspectiva venezolana.** (Energy sources: a Venezuelan perspective.)
Edited by Aníbal R. Martínez (et al.). Caracas: CONICIT, 1977. 141p.

A collection of papers, presented at a seminar in 1976, covering energy policy, research, and resources, and the applicability of various energy sources in Venezuelan conditions.

688 **The Amazon project of the Venezuelan Institute for Scientific Research.**
E. Medina, R. Herrera, C. Jordan, H. Klinge. *Nature and Resources*, vol. 13, no. 3 (1977), p. 4-6.

Outlines the research work of the International Centre for Tropical Ecology on the vegetation, soils and waters of the Río Negro area in the territory of Amazonas. A slightly fuller account is 'Studies on the ecology of Amazon caatinga forest in southern Venezuela', by Klinge (et al.), *Acta Científica Venezolana*, vol. 28, no. 4 (1977) p. 270-76.

689 **Venezuela.**
Marcel Roche. In: *Nuclear power in developing countries: an analysis of decision making.* Edited by James Everett Katz, Onkar S. Marwah. Lexington, Massachusetts; Toronto: Lexington Books, D.C. Heath, 1982, p. 239-43.

This discussion of the installation and utilization of Venezuela's first nuclear reactor at the Venezuelan Institute for Scientific Research, by the Institute's former director, throws interesting light on the nature of scientific activity in the country.

690 **Science and technology in Latin America.**
Edited by Christopher Roper, Jorge Silva. London; New York: Longman, Latin American Newsletters, 1983. 363p. (Longman Guide to World Science and Technology).

The section on Venezuela (p. 237-48) outlines the organization and financing of science and technology, and gives an annotated list of governmental and academic institutions involved. The appendices include various statistics, and a directory of academies and other relevant bodies.

691 **Ciencia académica en la Venezuela moderna. Historia reciente y perspectivas de las disciplinas científicas.** (Academic science in modern Venezuela. Recent history and prospects for scientific disciplines.) Edited by Hebe M.C. Vessuri. Caracas: Fondo Editorial Acta Científica Venezolana, 1984. 461p. bibliog.

Gives the proceedings of a symposium held in 1983 to review the state of academic teaching and research in Venezuela, with special reference to biology, engineering (chemical, electrical and electronic), computing, mathematics, chemistry, sociology and anthropology.

692 **Las instituciones científicas en la historia de la ciencia en Venezuela.** (Scientific institutions in the history of science in Venezuela.) Edited by Hebe M.C. Vessuri. Caracas: Fondo Editorial Acta Científica Venezolana, 1987. 388p.

Comprises a collection of fourteen essays on various scientific institutes, with fields ranging from physics to folklore and from dermatology to industrial technology.

143

Literature

History and criticism

693 **Spanish American literature: a history.**
Enrique Anderson-Imbert. Detroit, Michigan: Wayne State
University Press, 1969. 2nd ed. 2 vols.

This chronological account of Spanish-American literature includes brief descriptions
and appraisals of the works of Venezuelan writers Andrés Bello (1781-1865)
(p. 191-96); Rafael María Baralt (1810-60), Juan Vicente González (1810-66) and
Fermín Toro (1807-65) (p. 213-14); Jacinto Gutiérrez Coll (1835-1901) and Antonio
Pérez Bonalde (1846-92) (p. 260); Manuel Vicente Romero García (1865-1917),
Gonzalo Picón-Febres (1860-1918) and Miguel Eduardo Pardo (1868-1905) (p. 328-29);
Andrés Eloy Blanco (1897-1955) (p. 477); Rómulo Gallegos (1884-1969) and Teresa de
la Parra (1890-1936) (p. 518-23); and Arturo Uslar Pietri (1906-.) and Miguel Otero
Silva (1908-85) (p. 640-43), with shorter notes on numerous other writers.

694 **Venezuela.**
John Beverley. In: *Handbook of Latin American literature.* Compiled
by David William Foster. New York; London: Garland, 1987,
p. 559-77.

A succinct essay on the history of Venezuelan literature.

695 **Latin American poetry. Origins and presence.**
Gordon Brotherston. Cambridge, England; London; New York etc.:
Cambridge University Press, 1975. 228p. bibliog.

Includes (p. 27-36) a discussion of Andrés Bello's poem *América*.

696   **Andrés Bello: philosopher, poet, philologist, educator, legislator, statesman.**
Rafael Caldera.   London: Allen & Unwin, 1977. 165p. bibliog.
A brilliant prize essay, written when the author was only nineteen years of age, which combines a brief sketch of the life of Andrés Bello with an evaluation of his literary, philosophical and educational achievements. First published in Spanish in 1935, and subsequently in many other languages, this was the first short introduction to Bello's career and thought to appear in English. Caldera later founded the political party COPEI and served as president of Venezuela from 1969 to 1974.

697   **Rómulo Gallegos and the generation of *La Alborada*.**
Lowell Dunham.   *Hispania*, vol. 39, no. 2 (1956), p. 186-89.
A brief discussion on the short-lived periodical *La Alborada* (eight issues of which appeared in 1909 before it was suppressed by the Gómez government), which launched Gallegos on his literary and political career.

698   **Rómulo Gallegos: an Oklahoma encounter and the writing of his last novel.**
Lowell Dunham.   Norman, Oklahoma: University of Oklahoma Press, 1974. 100p.
A memoir of the author's association with the novelist between 1948 and 1963, focusing on Gallegos' months of exile, spent at the University of Oklahoma, where he drafted his last novel, *Tierra bajo los pies*, published posthumously (Barcelona, Spain: Salvat, 1971. 187p.). Dunham wrote and published a dissertation on Gallegos' life and work, *Rómulo Gallegos: vida y obra* (Mexico, DF: Ed. de Andrés, 1957).

699   **Doña Bárbara, legend of the *llano*.**
John E. Englekirk.   *Hispania*, vol. 31 (1948), p. 259-70.
Discusses Gallegos' visit to San Fernando de Apure in 1927, and the stories he was told there of actual events, characters and customs which formed the basis for his famous novel, *Doña Bárbara* (q.v.).

700   **Modern Latin American literature.**
Compiled and edited by David William Foster, Virginia Ramos Foster.   New York: Frederick Ungar, 1975. 2 vols. (Library of Literary Criticism).
An anthology of literary criticism, some from English-language sources, others translated from Spanish, which includes: eight items relating to Manuel Díaz Rodríguez (1868-1927) (vol. I, p. 300-05); twenty items relating to Rómulo Gallegos (vol. I, p. 347-63); three items relating to Mariano Picón-Salas (1901-65) (vol. II, p. 187-90); and eight items relating to Arturo Uslar Pietri (vol. II, p. 385-91).

701   **Studies in Spanish-American literature.**
Isaac Goldberg.   Port Washington, New York: Kennikat, 1968. 377p.
The final chapter (p. 307-59) discusses the work of Rufino Blanco-Fombona (1874-1944) in the context of his wider career and literary influences, and includes comments on his poetry, novels, literary criticism, and political writings.

702 **The meaning of** *civilización* **and** *barbarie* **in** *Doña Bárbara.*
Ernest A. Johnson, Jr. *Hispania*, vol. 39, no. 4 (1956), p. 456-61.
Discusses the concepts of civilization and barbarism in Gallegos' novel, and the vocabulary he employs to describe the struggle between them.

703 **Three Spanish American novelists – a European view.**
C.A. Jones. London: Hispanic and Luso-Brazilian Councils, 1967.
24p. bibliog.
The first half of this lecture explains some of the difficulties European readers may have in coming to terms with Rómulo Gallegos' *Doña Bárbara* (q.v.).

704 **Andrés Bello: the London years.**
Edited by John Lynch. Richmond, England: Richmond Publishing, 1982. 167p.
This comprises a selection of papers originally presented at an international congress on Bello. Those directly concerned with Bello or Venezuela are: Rafael Caldera's 'Bello in London: the incomprehensible sojourn' (p. 1-6); Miriam Blanco-Fombona de Hood's 'The London of Andrés Bello' (p. 49-55); José Luis Salcedo-Bastardo's 'Bello and the symposiums of Grafton Street' (p. 57-65); Stewart R. Sutherland's 'Andrés Bello: the influence of Scottish philosophy' (p. 99-118); Oscar Sambrano Urdaneta's 'The London chronology of Andrés Bello' (p. 153-64); and D.A.G. Waddell's 'British relations with Venezuela, New Granada and Gran Colombia, 1810-1829' (p. 25-47).

705 **The lost rib. Female characters in the Spanish-American novel.**
Sharon Magnarelli. Cranbury, New Jersey; London; Toronto: Associated University Presses, 1985. 227p. bibliog.
Much of chapter two 'Women and nature: in man's image created (*Doña Bárbara* and *La vorágine*)' argues that the character of Doña Bárbara in Gallegos' novel of that name does not emerge as a woman but rather as a myth created by the male characters as a personification of the barbarism of nature.

706 **The fauna of the works of Rómulo Gallegos.**
J. Riis Owre. *Hispania*, vol. 45. no. 1 (1962), p. 52-56.
An analysis of the skilful use of animals and birds for symbolic and aesthetic purposes, and of the frequent juxtaposition of humanity and the non-human world in the fiction of Gallegos.

707 **Venezuelan prose fiction.**
Dillwyn F. Ratcliff. New York: Instituto de las Españas, 1933. 286p. bibliog.
Traces the history and development of the Venezuelan novel and short story from the mid-nineteenth century to around 1928. Among the writers discussed are Arístides Rojas (1826-94), Francisco Tosta García (1857-1921), Fermín Toro, Julio Calcaño (1840-1919), Eduardo Blanco (1838-1912), Tulio Febres Cordero (1860-1938), Gonzalo Picón-Febres, José Rafael Pocaterra (1892-1945), Rufino Blanco-Fombona, Manuel Díaz Rodríguez, Teresa de la Parra and Rómulo Gallegos.

708   *Las memorias de Mamá Blanca*: a literary tour de force.
George D. Schade.   *Hispania*, vol. 39, no. 2 (1956), p. 157-60.
A brief study of Teresa de la Parra's novel published in English as *Mamá Blanca's souvenirs* (q.v.), and described as 'a small and sparkling gem of its type', emphasizing the excellence of its style, the vividness of its imagery, the keenness of its observation, the delicacy of its wit, and the warmth of its humanity.

709   **A new history of Spanish American fiction.**
Kessel Schwartz.   Coral Gables, Florida: University of Miami Press, 1971-72. 2 vols. bibliog.
Essentially a study of the development of the Spanish American novel, volume I deals with the period to around 1930, and volume II with later developments. Several Venezuelan writers are discussed within the analytical framework of each volume. There are useful bibliographies of critical works on Venezuelan authors (volume I, p. 406-11; volume II, p. 413-16).

710   **Gallegos: Doña Bárbara.**
Donald L. Shaw.   London: Grant & Cutler, 1972. 84p. bibliog.
(Critical Guides to Spanish Texts, no. 4).
A brief analysis of the origins, theme, structure, characters and symbolism of Rómulo Gallegos's famous novel on the conflict of civilization and barbarism in the *llanos*.

711   **Contemporary Spanish-American fiction.**
Jefferson Rea Spell.   Chapel Hill, North Carolina: University of North Carolina Press, 1944. 323p. bibliog.
Chapter IX, 'Romulo Gallegos, interpreter of the *llanos* of Venezuela' (p. 205-38), discusses the famous author's short stories and novels.

712   **Teresa de la Parra: Venezuelan novelist and feminist.**
Ronni Gordon Stillman.   In: *Latin American women writers: yesterday and today*. Edited by Yvette E. Miller, Charles M. Tatum. Pittsburgh, Pennsylvania: Latin American Literary Review, 1977, p. 42-49.
A discussion of feminism in Parra's novel *Ifigenia* (Paris: Casa Editorial Franco-ibero-americana, 1924. 522p.).

713   **The emergence of Rómulo Gallegos as a novelist and social critic.**
Louise Welsh.   *Hispania*, vol. 40, no. 4 (1956), p. 444-49.
Discusses Gallegos' first novel *El último Solar* (1920) as an analysis of the social and political defects of the country and of their disorienting effects on Venezuelan youth.

Bio-bibliographical works

714 **Bibliografía de bibliografías venezolanas: literatura (1968-78).** (A bibliography of Venezuelan bibliographies: literature, 1968-78.)
Horacio Jorge Becco. Caracas: La Casa de Bello, 1979. 62p.
Lists 250 contributions to Venezuelan literary bibliography published between 1968 and 1979, and gives brief descriptive annotations.

715 **Diccionario general de la literatura venezolana. Autores.** (General dictionary of Venezuelan literature. Authors.)
Lubio Cardozo, Ada Ojeda Briceño. Mérida, Venezuela: Editorial Venezolana & Universidad de Los Andes, Facultad de Humanidades y Educación, Instituto de Investigaciones Literarias 'Gonzalo Picón Febres', 1987. 2nd ed. 2 vols. bibliog. (Libros de la Universidad de Los Andes. Collección: Ciencias Sociales. Serie: Letras).
A comprehensive revision and updating of the first edition, compiled by Lubio Cardozo and Juan Pintó (1974). It contains biographical data; information on involvement in literary movements, journalism and politics; and bibliographies of works by and about each author.

716 **Seudonimia literaria venezolana.** (Venezuelan literary pseudonyms.)
Lubio Cardozo, Juan Pintó. Mérida, Venezuela: Universidad de los Andes, Facultad de Humanidades y Educación, Escuela de Letras, 1974. 114p. bibliog. (Centro de Investigaciones Literarias, Serie Bibliográfica, 6).
Lists the names of writers and the pseudonyms they used. Also reproduces as an appendix a series of articles on pseudonyms and anonyms in Venezuelan politics and literature by José E. Machado, originally published 1924-28.

717 **Bibliografía de la novela venezolana.** (Bibliography of the Venezuelan novel.)
Gustavo Luis Carrera. Caracas: Universidad Central de Venezuela, Facultad de Humanidades y Educación, Escuela de Letras, Centro de Estudios Literarios, 1963. 71p.
Aims to cover all Venezuelan novels published between 1842 and 1962, and lists 324 titles by 187 authors.

718 **Spanish-American women writers: a bibliographical research checklist.**
Lynn Ellen Rice Cortina. New York; London: Garland, 1983. 292p.
The Venezuelan section lists the names of some seventy women authors and the titles of their major works.

719 **A dictionary of contemporary Latin American authors.**
Compiled by David William Foster. Tempe, Arizona: Arizona State
University, Center for Latin American Studies, 1975. 110p.
Contains brief bio-bibliographical entries relating to José Balza (1939- .), Salvador
Garmendia (1928- .), Adriano González León (1931- .), Ida Gramcko (1925- .),
Guillermo Meneses (1911-79), Miguel Otero Silva, César Renfigo (1915-80),
Guillermo Sucre (1933- .) and Arturo Uslar Pietri.

720 **Latin American literature in the 20th century: a guide.**
Edited by Leonard S. Klein. New York: Ungar, 1986. 278p.
There is a very brief, but reasonably up-to-date, survey of literary trends in twentieth-
century Venezuela on p. 259-68.

721 **Women writers of Spanish America: an annotated bio-bibliographical
guide.**
Edited by Diane E. Marting. New York; Westport, Connecticut;
London: Greenwood, 1987. 448p. (Bibliographies and Indexes in
Women's Studies, no. 5).
Includes lists of works by thirty-five Venezuelan women writers, with more extended
notes on four of them.

722 **A bibliographical guide to Spanish American literature. Twentieth
century sources.**
Compiled by Walter Rela. New York; Westport, Connecticut;
London: Greenwood, 1988. 381p. (Bibliographies and Indexes in
World Literature, no. 13).
Includes, for Venezuela, brief descriptions of seven bibliographical works, two
dictionaries of authors, thirty-one works of literary criticism, and twenty-seven literary
anthologies.

723 **Bibliography of the belles-lettres of Venezuela.**
Samuel Montefiore Waxman. Cambridge, Massachusetts: Harvard
University Press, 1935. Reprinted, Ann Arbor, Michigan: University
Microfilms, 1959. 145p.
The main body of the work is an alphabetical list of Venezuelan authors and the titles,
dates and places of publication of each of their works. There are also lists of:
bibliographical reference works; literary collections and anthologies; and Venezuelan
literary periodicals. Unrevised since 1935, it naturally excludes all recent literature, as
well as modern editions of earlier authors and critical works relating to them.

Anthologies in English

724 **Some Spanish American poets.**
Translated by Alice Stone Blackwell, introduction and notes by Isaac Goldberg. New York; London: Appleton, 1929. 559p.
Includes (p. 428-43) Spanish texts and English translations of five poems by Rufino Blanco-Fombona, one by Andrés Bello, and one by José A. Calcaño (1827-97).

725 **Anthology of contemporary Latin American poetry.**
Edited by Dudley Fitts. Norfolk, Connecticut: New Directions; London: Falcon, 1942. 677p.
Gives parallel Spanish texts and English translations, which include three poems by Otto D'Sola (1908-75) (p. 304-09); three by Jacinto Fombona Pacheco (1901-51) (p. 280-90); and one by each of José Miguel Ferrer (1903-69) (p. 390-93), José Ramón Heredia (1900- .) (p. 522-25), R. Olvares Figueroa (1893-1972) (p. 158-59), Miguel Otero Silva (p. 294-95), and Angel Miguel Queremel (1899-1939) (p. 278-79).

726 **New voices of Hispanic America. An anthology.**
Edited and translated by Darwin J. Flakoll, Claribel Alegría. Boston, Massachusetts: Beacon, 1962. 226p.
This collection includes an English translation of Antonio Márquez Salas' (1919-.) short story 'Like God!', a tale of Venezuelan peasant life (p. 47-59); and parallel English and Spanish texts of Ida Gramcko's short poem 'Sueño' (Dream) (p. 197-99).

727 **Fiesta in November. Stories from Latin America.**
Angel Flores, Dudley Poore. Boston, Massachusetts: Houghton Mifflin, 1942. 608p.
This collection (which takes its name from the story by the Argentinian writer, Eduardo Mallea) includes Guillermo Meneses' 'The sloop *Isabel* arrived this evening . . .', a story of sailors and their women in La Guaira (p. 283-302); and Arturo Uslar Pietri's 'Rain' (p. 435-47).

728 **Index to anthologies of Latin American literature in English translation.**
Juan R. Freudenthal, Patricia M. Freudenthal. Boston, Massachusetts: G.K. Hall, 1977. 199p. bibliog.
Gives details of 116 anthologies, mainly covering several countries and authors, and consisting of short stories, poems and extracts. By using the geographical index to the alphabetical list of the 1,128 authors represented in the various collections, it is possible to identify thirty-five Venezuelan writers, and trace the particular anthology in which each of their translated pieces appears.

729 **Anthology of Andrés Bello.**
Compiled and introduced by Pedro Grases, translated by Barbara D. Huntley, Pilar Liria, foreword by Rafael Caldera. Washington, DC: General Secretariat, Organization of American States, 1981. 259p. bibliog.

This selection from the writings of the Venezuelan born savant includes examples of his poetry, his studies in linguistics, philosophy, law and education, his literary criticism and his journalism. The volume includes a chronology by Oscar Sambrano Urdaneta and a discussion of Bello bibliography.

730 **Latin American prose in English translation. A bibliography.**
Compiled by Claude L. Hulet. Washington, DC: Pan American Union, General Secretariat, Organization of American States, [n.d.]. 191p. (Basic Bibliographies, I).

A useful list of translations of various categories of prose literature, such as biographies, essays, histories, criticisms, novels and short stories, each arranged by country.

731 **Spanish-American literature in translation. A selection of poetry, fiction and drama since 1888.**
Edited by Willis Knapp Jones. New York: Frederick Ungar, 1963. 469p. bibliog.

Includes: Jacinto Fombona Pacheco's poem 'I announce the kingdom of the star'; an extract from Rómulo Gallegos' novel *Doña Bárbara* (q.v.); and Rufino Blanco-Fombona's short story 'Redeemer of the fatherland', which is a sort of summary of his satirical novel *Hombre de hierro* (Man of iron).

732 **Latin America. Fiction and poetry in translation.**
Compiled by Suzanne Jill Levine. New York: Center for Inter-American Relations, 1970. 72p.

Lists thirty-three anthologies, specifying the authors represented, and 190 individual works. Entries are indexed by author, original title, English title, and country.

733 **Hispanic anthology. Poems translated from the Spanish by English and North American poets.**
Edited by Thomas Walsh. New York; London: Putnam's, 1920. 779p.

Includes the editor's translations of Andrés Bello's 'Dialogue' and 'The agriculture of the torrid zone' (p. 389-94); Muna Lee's translation of Rufino Blanco-Fombona's 'At parting'; and Joseph I.C. Clarke's translation of 'Jesus' by Miguel Pimentel Coronel (1865-1905).

734 **The images of black women in 20th century South American poetry: a bilingual anthology.**
Edited by Ann Venture Young.   Washington, DC: Three Continents, 1987. 250p. bibliog.

Includes parallel Spanish texts and English translations of Andrés Eloy Blanco's 'Píntame angelitos negros' (Paint me little black angels); Miguel Otero Silva's 'La infancia' (Infancy); and five poems by Manuel Rodríguez-Cárdenas (1912-.). Introductory notes on each author are given.

Individual works in translation

735 **Philosophy of the understanding.**
Andrés Bello, translated by O. Carlos Stoetzer, introduced by Arturo Ardao.   Washington, DC: General Secetariat, Organization of American States, 1984. 325p.

This work, *Filosofía del entendimiento*, written in the 1840s, but not published in Spanish until 1881, or in English until this edition, develops the ideas of Locke and of the Scottish 'common sense' philosophers, and is the basis of Bello's reputation as the founder of Latin American philosophy. The fifty-page introduction by Ardao places the work in its historical, philosophical, literary and biographical contexts.

736 **Creole democracy.**
Rufino Blanco-Fombona, translated by Isaac Goldberg.   In: *Great short stories of the world.* Edited by Barrett H. Clark, Maxim Lieber. Cleveland, Ohio; New York: World Publishing Company, [1952], p. 918-22.

Tells an ironical tale of the *llanero* version of electoral party politics.

737 **The man of gold.**
Rufino Blanco-Fombona, translated by Isaac Goldberg.   New York: Brentano, 1920. 319p. (Brentano's Hispano-American Series).

Originally published as *El hombre de oro* (Madrid, 1916), this story of an encounter between miserly wealth and genteel poverty is enlivened by acute characterization, historical allusion and political satire, and contains interesting sidelights on manners and conditions in Caracas at the beginning of this century.

738 **Cumboto.**
Ramón Díaz Sánchez, translated by John Upton.   Austin, Texas; London: University of Texas Press, 1969. 273p. (Texas Pan American Series).

First published in Spanish in 1950, this fictional exploration of race and status relationships between blacks and whites on a coconut plantation in the vicinity of Puerto Cabello (where the author [1903-68] was born), was adjudged the most notable novel to appear in Ibero-America between 1945 and 1962.

739 **Canaima.**
Rómulo Gallegos, translated and annotated by Jaime Tello,
preliminary study by Efraín Subero. Caracas: North American
Association of Venezuela, 1984. 317p.

First published in Spain in 1934 (where the author, later to be President of Venezuela in 1948, was living in exile), this powerful novel treats of life and death in the Guayana hinterland of the Orinoco; of its latex-tappers and its gold-diggers, its rapacious merchants and its political bosses; of violence and affection, fear and machismo; and of how Canaima, the evil spirit of the jungle, affects the minds and bodies of those men who seek to penetrate it.

740 **Doña Barbara.**
Rómulo Gallegos, translated by Robert Malloy. New York: J. Cape
& F. Smith, 1931. Reprinted, Peter Smith, 1948. 440p.

This is the best-known novel by Venezuela's most celebrated author. It is a classic evocation of the harsh environment of the *llanos*, and of the barbaric lifestyle of its inhabitants, as exemplified by Doña Bárbara, the mistress of the plains, 'a compound of lust, superstition, greed and cruelty' (p. 46). Originally published in Spanish in Barcelona in 1929.

741 **Mamá Blanca's souvenirs.**
Teresa de la Parra (pseudonym of Ana Teresa Parra Sanojo),
translated by Harriet B. Onis. Washington, DC: Pan American
Union, General Secretariat, Organization of American States, 1959.
129p.

Originally published in Spanish as *Las memorias de Mamá Blanca* in Paris in 1929, this charming collection of sketches of life in rural Venezuela at the end of the nineteenth century, as seen through the eyes of a child, is based on the writer's own experiences, and presents subtle characterizations with artistry and wit.

742 **A cultural history of Spanish America. From conquest to independence.**
Mariano Picón-Salas, translated by Irving A. Leonard. Berkeley,
California; Los Angeles: University of California Press, 1962. 192p.
bibliog.

Originally published in Spanish in 1944 and frequently reprinted, this essay on the Spanish colonial legacy to Latin America is one of the finest works of a distinguished scholar, diplomat and man of letters.

743 **The ignoble savages.**
Mariano Picón-Salas, translated by Herbert Weinstock. New York:
Knopf, 1965. 168p.

A series of reflections on culture, literature and society, by a distinguished Venezuelan, denouncing the social climate of his times as one dominated by 'ignoble savages', who are unwilling to allow a new civilization to evolve and yet are unable to create one themselves.

744 **Windstorm. (A novel of the Venezuelan Andes).**
Luis F. Prato, translated by Hugh Jenks.   New York: Las Americas, 1961. 221p.

Originally published in Spanish as *Ventisca*, this story, set in the mountain state of Táchira in the Gómez era, brings out the character of the Andean people, their way of life in their harsh environment, their customs and code of honour, their myths and superstitions, and their attitudes to government and politics, love and death.

745 **The red lances.**
Arturo Uslar Pietri, translated by Harriet B. Onís.   New York: Knopf, 1963. 233p.

This historical novel, originally published in Spanish in 1931 as *Las lanzas coloradas*, is set in the period of the 'War to the Death' (1813-14), and portrays the chaotic and violent impact on ordinary people of the struggle for independence from Spanish rule. The author was a writer, academic, diplomat, minister of government and presidential candidate.

Theatre and Cinema

746 **Cine venezolano. Producción cinematográfica del Departamento de Cine
– ULA.** (Venezuelan cinema. Cinematographic production of the
Department of Film – ULA).
Edmundo Aray, Vicencio Pereira. Mérida, Venezuela: Universidad
de Los Andes (ULA), Dirección General de Cultura y Extensión, 1986.
181p.

An account of the work of the only department of film production in the Venezuelan
university system, from its inception in 1969, and a catalogue of around 100 films it
produced, with synopses in Spanish and English.

747 **Theatre and playwrights in Venezuela.**
Leonardo Azparren Giménez. *World Theatre*, vol. 16, no. 4 (1967),
p. 369-76.

Offers brief comments on the work of Román Chalbaud, José Ignacio Cabrujas, Isaac
Chocrón and César Renfigo.

748 **Cinema Venezuela.**
Kenneth Basch. *New Orleans Review*, vol. 7, no. 2 (1980), p. 185-89.

A succinct survey of film-making and film-makers in Venezuela, with comments on
some of the most outstanding productions.

749 **A bibliographical guide to the Spanish American theater.**
Compiled by Frank P. Hebblewaite. Washington, DC: Pan American
Union, General Secretariat, Organization of American States, 1969.
84p. (Basic Bibliographies, VI).

Includes twelve references to books or articles, all in Spanish, relating to Venezuelan
theatre.

750 **Behind Spanish American footlights.**
Willis Knapp Jones.   Austin, Texas: University of Texas Press, 1966.
609p. bibliog.

Chapter twenty-one, 'Independent Venezuela and its theatre', is a short history of Venezuelan drama to the 1960s.

751 **Centenario del Teatro Municipal de Caracas.** (Centenary of the Caracas Municipal Theatre.)
Edited by Marta Mikolan.   Caracas: Fundación Teresa Carreño, 1980.
264p. bibliog.

A lavishly illustrated collection of short essays reviewing the history of the Municipal Theatre from its inception in 1881, with a chronology of the highlights of the presentations of opera, music, drama, ballet, and variety over the century, and details of the 1981 centenary programme.

752 **Bibliografía del teatro venezolano.** (Bibliography of Venezuelan theatre.)
José de la Cruz Rojas Uzcátegui, Lubio Cardozo.   Mérida, Venezuela: Universidad de los Andes, Facultad de Humanidades y Educación, Instituto de Investigaciones Literarias, 1970. 199p. bibliog.

Lists 1,338 items, including unpublished plays and musical dramas, ordering them by author, date and title.

753 **South American newsletter: Venezuela.**
Honey Salvadori.   *Plays and Players*, no. 357 (June 1983), p. 46.

This very brief review gives an idea of the character and range of contemporary theatre in Caracas.

754 **Memoria y notas del cine venezolano, 1897-1959.** (Memoir and notes on Venezuelan cinema, 1897-1959.)
Ricardo Tirado.   Caracas: Fundación Neumann, [1987]. 350p.

An illustrated record of Venezuelan films and film-making from cinema's beginnings to 1959. A sequel relating to 1960-77 is due to be published.

Music

755 **Music in Latin America: an introduction.**
Gerard Béhague.   Englewood Cliffs, New Jersey: Prentice-Hall, 1979.
369p.
Includes a number of references to Venezuela, from the sacred music of the colonial
period to contemporary electronic music. Most attention is given to the 'nationalist'
composer, Juan Bautista Plaza (1898-1965).

756 **La ciudad y su música. Crónica musical de Caracas.** (The city and its
music. A musical history of Caracas.)
José Antonio Calcaño, introduction by Walter Guido.   Caracas:
Monte Avila, 1985. 515p. bibliog.
Originally published in 1958, this is the standard work on its subject, covering the
period from colonial times to the 1950s.

757 **Bibliography of Latin American folk music.**
Compiled by Gilbert Chase.   Washington, DC: Library of Congress,
Division of Music, 1942. 145p.
Includes fourteen items specifically relating to Venezuela.

758 **A guide to the music of Latin America.**
Gilbert Chase.   Washington, DC: Pan American Union, General
Secretariat, Organization of American States, 1962. 2nd ed. 411p.
The Venezuelan section (p. 366-83) includes a brief survey of the history of music in
the country, and a bibliography containing some 150 items.

759 **Music in the Americas.**
Edited by George List, Juan Orrego-Salas. The Hague: Mouton,
1967. 157p. (Indiana University Research Center in Anthropology,
Folklore and Linguistics, Inter-American Music Monograph Series,
vol. 1).

The published papers of the first International Seminar of Composers and the second
Inter-American Conference on Ethnomusicology in 1965 include items (in Spanish,
with illustrations in musical notation) on Venezuelan folk music by Isabel Aretz and
Luis Felipe Ramón y Rivera.

760 **Teresa Carreño "by the grace of God".**
Marta Milinowski. New Haven, Connecticut: Yale University Press;
London: Oxford University Press, 1940. 410p. bibliog.

A biography of Teresa Carreño (1853-1917), one of Venezuela's greatest musicians, for
whom the capital's modern concert-hall is named. A child prodigy in her early years in
Caracas, she became an international concert pianist of genius.

761 **Music in Caracas during the colonial period (1770-1811).**
Juan Bautista Plaza, translated by Conchita Rexach. *Musical
Quarterly*, vol. 29, no. 2 (1943), p. 198-213.

An account of the remarkable flowering of sacred music in the last years of the colonial
period, by one of Venezuela's leading composers.

762 **Indigenous music of Venezuela.**
Isabel Aretz de Ramón y Rivera. *World of Music*, vol. 24, no. 2
(1982), p. 22-37.

Describes the place of music in Indian cultures and the instruments used, and gives
short examples of the music of each of six tribal groups.

763 **La música folklórica de Venezuela.** (Folk music of Venezuela.)
Luis Felipe Ramón y Rivera. Caracas: Monte Avila, 1969. 234p.

A discussion of Venezuelan folk music, with over 100 illustrative examples set out in
musical notation, including children's songs, work songs, religious music, cult
drumming, carnival music, folk dances, and a brief section on the music of indigenous
Indians.

764 **Música indígena, folklórica y popular de Venezuela.** (Venezuelan
native, folk and popular music.)
Luis Felipe Ramón y Rivera. Buenos Aires: Ricordi Americana,
1967. 66p.

A brief account of various types of song and dance, with some illustrative musical
notations.

765 **Rhythmical and melodic elements in negro music of Venezuela.**
Luis Felipe Ramón y Rivera. *Journal of the International Folk Music
Council*, vol. 14 (1962), p. 56-60.
A discussion, with examples, of drumming rhythms used as accompaniments to singing
in various centres of black population in the country.

766 **Music of Latin America.**
Nicolas Slonimsky. New York: Crowell, 1946. 374p.
Includes (p. 288-94) a brief summary of the music and musicians of Venezuela.

Art

767 **Art in aboriginal Venezuelan ceramics.**
Alfredo Boulton. Caracas: The Author, 1978. 253p. bibliog.
This collection of splendid photographs of aboriginal pottery objects of all kinds, from locations in various parts of the country, has commentary and captions in Spanish and English. The pieces are presented from an aesthetic and artistic rather than an anthropological or archaeological viewpoint.

768 **Historia de la pintura en Venezuela. Tomo I – Epoca colonial.** (History of painting in Venezuela. Volume I – Colonial period.)
Alfredo Boulton. Caracas: Editorial Arte, 1964. 483p. bibliog.
Discusses the nature of the painting of the colonial period, with 112 photographic examples, and gives biographical details of 140 painters of the seventeenth and eighteenth centuries.

769 **Historia de la pintura en Venezuela. Tomo II – Epoca nacional.** (History of painting in Venezuela. Volume II – National period.)
Alfredo Boulton. Caracas: Editorial Arte, 1968. 416p. bibliog.
Places Venezuelan painting from the early-nineteenth century to the mid-twentieth century in its historic setting, The volume features 137 excellent illustrations.

770 **Historia de la pintura en Venezuela. Tomo III – Epoca contemporánea.** (History of painting in Venezuela. Volume III – Contemporary period.)
Alfredo Boulton. Caracas: Ernesto Armitano, 1972. 309p.
Outlines the historical background to Venezuelan art from the 1920s to the 1960s, considering the development of art education, criticism and institutions, and the main stylistic tendencies, with excellent photographic illustrations. Particular attention is given to the work of Marcos Castillo, Francisco Narváez, Héctor Poleo, Bárbaro Rivas, Mateo Manuare, Alejandro Otero, Carlos Cruz Díaz, and Jesús Soto.

771 **Art of Latin America since independence.**
Stanton Loomis Catlin, Terence Grieder. New Haven, Connecticut;
Austin, Texas: Yale University Art Gallery, University of Texas Art
Museum, 1966. 246p. bibliog.

Produced for an exhibition of Latin American art in the post-independence period, this
handsome volume consists of 116 photographs of exhibits (including six of works by
Venezuelans); comments on the charactistics of five sub-periods; and biographical
sketches of the artists (including thirty from Venezuela).

772 **El arte ingenuo en Venezuela.** (Primitive art in Venezuela.)
Francisco Da'Antonio. Caracas: Compañía Shell de Venezuela, 1974.
161p.

In this volume, magnificently illustrated with colour photographs, the naïve art of
Venezuela is reviewed, with special reference to the period 1948-74. Some fifty
primitive painters are discussed, including Feliciano Carvalho, Víctor Millán, Bárbaro
Rivas, and Víctor Guitián. There is a brief English summary.

773 **Art in Latin America today: Venezuela.**
Clara Diament De Sujo, translated by Ralph E. Dimmick, William
MacLeod Rivera. Washington, DC: Pan American Union, General
Secretariat, Organization of American States, 1962. 77p. bibliog.

Little more than a pamphlet, this item offers a very brief introduction to modern
Venezuelan painting, and some fifty black-and-white photographs of works by Otero,
Soto, Hurtado, Jaimes and others.

774 **Arte colonial en Venezuela.** (Colonial art in Venezuela.)
Carlos F. Duarte, Graziano Gasparini. Caracas: Oficina Central de
Información, 1974. 234p. bibliog.

Covers architecture, painting, sculpture, altarpieces, cabinet-work, and gold- and
silver-smithing, and is illustrated by 270 photographs, mainly in colour.

775 **Pintores populares de Caracas.** (Popular painters of Caracas.)
Peran Erming. Caracas: Consejo Municipal del Distrito Federal,
1976. 159p.

Good reproductions of the work of twenty-seven artists, almost all of which were
painted in the mid 1970s.

776 **Modern Latin American art. A bibliography.**
Compiled by James A. Findlay. Westport, Connecticut; London:
Greenwood, 1983. 301p. (Art Reference Collection, no. 3).

Includes (p. 251-63) bibliographical details of 123 items on Venezuela.

777   **Venezuelan painting in the nineteenth century.**
Cornelis Christian Goslinga.   Assen, Netherlands: Van Gorgum, 1967.
128p. bibliog.

A critical discussion, with many black-and-white photographic illustrations, of the
major Venezuelan practioners of the styles of classicism, neo-classicism, romanticism
and modernism.

778   **South American folk pottery.**
Gertrude Litto.   New York: Watson-Guptill, 1976. 224p. bibliog.

Includes (p. 186-205) a brief historical review of pottery in western Venezuela, and a
survey, with good photographic examples, of the kind of work still being executed.
Notes that the craft receives little public encouragement and appears to be dying out.

779   **Francisco de Miranda: el primer crítico de arte.** (Francisco de Miranda:
the first art critic.)
Rafael Pineda, translated into French by Michèle de Graume, Serge
Vintrin, translated into English by Jaime Tello.   Los Teques,
Venezuela: Biblioteca de Autores y Temas Mirandinas, 1986. 102p.
(Colección Cecilio Acosta, no. 9).

Presents the texts, in Spanish, French and English, of a lecture by the director of the
art collection of the Venezuelan ministry of foreign affairs. His subject is Francisco de
Miranda's reactions to the works of art he saw during his travels in Europe and
America.

780   **Diccionario biográfico de las artes plásticas en Venezuela siglos XIX y
XX.** (Biographical dictionary of plastic arts in Venezuela in the 19th
and 20th centuries.)
Venezuela. Instituto Nacional de Cultura y Bellas Artes.   Caracas:
Armitano, 1973. 300p. bibliog.

Gives alphabetically arranged short notes on Venezuelan practioners of this aspect of
the fine arts, with many illustrations.

Architecture

781 **The changing shape of Latin American architecture. Conversations with ten leading architects.**
Damián Bayón, Paolo Gasparini, translated by Galen D. Greaser.
Chichester, England; New York; Toronto, etc.: John Wiley, 1979.
254p.
Includes (p. 214-33) an interview with Carlos Raúl Villanueva, and twenty photographs of Venezuela and its architecture.

782 **Venezuela.**
Edited by Walter Bor. *Architectural Design*, vol. 39, no. 8 (1969), p. 425-47.
Comprises brief articles by Manuel Corao, Alan Turner, Anthony Penfold, and Jonathan Smulian, on various aspects of planning and architecture. Over eighty photographs appear also.

783 **New directions in Latin American architecture.**
Francisco Bullrich. London: Studio Vista, 1969. 128p. bibliog.
Includes a discussion and several illustrations of the work of the architect Villanueva.

784 **A history of Latin American art and architecture from pre-Columbian times to the present day.**
Leopoldo Castedo, translated by Phyllis Freeman. London: Pall Mall, 1969. 320p. bibliog.
There is a discussion of the architecture of Villanueva in Caracas in this volume (p. 277-82).

Architecture

785 **La arquitectura colonial en Venezuela.** (Colonial architecture in
Venezuela.)
Graziano Gasparini.   Caracas: Ediciones Armitano, 1965. 379p.
Describes and discusses the civil, religious and military architecture of the colonial
period, and illustrates it with 267 black-and-white photographs, twenty-four colour
photographs, and thirty plans and drawings.

786 **La casa colonial venezolana.** (Houses of colonial Venezuela.)
Graziano Gasparini.   Caracas: Universidad Central de Venezuela,
Centro Estudiantes de Arquitectura, 1962. 187p.
A discussion of the development of colonial domestic architecture from the Spanish
conquest onwards, which is lavishly illustrated with excellent photographs.

787 **Templos coloniales de Venezuela.** (Ecclesiastical architecture of colonial
Venezuela.)
Graziano Gasparini.   Caracas: Ernesto Armitano, for Banco Nacional
de Descuento, 1976. 2nd ed. 302p.
This magnificently illustrated compendium of colonial churches covers examples from
all parts of the country.

788 **Latin American architecture since 1945.**
Henry-Russell Hitchcock.   New York: Simon & Schuster, for Museum
of Modern Art, 1955. 204p.
Includes photographs and diagrams of buildings by Benaceraf, Bermúdez, Vegas y
Galia, Guinard, and Villanueva.

789 **Carlos Raúl Villanueva and the architecture of Venezuela.**
Sibyl Moholy-Nagy.   New York: Praeger, 1964. 179p.
An analysis, with text in both English and Spanish, of the nature and significance of
the work of Venezuela's best-known architect, with numerous photographs.

790 **Venezuelan vernacular.**
Federico Vegas.   Princeton, New Jersey: Princeton Architectural
Press, 1985. 88p.
A beautiful collection of colour photographs of Venezuelan vernacular architecture,
classified under town, street, house, ornament and church, and set in the context of
landscape, with a minimum of text.

Mass Media

791 **Latin American newspapers in United States libraries. A union list.**
Compiled by Steven M. Charno. Austin, Texas; London: University
of Texas Press, 1968. 619p. bibliog.
Records the holdings, in around seventy American libraries, of some 5,000 Latin
American newspapers. Those published in Venezuela occupy p. 584-610.

792 **El huésped alienante. Un estudio sobre audiencia y efectos de las radio-
telenovelas en Venezuela.** (The disruptive lodger. A study on the
audience for and influence of 'soap operas' in Venezuela.)
Marta Colomina de Rivera. Maracaibo, Venezuela: Universidad del
Zulia, Facultad de Humanidades y Educación, Escuela de Periodismo,
1968. 150p. (Centro Audiovisual, Colección Ensayos, no. 1).
A brief analysis of the content of a sample of 'soap operas', and the report of a survey
of the viewing and listening habits of 1,000 housewives in Maracaibo, and of their
reactions to the material presented.

793 **The Daily Journal. Venezuela's English-Language Newspaper.**
Caracas: Daily Journal, C.A., 1945-. daily.
A daily (28p.), containing Venezuelan and world news, with sections on international
business, sports, local arts and entertainments, and various features and advertisements.

794 **Public policy in the Venezuelan broadcasting industry.**
Fred Fejes. *Inter-American Economic Affairs*, vol. 32, no. 4 (1979),
p. 3-32.
Describes the development of radio and television broadcasting from 1930 to the 1970s
as a predominantly commercial enterprise, with little initiative or interference from
government. Analyses the structure and nature of the broadcasting interests of both

the private and the state sectors, and concludes that the imposition of a national broadcasting policy, conceived in the public interest, is unlikely in the current political and international context.

795 Handbook of Latin American popular culture.
Edited by Harold E. Hinds, Jr., Charles M. Tatum. Westport, Connecticut; London: Greenwood, 1985. 259p. bibliog.

The work is arranged analytically by branches of the field, with bibliographies for each section. There are brief references to Venezuela in the sections on popular music, television, sport, photonovels, film, festivals and carnivals, and the single-panel cartoon.

796 Comunicación y cultura de masas. (Mass media and culture.)
Antonio Pasquali. Caracas: Monte Avila, 1977. 4th ed. 611p.

A scholarly analysis of the content of radio and television, and of the outlook for the film industry, which stresses the need for a national plan for the mass media to counteract 'cultural under-development'. An appendix gives the texts of relevant laws and codes of conduct.

797 El humorismo gráfico en Venezuela. (Pictorial humour in Venezuela.) ·
Ildemaro Torres. Caracas: Ediciones Maraven, 1982. 494p.

Presents a lavishly illustrated history of cartoons, caricatures, strip-cartoons, posters, covers, and humorous works of art.

798 Zapata.
Ildemaro Torres. Caracas: Concejo Municipal del Distrito Federal, 1979. 230p.

A discussion, in Spanish, of the work of the Venezuelan cartoonist, Pedro León Zapata (1929- .), which is illustrated by numerous examples of his work.

Encyclopaedias and Directories

799 **Biographical dictionary of Latin American and Caribbean political leaders.**
Edited by Robert Jackson Alexander. New York; Westport, Connecticut; London: Greenwood, 1988. 509p.
Sketches of thirty Venezuelan politicians of the nineteenth and twentieth centuries are included among the 450 profiles in this volume.

800 **The Cambridge encyclopaedia of Latin American and the Caribbean.**
Edited by Simon Collier, Harold Blakemore, Thomas E. Skidmore. Cambridge, England; London; New York etc.: Cambridge University Press, 1985. 456p.
Each of the sections, on physical environment, the economy, the peoples, history, politics and society, and culture, contains some material on Venezuela.

801 **Who's who in Latin America. A biographical dictionary of notable living men and women of Latin America. Part 3. Colombia, Ecuador and Venezuela.**
Edited by Ronald Hilton. Stanford, California: Stanford University Press, 1951. 3rd ed. 149p.
This is still of some value for basic data on persons living in 1951.

802 **Diccionario biográfico, geográfico e histórico de Venezuela.**
(Biographical, geographical and historical dictionary of Venezuela.) Ramón Armando Rodríguez. Madrid: Imprenta de los talleres penitenciarios de Alcalá de Henares, 1957. 887p. bibliog.
In encyclopaedic form, and alphabetically arranged, this includes entries on persons, places and events.

803 **South America, Central America and the Caribbean, 1988.**
London: Europa, 1987. 683p.

The second edition of a survey and directory of the area, in which the Venezuelan section (p. 659-83) contains brief articles on history by Malcolm Deas, and on the economy by Paul Hackett (revised by Sue Cunningham), plus statistical tables and a directory.

804 **Biographical dictionary of Latin American historians and historiography.**
Jack Ray Thomas. Westport, Connecticut; London: Greenwood, 1984. 420p. bibliog.

Includes brief articles on Cecilio Acosta. Rafael María Baralt, Andrés Bello, Eduardo Blanco, Rufino Blanco-Fombona, Mario Briceño-Iragorry, José Gil Fortoul, Juan Vicente González, Felipe Larrazábal, Cristóbal L. Mendoza and Arístides Rojas.

805 **Enciclopedia de Venezuela.** (Encyclopaedia of Venezuela.)
Edited by Pascual Venegas Filardo, Lucas Morán Arce, Enrique R. Bravo. Barcelona, Spain: Editorial Andrés Bello, 1976. 2nd ed. 12 vols. bibliog.

The work is divided into three sections. The first, *History and Descriptions*, (vols. 1-6), contains extracts from classic accounts of Venezuela, ranging from Columbus' report of his discovery at the end of the fifteenth century to Augusto Mijares' survey of the country's political evolution from 1810 to 1960. The second (vols. 7-10) deals with Venezuelan literature, and comprises essays on six different genres, with illustrative examples of each from various authors. The third (vols. 10-12) consists of essays on different aspects of contemporary Venezuela: geography, fine arts, music, the armed forces, architecture, the economy, education, flora and fauna, politics, sport, folklore, the media, women, scientific research, the theatre, tourism, and religion.

806 **The world of learning, 1989.**
London: Europa, 1989. 39th ed. 1988p.

The section on Venezuela (p. 1831-41) lists academies, learned societies, research institutions, libraries and archives, museums, universities, colleges, and schools of art and music.

Bibliographies

807 **Catálogo de publicaciones oficiales 1840-1977.** (Catalogue of official
publications 1840-1977.)
Beatriz Martínez de Cartay.   Mérida, Venezuela: Instituto Autónomo
Biblioteca Nacional, Sección de Publicaciones Oficiales, 1978. 445p.
Lists the titles of 3,865 items, arranged according to the originating institution or
department.

808 **Latin America, 1983-1987. A social science bibliography.**
Robert L. Delorme.   New York; Westport, Connecticut; London:
Greenwood, 1988. 391p. (Bibliographies and Indexes in Sociology,
no. 14).
Includes (p. 307-12) seventy-four titles relating to Venezuela. The previous volume by
the same compiler, *Latin America 1979-83: a social science bibliography* (Santa
Barbara, California; Denver, Colorado; Oxford: ABC-Clio, 1984. 225p.) includes
(p. 164-68) around 100 books and articles on Venezuela, and remains of value.

809 **Impresos relativos a Venezuela desde el descubrimiento hasta 1821.**
(Printed books about Venezuela from its discovery until 1821.)
Ivan Drenikoff.   Caracas: Fundación para el Rescate del Acervo
Documental Venezolano, 1978. 233p. (Colección Manuel Segundo
Sánchez).
A single alphabetical list of 751 items relating to Venezuela, published in various
countries and languages before 1821. Gives bibliographical details of original editions
and also, in some cases, brief notes on content and/or author, on later editions and
foreign translations, as well as on library holdings and prices paid.

810 **Impresos y mapas antiguos de Venezuela.** (Early printed books and
maps of Venezuela.)
Ivan Drenikoff.   Caracas: Ediciones del Congreso de la República,
1975. 195p.

Lists 359 items printed in Venezuela between 1808, when the first printing-press was
set up, and 1821; and 132 maps of Venezuela, engraved or printed before 1800.

811 **Bibliografía venezolana.** (Venezuelan bibliography.)
Instituto Autónomo Biblioteca Nacional y de Servicios de Bibliotecas.
Caracas: Instituto Autónomo Biblioteca Nacional y de Servicios de
Bibliotecas, 1982- . 8 vols to 1988.

This serial publication gives basic details of items catalogued by the bibliographical
service, comprising works by Venezuelan authors (whether or not resident in the
nation), works published in Venezuela, and works about Venezuela produced by
foreign authors. Volume I relates mainly to 1980 items: vol. II, 1981; vol. III, 1981-82;
vol. IV, 1981-83; vol. V, 1983-84; vol. VI, 1984-85; vol. VII, 1985-86; and vol. VIII,
1986-87.

812 **Women in Spanish America: an annotated bibliography from pre-
conquest to contemporary times.**
Compiled by Meri Knaster.   Boston, Massachusetts: G.K. Hall, 1977.
696p.

Arranged analytically and geographically, and indexed by author and subject, the book
contains over sixty readily identifiable items relating to Venezuela.

813 **Bibliografía venezolanista: contribución al conocimiento de los libros
extranjeros relativos a Venezuela y sus grandes hombres, publicados o
reimpresos desde el siglo XIX.** (Venezuelan bibliography: a contribution
to the knowledge of foreign books relating to Venezuela and to its great
men, published or reprinted since the 19th century.)
Manuel Segundo Sánchez.   Caracas: Empresa El Cojo, 1914. 494p.

Organized alphabetically by authors, this work gives full bibliographical details, plus
comments on author and content, of almost 1,000 items relating to Venezuela that
were published in other countries; and adds an appendix, listing a further 500 titles,
which the compiler extracted from various bibliographies. It is most valuable for works
published before 1914.

814 **Dissertations and theses on Venezuelan topics, 1900-1985.**
Compiled by William M. Sullivan.   Metuchen, New Jersey; London:
Scarecrow, 1988. 274p. bibliog.

Lists author, title, degree, institution and date for over 1,500 dissertations, and in some
cases adds a synopsis. The entries are arranged under headings such as anthropology,
biology, economics, education, engineering, geography and geology, history and
politics, law, literature and the arts, meteorology, oceanography, mineralogy and
sociology. The volume is indexed by author and subject.

815 **Colombia, Ecuador and Venezuela. An annotated guide to reference materials in the humanities and social sciences.**
Gayle Hudgens Watson.   Metuchen, New Jersey: Scarecrow, 1971.
279p. bibliog.

Gives brief descriptions of 894 works of reference published up to 1970, divided into sections on bibliography (106 items), dictionaries (53), handbooks (15), art (35), language (35), literature (68), music (14), philosophy and religion (40), anthropology (59), economics (75), education (20), geography (78), political science (53), history (147), law (77), libraries (29) and sociology (11 items).

Indexes

There follow three separate indexes: authors (including editors, compilers, contributors, translators and illustrators); titles of publications; and subjects. Author and title entries refer either to the main items or to other works cited in the annotations. The numbers refer to bibliographic entries rather than to page numbers.

Index of Authors

175

176

Peeler, John A. 310-11
Penfold, Anthony 661, 782
Penn, Raymond J. 643
Penniman, Howard R. 335
Pereira, Vicencio 746
Pérez, Luis Jesús 464
Pérez, Omar Alberto 540
Pérez Sáinz, Juan Pablo 603
Pérez Triana, Santiago 69
Pérez Vila, Manuel 247
Pernalete, Patricia 612-13
Petras, James F. 567, 617
Petre, F. Loraine 254
Phelps, Kathleen Deery 132
Phelps, Jr., William H. 119, 130
Philip, George 618
Picón-Salas, Mariano 742-43
Pierson, Jr., William Whately 285
Pimentel Coronel, Miguel 733
Pineda, Rafael 779
Piñero, Eugenio 212
Pintó, Juan 715-16
Planchart, Enrique 58
Platt, Desmond Christopher St.Martin 418
Plaza, Juan Bautista 761
Pocaterra, José Rafael 286
Pollak-Eltz, Angelina 171, 450-53, 480-81, 483, 501, 508
Poore, Dudley 727
Powell, John Duncan 312, 679
Prance, Ghillean T. 133
Prato, Luis F. 744
Prieto, Luis B. 531

Q

Queremel, Angel Miguel 725
Quintero, Katherine Raup de 401
Quintero, Rómulo 401

R

Rabe, Stephen G. 405
Rabinovitz, Francine F. 358
Rafter, M. 229
Ramón y Rivera, Isabel Aretz de 478, 759, 762
Ramón y Rivera, Luis Felipe 759, 763-65
Ramos Guédez, José Marcial 454
Randall, Laura 619
Rasmussen, Wayne D. 439
Ratcliff, Dillwyn F. 707
Raup, Philip M. 643
Ray, Talton F. 313
Rayburn, John C. 629-30, 662-63
Reading, Reid 393
Reed, W.L. 346
Reissman, Leonard 534
Rela, Walter 722
Rexach, Conchita 761
Reyes, Antonio 93
Rheinheimer, Hans P. 455
Rhodes, Dennis 152
Rice, A. Hamilton 100
Rippy, J. Fred 255, 287, 557
Rivera, Marta Colomina de 792
Rivera, William MacLeod 773
Robertson, William Spence 231-32
Robinson, David James 26, 193, 499
Robinson, J.H. 233
Roche, Marcel 686, 689
Rodríguez, Gilberto 126
Rodríguez, Luis Felipe 541
Rodríguez, Ramón Armando 802
Rodriguez, Reynaldo 583
Rodríguez-Cárdenas, Manuel 734
Rodríguez Mena, Manuel 197
Rodríguez Roussú, Iraida 23
Rodwin, Lloyd 500
Rojas Uzcátegui, José de la Cruz 752

Rollins, John F. 43
Römer, Rene A. 481
Romero, Carlos Antonio 393
Romero, Jesús 509
Roosevelt, Anna Curtenius 144
Roosevelt, Nicholas 101
Roper, Christopher 690
Roseberry, William 288, 480
Rosenblat, Angel 474
Rothman, Harry 644
Rourke, Thomas (pseud.) 289
Rouse, Irving 17, 139, 145
Rout, Jr., Leslie B. 381, 456
Ruddle, Kenneth B. 635, 648-49
Rudolph, Donna Keyse 198
Rudolph, G.A. 198
Rugiadi Battini, Mario 112
Ruscoe, Gordon C. 532
Russell, William R. 102
Ryder, Gene 111
Ryder, Mary 111

S

Sáder Pérez, Rubén 620
Safa, Helen 668
Saffirio, John 504
Salas, Carlos 542
Salazar-Carillo, Jorge 560, 621
Salcedo-Bastardo, José Luis 256, 704
Salera, Virgil 557
Salgado, René 584
Salgado-Labouriau, María Léa 137
Salias, Vicente 346
Salti, Danielle 297
Salvadori, Honey 753
Sambrano Urdaneta, Oscar 704, 729
Sánchez, George I. 533
Sánchez, Manuel Segundo 813
Sanoja, Mario 146
Sardá, Juan 557

181

Index of Titles

A

Abolition of slavery in Venezuela: a non-event 457

Aboriginal cultural development in Latin America 146

Acción democrática: evolution of a modern political party in Venezuela 328

Accounts of nineteenth-century South America 67

Adaptive responses of native Amazonians 160

Adaptive strategies of Wakuénai peoples to the oligotrophic rain forest of the Río Negro basin 160

African experience in Spanish America, 1502 to the present day 456

Agrarian reform in Latin America. An annotated bibliography 652

Agricultural development of Venezuela 641

Agriculture of Brazil and Venezuela: business opportunities 637

Agriculture of the torrid zone 733

Ahora eres una mujer 179

Airlines of Latin America since 1919 656

Alborada 698

Alemania y el bloqueo internacional de Venezuela, 1902-1903 415

All the year round 60

Alliance for progress. President Kennedy's visit to Venezuela 409

América 695

American-Venezuelan private international law 342

Anatomy of a land invasion scheme in Yecuana territory, Venezuela 155

Andrés Bello: philosopher, poet, philologist, educator, legislator, statesman 696

Andrés Bello: the London years 704

Anthology of Andrés Bello 729

Anthology of contemporary Latin American poetry 725

Antonio José de Sucre (Gran Mariscal de Ayacucho). Hero and martyr of American independence. A sketch of his life 235

Anuario del comercio exterior de Venezuela, 1987 592

Anuario estadístico de Venezuela, 1987 593

Aquatic biota of tropical South America 126

Archaeological chronology of Venezuela 139

Archaeological survey of Venezuela 143

Archaeology of northwestern Venezuela 141

Area handbook for Venezuela 1

Armed forces in Latin America. Their histories, development, present strength and military potential 352

Arquitectura colonial en Venezuela 785

Art in aboriginal

Venezuelan ceramic 767

Art in Latin America today: Venezuela 773

Art of Latin America since independence 771

Arte colonial en Venezuela 774

Arte ingenuo en Venezuela 772

At parting 733

Atlas de Venezuela y del mundo 50

Atlas geográfico y económico (Venezuela visualizada) 49

B

Backpacking in Venezuela, Colombia and Ecuador. Treks in the northern Andes 108

Bailadores: an agro-social study of a rural Venezuelan region 40

Bandidos: the varieties of Latin American banditry 192

Behind Spanish American footlights 750

Bellermann y el paisaje venezolano, 1842-1845 11

Bibliografía antropológica venezolana 171

Bibliografía básica de etnología de Venezuela 159

Bibliografía de bibliografías venezolanas: literatura (1968-78) 714

Bibliografía de la literatura indígena venezolana 184

Bibliografía de la novela venezolana 717

185

187

Index of Subjects

A

Academies 690, 806
Acción Democrática (AD)
 264, 266, 272, 279,
 312, 316, 321-23,
 327-28, 334-36, 570
Acosta, Cecilio 804
Administration, public
 308, 349, 360-61, 573,
 593
Afrovenezuelans 171, 443,
 448, 450-54, 456-57,
 481, 734, 765
Agrarian reform *see*
 Agriculture
Agriculture 34, 40, 42, 50,
 54, 58, 70, 89, 104,
 308, 439, 480, 546,
 557, 559, 564, 574,
 593, 634-54
 agrarian reform 17, 312,
 634, 636, 641, 643,
 645, 647, 652
 agro-industry 636-37,
 650
 bibliography 652-53
 cacao 203, 212
 cattle-raising 68, 181
 coffee 288, 646
 co-operatives 149, 682
 credit 634, 637, 642
 development 634, 641,
 653
 education 634-35, 649
 irrigation 637
 labour 682
 land erosion 651
 land tenure 46, 642-43
 maize 144, 638, 640, 644
 manioc 144, 640
 production 641
 science 686
 shifting cultivation 640,
 648
 small farming 642
 technology 683
 see also Peasants
Air force *see* Armed forces

Aircraft 347
 see also Communications
Aliens 342, 418, 434
Alliance for Progress 409
Aluminium 626
Amacuro, delta 511
Amazon, river 66, 73, 75,
 144
Amazon Pact 411
Amazonas, territory of 41,
 89, 99, 125, 130, 133,
 150, 166, 181, 688
Amphibia 126
Andean Development
 Corporation 579
Andes 31, 40, 42, 46, 66,
 73, 84, 104, 148, 288,
 480-81, 510, 744
 see also Migration;
 Photographs
Angel Falls 87
Angostura 52, 214, 219
Animals 56, 61-62, 706
Anthem, national 346
Anthologies *see* literature
Anthropology 149-88, 815
 dissertations 814
 folk literature 184-88
 teaching and research
 691
 urban 485, 492
Antitrust legislation 344
Anzoátegui, state of 97,
 172
Apure, river 66, 68, 105,
 224, 278
Apure, state of 464
Aragua, state of 116, 666
Arauca, river 233
Archaeology 72, 138-48,
 455
Architecture 9, 11, 13, 16,
 191, 275, 774, 781-90,
 805
 see also Photographs
Arekuma 459
Armed forces 1, 267, 348,
 352, 362, 805
 air force 347, 352

army 208, 277, 347, 352
 navy 269, 347, 352, 359,
 415
 see also Military
Aroa 62
Art 11, 61, 72, 283, 455,
 767-80, 805, 815
 bibliography 776
 biographies 771, 780
 dissertations 814
 humorous 797
Artefacts 148, 466
 see also Archaeology
Asphalt 394, 407
 see also Mining
Asphalt Trust 407
Atabapo, river 105
Atlases *see* Geography
Audiencia 202
Auyan-Tepui 87
Aviation 347
 see also Communications
Avila 135

B

Bailadores 40
Balza, José 719
Banditry 192
Banking 564, 569, 593
Baralt, Rafael María 693,
 804
Barcelona 74, 77, 97, 324
Barinas 33-34, 219
Barlovento 451, 480
Barquisimeto 62
Barrios 178, 295, 313, 340,
 451, 484, 493, 498, 536
Bello, Andrés 693, 695-96,
 704, 724, 729, 733, 804
Beluche, Renato 221
Benaceraf 788
Bermúdez 788
Betancourt, Rómulo
 262-63, 272, 327, 359
 régime of (1959-63) 10,
 263, 273, 322, 550,
 555, 561, 654

197

347-48, 352, 356, 362,
    392, 415, 541, 570
  see also Armed forces
Millán, Víctor 772
Minerals 50, 70, 577, 602
  see also Mining
Mining 53, 72, 559, 564,
    574, 626-33
  asphalt 630
  bauxite 626
  copper 62
  diamonds 628
  gold 53, 627, 632
  iron 602, 626, 629, 633
  labour 628
  laws 628
  production 631
  resources 631
  taxes 628
  technology 683
  see also Minerals
Miranda, Francisco de 71,
    215-16, 227, 229,
    231-32, 234, 236, 238,
    779
Miranda, state of 451
Monagas, José 513
Morillo, Pablo 220, 229,
    237, 239
Motilón 84
Mountains 14, 19, 28, 31,
    41, 135, 137, 188
Movimiento al Socialismo
    (MAS) 325
Music 755-66, 795, 805,
    815
Mycology see Fungi
Myths 184-85, 187, 435,
    744

N

Naiguatá 135, 452
Naricual 77
Narváez, Francisco 770
National Securities
    Commission 587
Native peoples see Indians
Neblina, Cerro de la 41
Negro see Río Negro
Negro see Afrovenezuelans
New Granada 219, 229,
    239

New York and Bermudez
    Company 407
Numismatics see Coins
Nutrition 641, 650, 654
  see also Food

O

Oil see Petroleum
O'Leary, Daniel Florencio
    251
Olvares Figueroa, R. 725
Organization of Petroleum
    Exporting Countries
    (OPEC) 364, 401, 405,
    599, 614, 625
Orchids 121-22, 128
Orinoco, area 19, 38, 97,
    144, 157-58, 161-62,
    169, 429, 461, 739
Orinoco, delta 14, 176,
    181-82, 186-87, 460,
    511, 577, 635, 649
Orinoco, river 52-53, 58,
    65-66, 73, 79, 89,
    95-96, 105, 175, 214,
    219, 224, 233, 399, 657
  headwaters 154, 174, 181
  source 91
  upper 88, 99-100, 174,
    185, 640
Ornithology see Birds
Oro, Río de 47
Otero, Alejandro 770, 773
Otero Silva, Miguel 693,
    719, 725, 734
Otomac 175

P

Pacaraima 37
Páez, José Antonio 68,
    219, 278, 287
Panare 151, 157-58, 161
Pao, river 66
Parasites 126
Pardo, Miguel Eduardo
    693
Paria, Gulf of 372
Parima highlands 173
Parmana 144

Parra, Teresa de la 693,
    707-08, 712
Partido Comunista de
    Venezuela (PCV) 314,
    323
  see also Communists
Patameno 452
Paviche 627
Pearls 123, 209
Peasants 149, 288, 312,
    328, 453, 480, 485,
    510, 635, 657-58, 673,
    679
  see also Agriculture
Pemon 177, 459
  see also Languages
Pérez Bonalde, Antonio
    693
Pérez, Carlos Andrés 387,
    389
  régime of (1974-78) 306,
    525, 553, 567, 596
Pérez Jímenez, Marcos
    273, 292, 359, 398
  régime of (1948-58) 6,
    104, 266, 279, 299,
    533, 585
Perijá, Sierra de 39, 84,
    188, 466, 648
Petróleos de Venezuela
    (Petrovén) 609, 618
Petroleum 307-08, 546,
    548, 553, 569-70,
    601-02, 606-25
  administrative
    organization 612
  and the economy 288,
    619, 621
  and politics 266, 609, 624
  and society 172
  and US relations 397, 405
  bibliography 195, 622
  chronology 611
  development 301, 610,
    619
  exploration 606-07
  exports 611
  history 610, 613, 625
  international companies
    290, 602, 615, 624
  labour 615, 619, 667
  nationalization 306, 364,
    405, 595, 597, 604,
    608-09, 617-18, 624-25

203

Map of Venezuela

This map shows the more important towns and other features.

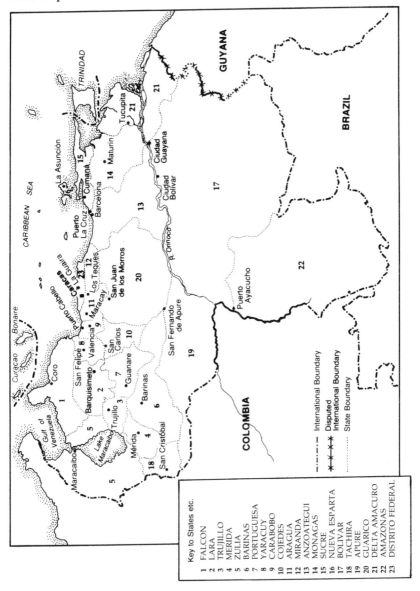

Key to States etc.

1 FALCON
2 LARA
3 TRUJILLO
4 MERIDA
5 ZULIA
6 BARINAS
7 PORTUGUESA
8 YARACUY
9 CARABOBO
10 COJEDES
11 ARAGUA
12 MIRANDA
13 ANZOATEGUI
14 MONAGAS
15 NUEVA ESPARTA
16 SUCRE
17 BOLIVAR
18 TACHIRA
19 APURE
20 GUARICO
21 DELTA AMACURO
22 AMAZONAS
23 DISTRITO FEDERAL

– – – International Boundary
––* Disputed International Boundary
·········· State Boundary

THE CABBAGE
PATCH

BY

NOEL LANGLEY

ARTHUR BARKER LTD.

30 MUSEUM STREET, LONDON, W.C.1

First Published in 1947
Cheap Edition 1949

MADE AND PRINTED IN GREAT BRITAIN BY
MORRISON AND GIBB LTD., LONDON AND EDINBURGH

CONTENTS

This Is The House

IF you were looking for Lady Buckering's house, you went in from the Finchley Road end and kept to the right.

Nobody lived in the house on the corner, and the next one had been turned into a boarding-house called 'Resthaven'; thereby betraying the how-have-the-mighty-fallen circumstances of the neighbourhood to even the rudest radical passing by in a bus; and the house after that was Lady B's.

All the houses were old, and sat fuddled together with their Victorian façades touching, watching the changing face of the street with uneasy eyes as more and more of their old landmarks came down to make way for blocks of flats. The trees in the front gardens sprawled over the windows and roofs like skinny boys in need of hair-cuts, tangling their gangly branches hopelessly with whatever they touched.

In the Spring, Lady B. raised crocuses and tulips in two little circular beds on each side of the front steps. Most of the tulips died in their bulbs of rickets and the botts, but the crocuses often achieved a peaky bud or two before the dog from over the road chased a cat across them. This sort of thing couldn't happen if Bicky, or whoever else it was, remembered Lady B's insistent request to shut the front gate after them when they came in or out; but do you think you could get them to remember a simple little thing like that? Not if you stood on your head and shouted yourself blue in the face. The front door had leaded panes of ruby diamonds and round bottle glass interweaved with water-lilies and morose storks, and rattled all through the house when it was slammed. Why the whole thing didn't fall out with a crash every time Bicky came in, Lady B. couldn't tell you; but if it ever did, Bicky would pay for it out of her allowance. So as long as that was tacitly understood, she could use her own judgment about it, even if she cared nothing for other people's nerves. There was a hang-dog, sway-backed cane sofa and two cane chairs on the front verandah, as weatherbeaten as retired Anglo-Indian civil servants; a leg was missing from the sofa, and a flower-pot, upside down, did duty for it. The flower-pot was broken, too, and the seat of the chair pushed farthest away from the steps wouldn't have supported an undernourished midget without bursting asunder.

Sometimes the door-bell worked, and sometimes it didn't. Dougall was working on it. Every so often, when he could get around to it, he sweated and swore, gave himself a series of violent electric shocks, and for a day or so following, the bell was ringable, provided one was listening hard. By some contrary instinct, anybody who came to the front door during these periods invariably knocked.

When the bell was *hors de combat*, everybody rang, and then went away in a rage.

Just inside the front door, on the right, was the hall table. Lady B. liked this to be kept clear and tidy, because of people's first impressions : did they want everybody to think they lived in a pigsty? Seven days in the week it was piled high with hats, library books, magazines, and mysterious parcels that lost their mystery when opened, being something someone had left some-where, or forgotten to return to someone. Above the table was an engraving of Napoleon in a bird's-eye maple frame. " That's

8

very valuable," Lady B. would tell a visitor. If pressed to estimate a figure, she would hint vaguely at a few round hundreds, though she bought it for ninepence in a junk shop in Penzance in 1919, and the damp had covered Napoleon with large brown spots the size of sixpenny pieces.

The rug on the hall floor had a crease through the centre that always tripped people. There was something malignant about the way it deliberately lay in wait for innocent prey; it was obviously proud of its contemptible record.

The stairway faced the door, and under it reposed a sullen powder-la-nose-room, where the hacking asthma of antique plumbing had earned for it the epithet of "The Last Resort." Visitors who wanted to wash their hands were always ushered upstairs to the first-floor bathroom, which bulged out of the back of the house like a bustle perched rakishly over the kitchen, and was modern and refined in its habits.

The hall had been covered with a gay floral wallpaper in 1923. That is, it had looked gay to Lady B. in the sample book; but once it had been spread across the wall, its gaiety had gone berserk, like over-ripe fruit scattering in confusion from the Horn of Plenty; and until Time—the great Leveller—had dulled the colours and brought it under some sort of restraint, the hall and stairs had always looked like a French hotel bedroom. Cathleen was wont to insist that all it needed to complete the illusion was a genuine bidé enthroned in all its artless glory on the landing. Up the wall of the stairs at reasonably equal intervals were "Cries of Old London" prints. Lady B. never called the same attention to them as she did to the print of Napoleon, for they had originally been advertisements for bath salts, but she did maintain it was practically impossible to tell them from originals—beauty being in the eye of the beholder.

The sitting-room was long and high-ceilinged. Two windows looked onto the street and one onto Resthaven's backyard, where a deep-dugged, piebald lady spaniel ceaselessly employed herself rearing broods of variegated puppies; was robbed of them; and began all over again.

There were two sofas, one small formal one reserved solely for guests, and one that had huge hollows in it and made a noise like a mutinous gong when sat in. It was always difficult to rise from its sunken depths and still maintain dignity and poise: Lady Buckering never sat in it unless she forgot. Usually she occupied a wing chair by the fireplace, from which vantage-point she could survey the room with the regal air of presiding over it.

Beside it was an unsteady gate-leg table, holding her knitting-bag and a lamp with a singed pink satin shade. The singed side of the lamp was always kept to the wall, but had a furtive habit of edging itself around the moment it detected the presence of guests. There were always three separate and unfinished sets of knitting in the bag; all, however, of the same wool. In moments of optimism and elation, Lady Buckering would work on a sweater; in moments of reverie, upon a scarf; and to keep her mind off pressing worries, a sock. Occasionally she would unravel the sweater to finish the sock, but more often she un-ravelled the sock to finish the scarf. It all worked out to the same thing in the end.

Over the fireplace, which was tall and ornate and white, was a coloured reproduction of Van Gogh's " Sunflowers." It went with nothing else in the room, but it gave its own wall a sort of Bloomsbury bravado. On the mantelpiece was a black marble clock with the minute-hand missing, shaped like a Greek Temple and smothered by a great deal of unanswered correspondence; two plaster-of-paris Venus de Milos offendedly turning their bottoms to each other; a Mabel Lucy Attwell calendar; two blue glass vases containing everlasting flowers, knitting-needles, hat-pins, and three unclaimed artist's oil brushes. There were bookcases on each side of the fireplace: the books you could see from the sofa were novels and classics; but the ones hidden by Lady B's chair and the gate-leg table were old business and telephone directories, put there for bulk.

A china cabinet stood between the windows. It wobbled neurotically when anyone walked past it, and was cram full of nondescript teacups and china souvenirs of watering-places, presided over by an open-minded china shepherdess being mischiefed by a purposeful but legless shepherd. All around them, in untidy piles, was a five-year accumulation of Christmas cards and an obscene yellow dog in a bowler hat won at a side-show and stubbornly hoarded by Bicky. Along the top of the bookcases was a jumble of family photographs; the ones without frames were tucked into the corners of the ones that were framed, obliterating them. One, of Bicky as a baby, had been turned to the wall; a hard-won compromise reached by Daisy in the face of Bicky's wish to remove it permanently after a boy called Esmond Dunstible had guffawed at it. The ceiling was elegantly scalloped in white plaster, except for a corner directly below Lady B's dressing-table in the bedroom above, where a bottle of Eau de Cologne had spilled and soaked through into a large round watermark shaped like South America.

The room was tattered and down-at-heel; but it still held all the bits and pieces Michael had liked. Daisy, Lady Buckering, had married Michael instead of Sydney Drew; and Michael had been dead fifteen years.

This Is Daisy

DAISY was still eighteen when Sydney had turned twenty-one, and they had grown up together. She was as pretty as a bon-bon on a pink dish at a Christmas party in those days; and Sydney's hair used to stand up in unruly tufts, defying all efforts to bring it to order. He was poor, and it took everything his parents could beg, borrow, or steal to put him through his medical training; so when he took Daisy out it was something of an occasion, planned and saved for over a period of weeks. They would go in the train to Hampton Court, or walk in Hyde Park, or go to the Zoo, strolling contentedly side by side while Daisy prattled gaily about trivialities and Sydney glanced at her with silent adoration, thinking with a bursting heart of the day to come when he could tack a brass sign on his door, present his credentials to her parents, and then ask her to marry him.

He never discussed marriage with her or talked of the future at all, but he was quite sure that her mind was so magically attuned to his own, that she already knew and shared all his unspoken hopes and ambitions.

Unhappily, though she was warmly fond of him in an easy-going sort of way, Daisy was far less mystically endowed than he fondly believed, and suspected nothing of his intentions. She looked forward to his visits and the outings, because he always made her feel exceedingly bright and vivacious, even when she was only being kittenish and talkative; and it was delightful to be so wholeheartedly appreciated; but she took him entirely for granted, and gave his heart about as much credit for emotional sensitivity as a watch.

One day, over tea, Daisy had said, without hidden meaning, "You'll have to be thinking about marrying soon, Sydney."

Sydney started, having read a hundred secret confidences into her voice, and felt himself blushing; he was utterly confounded now that the subject had eventually arisen.

"Oh, I don't know," he said in a gruff voice, scowling frightfully.

"Who will it be?" asked Daisy brightly. "A sort of Florence Nightingale would be best. You know—someone who could hold your patients' fevered wrists and stroke their brows while you were chopping them into little pieces. What about Nora Strudwick? She'd make a *wonderful* doctor's wife."

Sydney gazed at her in blank astonishment. If this was humour, it was baffling humour; and if it was serious, it was the news being gently broken to him that she was begging to be excused from any further plans he might have about her.

Instead of asking her point-blank which it was, however, he humbly accepted it as a thunderbolt, bowed submissively under it, and answered:

"Yes, she would. Not for *me*, of course; but she shows great promise. If you've finished your tea, I'll flip a penny: heads, the Zoo, tails the Park, unless there's somewhere else you'd like better?" And with a breaking heart he flipped tails and they spent an hour and a half listening to the soap-box orators at Marble Arch.

Destiny, running true to form, chose that afternoon to breathe a belated response into Daisy's carefree mind. As they were strolling for their bus it suddenly began to pour with rain. Sydney, displaying unsuspected romanticism, picked her up and ran with her to a cab, and when they were safely inside, Daisy found herself tingling delightedly at this new-found gallantry. He sat very quietly beside her, watching the shop-windows with elaborate attention and nursing a sensation of molten lead in his bosom; and Daisy, studying him for the first time in a new light, suddenly discovered with a small thrill of excitement that he was handsome in a rather specialised sort of way.

"I must be in love with him," she thought to herself in wonderment, and then, "I *am*! How perfectly funny! Does he know? Yes, of course he does; wise old Sydney, he knows everything. . . . I wonder what he thinks about it? He never *shows* what he's thinking . . . perhaps I'm just a sister to him!" Her heart sank. He had certainly never betrayed any signs of a tender passion; not so much as a kiss since the day they met. And yet he must care a *certain* amount, or he wouldn't take her out so consistently.

Concealing her elation and curiosity with a surface restraint, she began to lead the conversation gently towards a point that would make Sydney show his hand.

"Isn't it a shame I'm not the right type for a doctor's wife?" she asked with such careful lightness that it was over-light.

"Yes, isn't it?" smiled Sydney, as his last forlorn hope rolled over and died.

Daisy, hurt by his bluntness, cried when she had got home and locked herself in her bedroom until supper; and Sydney had sat down at his dining-room table, after his mother had cleared away the supper, and written to a hospital in Belfast applying for admission as an interne. It was both an impulsive and dramatic thing for the sober Sydney to have done; but it had its effect, for he was told to report in Belfast two weeks later. He had a pleasant and uneventful farewell lunch with Daisy, who had by now recovered her spirits, and ridiculed herself for supposing there was anything more than friendship between them ; and hurt him deeply, as a result, by displaying a complete lack of any surface regret or pity when she said good-bye.

After he arrived in Belfast he was kept so busy that he soon grew philosophical, even convincing himself that no struggling young doctor has a right to marry anyone as attractive as Daisy. Then Michael had written to him, thanking him for introducing him to such a wonderful girl, and Sydney put the whole thing behind him for ever and swore himself to eternal bachelordom.

Then there had been pictures in the papers . . . " Miss Daisy Etting and Sir Michael Buckering, announcement of the engagement of." . . . Sydney clipped one or two and put them away in a book. He never came across them again . . . must have been somebody else's book. Just as well.

He came to London on his first holiday, and called on Daisy the day before he went back to Belfast again. She was overjoyed to see him, very hurt that he had waited until his last day to see her, and told him a little too triumphantly that she and Michael were being married in three weeks. Anybody but Sydney would have detected a faint tremor in the triumph.

" Is he good enough for you ? " he asked banteringly.

" Sydney, he's *sweet* ! As a matter of fact, it's a funny thing, he's rather like you. Not to look at, I mean ; but deep down, you know."

" Too bad it's not me, then," said Sydney, hoping it sounded gay.

" You ? " returned Daisy, with a little bounce. " Any woman who wanted to see more than two minutes a day of you would have to spend her life thinking up things to be in bed about ! "

" That is somewhat of an exaggeration," said Sydney with grandeur, and they both fell unaccountably silent, though they knew they ought to go on talking brightly.

" I suppose I get an invitation to the wedding? " asked Sydney at last.

" Of *course*, Sydney ! " said Daisy. " And if I faint you'll be able to come to the rescue with a burning feather. . . . Sydney, don't look so mournful, please ! We're talking about my wedding, not my funeral ! "

" Mournful? Good heavens ! " returned Sydney stoutly. " I was just wondering what to give you as a wedding present "; and then, noticing with surprise that there were tears in Daisy's eyes, he said worriedly, " Why, Daisy, what's the matter? "

" Nothing, " said Daisy, annoyed with herself. " Excitement, I suppose. And I'm really scared to death, Sydney. So's Michael. We'll neither of us know how we'll ever walk up the aisle . . . though *he* doesn't have to, does he? . . . and I don't know why it should, but seeing you again has suddenly made me weepy for no good reason, except that I hate to think of you growing into a crusty old fogey, tapping people with your knuckles and telling them to say ninety-nine. "

" But you always said I was born to be a doctor ! "

" Yes, I know I did, silly, and you are; I'm just rambling on aimlessly. It's really because you're the nearest thing to an old beau that I ever had, so *naturally* it makes me sentimental ! "

" I wish I *had* been your beau, Daisy, " he said with a touch of wistfulness.

" Thank you, Sydney, " she said, and then looked at him with wide eyes. " Why, Sydney ! "

" Why Sydney what? " he parried defensively.

" You didn't *always* wish that ! "

" I did, " said Sydney unwillingly. " You mean it never showed? "

" Not a trace ! "

" Well, it's water under the bridge now, " said Sydney. " Though I came very close to proposing to you once. "

"When?" asked Daisy blankly.

"Oh . . . that time; *you* know. It rained. The afternoon I took you home in a cab."

Yes, Daisy knew.

So that was that.

They both looked at each other, and smiled; and Sydney looked across into the fire, and Daisy moved the tea-things vaguely, and after a moment poured them both a second cup of tea.

"I'm very touched, Sydney," she said when she was sure of her voice again. "I'll remember that."

"What on earth for?" asked Sydney.

"Because it was beautiful," said Daisy, "even if you never *did* actually say anything at the time."

Sydney had a sudden, revolutionary urge to ask her what her answer would have been. The question balanced itself dangerously on his tongue; Daisy realised she had invited it and was filled with sudden panic, and he asked for the sugar instead. Their mutual regrets, only half-aroused, came to heel obediently; they felt a wave of relief sweep over them, and drank another cup of tea.

So that was how it had been.

Daisy married her Michael and did splendidly.

Sydney moved into London and put up his brass plate, and they were all delighted to see each other again.

Then came the evening of the telephone call from Michael's theatre. Sydney had driven to Shaftesbury Avenue and found him lying on a sofa in his dressing-room; his dresser had loosened his tie and collar. They were on top of the world, then; and Michael had all his money in shares.

"Sydney, I'm in the worst jam of my life," he had said. "For God's sake give me a shot of something that'll carry me through; I've got to keep the play open; and get a film job on the side as well. Keep me going till I'm out of the rough, and then I'll go into a public ward or a strait jacket, or anything you say; but I *must* keep going !"

The shot hadn't been invented that Sydney could have given him.

"Mike, you're sick," he told him. "Get on home and go to bed, even if it means the bread line; it'll be cheap at the price."

"I can't," Michael answered, in not much more than a whisper. "Sydney, get me through the next three days, anyway."

"Do you want me to have Daisy come down and fetch you?"

In the end he got his way, and drove Michael back home.

They had been in their Portman Square house a year then, and the house was very gay and bright and fashionable.

When Michael was in bed, Sydney had told the worried and frightened Daisy, "Keep him there, if you have to sit on his head," and for three weeks Daisy kept watch over him, though he raved and fretted, and the play was closed without his knowing about it. At the end of the three weeks, Sydney let him see the market prices, and with almost superstitious wonder he found Derwent Aluminium still holding its own. The following Monday he went down to his broker's office, his pledge to Sydney being that he would only stay half an hour, and call him if he felt bad again.

That Monday Derwent Aluminium collapsed, too rotten with embezzlement to be nursed any longer. Michael worked frantically till four and then collapsed, bullied his broker into silence, rode home in a taxi, and died that night.

Daisy had displayed fortitude and courage. Sydney had been afraid that the sudden onrush of sorrow and problems and responsibilities would be too much for her; but with an unsuspected inner strength, she had worried them out for herself, going to no one for help; her pride being at its fiercest whenever Sydney offered to shoulder some of her problems.

He had watched the children grow, undisciplined and rather wild.

Sometimes he thought there was a danger of them straggling too haphazardly ever to prune themselves into their allotted place in society; but somehow or other they seemed to muddle through: his favourite picture was the five of them in a leaky boat, with Daisy bailing diligently . . . sometimes she was clear, and sometimes almost awash, but though he stood patiently on the shore, ready to help, she never once called to him for anything more material than professional support when grappling with flu and the mumps.

At regular intervals he had wanted to propose; he had his little speech all ready . . . "Considering I've spent the better part of my life without you because I was too slow on the uptake that time, the least I can do is ask you to share my Autumn with me." . . . But the years had made him shyer, if anything; and an occasion never seemed to arise when he could coax Daisy away from casual topics long enough to steer the conversation towards it. After all, it would have to be done in an atmosphere of peace and reverie, at an appropriate moment, carefully stage-managed. Even then he wasn't sure he'd be able to come out with it . . . there was something silly about an old man prancing about, proposing. He looked twenty years older than Daisy; fifteen, anyway . . . he had gone bald instead of distinguishedly grey, and hadn't worried about it at the time, though a Swiss barber had told him he could prevent it if he took massage and ate rhubarb.

One wouldn't be able to blame Daisy if she laughed in his face at the idea—though of course she wouldn't. She'd be very touched, the way she had been the other time, and say something charming; and what an old fool he'd think himself afterwards.

Now Doreen was having her first baby, and Daisy would soon be a grandmother.

It was absurd.

But it was their Autumn, all right. Daisy might never look like a grandmother, or behave like one; but she *was* one . . . all but for a day or so.

It made him feel like Methuselah.

This Is The Family

DAISY had four daughters: Doreen, Cathleen, Gerda, and Bicky.

Doreen was twenty-three. She was the quiet, responsible, rather ordinary one. She had married Dougall Pitchford because he needed looking after, and she looked after him very well . . . or had done, till her approaching motherhood had taken up all her time. She was rather sharp with him now. It wasn't like her at all; but he understood, being nothing if not excessively understanding in a clumsy, well-meaning way. Daisy was very fond of him: he had the faculty of bringing out the motherliness in her. He often reminded her of an apologetic spaniel that had made a small puddle and was anxious to do penance for it. He worked in an advertising office for five pounds a week, and they lived, in normal times, on a scurrilous old hulk moored in the Thames near Chiswick, to which they referred with restrained hauteur as their house-boat. You crushed your head on the cabin ceilings and fell down its perpendicular companion-ways, and the toilet was worked with an irresponsible hand-pump that behaved like a berserk oil-well when the mood so took it.

Daisy had insisted that they stayed with her till the baby was well established. They were unable to afford a hospital, and

Daisy was determinedly adverse to having her first grandchild born without a fixed address.

Cathleen was twenty-two. She was the sophisticated one; very worldly and self-contained. She was beautiful in an independent way, as if it mattered less than two hoots to her whether she was or not. She lived her own life, and made six pounds a week as a fashion-editor on a twopenny woman's weekly that catered unashamedly for the hoi-polloi. Daisy had the uncomfortable feeling that she hardly knew her at all.

Gerda was twenty, and was the delicate one. Even as a child she had been quiet and self-effacing and dreamy, and had taken life very seriously. She had married a young writer called Wilfred Marks, and learned how to talk very intently and intelligently: it gave Daisy the disconcerting feeling that Gerda was growing away from her, and trying to live up to Wilfred. . . . Wilfred, the genius of the family; the editor of a magazine at university, and very interested in Socialism, though he never discussed it at the house. And somebody was always just about to buy his play and make him famous.

Nobody in the family liked Wilfred, though Daisy tried her best; and Wilfred certainly didn't like anyone in the family. Daisy had once tried to read a play of his in blank verse called " Morons, Morons Everywhere," and thought that any school child could have done just as well; though Gerda insisted it was magnificent.

Gerda, who had never thirsted for anything deeper than *Winnie the Pooh* before she met Wilfred. Now she wore her hair combed straight to her shoulders, and slacks, and unattractive sports coats, and kept talking about economic revolutions, and damned the Conservatives without being a Liberal to make up for it, all with a glibness that made it quite obvious that she was just repeating Wilfred word for word.

There was something else about Wilfred that Daisy didn't

like ; not to do with his ideas. It was a furtive, elusive thing, a flaw right down in the actual make-up of Wilfred as a person ; something that made him fall short of being a good person, or even a real one. She didn't know what it was, except that it was there.

Bicky was seventeen—the baby of the family. She was small and looked as charming as a porcelain doll, with large innocent eyes and a demure mouth, and she had been spoiled by the others. She was the dramatic one.

Life was a continuous Drury Lane spectacle to Bicky, replete with train wrecks, volcanoes erupting, emotional crises and syrupy love idylls coming close on each other's tail. In those calmer periods of her life, that might reasonably have been treated as well-earned intermissions, she pulled drama out of thin air, and kept her senses in a twitter until life once more raised its curtain on further lavish excursions. The repercussions and reverberations of this insatiable zest for drama naturally affected the rest of the family : their own muddled and precarious patterns were perpetually prey to violent aggravation from the divers whirlwinds, monsoons, and earth tremors of Bicky's *agitato con molte*.

Love had come to her, too, in its most acrobatic form ; she had developed an attachment for an embryo Edmund Kean called Roland Wayne, whose emotional stability ran hers a poor second. They were problems.

Upon this unruly brood, Daisy perched like a lightweight hen, keeping her balance by sheer will-power. Even at the height of her despairing exasperations, though, she still burned with fierce loyalty and pride for all of them, and adored them singly, wholly and without reservations, with an inexhaustible fund of love and affection.

She had never been out of debt since Michael died. Her life was a giddy tight-rope walk among the placatable and

23

unplacatable tradesmen in the neighbourhood; and when Doreen and Dougall moved in, her non-existent cornucopia was rattled and squeezed to its last despairing inch to hire a trained nurse.

The trained nurse was called Miss Pynegar.

Whenever Daisy woke in the morning to the sounds of a firm, unfamiliar manly step striding the passage outside her door, it took her a moment to attribute it to Miss Pynegar, going to empty something or coming back from filling something.

Miss Pynegar was very expensive and very efficient, and didn't give in to patients. She preferred working in hospitals, and on private cases made a great point of doing her duty to a nicety and not a millimetre more. She belonged to a revivalist society, and had dreadful coloured pictures of saints ascending into the Aurora Borealis propped up on her dressing-table. She didn't eat meat, explaining to Daisy that animals were evil spirits; and that when she, Miss Pynegar, died, she had been guaranteed by the Ascended Masters that she would go up to heaven off a mountain in Wales, shoes and all. Daisy had had an anxious talk with Sydney about this, but Sydney had reassured her that Miss Pynegar never mixed metaphysics and business, and was the best nurse at the price that Daisy could hope for.

She could hear them talking through the wall, Doreen and Miss Pynegar, though not the actual words.

Poor Doreen, the strain was really beginning to tell.

Even Sydney hadn't expected the baby to be as long as this—five days late almost. She knew it couldn't help but disorganise the house when she first suggested it, but it had turned out to be much more inconvenient than she had expected, particularly in the way that the Pynegar had come to look on the bathroom as her own private domain, and banged on the door whenever anyone took longer than five minutes to bath.

She could have wished that Doreen would try a little more to make the best of it, too, although one was entitled to be humoured

24

a little before one's first baby was born. But demanding outlandish things like sweet Burgundy and fried shrimps in tomato sauce, and then refusing to eat anything else; and being so waspish to poor Dougall, who was in a desperate enough state of nerves as it was; it wasn't really fair on the rest of the household.

She remembered how romantic it had sounded, two years ago, when Doreen and Dougall had first told her about the houseboat; twelve shillings a week, and who cares about going without gas and electric light? Our grandfathers did all right; modern living had made people too soft. So they went and lived on the house-boat, which wasn't really a house-boat when Daisy had seen it and pinned them down; it was an odoriferous relic from some disbanded fishing fleet, with the mast sawn off, and four poky little cabins with bunks as hard and narrow as massage tables, and low beams that even Bicky had to watch out for: Dougall's forehead was a mass of scars: but he and Doreen had been so excited about being able to marry at last, and had kept interrupting each other to prove how they could live on three pounds ten a week and bank the other thirty shillings out of Dougall's salary; and Doreen had had a thousand ideas about decorating the place. Somehow, no matter how many misgivings one felt, one hadn't been able to advise them against it.

She could have dampened them. " What about the winter? " she could have said. " It's the hottest day of the year to-day, and it's as cold as a frigidaire down here. And suppose you have a baby? You'll have to watch it every minute, or it'll be into the river before you can say Jack Robinson."

But she pretended to be as happy about it as they were. . . . Perhaps she really had been. Perhaps she had never *actually* thought about it being cold in the winter until long after, when Doreen and Dougall arrived shuddering and blue with suitcases and stayed in the spare bedroom until May.

Now that she actually came to think of it, it had been Sydney who had thought of all the disadvantages; and everybody had shouted him down, Daisy along with the rest of them.

So in a way, it was partly her fault that they had ever taken the house-boat. But if they hadn't, they wouldn't have married, which they wanted to do so much. . . .

Then the day when they came in to see Sydney; and Sydney told them most certainly it was a baby and not some furtive-looking canned salmon Doreen remembered having eaten.

There had been a very grave conclave that evening down in the living-room. Doreen was still half unconvinced, feeling scared and important too; and Dougall had sat knitting his long legs and saying, "Well, gosh, Daisy, there it is, then"; not sure whether to be delighted or worried stiff—and terrified out of his wits.

He said one nice thing that Daisy had made a point of remembering. "I'm not scared of bringing a baby into the world just because it's in a mess," he said. "I think it's the job of people like Doreen and me to believe in the future enough to feel that when the baby grows up, things will have quietened down, and maybe he'll see a better world than we did. The bad things in life don't last as long as the good things, the way I see it; and, gosh, Daisy, if everybody suddenly decided to stop having babies till things got better, things never *would* get better, would they? I mean; how could they?"

"I think you're quite right, Dougall," Daisy had said warmly.

Not like Wilfred. "It's the death-throes of an obsolete reactionary system," were Wilfred's feelings, "and the coming home to roost of the economic revolution. Being fifty years too late, it'll destroy the innocent along with the guilty, impartially."

"Who is who?" Daisy would ask, but Wilfred would never say. It was very seldom he bothered to prophesy for Daisy, because he thought her scatter-brained, and usually read a book until it was time to go home, leaving Gerda to do the talking.

Gerda was never quite clear enough in her own mind to make what she was saying clear to anyone else, and usually had to finish up with, "Well, if you'd read Karl Marx you'd know what I mean," and Wilfred would snort disparagingly into his book, cynically amused by the childish minds about him.

There was, however, a vaguely familiar ring to Gerda's arguments. When Daisy had gone to the London University for a domestic science course, after leaving school, a lot of *her* friends had read Karl Marx and had become very excited about him. One young man in particular had nearly got himself arrested, Ted somebody. Now he owned a string of theatres, and lived in the Bahamas; and Julie Knox, Daisy's great friend of the moment, who had been so anxious to march on London and be handcuffed to the railings outside No. 10 Downing Street, married a banker and was a widow now, with her picture in *The Queen* every so often.

All Gerda really needed was a baby to mother, so that she could stop trying to mother strikers, by walking up and down in picket lines in dark glasses. Daisy had once run into her in Greek Street carrying a huge white card nailed up on a stick, outside an apologetic-looking restaurant. They had both been a little embarrassed, but Daisy had greeted Gerda quite naturally and said, " Hullo, Gerda dear, whatever are you doing here?" And Gerda had said, "Helping out," and Daisy had paused vaguely for a moment, and then said, "Well, see you Sunday as usual, then?" and smiled and hurried on.

No, she wasn't worried that Gerda would turn a weird social reformer; but she *was* worried that Wilfred's influence was a bad one, and getting worse all the time. " He doesn't get enough sun," she told Gerda. " You should make him drink orange juice, it has Vitamin A in it; and go out more, even if it's only to a movie."

" Wilfred despises movies," Gerda had explained, " except

27

French ones; and we very seldom have an evening free, you know. Wilfred's friends come round to the flat, and we talk."

"One of my daughters lives on a house-boat, and another in a Chelsea basement," Daisy would say sadly. "It makes me look towards the marriages of Cathleen and Bicky with undisguised misgiving."

There was a jingle of crockery outside in the passage.

Corder, the butler, with Doreen's breakfast. She heard him tap on the spare room-door, and exchange haughty good mornings with his arch enemy. He and the Pynegar did not hit it off.

"Milady, would you kindly speak to Miss Pynegar? I can't have her all over my kitchen, running it as if it belonged to her, and still guarantee adequate service."

"Very well, I'll speak to her, Corder."

"If your manservant co-operated a little, Lady Buckering, instead of meeting me with insolence and passive resistance, I'd find it easier to make a conscientious job of my responsibilities to Dr. Drew. If people are going to have babies in private houses instead of in hospitals properly equipped to deal with——"

"Yes, yes, Miss Pynegar. I'll speak to Corder."

I'll speak to Corder. I'll speak to Miss Pynegar. I'll speak to Corder. I'll bang your two silly heads together if you can't find anything better to do than snap at each other. And Corder's salary due again; three months of it now. And nothing to pay it with.

"*Your account, Lady Buckering*——"

"Oh dear, not overdrawn again?"

"*Well, yes, it is, I'm afraid. . . .*"

"I'll see to it at once."

See to what at once? Robbing the Mint? Counterfeiting a ew thousand pound-notes?

Thank goodness Simpson and Walsh never minded waiting for their bills. Not that she took advantage of it. As a matter of fact, she was more careful not to run up an impossible account there than she was anywhere else. And their sample models always looked wonderful on Bicky; no one could tell they only cost three or four pounds, particularly the beige coat and skirt. You couldn't match it at Harrod's for less than fifteen or twenty guineas.

" . . . Oh dear ! Bicky. . . ."

" Try not to worry so much, Daisy. She's just going through a difficult stage—midway between puppy fat and the awakening of womanhood."

" That's all very fine, Sydney, but what would you have me do ? Lock her up until the womanhood's awake ? It may take years, and meantime she's leading me such a dance, I don't know where I'm at. That horrible little Roly ! "

" Oh, he's all right."

" He's a spoilt little prig, Sydney Drew, and you know it. I only wish I knew what Bicky sees in him, if it isn't his money."

" Has he money ? "

" Well, not yet—but when he's twenty-five he will."

Quite a lot, as a matter of fact. The Waynes got their money out of armaments, though they didn't go broadcasting it to everybody. And he might turn into something presentable by then : five years to go. It'd be a pity to break them up now, and have them regret it later. There must be no sawed-off fishing boat for Bicky ; nor a mildewy basement flat, with half an inch of light creeping in from the top of the window, and no air.

On the other hand, they were both so irresponsible and excitable. They're not good for each other.

And the idea of thinking about Bicky marrying—two months away from eighteen. " . . . I mean, it's absurd, Sydney."

" Let her go on the stage then."

" Rubbish."

29

" All right, what else have you to offer? Anyway, there's plenty of time yet.   Wait and see."

" You said that about Doreen.   And Gerda.   And Cathleen."

And Cathleen'll be on the shelf if she goes on keeping to herself much longer. . . . Why?   It wasn't as if she was unattractive. As a matter of blunt fact she had more poise and beauty than the rest put together.   Was it because she was too distant with people? She didn't get it from her mother.   Or from Michael. . . .

Now my tea's cold.   Not that I really wanted another cup. Oh dear, I suppose I ought to get up.

If the Pynegar'll let me in that damn bathroom long enough to count ten. . . .

CHAPTER FOUR

This Is The Overture

THERE was a tap on the door and Dougall's long pensive face peered round it.

"Can I come in?" he asked humbly.

"Yes, dear," said Daisy. "How's Doreen this morning?"

"Well, she didn't sleep much," said Dougall, ambling into the room, still in pyjamas and a wrinkled and threadbare dressing-gown that ran out before it reached his knees.

"Oh, that's too bad," said Daisy. "Pull your sleeves down, dear."

"They're down," said Dougall.

"I keep meaning to buy some cheap linen and make you some pyjamas. Those have shrunk terribly. It makes you look like something out of Oliver Twist. Have you had any breakfast?"

"Not yet," said Dougall. "I'm not hungry, though. Pynegar thinks it will be to-day."

"What will?" asked Daisy. "Put my tray out on the chair in the hall, that's a good boy. . . . Oh, you mean the baby? Yes, I've got a feeling it will be, too, dear. That'll be a load off your mind, won't it? And everybody else's. Did you get any sleep?"

"I didn't like to. I snore, you know. Doreen had to lean across twice and hit me with her slipper; so I sort of half dozed. There was a nice sunrise this morning. Red."

"Red sky at night, shepherd's delight; red sky at morning

shepherd's warning," said Daisy thoughtlessly, and then tried to cover it up briskly. "You'd better get dressed and order something for breakfast."

"I will. I'm waiting for Pynegar to let me back in the room. Doreen's being washed. I'm not allowed to be there. Honestly, Daisy, Pynegar makes a fellow feel that being married and having a baby is unnatural."

"Maybe it is, to her," said Daisy.

"It shouldn't be to anyone," said Dougall. "It's a very beautiful thing . . . In retrospect. . . . I bet."

He wandered mournfully round the room, then sat on Daisy's rather carelessly folded dress.

"Not on there, dear," said Daisy.

"Sorry," said Dougall, and got up and wandered back round the room the other way.

"What time do you have to be at work?" asked Daisy encouragingly.

"I don't have to, if I ring Leftwich. As a matter of fact he said I needn't come till after the baby was born. That was pretty decent of him, wasn't it? It's so far away, you know. The office. From here. I mean, if I was sent for in a hurry; if anything went wrong——"

"Oh, pooh, pooh!" said Daisy cheerfully, "what could?"

"Nothing, of course," said Dougall without much conviction, "but the Pynegar was saying that there was never any guarantee, even with women who had had children before with no trouble. She knew a case where a woman had three, very easily, and died on the fourth."

"That Pynegar," said Daisy disparagingly.

"She told Doreen that if she had her way, everybody would have caesarians," added Dougall, who had come to endow the Pynegar with all the macabre infallibility of a morbid oracle.

"If she had her way," returned Daisy with spirit, "everybody would dig babies out of the cabbage patch fully dressed and able to say ma-ma !"

Dougall brightened momentarily at this defiance of the oracle, and wandered to the door.

"I'll go and see if she'll let me have my clothes now," he said, and smiled at Daisy. Daisy smiled back, and he went.

She sometimes got the feeling that Dougall was actually fonder of her than her own children—or at least didn't take her quite so much for granted—and his gentle, rather clumsy affection touched her very deeply, though if one was honest with oneself, he was as vague and as unpractical as she was, and between them they never did much more than double the muddle of whatever they were trying to unravel.

Even his office only kept him on because his boss was a senti-mentalist, and wrote Dougall off as an office-boy rather than fire him and get a real one for less money ; and yet no advertising copy-writer ever worked harder than Dougall.

"It's just that he hasn't found his place in the world yet," Daisy would explain with aggressive loyalty. "One day he'll fit in somewhere, and you'll hear from him. Nobody can work as hard as he does and not get *some*where !"

At least he made five pounds a week ; Wilfred didn't make anything : he had an allowance from an aunt in Dublin who had wanted to be a writer herself but had been made to marry a corn chandler instead.

She heard the Pynegar thubbering along the passage.

"Oh, Pynegar," she called, "is the bathroom free ?"

"For a while," said the Pynegar grudgingly, caught off-guard and unable to invent an obstacle.

Daisy put on her dressing-gown and slippers and went out into the passage.

From Doreen's room came a quiet flow of sullen complaints, and she tapped and went in.

"Good morning, Doreen dear," she said.

Dougall, half dressed, hopped behind a screen with one sock flapping, and Doreen stopped complaining and said good morning to Daisy.

There was an offended, wounded look in her eyes: she resented the indignity of her position keenly, and was aching for a hair-dresser and a manicure. Also, Pynegar had tried to make her drink Ovaltine again, and Dougall had refused to tip it out of the window. Doreen felt betrayed and forsaken by Nature and man, the victim of a cosmic joke at everybody's expense. Nobody else had ever felt as badly as she did, and they could all say what they liked, but it wasn't worth it. Never again, not for all the rice in China. If anybody had told her it would be like this. . . . She was trapped, bound hand and foot, betrayed. If only people wouldn't be so damned sentimental and fragrant about it. If someone would say: "God help you; you look like nothing on earth, and the whole thing's an imposition"; but every-body beamed fatuously, and said how happy she must be and how they envied her. And if Dougall called it Life's Most Sacred Mystery again she was going to hit him with the chamber-pot.

"Comfortable, dear?" asked Daisy, kissing her.

"Do I look it?" said Doreen bleakly.

"Let me puff up your pillows," Daisy offered.

"They've *been* puffed up, and they're not pillows; they're sand-bags, except for the one under my head now, which has gravel and old golf-balls in it."

"Shame," said Daisy sympathetically. "But it won't be for much longer now, dear. When I woke up this morning the first thing I thought was: this is the day."

"You said that yesterday."

"I know, dear, but this morning I heard the stork circling round the house."

" Oh, *Daisy* ! " said Doreen, exasperated.

" *I've* got a feeling it'll be to-day," said Dougall, helpfully, peering over the screen.

" Then it won't be ! " said Doreen, and scowled at him savagely.

Dougall, in an attempt to look benign and understanding at the same time ended up by beaming sheepishly instead. " Yes, it's *very* funny ! " she added, quick to seize upon his discomfiture, and Dougall at once stopped smiling and looked apologetic.

" Ah now, Doreen," he said humbly, coming out from behind the screen, " don't be angry with me any more. Gosh, I'd give anything to take some of this off your hands; you *know* I would ! "

" All right, then, go ahead and do it ! " said Doreen. " You have the baby instead of me, and I'll get up and go to a movie. I'm sure we can arrange it with the Pynegar."

" If only there *was* something I could do—" Dougall began earnestly.

" You can stop saying fatheaded things and getting on my nerves," Doreen informed him swiftly, " and go and have your breakfast ! "

" Okay," said Dougall sadly. " If you want me for anything, just call." He bent over hesitantly to kiss her, and for a second Doreen had an irritable urge to turn her head away. She conquered it, however, and kissed him impatiently but with a more amiable air, and patted his cheek.

" Now run along," she said; and Dougall, cheered at this indication that the old Doreen was not entirely lost to him, ambled off downstairs, humming off-key.

" I suppose you think I'm awful to him," said Doreen defensively.

" Of course not," said Daisy pleasantly, " nobody expects you to be absolutely yourself."

" Who *do* they expect me to be, then? Greta Garbo? I *am* awful to him, as a matter of fact; and it's not really fair, but I can't stop myself. I never *used* to nag him, Daisy. Do you think having a baby is going to make me a nagger? It seems to come so naturally, all of a sudden. It's out before I know I'm doing it. They always say you never know you're changing into a shrew till after you've changed, and then it's too late."

" I never heard such nonsense," said Daisy stoutly. " Why, to-morrow you'll be sitting up in bed eating whatever you want, as happy as a lark. You see if you're not."

The mention of food had been a tactical blunder. Doreen's eyes suddenly took on a fanatical glare, and Daisy could have bitten her tongue off.

" Daisy," said Doreen slowly, in something like a purr, " I want some fried shrimps, with some tomato sauce."

" No, you don't, dear."

" And sweet Burgundy. That Burgundy we had at the restaurant last June. It wouldn't be hard to get. Daisy, I've never wanted anything in my life as much as I want fried shrimps this very minute ! "

" I used to want curried eggs and marmalade," said Daisy, with a bright, carefree air, " but I thank Heaven that nobody ever gave them to me ! You must just try to be strong about it, darling."

" I *have* tried. It's no good. Something terrible will happen if I don't get them ! "

" Something terrible will happen if you *do* ! "

A terrible scowl drooped down over Doreen's face.

" I see. You're against me—along with all the others. My own mother. No, don't bother to say anything more. But if you're all sorry later, don't blame *me*. . . . If I'm still here to blame."

Daisy made a litttle clucking noise of reproach.

" Oh, really, Doreen ! No wonder Dougall's a bag of nerves,

if *that's* the way you talk to him," she said firmly. "Goodness me!"

A door slammed outside the passage. It was the bathroom door.

Daisy jumped up and hurried to the door.

"Was that you, Pynegar?" she called with a sinking heart.

"Yes," said Pynegar triumphantly from inside the bathroom.

Doreen had turned over with her face to the wall. Daisy half contemplated going back and trying to cheer her up, then tip-toed out quietly.

In the passage she made a detour and looked in at Bicky's door, but Bicky was fast asleep, curled up in a small ball in the middle of the bed.

She looked very pretty, and very young, not more than eleven or twelve.

In repose her face was trusting and serene, as if she had sublime faith in Fate's ability to steer her harmlessly and protectively through life.

Her clothes lay scattered in wild confusion; there wasn't a drawer in the pink and blue bedroom-set that wasn't half-open, overflowing with tangled stockings and rumpled underclothes. The waste-basket was housing Roly's picture and all his letters. Later they would be picked out repentantly and restored to places of honour, and a little later than that, back into the waste-basket they'd go. Roly looked very silly gazing dramatically up at her; he had posed for the picture with his hat pulled romantically over one eye, his overcoat collar swaddled around his neck, and a pipe glamorously gripped between his teeth, though he never smoked anything but du Mauriers. Rather an empty little face, no character at all, just smooth and round and vaguely handsome in a fuzzy sort of way.

Or was it that he didn't have a sense of humour? . . . You

37

couldn't actually *condemn* anybody for that, because one was either born with one or without one.

Daisy wondered if she had a sense of humour herself. She never actually laughed at her own misfortunes till long afterwards; but then she told them as jokes against herself—and Sydney always found her very funny.

She hoped she *did* have a sense of humour; and then wondered if anybody really did . . . one that worked twenty-four hours a day, that was . . . so that when one's whole world seemed to be tumbling about one in ruins, one could still sit back and shake with laughter. " *What a pippin of a story this will make, four months from now !* "

She half paused outside Cathleen's bedroom, but as there was no sound within, she went back to her own room and sat down to wait till Pynegar was prepared to let her have a bath.

No post that morning. Thank heaven. The bills wouldn't be in again till next month. " *Dear madam, we would respectfully bring to your attention your outstanding account with us.* " . . . Of course, there *were* the shares.

Daisy had been turning out Michael's papers to find something unimportant, and had come across some gold shares bought in 1927. The mine was South American, and so was most of the language printed on the shares, but they ranged in price from small ones worth twenty-five pounds to large ones worth three hundred. It never occurred to her that they were worth any more than the shoe-box full of Derwent Aluminium Byproducts Inc. that had robbed Michael of his nest egg; but with no conscious intent to defraud anybody, it *had* occurred to her that one or two of the tradesmen might be sufficiently attracted by the romantic sounding South American shares to take them in return for outstanding bills; and only two days ago, in a spirit of tentative experiment, she had offered one to Mr. Twudd the milkman, and he had turned it over in his mind dubiously for a moment, examined the share very carefully on both sides, and then reckoned he might take it as surety for the bill. Gladdened and encouraged, Daisy then offered a larger one to Corder, who had begun to grow restless for his wages; but Corder professed to have unhappy memories of traffic in shares; and though retaining the share, asked to be allowed to think it over before he gave a straight yes or no. Dignity had forbidden Daisy to do otherwise than consent to this, and there the matter had rested.

Indirectly this had led to a little scene that bewildered and worried Daisy.

Cathleen had come in in time to hear her talking to Corder, and, after Corder had gone out of the room, she had asked Daisy what she was up to now.

"Well, I'm simply trying to hold people off for a while, until I get some money," Daisy had said. "It's not as if I'm doing anything underhand. If they want to take the shares, it's their own lookout; nobody's forcing them to! For all I know to the contrary, they may be worth twice what it says they are."

Cathleen had at once behaved very strangely. "But you can't do that!" she had said in a strained voice. "It's as good as telling everybody in London that we're so poverty-stricken that we can't meet our obligations! It's—it's humiliating, Daisy! The milkman'll go around telling everybody! It's the principle of the thing! It's betraying one's own standards, and putting oneself on a level with Corder, and even lower, because we're supposed to know better!"

"But if I don't make *some* attempt to pay my bills, people will know we're poor anyway," Daisy had pointed out logically, "and I really don't see where it's humiliating or betraying standards, dear."

"Offering tradespeople phoney shares? Running the risk of being charged with it?"

" They only hold the shares as surety for the bills. Mr. Twudd told me so himself."

" And what happens if we never pay the bills and they go to cash the shares? "

" I think you're giving the whole thing an over-importance, Cathleen," Daisy had said with dignity, beginning to feel pangs of vague misgiving by now, but quite sure it was from natural worry and not from anything Cathleen was saying. " It isn't a crime not to be able to meet a bill occasionally, is it? " And Cathleen had said, " Yes, it is ! " and begun to cry.

" Why, Cathleen," said Daisy in amazement, sitting down beside her and taking her hand sympathetically. " What is it? Are you really as worried about it as all that? " And then a sudden thought struck her and made her heart sink, and she held Cathleen's hand tighter and said a little fearfully, " Is it something to be ashamed of? " and though Cathleen hadn't wanted to answer, and evaded the issue when Daisy asked her again, Daisy had felt very like crying herself. In a way, she knew what Cathleen was feeling; she'd felt it herself, in the first months after Michael died, when the first of the unmeetable bills had started coming in. Everything in those days had seemed to be united to destroy her pride and dignity. She used to imagine Griggs the fishmonger leaning across and whispering to other customers that she didn't pay her bills, and was after credit again; and had been unable to go to the back door to receive deliveries because she was sure the delivery-boys were covertly sneering at her. But that had been a long time ago; the novelty soon wore off, and Griggs had always continued to say " Good morning " with the same inflection, whether he was paid up or in arrears; it was all in the daily round, and trades-people apparently never expected anything else but overdue bills from the gentry.

It wouldn't help to explain it all to Cathleen now, though;

even if she made herself clear about it, which she seldom did. Besides, she had never suspected that Cathleen would be so sensitive about it, and the sudden revelation left her at a loss. Cathleen was usually so self-contained; even when she had been a silent, unobtrusive school-child. She lived her own sedate little life, apart from the other three, and never asked friends to the house. . . . But now, of course, Daisy knew that she was ashamed of the house.

She had decided that she would speak to Sydney about it.

" Where's your maternal intuition? " Sydney had replied, when she did. " She's in love."

" *Is* she? " exclaimed Daisy, delighted and relieved at the same time. " I wonder who with? I *do* wish she'd talk to me, once in a while; not extravagant confessions, you know—just enough to let me know if there's anything I could do to help. I don't seem to be much help to any of them, though; do I? They've all grown up rag, tag, and bob-tail, while I fluttered aimlessly on the sidelines. Like a hen."

" Oh no, Daisy."

" Oh yes, Sydney. Like an old hen."

" Very well, if you say so."

" That's *charming* of you, I must say ! Old world gallantry, no doubt? . . . Sydney, I *know* what's the matter with Cathleen ! Yes, of course that's it; how silly not to have thought of it before ! She always said she had higher hopes than being a wage-slave all her life; she was just working to prove to herself that she could adapt herself to any sort of job at a pinch; you know—as a stepping-stone; and now she's found it wasn't a stepping-stone after all, it was a dead end; and it's shaken her confidence in herself, and her belief in things in general. You see? . . . It *is* something I ought to be helping her with."

" How? "

" By teaching her to take the long view and be philosophical, and you needn't simper like that: I *can* do it, if I really set my mind to it."

But when she thought it over, and weighed the pros and cons, she felt it might drive Cathleen further into her shell if she suddenly came out of the blue with a lot of unsolicited motherly advice. It would have to wait till Cathleen came to her voluntarily, and they'd be able to sit down together and iron it all out.

Provided, of course, that Cathleen didn't go to anyone else. Daisy wished she knew the exact extent of Cathleen's feelings for her. Perhaps she didn't have any feelings at all.

Daisy tried to put herself into Cathleen's place and examine herself objectively. Would she come to herself for help and counsel?

Daisy thought very hard, but somehow she could only see herself as a hazy, rather blurred and unreliable figure, with no particularly outstanding characteristics one way or the other, and she suddenly felt very depressed.

Suppose that was the way all four of them saw her?

. . . A sort of Mrs. Micawber, waiting for everything to sort itself out right side up.

But Sydney would have warned her if he'd seen her making too much of a mess of everything.

Maybe he had! Perhaps, all during the times she had nodded impatiently and said, "Yes, I *know* all that, Sydney, but the point is *this* . . ." when he was trying to speak, he had actually been warning her that such-and-such would happen.

"Oh dear," said Daisy worriedly, and went and looked out of the window into the street, "I must do something about them all before it's too late."

And as if the Moving Finger had chosen this moment to write that it was too late already, there was an ominous knock at the door.

"Who is it?" said Daisy.

"Corder, Milady," said Corder. "A Mr. Grant Magill is downstairs to see you."

"Magill? Magill? I don't know anyone . . . what's it about?"

"The rent, Milady," said Corder.

"I'll be down," said Daisy with a brave front; but she sat down with her hands in her lap, because for the moment she felt quite faint with despair and fright.

This Is The Preamble To The Plot

CONCERNING the irregular habits and gipsy tantrums of Roland Wayne, his antecedents were not without blame in the matter.

The Waynes lived in indecent luxury in Cadogan Square, and Roland Wayne had two rooms of it to himself—a bedroom and a study. He had awakened, this especial morning, when Curtis brought his tea and *The Times*, with a positive sense of having slept on a problem and being no better for it. At first he hoped that it was a part in a play that someone had offered him, and which he couldn't decide to accept; but as the mists of sleep were clearing fast, the fatuousness of such a conceit lay all incongruous on the morning air.

Roland Wayne had not appeared before the public since the previous September at the Perranporth Summer Theatre, in his seventeenth year; where for his sins, and the immeasurably vaster sins of his fellow actors, he had played a galaxy of old men, butlers, party guests, and angry crowds muttering " rhubarb, rhubarb " off stage; but he did the rounds of the agents manfully every morning, and had once nearly landed an understudy in a play about the Atom bomb that lasted three nights.

Mr. and Mrs. Wayne were waiting patiently and indulgently for him to go into insurance. Roly was waiting patiently and

44

indulgently for Mr. and Mrs. Wayne to reassess his talents and give him two thousand pounds to give a small fat shoe-string manager called Parke-Bensche, who was prepared in return to stage a play about coal-miners with Roly as the star—forty-two pages in his part and two big love scenes. Who could miss?

This impasse was old history in the Wayne menage, and Mr. Wayne had stopped commenting on it caustically out of sheer ennui : the present bone of contention, tactfully and adroitly promoted by Mrs. Wayne, was the question of Bicky Buckering. The Waynes quite liked Bicky, and thought her a very sweet girl. As a friend, they could think of no one more suited to Roly's present phase ; but now that they were all being candid about it, Roly *did* realise, didn't he, that it would be very silly, and rather cruel to Bicky, to give it too much importance?

" Nobody's giving it too much importance except you and Dad," Roly had pointed out austerely.

" Well, naturally your father and I attach a lot of importance to your happiness, Boysie. We want to try and help you avoid some of the unnecessary mistakes all young people make when they're starting out in life."

" Well, that's pretty nice of you, Mother. Next time I see a mistake coming up, I'll call you in on it. But what's behind this fireside chat, anyway? Not bees and flowers, I trust?"

" Oh, Roly ! . . . Well," said Mrs. Wayne, talking as an equal and a friend, " to be quite open and above-board about everything, the other evening when Bicky was here, I just happened to be passing by your study and I couldn't help but overhear you talking about marriage, that's all. Now I *know* you weren't deadly serious about it, and the *last* thing I'd want to do would be to exaggerate its importance ; but sometimes young people drift into a certain way of thinking without quite realising it."

" We were just saying what a lousy thing marriage was, if you want to know," said Roly, simulating quizzical tolerance.

45

"Yes, dear, but that's not quite the attitude to take either,"· Mrs. Wayne had said with commendable understatement.

"Well, you don't catch me getting married in a hurry," he assured her grandly. "I wasn't born yesterday. It's a mug's game!"

"Not when the right girl comes along," said Mrs. Wayne with a wise and knowing smile.

"Were you Dad's right girl?"

"I think so. I hope so. Yes, of *course* I was!" said Mrs. Wayne, rattled.

Roly let this go uncontested. Mrs. Wayne bored Mr. Wayne to extinction; and he, in self defence, had built up an impregnable wall of reserve, and could come into the house, eat his meals, hear her talk and listen to her snore without it making the slightest imprint on his conscious mind. Roly was also aware that two or three other right girls had come along since. He had begun by despising his father for it, then rather envied him, and finally dismissed it as biologically unavoidable but undignified and vulgar in one of such advanced years.

He had had a shallow and negative upbringing; they had shaped no character in him, so what he did have was his own, acquired the hard way. He was unfortunately unaware that through never being given, or having been allowed to give, a real and comforting affection in his childhood, he had been cheated of something he needed badly now. Callow cynicism had come easily to him, as a forlorn makeshift for all the things for which he was lonely.

He prided himself highly on his fine independence and his flair for twisting a cryptic phrase. He had barely turned sixteen when he saw through his mother. So competent, and all-wise and serene; and underneath it, a cold, ruthless concern for her own body comforts, and not a trace of it for anyone else's. Always so pleased with herself. Always so right about everything; no

46

passion or compassion; no happy moments and no sad ones. The President of some marrow-chilling Women's Club, and a coy cheater at bridge. And everlastingly interfering, in that monotonous, melodious sing-song voice.

Bicky was his own affair. He had had no more idea of taking her seriously than flying; but he needed Bicky, somehow.. He could lord it over her, and always win in arguments; and though her tears and tantrums were boring at times, that was women for you. All women were basically the same clay as his mother. You could only go so far before you stumbled upon all their flaws and failings, so complacently and over-confidently hidden.

It was true that he and Bicky weren't ideally suited; they quarrelled far more often than they drifted in perfect peace together; when a better one came along, he would drop her quick enough. There was nothing maudlin or sentimental about *him* ! He had to watch that he didn't let her get him so excited, though: Bicky's hysterics were infectious; he often caught himself being just as undignified and violent as she was; and at the time he wouldn't be able to stop himself; instead, he'd pitch his voice even higher, as a sort of sardonic defiance of his own finer feelings.

" . . . Well, now, Roly, I don't want you to feel that I went behind your back, ever; this just came up naturally in the course of conversation; and as I say, all I'm doing is just talking it over with you conversationally and sympathetically. Bicky rang you last night when you were out; and we were talking about nothing much in particular, and then very naturally we were touching on the subject of you, and Bicky said you'd asked her to marry you, so I laughed and——"

" She said *what*? " said Roly galvanised into ferocity. " Why, the silly little twit, I never said anything of the sort ! *She's* the one that's always talking about marriage ! Why, she's crazy ! "

47

"Oh no, she's just a romantic child; but you *do* see what I mean now, don't you, Boysie?"

"No!" said Roly, very deliberate and hostile.

"Oh yes, you do, dear. Some absolutely natural slip of the tongue, some little remark in jest; and this little girl takes you seriously. Wouldn't it be better, now, to not see her quite so much—say for a week or two? I'm not trying to suggest anything drastic like breaking with her *entirely*: you know that, don't you? But Mother's older and wiser than you, Boysie; and sometimes she makes a tiny bit of sense."

Roly had not permitted the outrage to go any further. He retreated in a white-hot temper that confirmed her worst suspicions, and cloistered himself in his study. For Bicky to have told his mother—of all people in the wide and dreary world. The utter bad taste of it, the unwarranted presumption of it!

Anything, anything else that Bicky was capable of, he might have forgiven; but to tell his mother he'd proposed—it was the end. She had had it. Out upon it. He was through. He walked round his study very rapidly until he slipped on a polar-bear rug, then threw himself onto his back on the sofa and breathed fiercely at the ceiling. Then his rage reached boiling-point and he seized the phone and dialled Bicky's number.

This Is The Plot

GRANT MAGILL sat in the Buckering sitting-room looking at a dog-eared Lilliput and wishing it was all over. Every now and then a sinister figure in a nurse's uniform flitted through the hall with a *free-fri-fro-fruff* of starch; he didn't like to turn and openly stare, but caught it out of the corner of his eye, and when the butler came back, he made bold enough to say, " Is somebody ill in the house? Perhaps I ought to come back some other time——"

" It's only a baby," said Corder dispassionately.

" Oh," said Magill politely. " Girl or boy? "

" They don't know yet," said Corder, and walked out with an air of impartial detachment.

Magill took out a cigarette and leaned back in the chair, leaning hastily forward again when it made a low cracking noise.

The house was very quiet, except for a small glass chandelier in the middle of the ceiling, which tinkled gently every time someone in the room above walked over it. Now and then a door would open and shut with a far-away, muffled sound upstairs, but the sitting-room had a definite feeling of pensive isolation about it until the silence was suddenly shattered by the telephone. The noise zig-zagged through the house—a shrill, angry, insistent noise, like an old lady in a death-struggle for a three-way-stretch in a bargain basement. It rang for a full minute, and eventually he began an uneasy movement towards it himself.

As he did so, a long-suffering childish treble came rippling from the top of the stairs.

"Is somebody going to answer that damn telephone, or let it ring until I go mad?" it demanded torturedly. "Daisy! Cor-der! Answer the pho-oan!"

Magill picked it up obediently, and Bicky came hurling down the stairs in her pyjamas a second later.

"Hullo?" he said into the phone.

"Hullo," said a cold and stony voice, "is Bicky there?"

"Is Bicky here?" Magill relayed respectfully.

"Yes. It's me," said Bicky promptly, as if he should have known. "Who is it? Find out who it is."

"Who's calling? . . . A Mr. Wayne."

"Oh!" said Bicky, transformed, and was down off the stairs and had the receiver out of his hand before he could have snapped his fingers, adding, "'Scuse me like this, won't you?" as a belated tribute to decorum, and then, on the verge of answering the phone, thrust it against her middle and pressed her hand over the mouthpiece instead.

"I'll let him wait a minute or so," she said grandly. "He needn't think I *hurry*, just because it's *him*!" She perched herself on the arm of the sofa and eyed the ceiling with elaborate casual-ness; but as quickly as the resolve had frosted, it thawed and died, and a moment later she took her hand off the mouthpiece.

"Hullo?" she said, in a languid voice. "Oh, hullo, Roly. How are you?"

She struck Magill as a very pretty little thing, very full of *joie de vivre*; unrepressed, too. She'd taken him in her stride as if he'd always been around the house, in one capacity or another: no standing on ceremony about her. He had gathered that she was dealing with her gentleman friend, but was hardly prepared for the turgid human drama that now unleased itself like a tropic monsoon upon the room.

"*What?*" cried Bicky in such staccato horror that he jumped and dropped ash on his coat. "*I* told her that we were engaged? *I* did? Roly, I swear I never said anything like that to anybody, and certainly not to your *mother*!" This was clearly met by dogged onslaught from the other end of the wire, and she was only able to gasp, "Yes—but—yes—but—," until her forces rallied and she fired her answering volley. "Roly, *listen* to me for just one *moment*! It's no good getting hysterical about it"—at which an hysterical denial crackled over the phone and was ploughed under—"Yes, you are! You get hysterical about *everything*! . . . Why should it make *you* look like a fool any more than it makes *me* look a fool, if anybody *does*; and they *don't*, except in your *imagination*! . . . And *shouting* doesn't put you in the right! . . . Yes, you *are* shouting!" This was delivered from so dizzy a height of her own vocal register that her unwilling audience wondered whether he ought to retire to the hall before he was blown there.

Mr. Wayne, meanwhile, in a doughty effort to win a technical point before he sprang his fiercely cherished trump of hanging up, was as easy to hear as Bicky, and his context was not gallant.

"If I ever proposed to you," came loud and tinnily clear, "I'd go and have my head examined, and I'll thank you not to misrepresent me again in public, you nit-witted little neurotic!"

"Are you calling me a *liar*?" Bicky demanded with the dangerous note in her voice of one about to consult a good lawyer. "Because *if* you are, there happen to be one or two intances when you——" There was a loud clatter from the other end of the wire as Roly fumbled his trump.

At that moment he was shuddering with silent rage at having hung up at an undramatic moment of her conversation instead of the dramatic climax of his own. Still, hung up he had; and

Bicky, who had intended to be the one that hung up this time, stared disbelievingly at the phone, and then in a rising tremolo cried, " Hullo ! . . . Hullo ! . . . *Roly, are you there ?* "

Answer coming there none, she dropped the telephone numbly, ran her fingers up into her hair and stared tragically at an ash/tray.

" He hung up," she said at last in a very low voice, and stood quite still for a moment.

Magill tried to look sympathetic, and had begun to feel some/thing non/committal but consoling was expected of him, when she suddenly gave a long, wavering wail, called for Daisy twice, and swallow/dived head/first into a pillow on the sofa, where she abandoned herself to a potted götterdämmerung of Wagnerian grief.

" Oh, how I wish I was dead ! " she intoned. " Oh/ho/ho/ho, how I wish I was deh/heh/*ead* ! "

These alarums reaching Daisy as she was deliberately finding little things to keep her from going downstairs, she was inclined at first to attribute the hubbub to another round in the marathon bout between Doreen and the Pynegar, and ignore it ; but when she opened her door and heard Bicky's lusty dirge in the sitting/room below, she hurried down dutifully with her sewing/bag in one hand and a pair of stockings that she was about to tidy away in the other, too flustered to remember that a Mr. Magill ought to be lurking somwhere in the room too.

" Here I am, darling," she called comfortingly, " tell Mother what it is."

" It's Ro/ho/holy ! " cried Bicky, raising a wild and tear/stained face from the cushion for a moment.

Daisy threw the sewing/bag into her chair, pushed the stockings into the cuff of her house/coat, and sat down beside Bicky and took her hand.

" What's he done this time? " she asked, adapting herself

smoothly to *Routine One: Trouble With Roly Again.* "And why do you let him upset you, dear? Life's too short, I always say."

"He says he miffem-wuffum-riffum-wuff," keened Bicky into the pillow.

"I can't hear you, dear," said Daisy patiently.

Bicky lifted her head and raised her voice too obligingly.

"He says he never said he wanted to marry me, and that I'm a liar, and all his friends are laughing at him!"

"As if he *had* any friends!" said Daisy, catching some of the injustice of the slight. "Don't waste any more tears on him, dear. Anyway, it's *much* too early to be bothering about marrying anybody. You're still only a baby——"

"I'm *not*! I'm eigh*teen*!" returned Bicky, side-tracked for the moment, and ready to pursue it further; but at this moment the phone rang again, and she bounced in the air like a ping-pong ball. "If that's Roly again, I'm not going to speak to him!" she proclaimed atavistically.

"That's right, dear, of course you're not," said Daisy whole-heartedly. "Corder can tell him you're not in to him, and we'll forget all about him." The telephone continued to carol blithely, however, and at last Daisy swung majestically to her feet and called very grandly towards the hall, "Does *nobody* in this house know how to answer a telephone, for pity's sake?"

Magill, who had been tentatively standing up and sitting down ever since Daisy's entrance, now made a belated shuffle towards the phone, but as Corder had come in from the hall at the same moment, Daisy failed to notice him even then.

"It doesn't take people all *that* time to get from the kitchen to the phone!" she commented with acerbity.

"I came as soon as I heard it, milady," said Corder in an injured voice, picking up the phone.

"If it's for me, I'm not in!" Bicky instructed him sharply.

"That's if it's Mr. Wayne," Daisy amplified, and listened in as much suspense as Bicky to learn if it was.

"Lady Buckering's residence," said Corder, and then looked sphinx-like and added, "I'll call her."

"Who is it?" hissed Daisy and Bicky, as one voice.

"It's for Pynegar," said Corder, with quiet triumph, and went upstairs.

Bicky slumped back against the sofa.

"You see?" she said in the voice of one dastardly betrayed, "it *wasn't* Roly," and while Daisy was still trying to follow this sudden switch in logic, she added fatalistically, "he's never going to see me any more. I know it just as well as I know my own name. I may as well go and drown myself. What's the use of going on living? Oh, how I wish I was dead!"

Daisy, to whom this particular phrase of the *sturm und drang* always rang most false, stiffened a little.

"It's so *silly* to say that, Bicky," she said, hoping her voice sounded kindly, but aware that a note of criticism had crept in. "You know quite well you only say it because it *sounds* impressive. I only hope you never say it in front of people who don't know you very well. I don't know *what* sort of an upbringing they'll think you had!"

"There you go, talking like a snob," Bicky said bleakly.

"Why, *Bicky*!" said Daisy, wounded.

"Well, you hate Roly—all of you do, you never tried to hide it! You're all as pleased as anything because it's all over! You don't care about the disgrace and the cruelty and the insults of having the only man you've ever loved stab you in the back and betray you! You're probably gloating because at last it's all over, and I'm an old maid!"

Pynegar, having fruff-fruffed to the phone, now tried to make something intelligible of the chemist's voice at the other end.

"I'm not, and I don't hate Roly! When did you ever hear

54

me say such a thing? . . . And it would be too much to hope that it was all over as easily as this!" returned Daisy, still smarting.

"Is *that* all you can say about something that's ruined my life?" shrilled Bicky. "That's all it means to you to see my happiness destroyed, is it?"

"You *are* behaving badly, Bicky!" said Daisy, torn between maintaining implacable calm and showing Bicky that she couldn't scream at people and expect to be given in to. "And I wish you'd stop using that *absurd* way of talking! You're not at school any more!"

"I said, *We're expecting it any minute now!*" said Pynegar, with little red muscles beginning to show in her neck.

"If I'm not at school any more, stop treating me as if I was!" Bicky countered swiftly. "If you had any real sympathy you'd try to *help* me, instead of telling me I'm too young to have any feelings!"

"I *didn't* say that! I *am* trying to help you!" cried Daisy desperately.

"You'll have to speak up; there's a lot of *noise* going on in here!" said Pynegar in the modulated tones of the Singing Bull of Ushanti, glaring at Daisy; and Daisy, glad of the excuse, turned on her like a mongoose.

"Pynegar, tell them to call up some other time, and go away!" she said exasperatedly.

Pynegar clapped her hand fiercely over the mouth-piece.

"If people are going to have babies in houses instead of in hospitals where they ought to, necessities have to be ordered!" she returned volcanically.

"Well, the baby isn't here *yet*, is it?" countered Daisy testily.

"It *could* be, in the next ten minutes," snapped Pynegar, as if veiling a threat.

"Well, Doreen says it won't be here till Monday!" Bicky

intervened with battle in her eye. " And *she* ought to know ! She's *having* it !"

" She's the last person to know for certain !" Pynegar retorted, with a rattle of artillery.

" Don't be an alarmist !" Daisy chided her grandly.

Pynegar drew herself to her full height.

" This isn't the first time I've seen a baby into the world, Lady Buckering !" she said menacingly. Sparks flashed from her eyes, and Daisy quailed inwardly in spite of herself. Pynegar, having routed the foe, readdressed herself to the forsaken chemist. " Hullo ! I'll call you back later," she barked, and swept upstairs in a huff.

Her exit succeeded in demagnetising the atmosphere. Bicky lay back on the sofa with the pensive apathy of an expiring Traviata, and Daisy wandered rather aimlessly round in a half-circle.

Magill waited a moment, then gave a small cough.

Daisy gazed at him thoughtfully and absent-mindedly for a moment, and then moved away and began leisurely picking up her sewing-basket ; then she suddenly dropped it and looked back at him.

Magill smiled apologetically.

" I'm Mr. Magill," he said helpfully.

" I'm sure you are," said Daisy graciously. " Magill ? "

" Of Magill and Brand."

Daisy's brow cleared.

" Oh, of course, how *silly* of me !" she said brightly. " *How* do you do ? Do sit down ! This is my youngest daughter, Bicky. Bicky, this is Mr. Magill."

Magill bowed formally to Bicky, but Bicky remained supine and brooding.

" And now run along upstairs, my pet," added Daisy gracefully, helping her up off the sofa, " and we've forgotten all about that horrid little Roly, haven't we ? "

Bicky stiffened, and then suddenly ran purposefully towards the stairs.

"I'm going to jump out of the window!" she announced from the hall, and then banged up the stairs so violently that something fell off a shelf in the Last Resort.

"Bicky, you're not to be so *silly*!" Daisy called after her, and then turned to Magill with a disarming smile and added reassuringly, "She doesn't really mean it, you know."

"I'm glad," said Magill politely, and waited until Daisy had settled herself comfortably in her chair, and then sat down again.

"Of course she's driving me into a nervous breakdown," continued Daisy cheerfully. "Would you think she's only eighteen? She's only eighteen. She takes her emotions so *seriously*. I think that's only natural at her age, though, isn't it? They grow out of it. I hope. This boy Roland Wayne—he's really a *very* bad influence on her, but what can you do about it? He comes rushing in here, and they have the most ear-splitting fights and accuse each other of extraordinary infidelities"—here she paused, and added lightly, "harmless ones, of course—and then out he rushes again, till the next time; and the *telephone* calls! Well, I wish you could see our bill!" This time she paused very deliberately, then gave a casual little cough, and added delicately, "But hark at me! Did you come about the rent?"

"I'm afraid I did."

"Oh dear, are we months and months behind?" she asked disarmingly.

"Four, to be exact," Magill replied, disarmed.

Daisy made a little tuttering noise.

"Isn't that *simply* scandalous?" she inquired of the room at large. "It's a wonder you haven't thrown us out into the street weeks ago! And it's nothing but forgetfulness; except that I've been so busy with my family that the rest of my life has just gone to pieces! Doreen, that's my eldest married daughter, is having

57

a baby. Right upstairs. We're expecting it any minute now. Her husband's in an advertising agency; he writes the things you see on posters, at least he writes the things the other writers rewrite. I was amazed how little future there is in it. . . . How much do we owe you?" This was tagged on with such adroitness that for a moment Magill mistook it for part of Dougall's problems, and answered to a late start.

"Eighty pounds."

Daisy was silent for a moment, then fell to rearranging her sewing-bag on the table beside her, and finally, in a carefree, inconsequential voice, remarked, "A friend of ours has two thousand pounds tied up in a Czechoslovakian cement factory."

"That's too bad," said Magill sympathetically.

Daisy nodded her acceptance of this civility, noticed the stockings in her cuff, and unobtrusively moved them to her pocket. She displayed no anxiety, but also no apparent distaste, to pursue the question of the eighty pounds. There was an air of graciousness and hospitality in the room. Magill felt the situation ebbing pleasantly but firmly out of his control, and began to develop a definite respect for Daisy.

"I suppose," she said sweetly at last, stroking a curl off her forehead, "you want a little something down on account?"

"I'm afraid they want all of it," replied Magill, feeling boorish.

"Oh," said Daisy mildly, "they do?" and folded her hands gracefully in her lap, as if it was up to him to go on from there.

He was painstakingly choosing the right words to explain that they wanted it in cash too, when the front door opened and hit the hall table with a resounding thud, and a girl with a slightly unconvincing cheerfulness called out, "Anybody at home? Daisy, where are you?" and Gerda and Wilfred entered the sitting-room.

Gerda was wearing a bright handkerchief over her head, which she now took off, and was dressed in grey flannel slacks and a light sports coat over a grey-turtle neck sweater. She was very fair, with a quiet over-sensitive face, and struck Magill as being delicate. She was the first of the family he had seen that had a curiously pathetic air about her, as if someone ought to take her in hand quickly and straighten her out before it was too late and she turned into a negligible nobody. Wilfred proceeded straight to the bookcase, where he took out a copy of Carlyle's *History of the French Revolution*, settled himself down with his back to the room, and prepared to immerse himself in merciful oblivion till it was time to go home. As neither Daisy nor Gerda commented on this, Magill presumed it was a familiar ritual.

When Daisy introduced her, Gerda smiled at him with a natural friendliness, almost as if she was overdoing it a little to offset Wilfred's unsociability, and shook his hand.

" This is Mr. Magill, dear. My daughter, Mrs Marks," and then with a note of faint regret in her voice, " and that's Mr. Marks."

Mr. Marks continued to show them the back of his head, and Gerda had to call him to order.

" Wilfred, this is Mr. Magill."

" How do you do," said Wilfred to the book, searching for his place in it.

" Wilfred's the genius of the family," explained Daisy quickly, craftily disguising an apology. " He's writing a book. What's it called again, Gerda? "

" Oh, Daisy, you know how he hates you to talk about what he's done in front of him," said Gerda easily.

" Well, I like to explain, dear," returned Daisy innocently, " then people understand. Oh, yes. . . . *Morons, Morons Everywhere*."

Gerda laughed and offered Magill a cigarette.

" We rather bewilder poor mother," she said easily. " She

thinks we're a couple of bomb-throwing Communists, but we're really quite civilised." Magill declined the cigarette but lit her own, and as she leaned forward she disconcerted him by adding, "How did you get trapped in here? Are you courting one of the brood?"

"Oh, Gerda!" said Daisy reprovingly. "Mr. Magill owns the house. At least his firm does, and it's not that I want to chase you away, but why not go upstairs and say hullo to Doreen, dear? We were talking business." She inclined her head meaningly towards Wilfred.

"Oh, sorry," said Gerda cheerfully. "I'll vamoose at once. And you needn't worry about Wilfred; he's lost to the world for the morning."

At this moment the front door banged open again, and Roly Wayne leaped like an ersatz Nijinsky into the hall.

"Is Bicky home?" he demanded sharply.

"No—yes—no," said Daisy, taken off her guard, and then as Roly rushed up the stairs two at a time, she gave a gasp of exasperation, and was about to say something acid about Roly when Dougall came stumbling down the stairs calling frantically for Pynegar and hugging himself anguishedly.

"Daisy!" he cried from the banisters, almost in tears. "The baby! It's started! It's started! Oh, come quick! Where's Pynegar? Oh, *hurry*!"

Daisy ran into the hall and called loudly for Pynegar while Dougall hopped despairingly on the stairs, wringing his hands and baying, "Oh, quick! Oh, it's awful! Daisy, make her hurry!"

"Be *calm* about it, Dougall!" Daisy exhorted, as flustered as he was. "You mustn't let yourself get upset! Pynegar, where *are* you? Are you *deaf*? Gerda—get Dr. Drew on the phone and tell him it's started!" and then as Pynegar came measuredly from the kitchen with her mouth full of toast and started languidly up the stairs, " Well, *hurry*, for heaven's sake, Pynegar ! Shall I call Dr. Drew ? "

" Not till I know it's not another false alarm," returned Pynegar anti-socially.

" Of *course* it's not another false alarm ! She's in agony ! It's *dreadful* !" cried Dougall vehemently.

" I'll make sure first !" said Pynegar in a voice of iron, and hove out of sight with Dougall babbling incoherently at her heels. " And kindly do not *push me* !"

Daisy hovered to and fro undecidedly at the bottom of the stairs and then, swept up in the excitement, said, " Excuse me, will you ? " to Magill, and hurried upstairs after them.

As their voices died away and finally stopped as a door shut, Magill looked across to Gerda and said mildly, " I think I'd better call back some other time when Lady Buckering isn't so busy."

Gerda laughed casually.

" Oh, Daisy isn't busy ! " she assured him. " You may just as well stay. You'll never come into this house when there *isn't* a domestic crisis going on. Or starting—Or ending."

" Yes, but there's a baby being born," Magill said helplessly.

Wilfred suddenly looked up from his book and gazed coldly through his spectacles at him.

" There are probably something like sixty babies being born all over London at this second," he estimated in an impartial voice, as if that put an end to any nonsense. " We're a nauseatingly overpopulated island."

" Just the same," said Magill, " I'm only in the way——" He broke off as he heard Cathleen's voice in the hall, recognising it with a start of incredulity.

She saw Gerda from the stairs and said with mock determination, " I'm going out for a long, long walk ; and I won't commit myself now, but I doubt if I'll ever come back again.

Hullo! Gerda," and Gerda having replied in kind. "Hullo! Wilfred, you intellectual little prig," which Wilfred ignored; and then she saw Magill, and stood still.

"Hullo," she said quietly, applying all her attention to pulling on her glove. "What are you doing here? Come to cut off the gas?"

"Oh, you know each other, then?" said Gerda.

Magill, seeing that Cathleen was still at a disadvantage, smiled and nodded. "In a way. We're always running into each other at other people's parties," he said lightly.

"Yes," said Cathleen gravely. "It seems all wrong to see you in the daytime!"

"My, oh my!" said Gerda frivolously. "I'm glad it's all right to see him at night! And how lucky for everybody. Now you can't throw Daisy out into the snow, can you, Mr. Magill?"

Cathleen looked at him with a puzzled frown.

"Is that why you're here?" she asked.

"Well, not entirely," he said guardedly.

"Does Daisy owe you money?"

"Not me; my firm."

She began pulling on the other glove. Gerda, who had sensed the constraint, changed the subject.

"What's the latest bulletin from upstairs?" she asked. "I'd have thought they'd have kicked Dougall downstairs, if the balloon's going up at last."

"Oh, it's nothing. Every time a lorry goes by out in the road, Doreen thinks her hour has come. Bicky and Roly are yelling each other's heads off in her room. And watch out for the Pynegar. She creeps up on you from behind and attacks you with Dettol from a spray-gun at the drop of a hat."

She had regained some of her poise; stopped at the mirror and set her hat a little more jauntily, then turned to Magill. "Well,

I hope you'll get paid," she said. "If you're going to take it out in furniture, do me the favour of taking that umbrella-stand in the hall first, will you?"

She had lingered too long, however, for now her retreat was blocked by Roly and Bicky descending the stairs in a thundering avalanche.

"Throw him out, somebody! Thrash him, somebody!" Bicky was entreating wildly, though keeping a grip of iron on Roly's sleeve. "He comes in here and insults me, and then he tried to hit me!"

"I did not!" cried Roly fiercely.

"You did! If I had a father he'd have horse-whipped you! Only you wouldn't have dared to insult me, if I had; you'd have been too scared! You took advantage of us being a lot of helpless women!"

"That's a damn lie! The place is swarming with men!"

"Don't call me a liar! I'm not a liar!" screamed Bicky, circling round him and herding him into the sitting-room.

"Yes, you are! You're a horrible little liar!"

"I'm *not*!"

"Stop *screaming* at me! I'm deaf already!"

Bicky flung out her arms to Magill and the unresponsive Wilfred in tragic appeal.

"Well, *do* something, don't just *stand* there!" she wailed, and added scathingly to spur them, "if there was half a man among you, you'd throw him out!"

"If he was half a man he'd throw himself out," Cathleen countered caustically.

"Don't worry!" returned Roly, stung. "I'm *going*!"

He made a half-hearted attempt to reach the hall, and Bicky seized his coat-tail with a sob, and dragged him to a halt. "If you go away and leave me, I'll kill myself; I'll throw myself out of the window, I swear I will!" she declared wildly.

"She's mad!" said Roly frantically to Magill. "She ought to be locked up!"

"He says he's never going to see me any more!" wailed Bicky, hooking his arms into a half-Nelson.

"Get it in writing," said Gerda.

Roly wriggled himself into view and put his case to the quorum. "She's made a laughing-stock of me in front of the whole of London, that's all!" he announced with pardonable emotion. "I can't walk down Shaftesbury Avenue any more, without everyone grinning like looneys!"

"When did you first notice this?" asked Cathleen sceptically.

"Well, I'm sick of being smothered by an hysterical obsession! I'd sooner be locked up and be done with it, see?" he announced querulously.

"Shut up," said Wilfred in a low but penetrating voice from his book.

Bicky drew back with a shuddering gasp and confronted Roly, ablaze with outraged sensitivities.

"You *beast*!" she said, "you wicked, wicked beast!" and seizing his hat in both hands, she rammed it down over his eyes with a thud. "I *hate* you, *hate* you, *hate* you!"

"Stop that!" ordered Roly masterfully from under the hat. "Stop it at once, do you hear?"

He pulled the hat free and fell away panting, trembling at the vandalism of it. "Look what you did to my hat!" was all he could say, in a voice more eloquent than anything had been up till then. "By God, look what you did to my hat!"

For answer Bicky smacked it smartly out of his hands, and when he bent to rescue it with a muffled roar, she pushed him with such animal vitality that he fell upon it with a wallop that shook the room, crushing it flat. Intoxicated with power, she drove home her victory by planting her knees on his lunch, and banging his head on the floor until Cathleen and Gerda pulled her off, whereupon she looked frail and wept.

Roly lay on the floor, winded; and without making any effort to get up, reiterated mournfully, " This is the end. I call on you all to witness, this is the end ! "

Red-faced and outraged, Dougall now pounced down the stairs, struck a wild attitude in the hall-way and demanded in an oratorical frenzy, " Does it mean anything to any of you that somebody's trying to have a baby in this house, or are you all too self-centred to care? "

" You go to hell ! " returned Bicky, uncontrite.

Dougall, spurning repartee, dived swiftly towards Daisy's desk, soliciting Dr. Drew's telephone number from the room at large. " Why doesn't somebody write down a vital number like that? Where's the telephone book? Who's been messing around in here and muddled everything up? " he stormed incoherently. " My God; a baby's being born, and nobody knows the tele——"

" All right, Dougall dear, we don't need Dr. Drew for a while," Daisy interrupted, pursuing him from the stairs like a soothing zephyr. " Sit down and have a little rest," and then, as he subsided she turned reproachfully to the wheezing and exhausted lovers, " Bicky, Roly, how *could* you? I turn my back for *one* minute——"

" Girl or boy, both or neither? " Cathleen interrupted flippantly.

" Neither, dear; just a very understandable false alarm," returned Daisy. " You shouldn't really joke about those matters, darling. . . ."

" Oh, it's all very well for everybody to be inconsequential about it ! " the wretched Dougall said with heavy sarcasm. " I only wish a few other people around here would try having babies and see how funny it is ! "

The lightness went out of Gerda's eyes for a second, and Daisy patted Dougall gently and said, " There now, Dougall, everybody feels for you—you *know* that."

" Well, it's only Pynegar's word that nothing's happening ! " he averred, excitably. " Dr. Drew ought to be here all the time, now ! I bet you it *does* happen when he's off playing chess in a club, or something ! And apparently nobody gives a damn that people about to have babies are entitled to a little peace and quiet ! Oh, no ! Life's greatest mystery, and people fight all over the floor, and make jokes about it ! That old bag Pynegar doesn't know what she's talking about, anyway ! " Having got that much off his chest, and feeling correspondingly better, he shuffled back upstairs again to resume his faithful vigil by Doreen's bedroom door.

" I thought you were going home? " said Bicky to Roly with an unladylike sneer.

Roly, who had been listening raptly to Dougall, jerked his shoulders indignantly.

" If I tried, you'd start screaming the house down again ! " he returned discourteously.

Daisy took up a strategic position between them.

" Don't you think, *both* of you," she said carefully and reason-ably, " that for a mole-hill that should have never been anything more than a mole-hill, the five hundred different sorts of mountain that you two have made of it ought to be enough for one day? "

" That *I've* made of it? I like that ! " snorted Bicky in an injured voice.

Roly drew himself up austerely.

" Lady Buckering," he said with quiet hauteur, " nobody regrets more than I that a purely private difference of opinion should have concerned and inconvenienced anyone but Bicky and myself; but the use of ' mole-hill ' seems to me a peculiarly

66

unfortunate choice of simile. I shall not trouble any of you again. Good morning!"

He paused only long enough to guard against any shock tactics from Bicky, then turned on his heel and strode magnificently from the room and out of the front door, swinging it to behind him with a clatter.

As he walked down the front steps his soul was singing. What timing; what an exit!

Left with her thunder stolen, Bicky stood inanimate in the middle of the sitting-room, staring enigmatically away into the beyond, wondering if there had been something worse that she could have done to him before he got away. How squalid life was.

"You're not going to let him get off as lightly as that, are you?" asked Cathleen disbelievingly.

Bicky bequeathed a look of lofty resignation upon her.

"What's the use?" she said tragically; though the question was rhetorical, not calling for an answer. "What's the use of anything any more? Something just died inside of me here. I felt it. You can only suffer so much pain; after that something snaps, and you go numb."

Upon this ethereal and sombre note, she turned and walked unhurriedly and disconsolately towards the kitchen, to see if Corder had salvaged anything acceptable in the way of breakfast.

This Is The Romantic Interest

"WELL," said Gerda, "Mr. Magill's still waiting patiently to serve Daisy with his papers. I'm going up to Doreen. Coming, Wilfred?" she added half hopefully.

"No," said Wilfred, not looking up from his book.

"Oh, I do think it'd be nice, just this once, Wilfred," said Daisy cajolingly.

"Don't take any notice of him, Daisy," said Gerda quickly. "You know us, we're not the type for Doreen anyway, at the moment," though this cryptic remark seemed to be for Wilfred's benefit more than theirs, for he got to his feet long-sufferingly.

"Oh, all right," he said, "I'll go into the dining-room till you're ready to go home." He rose with a poor grace, and wandered off without a glance at anyone in the room.

"Were you going somewhere, dear?" Daisy asked Cathleen.

"Yes," said Cathleen, "unless you need moral support."

"No, of course not. Will you be back for lunch?"

"Probably," said Cathleen, "if I don't find a nice, dirty old man in the park who'll buy me one," and made her departure from the house with the briefest and most casual of good-byes to Magill.

Daisy, alone with Magill at last, came to the point far quicker than he had hoped.

" What a dreadful long time you've had to wait for what you came to see me about," she said sympathetically, " but now we can get it over informally and pleasantly."

She paused to show him how informal and pleasant everything was, then continued amiably. " I don't have eighty pounds in the bank just now, so it's no good writing you a cheque for a few days; but what I *do* have—I know how silly this is going to sound—are some shares; I fetched them when I went upstairs just now—in case you think I always carry them round in my bag !"

She brought them out, unfolded them with reverence, and passed one across to Magill, who took it with mixed feelings and wondered silently how one told a good share from a bad one.

" My husband bought them a *long* time ago, and I never liked to cash one unless I absolutely *have* to," she explained charmingly. " That one you're looking at is marked a hundred and fifty pounds, and these two are three hundred each, and there're two more somewhere. . . ." She let her voice trail off gracefully, and watched him as he read through the Spanish, which fortunately he understood.

" It seems to be all in order," he commented guardedly after a moment. " I don't know the mine, right off, but it'll be easy enough to check on it."

" Well, then," said Daisy beaming, " I thought that if you liked to take *that*, you could give me a receipt, and credit me with the difference against the next payment ! I'm *so* glad everything worked out so easily !"

Magill smiled, but his baser suspicions still twitched restively.

" But are you sure it's wise to turn in one of these? " he asked tactfully. " They may be worth keeping. Suppose they increase in value? "

" Oh, I'm sure they won't," said Daisy briskly. " But even if they *do*, it can't be helped. . . . I can't go *on* owing you all that money ! I feel so *guilty* about it !"

"Well," said Magill, folding the share, "with your permission, I'll take these to our brokers, and mail you the receipt as soon as they turn it over."

"Oh dear," said Daisy with a comic face. "You mean you don't trust me till you've cashed it?"

"I assure you, it's not a question of that!" he replied quickly.

"Then what is it a question of, or shouldn't I ask?" said Daisy ingenuously.

He made a sudden reckless decision and acted on it.

"It was just a matter of form," he said. "If I may use your desk, I'll give you a receipt for it now."

Daisy, pleasantly surprised, rose without undue haste and led the way to the desk. "You'll find everything there," she said hospitably, "but don't use the red pen, I just keep it because it's pretty . . . the little black stocky one writes. . . . Oh dear, I should have warned you! You always get a blot first!" She busied herself politely about the room till he had stopped scratch/ ing away with the stocky black pen and put it down, then walked back and said, "Finished?"

"There you are," he said, handing her the receipt. It acknow/ ledged the payment of eighty pounds and a credit of seventy. It made no mention of any shares.

"Thank you *so* much," said Daisy cordially, taking it and throwing it back on the desk without even reading it, "you *have* been nice about it—most people aren't; and any time you're passing. . . . I don't know *what* you'll go away thinking of us, of course. . . ."

Out in the street his mind began to clear, and he realised that his father, not sympathetically inclined towards the mixing of sentiment and business, would probably fire him when he learned how the job had been handled. He wandered along the pavement, wondering what had made him do it—a quixotic gesture for Cathleen's sake, or an impulsive fascination for Daisy, who could have charmed the shirt off his back if she'd set out to do it.

She was a wonderful old girl; anyone who could handle a houseful of difficult brats, and keep on her toes with all that enthusiasm, was all right. Try selling it to old Magill, though.

"*Where's the money?*"

"I took it out in shares, because I liked the old girl too much to serve her notice."

Then the fur would start flying.

He felt for a cigarette, found his case empty, and turned into a small tea-room. As he was buying a new packet, he saw Cathleen at a table in the corner. His heart quickened, and he went over to her.

"May I join you?" he asked hopefully.

She looked up quickly, and then nodded.

He sat down beside her, and she moved her feet carefully away, as if it would be indelicate if they touched his.

"Well?" she said in a slightly hostile voice. "Does Mother go to jail or did you compromise?"

"We compromised," he assured her. "Will you have a cup of tea with me?"

She shook her head and he ordered one for himself.

"What was it about?" said Cathleen at last, in a low, unwilling voice.

"Oh, just the payments on the house."

"It's not worth what she pays for it," said Cathleen aggressively.

"I know. It's all settled, though. I didn't know it was your house till I got to the door."

She let this go by without comment.

"Are you still as through with me as the last time you said you were?" he asked casually after a moment. "It was fate that brought us together again, you know—even if the omen *was* a bill!"

"How was it settled?" asked Cathleen unwillingly. "Did she . . . pay you?"

"In full."

She looked at him very directly for a moment, but there seemed to be no evasion in his eyes.

"I haven't been the same man since you told me you never wanted to see me again," he informed her gravely.

"I'm sorry."

"You wouldn't lift the ban, say, for one night every six months, would you? . . . starting to-night?"

Cathleen's heart gave a little bound of response, but she waited till it was calm again, and then said, "It wouldn't be any good, honestly it wouldn't, Grant. I won't change my mind, I'm afraid."

He pondered this for a second.

"Then, don't," he said easily. "Come out hating yourself, *and* me, but anyway, come out. Maybe, by the end of the evening, whatever it was that suddenly went counter-clockwise will give a loud whirring noise and start going clockwise again."

"And then?"

"And then we can get married, and you can help me turn people out into the street at 3 per cent. of what you collect and a minimum guarantee of eight quid a week."

She was unable to help smiling.

"It's not very inviting," she said. Her throat suddenly constricted with the things she wanted to say, and she felt ineffectual and miserable.

"Look," said Grant gently, "I'll tell you what we'll do. I'll come round to the house about seven-thirty. If you still don't want to come, just tell your butler to slam the door in my face. If you've changed your mind, out we'll go. That's fair enough, isn't it?"

Rather than trust her voice, she nodded.

This Is The Doctor

DR. SYDNEY DREW pulled his car up in front of the house with a protesting squeak of brakes that everyone in the house recognised at once; and as he walked up the front steps Daisy opened the door and said, "Hullo, Sydney. Late for your own funeral again."

"Why?" he inquired, unruffled. "Stork hasn't beaten me to it, has it?"

"No," said Daisy, closing the door after him, "but your responsibilities don't start and end with someone who isn't here yet. There's no one to protect us·from Pynegar when you're out of the way."

"And how is Dougall?" asked Sydney, taking off his coat and folding his gloves neatly and popping them into his hat.

"Well, he had rather a bad night, but he's better this morning," said Daisy.

"Good," said Sydney, "I'll probably be able to pull him through. And·how's the rest of the devil's brew? Any more cases of delirium tremens? I see Wilfred's here," he added, as they went past the dining-room. "Gerda all right?"

"I don't know," said Daisy seriously. "And of course you couldn't get her to *admit* anything was wrong with her if she was at her last gasp. Are you going straight up to Doreen?"

"May as well," said Sydney, and took a last look in his bag to check everything. "What have you got for dinner to-night?"

"Oh dear—Saturday. Do you mind a stew?" asked Daisy apologetically. "We could get something special in for you, if you liked."

"Stew's fine," said Sydney cheerfully, and was about to start up the stairs when Bicky came rushing down, hatted and coated, and tore past them out into the street, where she hailed a cruising taxi, leaped into it, and was whisked away in a proud clatter.

"Bicky!" cried Daisy, as the front door crashed open behind her. "Where are you going? Come back here this minute! That child! *What's* one to do with her? Look at her getting in that taxi! *Who's* going to pay for it? I *know* she hasn't got any money!"

Sydney pondered a moment and then shook his head reflectively.

"It's a problem," he admitted as he went up the stairs. "She gets more like you every day, Daisy; more like you every day."

"I'll take that up with you later," Daisy called after him, shutting the front door tenderly and feeling it to see if any of the panes had been shaken loose.

Upstairs, Sydney met Gerda coming out of Doreen's room, with Pynegar wielding an invisible sword of fire in the rear.

"Hullo, Sydney," said Gerda, giving him a hurried and rather self-conscious kiss on the cheek, "I'm just going out to buy Doreen a pound of shrimps and a bottle of Burgundy."

"You do, my girl," Sydney returned sternly, "and I'll wish triplets on you. How are you these days? Getting enough to eat?"

"Of course I am! What were you going to advise: brimstone and treacle?"

"Wouldn't hurt, wouldn't hurt at all," said Sydney, patting her and ambling past. "Morning, nurse; everything well in hand?"

"Yes, I think so, Doctor," said Pynegar in an unfamiliar voice of dulcet respect. "Temperature normal, but a tendency to restlessness; very adverse to exercise."

"She just threw a book at Dougall's head," supplied Gerda from the top of the stairs. "I think it was a Marie Stopes."

"I'd like a word with you, Doctor, before you go in," said Pynegar in a professional undertone.

"Very well," said Sydney accommodatingly. "What about?"

Pynegar glanced at the retreating Gerda and then at the bed-room door, as if the walls had ears.

"It's about the patient's husband."

"Ah," said Sydney.

"It'd simplify my duties more than I can say, if he could be persuaded to go for a walk in the park occasionally. To my certain knowledge he hasn't set foot out of that door for the last three days—except to cry Wolf."

"I'll speak to him," Sydney promised.

"Thank you," said Pynegar, with a kind of acid complacency.

Sydney opened the door of the bedroom and walked in.

Dougall stood by the window, doggedly clinging to his post. Doreen lay glowering at him, as if he had only to move an eyebrow to bring another book at his head. They both turned to Sydney with much the air of unhappy rabbits caught in a snare and awaiting doom.

"Well, *well*!" said Sydney, cheerfully disregarding their woe-begone expressions. "Another new day, and still no prodigy? I guess he missed the early stork and had to come by parcel post. Have you had breakfast, Dougall, my boy? You look hungry."

Dougall, who knew that the last thing he looked was hungry, said tersely, "I'm not. I ate."

"Good," said Sydney. "And now if you'll run along for a few moments, Doreen and I will read the minutes of the last meeting and compare a few notes."

75

Dougall stood his ground for a moment, a well-rehearsed speech all ready to be flung at Sydney. . . . "I think I'm entitled to know the gravity of the situation. I should be allowed to stay by my wife's side when matters of this seriousness are being discussed. I refuse to be kept in the dark!"

Instead he lost his nerve, as he always did when Sydney eyed him with that bright, intelligent eye, making him feel small.

"Okay," he said dispiritedly, and walked with leaden feet to the door.

"You don't have to take all day about it!" said Doreen waspishly.

He gave her a wounded look, and went out.

As he closed the door he heard her first words to Sydney.

"I want some fried shrimps and Burgundy," she said with quiet determination.

When he reached the bottom of the stairs, Wilfred came out of the dining-room and went into the sitting-room, where Daisy and Gerda were talking. He had to cross in front of Dougall, but ignored him so impersonally that for a moment Dougall wanted to kick him. Instead, he trailed into the sitting-room behind him docilely.

"Isn't it time to go home yet?" Wilfred asked bleakly, interrupting Daisy in the middle of a worried story about Bicky.

"Yes, precious, in a minute," said Gerda.

He sighed and strode over to the bookcase, making no attempt to conceal his boredom.

Dougall sank gloomily into the broken chair, and Daisy smiled benignly at him.

"Feeling happier now, dear? *That's* good!" she said wishfully. "Why not go for a little walk to the park and back? The fresh air'll do you *so* much good; you haven't been out for *days*."

"I was out yesterday," returned Dougall self-righteously.

76

"Well, it *seems* like days," Daisy compromised, and then, in an open appeal for moral support, "Gerda," she suggested brightly, "make him walk to the bus stop with you and Wilfred."

Wilfred slowly turned his face from the bookcase. "Are we our brother's keeper?" he inquired glassily.

"Oh well, never mind. It was only a suggestion," said Daisy, rebuffed.

"Don't worry," said Dougall with dignity. "I wouldn't disgrace the great Wilfred by walking on the same side of the street with him!" and with growing indignation, "or with any other misanthropic snerp who thinks it's disgusting to have babies!"

Wilfred eyed him with aloof condescension.

"Why does it follow I think it's disgusting, simply because I fail to go into mauldin ecstasies over an excessively dreary animal function?" he inquired coldly.

"Oh, don't let's start all that again!" said Gerda hurriedly, rising and taking Wilfred by the arm. "Let's go home."

Wilfred drew his arm away.

"As a matter of fact, seeing that you brought it up, I *do* think it's disgusting," he continued provocatively. "Any objections?"

"None," returned Dougall heavily, rising to the bait. "Everyone's entitled to his own opinions; but if that were mine, I'd jump in a lake!"

"Why, Dougall," said Wilfred, gently reproving, "you never had an opinion in the whole of your life, you middle-class monument to habit!"

"Wilfred," cried Daisy, dropping her olive branch and taking sides. "How could you? That's *unkind*!"

Dougall tried to look impervious, and made a big show of shrugging.

"Well, I'd sooner be a middle-class monument to habit than

a waterglass-egg genius," he said, trying to copy Wilfred's delivery. "At least I earn my own middle-class living!"

"Ha," said Wilfred with a tolerant smile, "there's that jealousy again. Copy-writing the glories of cathartics and pimple-removers isn't complete enough expression for your artistic little soul, so you ease it by belittling the unattainable; eh, Dougall?"

"Oh, stop it," begged Gerda. "You're both as bad as the other!"

"What do you mean 'both'?" said Wilfred superciliously.

"You needn't think I want to be classed with *you*!" Dougall replied hotly, groping for repartee equal to Wilfred's. "And I wish to God you'd find someone worthier of your brittle wit! I've had a belly-full of it!" He appealed to Daisy, in exasperated protest: "Every time he comes into this house. . . ."

A loud and unworthy noise froze him with surprise and outraged indignation.

Wilfred the thinker had blown a raspberry; even Daisy was stunned.

Spontaneously, Dougall blew another back, discovering to his secret gratification that he blew louder ones than Wilfred.

"Well, you're not going to solve anything by doing *that*!" said Daisy severely. "After all, you *are* married into the same family, for better or worse. . . ."

"For worse!" Wilfred assured her.

"I thought *I* was the one that made the obvious remarks?" Dougall commented ironically.

"Someone else still has to have made them first!" Wilfred made swift answer.

"Oh, stop it, *do*!" Daisy beseeched, her head having begun to swim. "Gerda, darling, for *goodness'* sake take him home; and Dougall, sit down and read the paper or something, but stop being so *jittery*!"

Dougall obeyed remorsefully, and Gerda speeded Wilfred on

his way to the hall. As he was picking up his hat, he called over his shoulder with a moderately good grace, " Good-bye, Daisy. No offence intended."

" Good-bye, Wilfred," returned Daisy with equal moderation. " Not very much taken."

" Come on," said Gerda firmly. " Good-bye, Mother. I hope Doreen does well for herself."

The front door closed on them, and Dougall leaned back on the sofa and scowled fearfully.

" My," he said with a certain pathos, " I'd like to take a sock at him," adding defeatedly, " if I thought it'd do any good."

He gazed apologetically at Daisy, who had moved to the window, and was gazing pensively out at the sky.

" I'm sorry, Daisy," he said sincerely. " I *do* try not to rise to him : I don't usually lose my temper, you know that. But he gets me so mad I don't know what to do with myself ! "

" Yes, dear, I know," said Daisy absently. " It's just a great pity, that's all, and a little hard on the rest of us."

" Rubbish, Daisy," said Sydney unexpectedly from the door, " you revel in it ! "

" I do *not* ! " said Daisy indignantly, drawing herself up in a stately manner.

At the sound of Sydney's voice Dougall had spun round, and now lolloped over to him with a face as careworn as a beagle.

" Is Doreen all right ? " he asked rapidly. " How long will it be now ? Is there any danger ? More than normal, I mean ? Do you think we ought to get another doctor in ; not in any way as a reflection on you, but just to be on the safe side ? "

" You can call in the whole of Harley Street, if it'll make you any happier," said Sydney accommodatingly, tucking his arm into Dougall's. " Though, as a matter of fact, she's doing fine, my boy, just fine. I couldn't say off-hand how long she still has to go before young Percy Pieface shows up—any time now, really—but she couldn't be in better shape. All over in ten minutes, once it starts." He turned Dougall's face to the light and examined it professionally. "H'm," he diagnosed. "Dilated pupil. Why don't you go for a nice swim, Dougall?"

"A *swim*?" echoed Dougall incredulously. "Me? *Now*?"

"Yes. It's only an hour by train to Brighton."

"To *Brighton*?"

"Well, a good movie, then," said Sydney persuasively.

"I don't want to go to a movie," said Dougall, a mulish note creeping into his voice.

"Why, Dougall, you know you just *love* movies!" Daisy put in brightly. "*Mickey Mouse*?"

"Not at the moment I don't," returned Dougall. "Not with Doreen in pain, alone up there!"

"She isn't alone. She's got Sydney, and Pynegar, and me," said Daisy practically. "And looking at it fairly and squarely, dear, no matter what sort of frenzy you lash yourself into, you can't *both* have that baby. So why not relax and let things take their natural course?"

"Jolly well put," said Sydney in approbation.

"I'm sorry," said Dougall, firm as a rock, "but I don't want to go out."

"Then let me put it to you this way," said Sydney, with the patience of Job. "As an unselfish favour, just to oblige everybody else in the house, will you go down to the pub and play darts for half an hour, just for the change of scene?"

"Now that's a *wonderful* idea," Daisy confirmed warmly.

"Why?" said Dougall slowly, backing away from Sydney and beginning to eye him with awful suspicion. "Why are you suddenly so anxious to get me out of the way?"

"What's sudden about it?" countered Sydney reasonably

"Something's wrong!" said Dougall, his worst suspicions confirmed. "Something's gone wrong and you won't tell me

what it is ! But I *insist* on being told ; I've a *right* to know !
I'm her husband, aren't I ? I *demand* to be told ! I *knew* something was . . ."

" If you *must* know the truth," announced Sydney bluntly,
" you're getting so much on Doreen's nerves that every minute
you're away at the pub's worth its weight in gold to her."

The truth rang clear enough to allay all Dougall's fears, and
he subsided meekly and rubbed his toe into a furrow in the
carpet.

" Well, I suppose if that's how it is," he said in a small, forlorn
voice, " I'd better go and play darts."

" Here," said Daisy generously, digging down into her bag,
" I've got *lots* of pennies. . . . At least I *did* have. . . ."

" That's all right, Daisy, I've got half a crown," said Dougall
forgivingly, and turned towards the hall with the noble air of
Sydney Carton going to his tumbril.

At the door he paused and added, rather timidly, " If anything
went wrong. . . ."

" Corder will ride like the wind to fetch you," Sydney promised.
" But we'll be becalmed till well into the stilly hours. It won't
take you all that time to best the champion."

Dougall produced a ghost of a smile and wandered sadly out.

" Well, *that's* a step in the right direction !" said Daisy, subsiding into her chair, and picking up her sewing-bag with a sigh
of contentment. " Now if only I can get five minutes to myself
before lunch, I'll be able to last through the afternoon. What
a day !"

" You're being deceptively calm about your approaching
grandmotherhood," remarked Sydney flatteringly.

" Don't be silly," said Daisy gaily. " I'm always calm about
important things—and why should I be anything else? You
brought all my children into the world." She paused to thread a
needle. " C.O.D.," she added sweetly.

" That's good, coming from you ! " said Sydney. " You still owe me four pounds ten on Bicky ! "

" Oh dear, Bicky ! " said Daisy, brought back to realities with a bump. " Sometimes I wonder where she'll eventually end up, Sydney. I really do."

" Leave 'em alone and they'll come home, wagging their tails behind them," said Sydney.

" *Will* they? It'd take a lot off my mind if I could really believe that. I don't think Gerda would. She's the one I'm really worried most about. I've thought something for a long time, Sydney; and to-day I made sure of it, just watching them. She's frightened of that horrid little Wilfred."

" Oh? " said Sydney, not fully impressed. " I wonder. If he wasn't trying his best, she'd probably walk right out of that flat and leave him to shift for himself."

Daisy gave him a pitying look.

" You're lucky you don't have to cover psycho-analysis in your branch of medicine," she observed disparagingly. " I'll tell you something you don't know about hypersensitive women who get a morbid fascination for people like Wilfred. The worse he got, the more she'd want to stay around and see how much worse he *could* get ! You can't tell me anything about my own son-in-law. I don't believe Wilfred has the feelings of a caterpillar."

" A caterpillar has feelings."

" No, it doesn't."

" I'm sorry to differ, Daisy, but it does."

" Well, this particular caterpillar *I'm* speaking of doesn't," said Daisy with a touch of asperity in her voice.

" There is no such caterpillar," said Sydney ruggedly.

Daisy shot him a look, and he chuckled amiably.

" Anyway," he added, " I remember when you were tickled to death because Gerda had got herself a genius."

" Everyone *said* he was a genius," Daisy defended herself.

" How was *I* to know it was just permanent adolescence? *I'm* not an old saw-bones ! "

The tranquillity of the house, so newly wooed, was suddenly blown asunder. Pynegar came running to the top of the stairs just as Roly dashed in through the front door and pelted up to Bicky's room. They met in mid-stair, and Pynegar's call for help was knocked back into her diaphragm.

" *Look where you're going !* " she grunted ferociously, and then, half over the banister : " Dr. Drew ! Please come at once, will you? I think the baby's started ! "

" Crumbs ! Already? " said Sydney, bouncing out of his chair. " Daisy, keep calm ! "

Daisy felt the first tendencies to panic creep over her. As Sydney disappeared, she rose and went into the hall, in time to confront Roly, having found his bird flown, bounding down the stairs again.

" Lady Buckering, where's Bicky? " he demanded tersely.

" She went out, " said Daisy, trying to brush him aside, gazing upstairs worriedly.

" Who with? " rapped Roly. " With whom? "

Daisy put her foot on the first step of the stairs and answered impatiently, " I don't know, " and then beseechingly, " Roly, some other time . . . things are *happening* ! "

Roly dug his fingers into his hat.

" If she went out with somebody else I *must* know who ! I'm deadly serious ! " he announced earnestly.

Daisy, exasperated too far, suddenly turned on him.

" She's out with a beautiful young man with a tip-tilt nose and a sense of humour, playing a cornet ! " she said irritably.

Roly smacked his forehead with his hand.

" His name ! " he cried. " Who is he? "

" I don't know, " said Daisy heatedly, " but he doesn't spend his life pulling wings off flies, so it must be a very nice change ! Now run along, will you, Roly ? The baby. . . ."

She began hurrying up the stairs ; but a long drawn-out banshee-wail from Roly arrested her, and she turned round in alarm.

His little face looked as if it would explode under the strain.

" Do you realise what he's *destroying* ? Do you realise how *far* it had gone ? " he roared unsteadily. " When I find him, I'll kill him ! I'll *kill* him ! "

He swung round and dashed out of the front door, all but breaking his neck as he took the front steps in two jumps.

" *Roly !* " cried Daisy, stabbed with misgiving. " Roly, come back ! Good heavens ! How far *has* it gone ? "

She was talking to the empty hall.

" Oh dear," she said, flustered and confused. " The silly little . . . what was happening when he interrupted ? . . . Doreen. . . ."

But there seemed no point in going upstairs now. She had better wait quietly in the sitting-room and sew, as Sydney had instructed.

How that boy shouted : her ears were still ringing from it. What on *earth* did Bicky see in him ?

She settled herself in her chair and picked up her sewing, then changed her mind, put it away, and took a sock out of the knitting-bag. She had hardly had time to start worrying it, however, when Corder entered with a catlike tread.

" When shall I serve lunch, milady ? " he asked.

Daisy started nervously.

" Oh, it's you," she said. " What ? Lunch ? Will it keep ? I don't want any, and I'm sure nobody else in the house does either, at the moment."

" Very good, milady," said Corder, " and the other thing was, I'd like to tender my notice."

" Oh ! " said Daisy blankly. " Aren't you happy here ? "

"I'm going into the Civil Service," said Corder, preferring to leave the other issue unanswered. "So if it won't inconvenience you, I'll leave to-morrow."

"Well, it will rather," said Daisy frowning, "but I suppose if you're going, you're going. Do I owe you a great deal of money?"

"Two weeks'. And I'd be very obliged if you could see your way to taking back those shares you gave me, and let me have a cheque for my full services, milady."

Daisy looked up from her knitting.

"Why? There's nothing the matter with the shares, is there?" she asked with a good try at insouciant innocence.

"I haven't checked yet, milady," said Corder smoothly. "It's only that an acquaintance of mine, also in domestic service, got caught with some shares just recently, and I wouldn't like to be in the same position. The Market isn't what it was, ma'am."

"Absurd. It was never better," returned Daisy with spirit.

Corder coughed again, without changing the smug obliqueness of his expression. His poker face got on her nerves, though she had hired him originally because of it; he had looked so like Charles Laughton that the distinction it lent him was worth the money alone.

"At the risk of differing from you, milady," he said politely, "anything not gilt-edged is a highly speculative venture for anyone, much less a butler. I wouldn't be surprised but that Mr. Magill will be no more successful with *his* shares than I would be with mine."

A wave of helpless displeasure caught hold of Daisy, as it always did when Corder overstepped his place. With all the coldness and severity she could muster, she said, "How do you know Mr. Magill has any shares?"

"One picks up snatches of conversation in the course of one's duties," replied Corder easily, "whether one wants to or not."

85

She sat very upright and raised her eyebrows. "I don't know what," she said forbiddingly, "you mean by that," weakening the effect somewhat by adding, "If the shares were good enough for Mr. Magill to accept, that should be good enough for most people, I would have thought."

Corder conceded her right to her own justifications by a civil incline of his head.

"Nevertheless, I would prefer a cheque instead of the shares, milady, if not too inconvenient," he said, with a great deal of quiet intimidation behind it.

"It won't be inconvenient at all," returned Daisy proudly, left with no alternative. "When you're ready to go, you can return the shares and the cheque will be ready for you." For a terrible moment she thought he would change his mind again and ask for cash, but he appeared satisfied.

"Thank you, milady," he said and withdrew.

She toyed uneasily with her knitting for a moment, then laid it down and sighed.

No peace for the wicked—though she wouldn't have called herself wicked. Her mind began darting about, pessimistically anticipating all the things ahead that could go wrong and make trouble. They hovered like a cloud of gnats in front of her. . . . Bicky . . . Doreen . . . Gerda . . . Cathleen . . . "leave them alone and they'll come home, wagging their tails behind them." . . . Corder, inscrutable, like the Chinese . . . perhaps he was a murderer, hiding in their house, and going out at night when the moon was full, killing strangers with a long, thin knife, which he hid in his mattress the rest of the time . . . right here in this house. And perhaps Magill would find the shares were illegal, and arrest her. . . . "*I'm sorry, madam, but we've got orders to place you under arrest* . . . "May I pack a small bag first?" . . . "*You won't need it, where you're going.*" . . . "But there's a baby being born; Doreen's. . . ."

Baby. Doreen. Good heavens !

She jumped to her feet and hurried to the hall to listen for noises, nearly colliding with Sydney, who was strolling casually into the sitting-room.

She gave a startled cry and jumped away from him.

"What's the matter? Did I scare you?" he asked solicitously.

"No, but how *quick* you've been !" said Daisy shakily.

"Doing what? Pynegar got me up there under false pretences, the befuddled old duck !" returned Sydney with professional contempt.

"Oh, did she?" said Daisy lamely. "Oh, she *did*? . . . Oh!"

He eyed her narrowly.

"Yes," he said at last. "A teaspoon of bicarbonate of soda in half a glass of warm water for you, my girl."

"That won't help my nerves !" Daisy answered tartly.

"I wasn't treating you for nerves, I was treating you for nervous indigestion," said Sydney, adding, as she drew herself up haughtily, "but if you want your nerves treated, you only have to say so."

"I do say so, then," said Daisy, only slightly mollified.

"Ah, well, then, in that case, take a teaspoon of bicarbonate of soda in half a glass of warm water." He patted her on one cheek affectionately, kissed her on the other, and trotted off into the hall for his hat and coat. "Bye-bye. See you at dinner."

"You dreadful old man," said Daisy, but she felt better already. Dear Sydney.

This Is Human Drama

WHEN Daisy had told Roly to his face, in so many words, that Bicky had made him a theoretical cuckold, he had fled the Buckering house with his mind a pretty to the Furies.

The idea of any other living man looking at Bicky twice, let alone attending upon her amorously, was something so fantastic that it had never before occurred to him to guard against it. That he himself felt an affinity for her, was one thing : there were reasons for that : it could be explained ; but Roly had always seen himself as a young King Cophetua making his light to shine upon the beggar-maid, secure in the conviction that to other eyes she was just another beggar-maid.

And now some furtive masher had come along, seen through the disguise of metaphorical rags, and tried to steal her.

It made him so angry that his stomach felt hollow.

Whoever the fellow was, he would thrash him to his knees, grind him underfoot and then jump on him, and Bicky would be there to see it.

Her treachery began to stun him with its magnitude ; her wicked, calculating deceit wracked him with disillusion.

All that show of tears and constancy had been a brazen façade, behind which she plotted and coquetted with other men !

Other men.

How long could it have been going on?

He shuddered, not even daring to estimate.

What a fool he had been ! How right his mother had been, and how much worse that made him feel !

Betrayed by Bicky Buckering. . . .

. . . "Betrayed by Bicky Buckering. . . ."

. . . *The Betrayal*, a 20th Century-Fox picture, starring Roland Wayne, with Vincent Price, Linda Darnell, and Maria Ouspenskaya.

"*Mr. Wayne played with a depth and intensity seldom before seen in the annals of motion-picture history. The preview audience rose to its feet at the conclusion, and gave the star an ovation unprecedented in the annals of motion-picture history.*"

Hot indignation swept aside this fleeting sedative; annihilated pride cried out afresh for vengeance.

He must be cold and calm and clear-thinking; plan every move; weave a net and ensnare them in it.

Too bad it couldn't be a duel with rapiers, by candle-light, in satin shirts, and neatly stockinged legs. Or in the cleared street of a mining town; Roly starting from one end and the masher from the other, while the population hid behind the bar-counters and walls.

Bang-bang-bang ! The masher's gun.

Bang ! Roly's gun. One deadly bullet, and then a running jump into his saddle and off across the purple sage into the technicolour sunset, while Bicky watched, blinded with tears, from an upstairs window of the saloon.

Wait till I lay my hands on that masher. I'll kill him.

He was not yet quite clear in his mind as to how one went about it, however. It was impractical to attempt to comb London for her right away; and her mother had craftily concealed her movements, fobbing him off with deliberately vague answers, making some feeble excuse about babies being born.

As if she had fooled him for a moment! Who? him? Roland Wayne, the man with the X-ray brain; the George Sanders of Grosvenor Square? Ha, ha.

He went home and cloistered himself in his study, aware that his mother was snuffing about in the hall outside, eaten away by curiosity.

A pox on her!

This was the birth of the great impasse, the Trojan siege between him and Bicky. . . . Bashing up that hat, and making an ass of him in front of all those silly jiggers! . . . this was no ordinary tiff! It was the knock-down, drag-out final battle for moral supremacy.

He flung himself back on the sofa again and breathed hard at the ceiling, studying strategies and devising tactics. He found his concentration seduced by vivid and spectacular mental panoramas, however. He could too easily envision the contrite and agonised Bicky sobbing uncontrolledly on her pillow; refusing food, and surrounded by a scared and anxious family; and though he hardened his heart against the unsettling vision, his conscience wasn't as easy as it ought to be, considering that she had brought it on herself, and would no doubt be the wiser for it in the end.

Next he saw her vainly calling him on the phone, and being told he was out to her, by Curtis the butler.

Her face was heart-breaking in its stricken woe, now. She stood at the phone, numb; then tried to whisper his name, but no sound came.

He rolled about uncomfortably, and half thought of going out to get a hair-cut; then, scornful of his own maudlin misgivings, began to think up magnificent chapters of his life to be, when he was married to a beautiful actress and lived in Beverly Hills, a star in his own right.

The vision was strangely lacking in realism for once. At the moment it felt as silly as if he had described it aloud in front of his mother.

Bicky came back into the picture.

She was standing in her bedroom, with a frozen, terrible expression on her face, and she held a small bottle of poison in her hand.

She was lifting it to her lips.

" *Roly,*" she cried brokenly.

There was a crash as he burst in through the door, knocked the bottle spinning harmlessly from her hand, and caught her unconscious body as she swayed into his arms, lowering her tenderly to the bed. . . .

He growled irritably and rolled over onto his stomach. His heart was beating very fast, he felt hot and stuffy, and severely contemptuous of himself; not that it helped. This is what *always* happened to him. He always weakened. He let the soppy, sentimental side get the better of him.

Not this time, though. He was darned if he phoned her, particularly after telling Curtis he was out to her. If he let himself down and *did* call her in the end, it certainly wasn't going to be before a couple of days: long enough to discipline her.

And he had made such a bungle of everything that morning, starting with the phone call. " Hullo ! " he should have said with impeccable *savoir-faire.* " This is Roland. I understand you told my mother I'd proposed to you. Is this true? . . . Never mind the ' buts,' that's all I wanted to know." *Click.*

Hanging up gave one a magnificent exhilaration; a sense of mastery and power. There was a special art in the timing of it, a question of split-second precision, or the effect was lost, even cheap. A fat lot of good, thinking of it now.

Bicky was back with the bottle of poison again.

This time nobody burst in the door; she drank it; and Roly

twitched spasmodically. She fell with a dull, heavy thud, and the bottle rolled away from her lifeless hand.

Exhibit A.

He stood facing the coroner's jury.

"*Yes, I drove her to it. I never thought she'd do it. Yes, if I'd telephoned her that night, she wouldn't have done it.*"

A monster; an outcast; people drawing away from him. . . .

Anyone'd think he was in love with her, instead of just going around with her. Just turned eighteen, and she's talking about marriage. What was he supposed to be, a cradle-snatcher?

Marrying an irresponsible kid like that.

Where would they live? Where was the dough coming from? Not from his mother, that was a certainty. A cheap flat in the suburbs, somewhere. She couldn't even fry an egg. He'd like to see the state of any flat she'd try to run, after a week of it. She was a helpless, unpractical baby-doll. Somebody had to be watching her all the time.

When he eventually did get around to marrying, it was going to be a gentle, responsible woman with grave-gay eyes and a knack of knowing just what to say and do to make him feel happy and appreciated. She would be famous in her own right, but would renounce her career to set up his home for him —a model home, with everything perfect; friend, wife, and lover. Not a little nit-wit who was always making him behave without dignity in front of people; and weeping, and tormenting herself and him at the drop of a hat.

He gave a groan of exasperation, rolled onto his back again, and began to read a novel wildly, skipping great paragraphs at a time.

CHAPTER TEN

This Is Human Melodrama

WHEN Bicky fled the Buckering house, her first intention had been to present herself at Roly's front door and have it out with him, then and there, and not stop till he was grovelling for forgiveness; but on the way in the taxi, discretion replaced valour; and when she reached Marble Arch, she changed her mind and went to the Regal, where she spent her last half crown on a good cry at Stewart Granger and stayed to see the supporting film too—a thing about an intelligent dog.

When she came out, it was four o'clock, and she felt aimless and rather small and futile; in no mood to lock horns with an impenitent Roly; so she strolled across Hyde Park in the direction of Gerda and Wilfred's. Primarily, she wanted to pour out her troubles to Gerda: they could have a good chat over tea, and then she could borrow her bus fare home; but there existed, besides, deep in Bicky's mind, a guarded respect for Wilfred, and it would be nice to see him for a minute or two.

She was always very quick to assure herself that this respect in no way meant she approved of Wilfred; there was something far too forbidding and conceited about him for that; nor did she endorse the indiscriminating way he condemned the whole family as beneath his notice; but often, on the rare occasions when he aired a view in their presence, she had felt herself respond intellectually to the logic of his reasoning.

She guessed that he probably thought her the dullest of the lot; but she had slowly developed a yearning to startle him one day by taking up the thread of one of his arguments and developing it with him on an equal mental footing.

She could visualise so clearly the mixture of surprise and grudging admiration on his face, soon giving way to respect and cordiality as he found himself matched against an opponent worthy of his mettle. The exact subject upon which they would debate was not wholly clear to her at the moment: abstract philosophy, or metaphysics, no doubt. That she knew nothing of either, dismayed her not at all; she was sure that once she was into her stride, she would talk spontaneously and enlightenedly, the cynosure of all and any other eyes present at the time.

It was a side of her that would never be brought out by Roly . . . but then, he was different: he was unique and beyond the pale, taking the habits and form of man merely as a convenience; and no matter how she hated him one minute, she couldn't live without him the next; and she knew their souls were so beatifi-cally unified that the greatest dread of all was that life wouldn't be long enough, and she would die still wanting to be loved by him as idealistically and desperately as she did now.

Such a love it was ! . . . a great unmanageable balloon of an emotion, dragging them this way and that at its whim and will; overpowering their attempts to control and guide it. Such a love had never been before; such a spiritual intensity had never been anybody's but theirs . . . a spirituality almost too bright and fierce for their mortal clay.

Perhaps it would eventually burn them up; like radium did.

How awful it was that no one understood that; except her, and sometimes Roly, in brief flashes.

The responsibility of it could sometimes be very crushing.

And how simple everybody else's lives were. Other people went about their little problems with all the egoism and fuss of tugboats, with glib and pat answers for everything, neatly docketed, all ready to be popped at you platitudinously; as if a little bottle of pills was all that was needed to cure the ills of the universe.

Nobody except Bicky really understood the terrifying vastness of the universe. Sometimes she was convinced that her spirit often soared up into the spheres, serene and all-wise, and looked back down to where the earth flickered like a pin-prick in a mighty nothingness; and she would be filled with a compassion and a pity for the people who ran about so busily, no more important than ants, thinking that the world began and ended with what they could see and hear in the course of a day.

She found herself outside Harrods, and came out of her reverie at the sight of a black strapless evening gown in the window.

There it was; made for her, and some little upstart bureaucrat's daughter would get it instead, and look like an overflowing sack of potatoes in it.

She ordered herself to dismiss it and move on, but instead, was irresistibly impelled to go in and try it on.

She would tell them quite frankly that she was only looking around, and had no intention of buying anything.

Harrod's soothed her: inside its portals she felt at home, in her natural environment.

As she went up in the lift she pretended she was Mrs. Harrod and had come in to take anything she fancied. How pleasant it was when the shop girls all hurried up and competed with each other. . . . " *Good morning, Mrs. Harrod!* " . . . " *Excuse me, your Highness, but I'll have to leave you for a moment—Mrs. Harrod has just come in and she always likes me to wait on her. . . .*"

She walked into the department with such an air of unconscious majesty that she was treated with instant respect, and it was nearly six when she regretfully climbed back into her tweeds and departed. She was hungry now, and had begun to worry about Roly again. Her first impulse was to hurry home as fast as she could to learn how many times he had called while she was out; but pride stayed her. Let him go on calling. Perhaps by evening he would have had time to cool down and regret the exhibition he had made of himself that morning.

She turned and set off for Gerda's flat.

As she set out for the King's Road, Fate moved its inexorable finger, and Roly, on his way home from his haircut, sped by her in a taxi. She passed so close that he could have leaned out of the window and caught her arm; and in a flash his brain became cold, clear and calm. He stopped the taxi, paid the fare with jittering fingers, and scrambled out onto the pavement outside the Knightsbridge Tube entrance.

A moment later Bicky felt herself caught masterfully by the arm and brought to a halt.

"I've been looking all over for you!" said Roly sharply, nearly scaring her out of her wits.

"I'm sure I don't know why!" she returned haughtily, recovering her poise. "And are you in the habit of shouting at people in the street as if you were in the privacy of a house?"

"Who's this masher?" returned Roly succinctly.

"What masher?" said Bicky coldly.

"All right, relax, Miss Garbo," said Roly with biting sarcasm. "You know who I mean! The squirt you're running around with! And don't think I don't know all about him, in case you still want to fence! Your own mother told me about him!"

"Really, Roland; I think you're dangerously insane," returned Bicky with a pitying smile.

"I'm giving you one chance," said Roly menacingly. "Are you going to tell me who this squirt is?"

" No ! " said Bicky fiercely. " And kindly move out of my way ! "

" Okay ! " said Roly. " If that's how you want it to be ! But you're not so smart ; nobody can make a fool of *me* and get away with it ! I'll find out who that squirt is and when I find him I'll break his neck. Do you follow me ? And I hope you're there to watch ! "

At this incomprehensible outburst, Bicky gave him one searching look of supreme contempt.

" Is that all ? " she asked coldly.

" Yes ! " said Roly.

" Then good-*bye* ! " said Bicky, and walked away.

He stood quite still and watched her.

At the next crossing she was unable to resist a furtive look over her shoulder, but seeing him still gazing at her, she stiffened and quickened her step.

He stood scowling at a pillar-box a moment longer, while his good self battled with his bad self and retired beaten ; then, with a professional *élan* that would have done Humphrey Bogart credit, he began to shadow his erstwhile beloved.

CHAPTER ELEVEN

This Is The Villain

WHEN Wilfred Marks was ten, his father, who was a lawyer, was shot and killed on his way home from his offices by an emotionally unstable Ulster laundry-man against whom Mr. Marks had obtained a conviction for starving his horse.

On the money from the estate, Wilfred had been sent to a good private school. When the money ran out, his aunt saw him through an inexpensive college. His aunt was a recluse who made rugs all day; and Wilfred, feeling himself beholden to no man, had come to London prepared to make the world hear from him.

He had an excellent classical education, no creative instinct, and a cold and bitter mind which, though brilliant, worked like a light-house. For every moment of intermittent brightness, in which he gazed forth upon the world, there was an equal moment of blackness, in which he saw nothing but the strange and haunted images of his own imagination, without knowing the difference.

This gave him what he thought was a superiority complex, and what Sydney had recognised as a sadder thing, a persecution complex.

He was tall and thin, not handsome; but his superficial self-assurance and aloofness gave him a sort of attractiveness to the easily-awed. He appeared, too, to have an utter detachment, as if there were no room in the flower of his brain for anything except his genius. He had chosen Gerda because she was the perfect example of conventional ordinariness, the exactly suited contrast to him, lending a decorative value to his legend. He sincerely believed that he needed, and was able to feel, affection; he even persuaded himself that the condescending attentions he showed to Gerda were the gestures of a warm and sensitive regard for her. He liked, when talking of his youth, to imply that those early nightmare years had destroyed all love and pity in him for anything except himself; but this was for the gratification of being argued out of it—if he could have suspected even remotely that he was stumbling on the truth, his whole world would have shattered about his ears.

He had courted Gerda with high-sounding analyses and social maxims, and Gerda, hungry for distinction and culture, had been as enamoured of it as if he had waltzed her to the " Blue Danube " and kissed her on a petal-strewn balcony by moon-light. She saw Wilfred as an Aldous Huxley come to judgment, a presence who would lead her by the hand out of her humdrum existence to the heights. She obeyed and believed in him uncon-ditionally, saw all his faults as facets of his genius, and so dazzled herself with her own concept of him, that she had no chance of learning either what he really was, or what she really thought of him.

She lived like a sleep-walker balanced on a wall, secure while she slept but in danger if she woke; and even now her sleep was fitful and disturbed.

While Bicky was walking blissfully from Sloane Square into the King's Road, Gerda was alighting from a bus in Finchley Road, from whence she made her way back to Daisy's house. A thin fog had rolled in from Hampstead and the lights were blinking on in the houses when she went up the front steps and pushed the front door open.

Daisy's voice came from the sitting-room in resigned anxiety.

"Bicky, is that you?"

"No, Daisy," said Gerda, taking off her coat. "It's me again."

Daisy came into the hall with a handful of darning trailing at her side, and in the middle of saying a cheerful hullo, noticed that Gerda was oddly quiet, and felt a quick sense of concern.

"Why, Gerda!" she said, closing the door and drawing Gerda into the light, "What's the matter?"

"I'm tired, that's all," said Gerda briefly.

"You've been crying," said Daisy gently. "Gerda, what is it? Is it Wilfred?"

Gerda shook her head and looked away.

"I'll be all right when I've had a cup of tea," she said evasively. "Can I use your powder?"

"Of course. You'll find everything you want in my room," said Daisy warmly. "Is there anything I can do to help?"

Gerda shook her head, gave her a quick impulsive kiss on the cheek, and went upstairs to the bedroom. Daisy puttered indecisively in the hall for a moment, and then followed.

Gerda was sitting at the dressing-table, making a half-hearted attempt to look at ease.

"I can't do anything with my hair," she said when Daisy came in. "It's like string."

"It looks wonderful," returned Daisy. "Is that the new rinse you were telling me about?"

Gerda nodded and took her comb out of her bag.

Daisy stood looking at her with such obvious concern that her reserve suddenly dissolved, and taking out her cigarettes, she said quite conversationally, "I'm rather on Wilfred's nerves."

"Yes?" said Daisy.

"I've worked it out," said Gerda with a little rush, trying to keep the feeling out of her voice. "I've made a failure of my marriage. And I can't leave him : that's the terrible thing. I *ought* to leave him. I'm not right for him. I've been holding him back." She was careful to make it a simple and flat statement of fact.

"Has he said so?" asked Daisy evenly.

"No. But he didn't have to." She looked at Daisy with a wounded, deep humiliation in her eyes. "It's obvious, isn't it? He *isn't* getting on."

"Are you sure it's your fault?" asked Daisy directly.

"Who else's could it be?"

"It could be his," said Daisy, though she knew it was her duty to keep impartial.

Gerda shook her head with unassailable conviction.

"No," she answered with a protective note coming into her voice. "There *is* something there . . . a sort of fitful fire. . . . He couldn't be so *sure*, if there wasn't," and then, as if it were vital that Daisy be persuaded it was so, "If you took away his sureness, there wouldn't be anything."

Daisy considered this a moment, and then observed, "There'd have to be something."

"Not with Wilfred," Gerda insisted, half anxiously, as if the disproving of her logic would leave her with no way to turn. "He's built his whole life round what he's *going* to be. And he can't do it alone. Nobody's ever done it alone, have they?" She paused, and dropped her voice to a quieter key. "I ought to be helping . . . and I'm no help."

"It's not going to be easy," thought Daisy. "Not a word against Wilfred." She sat on the corner of the bed.

"You're still very much in love with him?" she said at last. Gerda looked at her and nodded, and then looked away again. "Or are you in love with what he's going to be?" No, that was too blunt; she shouldn't have said that. . . . But Gerda had accepted it gravely, and answered quite naturally. " That too, of course," and her eyes betrayed some of her loneliness and bewilderment for a second.

" Has he ever been . . . do you think he's interested in someone else?" asked Daisy at last, and it was clearly the last thing she should have asked, because suddenly Gerda regained her authority, and answered almost lightly, " Oh, *no*, Daisy ! He isn't like that at all ! His work's the only thing that means anything to him . . . his writing !"

Daisy wisely left this uncontested, and wracked her brain for a gentler approach. Strangely enough, it was Gerda who supplied it, for, unprompted, she suddenly said, " I thought, once, that he needed other things to turn to. I was wrong."

" Why were you wrong?"

" I was going to have a baby," said Gerda, in a funny, hard little voice, and looked over her shoulder out of the window. " I knew he hated babies, but I was sure our own would be different. . . . That it'd fill something inside his heart that needed to be filled."

She stopped short, and then added almost harshly, " I didn't have any right to think that."

" What do you mean?" asked Daisy, filled with sudden misgiving.

" He made me——" began Gerda, and then lost courage and stopped. Then, more afraid of remaining silent than speaking, she went on hurriedly and unsteadily, " No, he didn't *make* me . . . it *had* to be done . . . but they didn't give me any anaesthetic . . . and something went wrong."

She turned to Daisy, almost childlike in her earnestness. " I *did* try not to make a fuss, Daisy, I swear I did. I knew that it was all my fault, and I was being punished for it . . . but it hurt so much. I used to *have* to cry sometimes; or I'd have screamed instead . . . it wasn't done right, you see . . . we had to go back a week later. . . . But it got on his nerves; he went away one week-end, because he couldn't work, because I was on his nerves."

"Who was with you?"

"Nobody. It was only for two days. There was plenty of food, and I could have called to the woman upstairs if anything had gone wrong." She paused and then added in a small voice, "It was just that I was frightened at night. I thought that if I died, there wouldn't be anyone near."

"Why didn't you tell me?" begged Daisy, almost in tears.

"You have enough trouble with the rest of them! . . . It's nothing to worry about, Daisy. It's all over now. Talking about it has made it something I can begin to see more clearly. I just needed a shoulder to cry on."

She got up and went to the window, her face in shadow, and finally smiled a little self-consciously.

"I don't think it's as simple as that," returned Daisy with expressive feeling, still aghast at what she had heard. "Are you sure you don't want to leave him, Gerda?"

Gerda gave her a brief, positive nod.

"Even though it might turn out to be the best thing for both of you?"

"I can't be sure of that," said Gerda inaudibly. "I can't leave him, because he—he really needs me. . . . In his own kind of way, without knowing it . . . as much as I need him."

"Suppose *he* left *you*?"

Gerda drew herself up defensively, as if Daisy had trespassed onto forbidden ground.

"That'd be different," she answered at last.

"I think it's something you ought to bear in mind," Daisy said steadily. "It's something that needn't be allowed to happen."

"He'd come back again, even if he did," said Gerda at last, as if it had been a struggle to discover a convincing reason. "It wouldn't be because of another woman, you see. It'd only be because he was trying to work out something. He'd come back in the end."

"You're very sure he's not interested in other women," said Daisy, unreassured.

"I almost wish it *was* another woman. That sounds phoney, doesn't it? I didn't mean it quite that way. . . . But other women: I'd be able to *cope* with that. It'd be. . . ." She tried to grasp for words, but they eluded her. " . . . . it'd be matter-of-fact, and *ordinary*. I'd almost welcome it."

"Oh no, you wouldn't," said Daisy sadly.

"I think I would," Gerda said, unconvinced. "After all, Daisy, I *am* ordinary. That's what's been wrong all the time. . . . . I've tried to pretend I wasn't."

"My hat!" said Daisy stoutly. "If anybody's ordinary! . . . Well, if Wilfred's extraordinary, there's a lot to be said for being the opposite! Oh dear, Gerda; I'm such an old fuddle-bag. I'm not being at *all* the wise mother who knows just what to say. . . . It's not that I'm afraid of interfering, either; because if I thought you were being made unhappy, I'd interfere like twenty charladies armed with brooms, and bang about like one o'clock till things were straightened out. But at least I *do* love you, my darling; and we'll sit down and see what we can make of things. I'll go and make you a nice cup of tea, and you can curl up in here with a book or something if you like; and I'll just potter about, and if you need me, I'll be just round the corner. . . . I'm glad you're here, anyway, for moral support . . . so you don't have to rush away, or anything; just make yourself cosy, my love. Everything will work out, you know . . . it always does. It's amazing what the human system can stand up against, and survive, and even thrive on!"

She smiled, and kissed Gerda, and Gerda smiled and returned the kiss gratefully; but when she was out in the passage on her way to see about the tea, a sharp, uncomfortable pain dug at her heart . . . partly sympathy for Gerda, but partly an awful, shameful terror that it was really all her own fault in the beginning for not having given Gerda a safer and more stable upbringing. . . . . All that insecurity, and no real discipline in the running of the house . . . and no father. . . .

" Oh dear, oh dear, Gerda," she thought to herself miserably, " have I bungled it for you too ? "

CHAPTER TWELVE

This Is A Regrettable Incident

WILFRED was at his typewriter in the middle of a realistic and sober intrusion into the realms of James Joyce, whose style was for the moment his beau ideal in his unflagging pilgrimage to the heights of literary prowess.

The front door-bell pealed stubbornly through the pall of his inspiration; and much aggrieved, he dragged himself away from his masterwork.

When he saw Bicky on the doorstep his first reaction was one of irritation.

" Hullo," he said ungraciously, " looking for Gerda ? "

" Yes I was," said Bicky.

" She's not here."

" Oh. Did I interrupt you at your writing, Wilfred ? "

" I *was* writing," Wilfred admitted aloofly.

" Oh, I *am* so sorry ! What a bore ! You must be madly fed up with me ! I know if one breaks a train of thought it's absolute death to try to get it back ! "

" Oh, well," said Wilfred, not anxious to create the impression that he had struggled too hard for noble syntax, " it's not as bad as all that. Do you want to come in and wait for Gerda ? I don't know where she's gone. Wives never bother to tell husbands these little things. Shove your things on that table. Have you had tea?"

"No!" said Bicky, following him into the cupboard they used as an entrance hall. "Shall I make you some, Wilfred?"

He privately doubted her ability to make anything as complicated as a decent cup of tea, and shook his head in dismissal of the idea. He had unbent a little, however, at the sound of the respect and desire to ingratiate in Bicky's voice; and being prey to a mood of nagging inner discontent, the cause of which evaded him, decided that he could do worse than exchange a few desultory minutes of small talk with his sister-in-law, who, if addle-pated, was at least comely to the eye.

"I've got a drop or two of sherry somewhere," he said. "We can kill that. What brings you into this part of the world? The last I saw of you, you and that little twit Roly something-or-other were trying to wring each other's necks."

Bicky drew a pained breath. "I'd just as soon not talk about him, if it's all the same to you, Wilfred," she said, speaking in the hushed tones of a mourner for someone long since gone.

Wilfred eyed her caustically and fetched the sherry from a cupboard. The basement was divided into two rooms, both as dark as crypts and permanently cold, and a kitchen and bathroom had been casually attached to the area in the rear, at the bottom of the ventilating shaft of the houses above. The smaller room served as Wilfred's study, and the larger as the living-sitting-bedroom for them both. It was furnished with old scrap, painted olive green, and lined with rickety bookshelves and reproductions of modern art. There was a large box-spring in one corner, covered with a dyed hessian spread in the daytime, and strewn with damp and lumpy cushions; an old Victorian armchair, covered with the same hessian; and a mirror with somebody's Stout and Ale engraved across it. The lamps were made of bottles, and the lamp-shades had liqueur labels glued haphazardly over them as decor. Over the fireplace were two battered duelling pistols, a particularly unlovely piece of Staffordshire of little girls holding hands, and a small wax mask, apparently Japanese, which squinted and had two teeth missing. Under it Wilfred the wag had pencilled, " *Rain. No Play*." Above the door to his sanctum was a card which read, " Abandon All Dope Ye Who Enter Here," and in the sanctum itself was a desk made of packing-cases, another box-spring covered with more hessian and damp cushions ; a long low chest with two brass candlesticks upon it ; a chest of drawers scraped to suggest natural oak, and more bookshelves. The walls were covered by charcoal drawings of nudes done by a friend who was a genius, soon to be recognised by the art world, but at the moment hard put to raise the price of his conté. The nudes were of both sexes, though in many cases it was difficult to define which ; and where more than two shared a composition, their arms, legs and charivari wound up in places that were anatomically unpardonable.

It was into his sanctum that he was now gracious enough to usher Bicky, pulling the hessian curtain across the door to complete the illusion of detached retreat from the mundane world without. A gas-fire hissed morbidly in the corner, giving the room the advantage of a fuggy humidity as opposed to the icy discomfort of the other one, and Wilfred's deathless prose lay scattered in austere grandeur about the desk.

" *Oh !* " said Bicky worshipfully, " is that the new book, Wilfred ? "

She approached the desk respectfully, and gazed with awe upon the disgruntled typescript.

Wilfred, warming at once, nodded offhandedly. " It's still in the rough," he said, in the benign tones of God belittling the solar system, " and I suppose it's going to be too obscure for most of the prodnoses who call themselves publishers."

"What's it about?" asked his admirer. "Would I *be* too stupid to understand it?"

"I don't see why," said Wilfred with lofty magnanimity. "It's not as if I was some Bloomsbury snob who was *trying* to be obscure. It's actually the flow of subconscious in a half-wit stable-hand's mind, at stud."

"Oh," said Bicky, going a little pink in spite of her worldly poise; and to save face, sipped her sherry and asked in the impersonal accents of the true literateur, "could I read a little of it, or don't you like people to see anything before you've absolutely finished it?"

"Well, as a matter of fact, I don't usually," Wilfred admitted, "but I'll read you a bit that's pretty well polished and ready for all comers."

"Oh *thank* you, Wilfred!" cried Bicky, deeply flattered. "Where shall I sit? Here?" She scrambled onto the boxspring and tucked her legs under her; and Wilfred pontifically sorted the riff-raff on the desk till he came across the passage he sought, then sat facing her, drained his sherry, and threw her a cigarette.

"I have to explain," he said almost kindly, "that it's the *flow* that you have to concentrate on; not the actual juxtaposition of words themselves. It's the concerted sum-total of the sounds and thoughts that make the picture." He paused and refilled her sherry glass from the bottle.

"Oh, I oughtn't," said Bicky contritely.

"Oh, go on," said he. "May as well finish what's there."

"But I don't like to drink up all your sherry. It's a waste."

"You may as well have your nip of it as anyone. Gluxman'll polish it off if we leave any, and Gluxman's a scrounger. He did those drawings."

"Yes, I know. I remember you telling me. They're awfully good."

"*I* think he's got something."

" I love that one over there."

" Oh yes, that one. The woman's a bit false, though. I mean, the abdominal muscles—they're too exaggerated. Of course he was trying to capture the spasmic. He's got it in the man all right; but I think he missed in the woman. Too slick . . . not enough depth. That's his one flaw. He'll have to watch it, when he's successful."

" I *do* see what you mean ! "

" He's going to do a series of line engravings for this book when it's finished."

" How *wonderful*, Wilfred ! "

" Abstract, of course."

" Yes, of course."

" Well; this is the bit where the stableman's piling manure, and the woman comes out of the house and brings him a stoup of ale." . . . " ' Cucumber cucumber thudding thudding hot boots steaming downright horse blanket fleas bloody fleas here fleas there and the sky down derry and a derry derry down ninepence tenpence change from two shillings cucumber dandle down dandle down plums plums wasps sting rabbits bobbing hot boots steaming. Door door door—knob knob here knob there cucumber. Oh the fine scent of it oh the rich muck and the beer and the beer dry gullet dry gut she comes with the beer with the beer with the beer barefoot huge feet fat legs apron : apron bursting with autumn laugh teeth laugh teeth cucumber plums wasp nest : nest nest pump beer who but a fool aye who am I but a fool nay no fool off apron off apron hay hay hay hay : handle tight fork deep hot boots steaming plums.' How do you like it, so far ? "

Bicky, divining that the last, being a question, could not be in context and therefore must be addressed to her, nodded warmly.

" It's wonderful, I can see the whole thing," she said earnestly.

"Have another sherry," invited Wilfred, with increasing cordiality.

"No, really, thanks."

"Oh, come on. It won't kill you. You can hold your drink, can't you?"

"Of course I can!" said Bicky, caught on a point of deep pride, and dismayed at the prospect of being considered a green adolescent instead of a mature woman of the world. Two glasses of sherry had seemed dashing enough, and one more than she had ever tackled at one sitting before; but to refuse the third would be to relegate the intellectual mood of the afternoon to the nursery. Would Wilfred read advanced literature to someone who had just reminded him that she was barely out of school? No. She held out her glass, and Wilfred filled both their glasses from the bottle and shot his own drink down his neck with an easy, care-free toss of the wrist.

Bicky followed suit.

The room quivered spasmodically before her eyes for a moment, like a reflection in water that suddenly wobbled, and her stomach felt very warm indeed.

"I think it's wonderful that you're reflecting the times we live in," she said profoundly. "So few writers are doing it, or even attempting it, are they? And it's the most terrific period of the world's history—at least, so I would have thought—I mean, it's a world revolution, isn't it? Not only politically, but socially and morally. I mean, we, as a race, are facing as enormous a change as the jellyfish did before they developed into the next stage. And nobody's writing about it, except you, Wilfred. No, I *mean* it: most writers are either flummoxed by it, or just get cynical and say we're all going to go up in smoke. I mean, look at the condition of the theatre, and films. I mean, they're so far behind the times that they don't reflect realism any more! That's why I think it's so wonderful that you're sitting there, getting on with your work; saying something *about* life at the moment: not skirting it, or rehashing stale old stuff that the reactionaries wrote before we were born, I mean."

Wilfred looked at her with conflicting feelings. Though much of what she said was meticulous re-editing of his own rhetoric, he was startled to find that she had absorbed so much of it. By the same token, however, the last thing in his mind was to tackle anything so ferocious as the literary recording of the tempo of his times, which appalled and nauseated him; and certainly one had to stretch a point to find topical social comment in the subconscious flow of a broody stable-hand with his mind on beer and stud.

He was nothing if not open-minded, however; and it now occurred to him that perhaps hot boots and steaming cucumber might indeed be significant ciphers, and as good a comment as any on the swivel-witted hari-kari the world seemed drunkenly intent upon committing.

"Ah," he said with restraint. "There's a lot in what you say. It's a pretty vast canvas, of course. One feels one's facing a Herculean task . . . like cleaning out the Augean stables."

"That's *exactly* it!" said Bicky enthusiastically. "The Augean stables. That's *exactly* what the world's like to-day! Bureaucracy *everywhere*! Third-rate leaders pushing the first-rate brains about and stifling them, and cutting off their own noses to stop the dustbin smelling!"

"I didn't know you took all this interest in civics," said Wilfred, with unwilling admiration.

"Oh," said Bicky loftily, "I don't talk like this at *home* much! They wouldn't know what I was getting at, poor dears!"

"I can hardly visualise Dougall lending an enthusiastic ear," admitted Wilfred, finding himself warming towards his sister-in-law, and observing her as a woman for the first time. "What I don't see is, if you're intelligent and serious about things, how you can put up with that little squirt that's always yelling the place down!"

"That was just a very unfortunate interlude," Bicky explained earnestly. "It's all over, I *assure* you, Wilfred. It belongs to what I call my transition period."

"Ah," said Wilfred, "and now you're safely through it?"

"I won't say there isn't room for improvement," said Bicky fairly, "but I *am* going forward; and Roly isn't. I don't know why, because the boy has some very sterling qualities; but he just doesn't seem to co-ordinate."

"Why should he?" said Wilfred. "He's rich, isn't he?"

"Yes, I know; but he has sterling qualities in *spite* of it."

"He's an obsolete adhesion to a worn-out social pattern," said Wilfred informatively. "If ever I saw the Œdipus complex, diluted with dill-water, he's it. He's a typical case. The fault lies in the mother. Smother-love; it's a privilege of the idle classes. A nit-witted woman hooks a man because he's a rich catch, by lying and ogling and pretending to love him, when all the time she'd sooner play with snakes. What happens on the nuptial night? She'd have been better off with snakes. She takes a violent revulsion to all sex, and stops it if she can, and submits mutinously if she can't. A child is conceived, more by bad luck than judgment—but also to insure the woman against desertion or divorce—and her natural sexual passion, which should have been absorbed by her husband, is poured onto the offspring. He gets a frustrated, mature, carnal love instead of a motherly one; his ma is so wildly possessive that she can't keep her fingers off him; always hugging and kissing and rubbing him up and down. She's his best pal. There's no secrets between them. They snigger and giggle and talk grown-up like two backward shopgirls out on Bank Holiday without drawers; and by the time he gets to puberty, his own sex development has been smothered by his mother, and never even gets a start. He'll never go near another woman, or want to behave like a natural healthy animal, because subconsciously his system has revolted at his mother's domination, and he hates all physical contact with women. That Roly is a potential pansy. I don't say he'll ever actually *be* one, but it would be just as well for him if he was: it's half a dozen of the one and six of the other: active or non-active, he's a poof just the same, with a mind doomed to permanent atrophy. A drone, a capon, a eunuch, a sissy. No wonder he's a mass of neurosis and hysterics. I dare say you find me blunt, but a spade's a spade, and the sooner the world looks at it that way, the fewer biological freaks will impede the development of the species. What use is Roly to any community? None. Take away his money, and what could he do? Sweet bugger-all; except suck up to old ladies and be a high-toned gigolo; like those Mittel-Europe misfits that rich American women adopt—Count Sagbag von Tikkeltitzen, pride of Montmarte; all kinds love made, fees cash, gold cigarette case in advance."

Bicky gazed at him in open wonder, her eyes as large as florins; and conscious of the rapt attention he was commanding, Wilfred rose and fetched a bottle half-full of vermouth, and off-handedly filled their glasses while he talked.

"The social structure is built on humbug and ignorance," he said, taking the broad view. "And where does it all start? In childhood. Read Nietzsche. Read Schopenhauer. All the damage is done before they're twelve years old. Ignorance. No problems explained. Babies come in little black bags, and it's wicked to peep at papa's tea-pot through the bathroom keyhole. Everything's hush-hush. Sex is wicked. The doctrine of original sin, no less; right here in this day and age of progress and reason. Look at me. I learned the facts of life behind W.C. walls, from scruffy, sniggering little morons. It couldn't have been more unsavoury and unappetising. It's a wonder I'm not as foxed-up as your Roly; except that I had a solid streak of common sense and a desire for logical answers. Has Daisy ever had a real heart-to-heart about the facts of life with you?" Bicky shook her head bewilderedly. "No, I thought not. I suppose *your* mind is a fuzzy tangle of confused half-truths and misinformation; just like ninety per cent of everyone else's. I tell you, it's the major crime of our social system. It's the cause of the inferiority complex; and the inferiority complex is the sire of the persecution complex; and that's what caused social conflict; and social conflict has caused wars and famines. Tell me, Bicky, have you ever asked yourself if you're really honest with yourself?"

"I've tried to," confessed the whirring Bicky.

"And what was the answer?"

"I *think* I am," she said without much confidence.

"Ah! Well, that's a healthy sign, anyway. But you're *not* honest with yourself. No one is. We're all humbugs of one sort or another—the good, the bad, and the lily-livered. The bad are nearest to honest, because they don't pretend to the moral rectitude that the good and the lily-livered do. Here, have some more vermouth; it won't hurt you. No; go on; there's lots here for me. And grab a cigarette. Everyone in life is a semi-failure. Why have they failed? Because theoretical perfection doesn't exist, even as theory."

"You're not an agnostic, I hope?" said Bicky tentatively.

"God, no! An agnostic is just a coward who can't look at the firmament without getting vertigo. No, no, I accept God. Obviously He's right in the long run, because He made the earth, so He knows how it has to operate; but who's going to get the chance of seeing how it operates in the long run? Stop me if I start getting too deep."

"You're not a *bit* deep," Bicky assured him rapidly. "I know *just* what you mean, Wilfred!"

" You see, I've been through the phases of disillusion, and lack of confidence in life *and* myself, and having no object or ambition; and I've got over shallow cynicism, and cults and philosophies, and now I'm *me*: Wilfred Marks, no more and no less. I answer to myself. That means I can't hoodwink myself like other people can. I cannot rest until I've pursued truth to its highest common denominator. In short, I am no longer trapped in permanent adolescence. The same is not true of Roly."

" Will it be true of me? " asked Bicky anxiously.

" Ah," said Wilfred, reserving judgment, " that depends on you."

" I don't *want* to be permanently adolescent ! "

" The principal symptom is that you would never know you were."

" Then I haven't got it? "

" Never, while you're prepared to listen to the still, cold voice of reason."

" Can we have *lots* of talks like this, Wilfred; so that I can develop my mind and not let it go to seed? "

" Well, as a matter of fact, you're jolly bright for your age, Bicky. I'll confess that you've surprised me. This is a side of you I hadn't suspected."

" I've never had a chance to talk to you like this before," Bicky pointed out with only a slight note of reproof.

" No, that's true. And you're through with Roly for good, eh? "

" *Absolutely* ! "

" Ah ! Well, what'll you do about a soul-mate, then? It's not natural for a girl of your age *not* to have some kind of soul-mate."

" I'll get someone who's intelligent this time ! "

" They don't grow on trees."

"You find me someone, then, Wilfred. You're the wisest person I know. I never knew anyone as wise as you."

"Too bad Gerda doesn't see eye to eye with you," said Wilfred with saturnine mystery.

"Why?" asked Bicky in surprise. "Doesn't she think you're wise?"

"Not so as you'd notice."

"Maybe she just doesn't say so."

"Frankly," said Wilfred, in a sudden burst of intimate confidence, filling Bicky's glass, "not to go further than you and I, the marriage couldn't be more of a dismal flop."

"Oh, I *am* sorry," said Bicky in distress, weaving a little as she leaned back, and noticing a tendency on the part of the room to swim about slightly.

"I'm the wrong man for her. She needs someone suburban, with a tatty little semi-detached house, and stiff collars, who always keeps his contraceptives locked up, and never undresses in front of her, and plays bridge with the neighbours, and cricket on Sunday. A chap like that wouldn't be any problem to a woman; and she wouldn't be a millstone around his neck. They'd have a whale of a smug little time, and breed offspring with weak eyes and watery noses for the Civil Service. You know what the basic trouble with men and women is? A man tends to marry his inferior, and a woman goes all out to marry her superior—mentally I mean. Then she spends her life bringing him down to her level. She thinks she does it subtly, so that he never knows what's going on; but it breaks his spirit; it cows him: takes away his self-respect and his confidence in himself. And does she replace them with anything? No. She just weeps with self-pity because the marriage didn't turn out the way she hoped it would, and of *course* it's all the husband's fault— it couldn't be *hers*: perish the thought! So now she's a martyr: Saint Cecilia of the Paper Flowers, with an itty-bitty halo that can be seen a mile off on clear days; and he's the hairy Woogley from Hell, sent to try her. Mind you, I'm not blaming her any more than I'd blame an orange for not being square. It's this awful flaw in human selectivity: no one ever picks the right soul-mate: everything's compromise, and making do with next-best and keeping a stiff upper lip.

" That's why you're better off than most. You've twigged that this pimp Roly is a parasite moron stuffed with sawdust. You've had a flash of clarity; and pulled yourself out of a mouse-trap. Plenty of other neurotic biddies would have hung on to him, rather than admit that their own taste in men had double-crossed them. He just brought out the potential mother-instinct in you, years ahead of its time. That's why I say you have a *chance* of becoming a rationalist, and you ought to seize onto it and hold it like grim death !"

" I will ! I will !" cried Bicky earnestly. " I *do* want to be a worthwhile sort of person, *and* honest; Wilfred; truly I do ! I often feel so silly and nit-witted and everything that I think I'm awful, and hate myself, and behave like a pig to people; but I *do* hate it, Wilfred ! I don't want to be a silly ineffectual nit-wit all my life !"

Two tears trickled down her cheeks, and she stretched her face by opening her mouth, and wiped them away with the side of her hand.

" Tut, tut," said Wilfred kindly. " You've got nothing to cry about yet. You're doing fine. Have some more vermouth. Tell me—I'm not asking out of vulgar curiosity, but to try and help you—did you and Roly ever have a scuffle in the buttercups together?"

" No," said Bicky, a little startled, and obviously telling the truth. For a moment a faint pink of embarrassment rose in her cheeks and she looked down uncomfortably.

" Good," said Wilfred reassuringly. " I didn't think you had, but these days one can't be certain of anything. Well, that's all right, then. Do you mind if I talk on the taboo subject of sex?"

"No, not a bit," said Bicky, rather faintly, but putting up a brave show of sophistication.

"It's wildly important; to get it in the right perspective, I mean. As long as the dog wags the tail, all is well; but when the tail begins to wag the dog, look out! It would have been absolutely fatal to have popped into bed with Roly. He'd have probably bungled it, and you'd have loathed it, and him, and yourself, and got a string of complexes about it, and maybe ruined your whole life. It's happened often enough; and once the harm's done, it's done. It's something you can't be too fastidious and objectively rational about. Have you ever given it much thought—*honest*.thought?"

"Well, I suppose I *have* wondered about it a bit, sometimes," admitted Bicky, constricted with shyness.

"And you're scared of it, I bet?" nodded Wilfred all-wisely.

"Well, yes, I am, I suppose. I suppose most girls are, aren't they?"

"The nice ones are supposed to be. But it's no good being scared of it, simply because one's ignorant of its real relationship to one's life. I've got some jolly sensible books here on the subject: they put the whole thing scientifically. It's just like any other science, really. If you go at it the right way, you can handle it easily, and not let it handle you. It's a good servant, and a bad master. The trick is, you have to be absolutely level-headed and dispassionate about it; and of course no one ever is . . . Does all this embarrass you?"

"No, of *course* not, Wilfred! I'm only too willing to learn all that I can about the important issues of life," averred Bicky stoutly.

" Well, the basic law is never to mix sex with emotion. Not at first, anyway ; not till you're master of it."

" Then how——" Bicky began, and stopped, feeling the question was hardly seemly.

" How do you master it ? " Wilfred supplied accommodatingly. " Simple. Try it out with someone you trust ; who knows his way about in it and can't scare you : so that you get a clear picture of it, on the credit side, with no risk for yourself."

Bicky went very pink indeed.

" Would that be the *only* way ? "

" It's the wisest."

" But who . . . I mean, how. . . . Are you *sure*, Wilfred ? "

" I wouldn't be filling you up with a lot of dangerous theory, would I ? What would I have to gain by it ? I'm trying to help you. These are proven facts I'm telling you. I mean, I'm talking to you as an equal, Bicky . . . that's what you wanted, wasn't it ? "

" Oh yes ! "

" Well, there you are, then."

" And you feel—you think that I really *need* to know about . . . sex, then ? "

" You're not a kid any more. Not mentally You're advanced for your age. That's all the more reason why you should defend yourself against making unnecessary mistakes in judgment and taste. You don't want to go *on* falling in love with poops like Roly, do you ? The only reason you will is if you don't *know* yourself ; and *why* you feel a certain way. Look, Bicky. I'll make a deal with you. I realise that it's a tricky proposition for you to go out in the high street and pick the right sort of man to experiment with, and you *could* pick one that wasn't exactly right from no fault of your own ; so if you like, just to keep it *really* dispassionate and level-headed, I'll show you the ropes, if you like. For God's sake don't think that I'm just being foxy and trying to seduce you; I'm not. But if I can help you that way, it's no skin off *my* nose; and at least you'll be safe if you put yourself in my hands."

Bicky stared very hard at her lap, feeling almost aghast and aware of a burning sensation in her ears.

"But I——" she said inaudibly. "It's very kind of you—but I—I mean, Gerda——"

"Ye gods!" said Wilfred grandly. "It hardly comes under the heading of infidelity, Bicky! This is something that concerns and affects no one except you and me; didn't I say it was a dispassionate experiment? I mean, if we were in *love* with each other, then it *would* be an emotional issue that concerned Gerda. It's just scared you, that's all."

"You . . . I mean . . . you weren't thinking of doing it right away, were you?"

"Not if you don't want to."

"I *would* like to think it over a bit, first."

"Why not? Never do anything before you're ready, I always say; particularly the first time. . . . But don't weaken, either; once you've set your compass, steer straight; never drift, or you're lost. Has the whole idea horrified you?"

"No," said Bicky slowly and diffidently. "It'd be silly to be horrified by something serious and constructive. . . . I *do* see what you mean about it not being emotional—and not being unfaithful to Gerda. . . . If one's honest, one *does* admit that one *is* curious about one's reactions to being made love to. . . . And if *you* think it isn't too early, you must be right, because you *are* wiser than I am. . . ." Then, in a little nervous rush, "Is it true one hates the person afterwards?"

"Not unless he was an offence to one's sense of taste in the first place."

"It *does* scare me, Wilfred. But I won't wriggle out of a thing just because it scares me, if I *feel* it's right to do it. . . . I know what you mean about steering straight, once you've set your course. Not many people do it, do they?"

" Too damn few. The world's full of people who've lost their bearings, and go bumping into one another, and landing on the rocks."

She nodded wisely, and then put out a slow, careful hand and wriggled off the divan. " I think I ought to be going now," she said very sedately, " before Gerda comes home. . . . I wouldn't like her to see me at this very moment——"

She stood up, and swayed so top-heavily that Wilfred jumped up and steadied her.

"Oh dear !" she said unsteadily. " Was that me? I'll be all right in a minute."

" You didn't have one too many?"

"No—oh no ! No; it's just that I need a little fresh air, I think. . . ." The room did a swallow-swoop to the left and then to the right, and she leaned her head dizzily against Wilfred's chest. He tightened his arms round her.

" Okay," he said kindly. " Take it easy. You'll be all right."

" Yes, of course !" said Bicky. He lifted her chin and kissed her lips in a very practised manner. A warm, melting feeling of inadequacy and languor filled her, and she made no resistance, though neither did she respond. Vaguely she felt her weight being taken off her legs, as Wilfred's arms lowered her back on to the divan. There was something cosy about Wilfred being all over her and round her—like a big motoring rug ; it was rather nice being kissed . . . he kissed beautifully. . . .What a very kind sort of person he'd turned out to be ; it just showed how wrong everybody had been . . . and it was nice to be hugged, so that one tickled and tingled all over.

Then, without any warning at all, she felt a wave of cold fright run through her. . . . Wilfred had unbuttoned her collar, and his hand had slipped through her dress. She gave a little gasp and wriggled till she was free of his hand, and felt her heart hammering loudly.

"I must go home," she said in a small voice. "Daisy'll be wondering. . . . Not now, Wilfred . . . you promised you'd let me think about it first. . . ."

"Don't be a coward," said Wilfred softly. "Relax and enjoy yourself. You're in safe hands."

"No," she said firmly. "No, no! Please, Wilfred. You promised. You promised you'd let me think it over first. I wouldn't like it if you did it now. . . . I wouldn't really, Wilfred. . . . It wouldn't be level-headed and dispassionate. . . ."

"Of course it would!" said Wilfred with authority. "You're doing just the thing you shouldn't be doing—you're getting in a panic. Just relax, and trust me. Put yourself in my hands. . . ." He slipped her dress down off her shoulder so expertly that she was distracted for a moment with surprise that it could come away so easily, and by the time she grasped the situation again, he had bared both her shoulders.

"No, *please*, Wilfred!" she protested tearfully. "*Please*, Wilfred, don't. . . ."

He silenced her with his lips, powerfully this time; and she found he was too strong to push away. Then the telephone bell rang so loudly that they both jumped, and when his grip relaxed, Bicky scrambled away and sat on her knees at the far end of the divan, hurriedly and clumsily pulling her dress on again.

"Damn that telephone to hell and blazes!" said Wilfred with feeling, pushing the hair back off his eyes and rescuing his glasses from behind his left ear. "I usually remember to take off the receiver. Don't be an ass, Bicky. I'd better answer it, now it's ringing. You can be slipping your clothes off." He got up and crossed to the desk and picked up the phone; and Bicky's head suddenly cleared. She slid off the divan and wafted like a small wraith into the hall, struggled into her coat and hat, and slipped out of the front door before Wilfred had even noticed her disappearance from the room.

CHAPTER THIRTEEN

This Is Gallantry

THE shops on the King's Road were beginning to put up their shutters, and the toilers were wending their way home in droves; there was a cheerful atmosphere in the air and life appeared to be pursuing its normal course.

It was twenty-five to eight by Roly's watch, and Bicky had been in Wilfred's flat since twenty-five past six.

He had maintained a ceaseless vigil from the vantage-point of a grocery store, his face as grim and set as the Count of Monte Cristo's, biding his time and nursing his vengance. He was waiting for her to leave the flat with the masher, and then confront them in the street. "I want a word with you," he was going to say grimly to the masher, and had already picked out the side-alley down which they were going to retire together and fight to the death. Then he was going to stride past Bicky without a word or glance, and drive off in a taxi. That was going to be the final scene between them.

His first impulse, when he saw her disappear into Wilfred's flat, had been to follow hot upon her heels, announce himself with sarcastic politeness, and request to be presented to the foiled masher, who would be standing cowering in the background. When he had changed his mind and decided to wait in the street, so that no furniture could be broken or hostile family loyalties involved, he had done so without allowing for the fact that two hours were going to play havoc with his patience.

This they had done.

He had conjured up a million different pictures of what was going on in the flat, and his face had taken on so many savage contortions that an assistant had come out of the store twice and eyed him with open misgivings: indeed, since six-thirty he had been as closely watched from inside the store as he was watching the flat, and it was only when he moved away from the open fruit displays that the assistant decided against calling a policeman, and wrote him off as a harmless nut.

At twenty to eight the doomed Bicky came up the area steps and out into the street, moving with undue buoyancy and aplomb; but to his mortification and surprise she was quite alone, and had mingled with the crowd and disappeared before he could remuster his scattered plans.

He kicked a fire hydrant in his rage, then his brain cleared: naturally they were too smart to leave together; the masher was still in the flat!

With a racing pulse he flung himself across the street and clattered down the area steps, his breath twizzling ferociously through his nose, and banged loudly three times on the green enamelled door, lost to all the niceties of circumspection.

There was pause, and then the door was flung open.

Roly danced forward, then had to catch himself in mid-air and dance back again when Wilfred opened the door and confronted him.

" Oh, it's *you*," he said irritably, blurring his words slightly. " What do you want? "

" Is there anyone else here? " asked Roly, struggling to remuster his demoralised verve.

" Only a talking dog and a couple of Burmese midgets,"

returned Wilfred aggressively, "but you're not dressed for it. Go home."

Roly clung valiantly to the door-post.

"Bicky was just here," he said resolutely. "I demand to know who was with her!"

"Oh, shove off!" said Wilfred, and began to close the door on him. Roly put his shoulder against it and stood firm.

"You won't gain anything by trying to shield her!" he warned. "I advise you not to interfere! Who was with her? Where's he now?"

Wilfred, too imbued with the grape to pursue discretion, lost his temper.

"You're talking to him!" he said provocatively. "Is there something you want to do about it? An alienation suit, perhaps?"

"*You?*" said Roly incoherently, as his theories collapsed and his ears sang foolishly. "You mean . . . you and Bicky? . . . You mean Bicky and you? . . ." His valour revolted at the thought, and he pushed his way into the hall. "You're lying! She wouldn't. . . . How dare you?"

"Listen, Misfit," said Wilfred. "It's about time you stopped annoying little girls with your dementia praecox, or you're liable to get yourself shut up in an institution; and merely for your own information, the sooner you stop seeing Bicky the more trouble you'll save yourself."

"Why?" said Roly, thrusting out his jaw.

"Because she's through with you."

"How do you know?"

Wilfred leaned against a book-case with a studied deliberation, and answered: "Because I arranged it that way. Is that good enough for you?"

"No!" said Roly, beginning to shiver with rage.

"All right, then; she's through with you because fruit that is

127

ripe for the plucking should be plucked by experts and not inverts," said Wilfred with classic delivery.

" Meaning me?" asked Roly dizzily.

" Meaning you."

" And you're the expert?"

" Draw your own conclusions. Who cares?" said Wilfred contemptuously, and Roly hit him solidly in the left eye.

Wilfred, taken by surprise, lost his balance, and sprawled ungracefully on his back.

" Get up !" exhorted Roly, with a wild light in his eye, dancing from one foot to the other, and doing a waltz round him. " Get up, you snake, and I'll kill you !"

Wilfred lifted himself slowly to one elbow and gingerly felt his eye.

" You bloody fool !" he said querulously, sobered by the blow and realising belatedly the full stupidity of his boasts. " I'm bleeding ! Get the hell out of here !" His voice cracked and went very shrill, but he stayed on the floor, making a great show of nursing his eye, and was, as a matter of fact, still a little too drunk to think of anything more heroic.

Roly lowered his fists and snorted, secretly filled with wonder at Wilfred's fear of him.

" Are you going to fight or aren't you ?" he demanded with Olympian scorn.

" Not now," said Wilfred owlishly, blazing venom from his good eye. " But I'll make you sorry you ever started this !"

" Any time, any place," said Roly grandly. " But just let me hear you've seen Bicky again, that's all, and I'll come right back here and murder you, see? And try another crack about me being an invert, and I'll tear your ears off your head, you elongated son-of-a-bitch !"

He jerked his hat on with an air of succinct finality, and swaggered out into the hall. As he reached the door, a bottle whizzed past his ear and burst like a bomb against the wall. He leaped into the air spasmodically, took a full moment to realise the heinousness of the crime, and then made a running dive onto Wilfred, who was scrambling for his study door with a sort of gruff whimper, having swiftly repented his hysterical deed.

They now began scuffling confusedly on the floor, grunting and bumping, until Wilfred, gaining a new strength from sheer terror of being murdered, managed to fold his knee into a flying wedge and then bump Roly's chin with it.

He heard the heartening clatter of Roly's teeth as they came together, and began groping for his neck, snuffling and sobbing with desperation. Roly, winded but ecstatic with fury, rolled free, gulped noisily, and then leap-frogged onto Wilfred and slapped his head so hard against the concrete floor that it made a noise like a kettle-drum.

Wilfred caught a fleeting vision of mauve electric sparks swimming kaleidoscopically in the ether, and then drifted peacefully into a pins-and-needles of soothing oblivion.

Finding a passive form beneath him, Roly scrambled suspiciously to his feet, rubbing himself tenderly on the chest and pushing the hair away from his eyes.

His lower jaw felt absent, but returned with a spasm when he touched it.

"I shall lose my teeth," was his first conscious thought. "False ones. Disfigurement. Character parts."

He picked up his long-suffering hat, which had been rolled upon again, and then waited expectantly for Wilfred to sit up.

Wilfred, however displayed no signs of human habitation.

His thin straggly body lay supinely spread-eagled, and his face, save for a rapidly developing bruise under his eye, had a disconcerting serenity about it. He hardly seemed to be breathing at all.

Maybe he wasn't!

The heat of the encounter suddenly evaporated and left Roly chilled and uneasy.

. . . *He had killed Wilfred Marks.*

. . . Murder?

Manslaughter?

When they put him on the stand he would have to shield Bicky, even at the supreme cost.

He could see the court-room.

The jury filing in; inscrutable.

The judge; inscrutable.

Roly; inscrutable.

The verdict. Guilty of unprovoked homicide.

A stricken cry from Bicky at the back of the court-room. . . . " *You can't! You can't send him to the gallows! It was my fault! All mine!* "

" Be quiet, Bicky! . . . Your Honour, pay her no attention! Order her out of the court! She has nothing to do with it! "

Sensation in court! . . .

He moved closer and examined Wilfred's tranquil form.

" Hey, Wilfred," he said uneasily.

When no answering flicker betrayed itself on Wilfred's face, his collar was suddenly too tight, and he said almost ingratiatingly: " Wilfred, you big ape, snap out of it, will you? "

Maybe he'd better get a mirror and hold it against his lips.

No. . . . Water; water first; *then* the mirror, if there was no result from the water.

He went through into the kitchen.

It was very small and untidy and squalid; there were two empty eggshells in the sink. He filled a jug with water and hurried back with it, his anxiety and fears mounting steadily.

He thought anguishedly of John and Lionel Barrymore in *Rasputin*.

If Wilfred had a beard he would look exactly like Rasputin.

He hoped fervently that he would prove as hard to kill; and tipped the full jug over his face. It splashed off gaily, like a small cascade, and a lot of it ran over his shirt and down his collar.

The slumbering blank of Wilfred's mind began to fill with dim images of sea and mermaids; and he heard faint but distinct celestial music, which he attributed to the Sunken Cathedral. Then a wracking pain bumped through his forehead, the mermaids scattered in confusion, the music stopped dead, and reality called to him in harsh accents. When he tried to open his eyes, water trickled in and blurred his vision. Some of it had even got up his nose.

Far away he heard Roly's worried voice saying, "Come on, Wilfred, snap out of it, will you, there's a good chap. Oh, gee! What'll I do?"

It all came back to him.

A fight.

He had never been so scared in his life. . . . The first time anyone had ever tried to fight him. . . . A paroxysm of helpless anger seized him as he remembered his terror. . . . Abased and beaten by an adolescent little prig, half a foot shorter than he was. . . . Over Bicky! . . . *How the hell did Bicky come into it?* . . . *Oh yes.* . . .

He felt very tired; too tired to get up, or answer Roly, who was still chittering at him. A second jug of water descending onto his face changed his mind for him, however; and he groaned and rolled over on his side, half expecting to be dragged to his feet and socked again. Instead, he heard an audible sigh of relief, and then retreating footsteps; the front door opened and shut, and he knew himself to be alone.

Wilfred, the thinker, the stoic, the aesthete, crawled slowly to his feet, limped to a mirror, and looked at himself.

The farcical wreck that gazed back at him turned him sick

and numb. The water trickled spitefully down his chest and into his underpants; his head was splitting, and his eye looked like a baked potato. It was as if the Furies had stripped him of all his protective insignia, smashed his idols, mocked his beliefs, and left him naked in a howling gale of brutal reality.

With a twitching conscience he recalled the scene with Gerda that morning, when he had overstepped his cynical mark, and she had turned and walked out of the flat without a word; something she had never had the temerity to do before, profoundly shocking him. He had been so sure that she would come home quietly, about half an hour later, and apologise abjectly for her fleeting show of disobedience. He had his verbal castigation all prepared; he knew it was barbed enough to make her cry; but that was only to be regretted, not taken into account.

And then the hours had gone by, and his indignation had subsided a little: he was now inclined to look upon it as a grievous peccadillo, to be met with analytical reproof and impartial criticism, calculated to refresh her awareness of her own shortcomings without labouring the point unduly.

Then Bicky had suddenly arrived without any express motive, but obviously to talk. At first he had been irritated by her intrusion; and then, sadly in need of an audience, he had begun to talk, and then the talk had suddenly begun to take its own course, and he had drunk sherry and vermouth, and now for the life of him he couldn't remember what had gone on with any clarity—glib talk mostly, that he had rolled out parrot fashion; familiar saws and sophistries that came easily because he had said them so often before; and an awareness of Bicky's legs, tucked up on the sofa, and her youthful body. . . . A green sapling, moving with every breeze. . . . Something had got into him and warmed him, a flickering excitement. He had felt that he was on one side of a picket fence with "*Keep Off*" notices on it, and Bicky was disporting nymph-like in the sanctuary of the green pastures beyond. He remembered discussing Roly with her as if the subject was actually important . . . and then what? . . . Had he tried to kiss her? . . . Oh, God, he couldn't have! . . . but his conscience was leaping like a spring-kissed salmon, and he began to piece together fragments of a sequence of approaches that he had been mentally assembling. . . . With a little click his mind recalled that it had been a lot more than mental . . . he had tried to get her dress off. . . . And then bragged to Roly. . . .

He leaned against the wall and pressed his swimming forehead against the mildewy plaster; then moved painfully into the bathroom and took three aspirins.

Wilfred the Thinker was badly scared.

CHAPTER FOURTEEN

This Is Tension

DAISY was changing for dinner when she heard the front door open and shut, and she put her head out of her door and called hopefully down the stairs, "Bicky? Is that you, just come in?"

"No, milady," Corder's voice answered. "It's only Mr. Magill."

"Oh," said Daisy, disappointed; and then, hurriedly remembering her manners, raised her voice to a cheery note of hospitality. "Good evening, Mr. Magill! I'll just tell Cathleen you're here. Isn't it dreadful? Bicky's been out all day. We can't think *what* can have happened to her, or *who* paid the taxi—if it *was* a taxi. Offer Mr. Magill a cocktail, Corder. Do make yourself at home, Mr. Magill!"

She wandered down the passage to Cathleen's room and tapped on the door.

"Cathleen, dear," she called. "Mr. Magill's here. Are you nearly ready?"

"Of course not!" Cathleen's voice answered her in tones of muffled indignation. "Pynegar never let me into the bathroom till half an hour ago! Tell him I'll be as quick as I can."

"Yes, dear, I did," said Daisy soothingly, and went back to her room to look for her other shoe.

"Thank goodness," she thought to herself, as she peered under the bed, "thank goodness Cathleen, at *least*, isn't in a dreadful muddle ! At least I can take comfort from *that*. Going out to a theatre . . . nice young man. . . . Thank goodness she has good taste; and doesn't go in for mousy boys like Roly, or furry caterpillars like Wilfred. Cathleen is my steady one— my anchor. Responsible, that's the word . . . the only *really* responsible one of the family. What a blessing there is at least *one* with their head screwed on the right way. Where on earth *is* that silly shoe? . . . It's really *too* bad of Bicky . . . staying out to all hours, without ringing up. . . . Wait a minute, did I leave that wretched little shoe in the linen-closet? No, I didn't; it's in here *somewhere*. . . . Gerda's sleeping, or *was* sleeping last time I looked . . . worn-out; nervously exhausted. . . ."

What an inhuman thing for Wilfred to have done. . . . So unnatural and cruel. No wonder poor Gerda had been looking unhappy. . . .

She'd *known* she was right, in spite of Sydney's reassurances.

A mother knew, instinctively, when things weren't right with her children; anyway, a mother worth her salt did . . . the point being, *was* she worth her salt?

She was almost afraid to ask herself that question. Yet she had *tried*. . . . Apparently trying wasn't enough. . . . " The word *something something* for the deed."

What was Michael thinking, from wherever he was? Was he in an agony of worry for the children? . . .

The thought suddenly made her feel lonely and inefficient and useless and very old, and she sat on the bed and cried a little.

" I *have* made a mess of everything !" she said forlornly. " Are you angry with me, Mike? It must be worse for you than it is for me really. . . . Not being able to *do* anything: just having to watch; and see me getting deeper and deeper in the soup, and falling down on my job; and the children getting more and more confused and mixed up. Oh goodness, *why* does anyone ever have children? . . ."

There the shoe was, right under her nose the whole time, lying by the suitcase. And what was the suitcase doing there, anyway? . . . Of course, it was Doreen's. She'd unpacked in the room when she first arrived, and no one had bothered to put the suitcase away since.

Things were suspiciously quiet in Doreen's room, now she came to think of it . . . even Pynegar had been lying low, instead of stalking human prey in the bathroom, or clomping about in her seven-league boots, or rattling china.

She pulled on her shoe and put her head out of the door. A dull, colourless mumble came from Doreen's room, like the drone of a tone-deaf bumble-bee. Dougall was reading aloud from *Quentin Durward*.

"If there's two things calculated to drive me half-mad," Doreen had once confessed, "it's Walter Scott and Dornford Yates; and Dougall worships them as if they were a couple of the lesser apostles; and I might be able to cope with *that*, except that I get them read aloud to me at the drop of a hat!"

A bottle fell off the dressing-table in Cathleen's room, and she heard her say: "Damn and blast to ruby blazes!" in tones of real anguish. It must have been the end of the Chanel Number Five that Bicky was always sneaking for the backs of her ears. . . . Oh, Lord, that young man's been sitting downstairs all this time—how *rude* he'll think us!

Daisy dabbed wildly at her nose with a stray puff, raised and lowered her eyebrows very rapidly to see if her eyes looked all right, pulled in her stomach and patted it to show it she was still its master; and sailed gracefully along the passage and down the stairs.

She entered the sitting-room and surprised Magill in the act of looking in the wrong bookcase.

"Ah," she said sweetly, "*there* you are! *Good* evening! Did Corder look after you properly? I hope we hadn't run out of whatever it was you wanted. . . ." She skilfully pushed the lampshade round till the singed side faced the wall again without breaking her flow. . . . "Fancy you and Cathleen knowing each other all the time; and owning the house too. *What* a small world, taken by and large! Why didn't you tell us this morning? We'd have tried to make you feel *much* more at home!"

"I doubt if you could have, Lady Buckering," replied Magill gallantly.

She beamed at him cordially, and settled herself in her chair, motioning him to sit too.

"And now you're going to the theatre together," she said contentedly. "I never get time to go to a *thing* these days. I still like Sybil Thorndyke in *The Corn Is Green* the best. Is Corder getting you a drink?"

"Thank you, no," said Magill politely.

"You don't drink?"

"Not very often."

"You're not just *saying* that, I hope? I mean, we *do* have *some* kind of something-or-other in the house. *My* man gives me two bottles of gin a month, and Sydney—that is, Dr. Drew—brings whisky, because occasionally his patients give it to him and he only drinks sherry, so we're much better off than most people—more so than usual at the moment, as a matter of fact, because of Dougall: Sydney and I laid in extra supplies, just in case. I dare say you think it's rather Edwardian of us to have the baby in the house and not in a hospital?"

"Not at all——"

"I'm so glad. You're sure you won't change your mind about the drink?"

"No, really, thank you."

"You will smoke, though? We're *very* well off for cigarettes."

"Thank you," said Magill, raising his cigarette. "I *am* smoking."

"*So* you are !" said Daisy brightly, laughing gaily in the hope that it would extinguish the subtle note of mutual embarrassment that seemed to have crept into the conversation. "Well, Cathleen won't be very much longer now, I don't think. Pynegar—that's that nurse—is always in the bathroom just when we need it most."

"I was early," said Magill chivalrously, and looked at his cigarette as if garnering courage to take a metaphorical bull by the horns. Daisy, divining the presence of metaphorical bulls, wracked her brains helplessly for a brilliant subject, but could only think of irrelevant idiocies; and Magill, realising that the floor was his, seized it and said awkwardly, "Lady Buckering, I hate like the dickens to bring this up at a time like this; but those shares you gave me this morning . . . our firm . . . I'm afraid we can't accept them. My father's a dyed-in-the-wool old reactionary, I'm afraid. You know. The business has to be run to set routine, come hell or high water; and he'd prefer a cheque for the eighty pounds—not *immediately*, of course—in the next few days."

Daisy looked at him reflectively and then sighed.

"The—*ahem*—shares," she said in an apologetic voice. "No good?"

"I'm afraid not," he said regretfully.

She nodded sadly.

"I was afraid of that," she admitted, and then very simply and with a kind of dignity, added, "I'm afraid I don't have eighty pounds, Mr. Magill."

Magill, touched, wrinkled his brow in concern.

"You mean . . . none of it?" he asked delicately.

She shook her head in forlorn confirmation.

"I suppose that means you'll have to turn us out?"

"Oh, that musn't happen !" he said with animation.

" Couldn't you. . . . Forgive me . . . borrow something from somebody? "

She gave him a glance of mild reproach.

" Have *you* ever tried to borrow something from someone? " she asked.

" I know what you mean," he agreed with feeling. " Well, couldn't you. . . . Forgive me again. . . . But there *are* pawnshops. . . ."

" I know many of them personally," said Daisy with quiet restraint. " What could I pawn? They give you so little."

" Yes, I know. I was just trying to think of ideas."

" It's very sweet of you."

" You haven't any old jewellery? "

" That went *long* ago ! All I have is Victorian paste now. This ring, for example. You'd think it was diamonds, but it's not." She held up her hand, as small and slender as Bicky's, and displayed a formidable cluster of brilliants. " My husband gave it to me in Paris in nineteen twenty-seven. The franc wasn't worth much then, as I recall it. . . ."

" May I see it? " asked Magill respectfully, and Daisy removed it obligingly and handed it to him.

" I shouldn't think they'd bother to put cheap stones in an eighteen-carat setting," he said at last, holding it under the pink lampshade.

" *Is* it eighteen carat? " asked Daisy in surprise.

He nodded.

" Well, fancy that ! " said Daisy amiably.

" I think they must be real diamonds, Lady Buckering," he decided with a certain amount of authority. " Not that I'm an expert ; but I'd bet even money you could raise eighty pounds on this without lifting a finger."

" No ! " exclaimed Daisy, transported. " *Could* I ? Could I really? Do you *mean* that? Why, that would solve everything, wouldn't it?" She bounced delightedly and clasped her hands together. "How *clever* of you, Mr. Magill! I'll take it to one of those shops to-morrow! *Oh*, what a weight that's taken off my mind!"

Magill, equally relieved, handed it back.

"I'm only glad to have been any help," he assured her heartily, offering up a silent prayer of thanks for his own reprieve. His heart had been cluttered with waltzing mice ever since his father had told him to get the money or throw them out: the scene had been ugly, and he had come off a poor worst.

"Now I mustn't go and forget," Daisy vowed, twiddling the ring in her fingers. "I always *do*, you know; my memory's like a *sieve*. I know. . . . I'll put it in an envelope marked ' Pawn Shop,' and leave it under my own nose on the desk, so that I *can't* forget. . . ." She rose and hurried to the desk and began scuffling vaguely for an envelope.

"You'd think you'd be able to find an envelope. . . . Everyone uses this desk. . . . One just doesn't have any privacy at all. . . . Ah, here we are!"

She unearthed an envelope, scribbled PAWN SHOP on it in large capitals, put the ring inside and licked the flap. "*There*. My goodness, I feel ten years younger already! What *would* we have done without you, Mr. Magill!"

"I feel ten years younger myself," Magill admitted pleasantly, and drew the shares out of his pocket. "I brought these back, by the way. . . . I hope they *do* turn out to be valuable. I'm sure they are. . . . And I wonder if you'd be kind enough to— er— Could I have the receipt back? I really *can* feel myself blushing now; but I have to give it to my father to-morrow morning, or go to the treadmill!"

"Receipt?" echoed Daisy vaguely. "Oh yes, of *course*! I'll be forgetting my own name next! Now I'm blushing too! You'll think it's all a sticky plot on my part to live free!"

She plunged back into the chaos of the desk and dug like an enthusiastic terrier. " Receipt, receipt, receipt. . . . Here we are. . . . No. . . . Ah, this is it ! . . . no ! Well, look at *that* !" she said suddenly and irrelevantly, holding up a card. " Our seats for the Coronation ! I *knew* I hadn't lost them ! . . . That receipt was right on top of everything this morning, but anyone'd think I kept chickens in this desk, the mess that every' thing gets into. . . . Ah, here it is. . . . ' *Dear Bicky, who the hell do you think you are, Bola Montez* ?' That wretched little Roly ! . . . I'll find it in a minute——"

Cathleen, dazzling in a smooth red evening dress, came down the stairs and into the sitting-room, looking beautiful and serene, and Magill turned and gazed at her delightedly.

" Hullo, Grant," she said easily. " Have I kept you waiting for hours ? Our clocks are all horribly slow—when they go at all."

" Hullo, Cathleen," he said worshipfully. " No, I was early. I say, you look wonderful !"

" Do I ? Thank you !"

Daisy shook herself free of the cluttered desk and wafted purposefully towards the door.

" Don't go for a minute, darling," she exhorted Cathleen. " I just want to look upstairs for something for Mr. Magill—I won't be two seconds. I must have taken it upstairs with me when I went to change——"

Her voice trailed away as she started up the stairs, and Cathleen looked at Magill questioningly.

" What's Daisy trying to sell you ? A gold brick ?" she inquired lightly, taking a cigarette from him and tapping it on her wrist while he grappled with a rogue lighter.

" Good Lord, no !" said Magill uncommunicatively. He held the lighter while she lit her cigarette from it, then lit his own and snapped it shut.

"What, then?" pressed Cathleen with a note of firm insistence in her voice.

"Still in love with the Austrian?" parried Magill.

"No," she said flatly.

"Where is he now?"

"Still in prison, I suppose."

"You say it as if it were a Turkish bath."

"Well, how do you want me to say it?" asked Cathleen with an edge to her voice. "To slow music? Anyway, why bring it up in the first place? There's been a lot of water under the bridge since then, hasn't there? Everyone's entitled to make a mistake now and again—and be allowed to forget it."

"I'm darned glad you *have* forgotten it!" he said cheerfully.

She looked at him oddly, and then away.

"Look, Grant," she said levelly. "It's a pity you found me again, and I'm an ass to be going out with you to-night; but it's strictly formal and impersonal and neat, and we aren't going to rehash the past like a No. 3 tour of *Private Lives*. I wouldn't be coming out at all if I hadn't been on the verge of going off bang . . . but I've been moping for eight months, and I'm sick of this madhouse, and I just suddenly must get out; so I'm only using you quite cold-bloodedly as an escort. Could a girl be franker?"

"You're in a bad way, aren't you?" he said lightly.

"Yes. But you won't have to do anything about it," said Cathleen brusquely.

Daisy came down the stairs again, her face worried.

"It's no good—I can't find the silly little thing *anywhere* in my room!" she announced positively. "It *must* be in the desk. . . . I'll take one last look. . . . I *had* it this morning! It can't have *walked* away!"

"It doesn't matter now, Lady Buckering!" said Magill quickly, "Some other time will do just as well——"

" But you said your father wanted it to-morrow morning or you'd go to the treadmill," said Daisy unthinkingly. " No—let me have one more quick look. . . . I feel so *guilty* about it ! "

Cathleen came over to the desk, frowning.

" What are you looking for ? What's it all about ? " she asked reservedly.

Daisy darted her a hunted look and began digging in the desk again with unconvincing preoccupation.

" Now don't you start flustering me, there's a dear," she begged, trying to make light of the whole issue. " Mr. Magill happened to give me a receipt, and now his father wants it back, that's all."

" Why does he want it back ? "

" Because—oh, well, because I haven't paid the rent yet, though I'm going to ; it was simply that his father didn't want the shares."

Cathleen's voice rang coldly on the room.

" What shares ? " she asked ominously.

" *You* know . . . *those* ones," said Daisy helplessly. " The ones your father bought that time . . . it's the *receipt* I'm looking for."

" It's not as urgent as all that," interceded Magill in her support. " We'll be moving along, and if it turns up, you can leave it where we'll see it when I see Cathleen home."

" Oh, will that be all right ? " said Daisy, brightening. " I'm *sure* to find it before you get back ! "

" Of course you will," said Magill reassuringly. " Cathleen . . . shall we go ? "

Cathleen, standing very straight and erect, looking as austere as Venus, answered in a level, matter-of-fact voice that was nearly hard, " Of course we can't go till my mother finds that receipt. I'll help you look."

" Why, Cathleen," exclaimed Daisy bewilderedly, " you'll be late, if you're going to a theatre, won't you ? "

" That's unfortunate."

" Oh, come, Cathleen," said Magill reasonably. " After all, it's not as important as all that——"

" *I* happen to think it is," said Cathleen coldly, going to the desk.

" But I *know* I'll find it !" Daisy said wistfully. " Don't be difficult, Cathleen darling, there's a dear."

" I'm sorry, Daisy, but it'd be silly to go out with the thought of having to face an irate father hanging over Grant's head all night."

Magill stiffened and frowned slightly. " That's taking rather an absurd attitude, Cathleen," he protested.

" If it is, I'm sorry," she retorted, angry pride creeping into her voice, " but I'm not going out with you as long as there's a misunderstanding about money——"

" What misunderstanding?" he countered sharply. " All that's happened is that a receipt's been mislaid. Where's the misunderstanding in that? It happens everywhere, every day, all over the world. Doesn't it, Lady Buckering?"

" Yes," said Daisy gratefully.

" Then tell me why you didn't accept those shares," demanded Cathleen uncompromisingly.

" Because of the way the office is run !" Magill answered.

" Then you must have known they wouldn't be accepted when you took them !"

" Not for certain !"

" What was wrong with them?" she asked bluntly, and Daisy who had been watching them as if they were a ping-pong match, gave a little gasp of distress.

" There was nothing wrong with them !" said Magil angrily. " What are you trying to do, Cathleen? *Pull* a misunderstanding out of the air?"

" Those are worthless shares, aren't they?" returned Cathleen, stubbornly.

" How the hell am I supposed to know?" he demanded indignantly. " By biting the edges?"

Cathleen whirled on the hapless Daisy and fixed her with a Medusa-like stare. "Of all the people in London that you could have given those shares to," she said bitterly. "Why did you have to pick on *him*?"

"Holy Moses!" Magill burst out. "Can we *please* forget about that receipt altogether? I give you my word it need never be mentioned again, *or* the shares, *or* the money. I'll wipe it off the books myself, if it'll do a little towards making you come down off your high horse!"

"Do you know what he's delicately hinting?" Cathleen demanded of Daisy angrily. "He means he's going to let you live rent-free, as a sop to his conscience!"

"To his what?" asked Daisy, befogged.

"Oh, *hell*!" said Magill in exasperation.

"Whatever *do* you mean?" Daisy inquired despairingly. "Truly, Cathleen, I don't know what's got into you! Why on earth should *I* be on *his* conscience?"

"It's not you! It's me!"

"You?" repeated Daisy, floundering deeper and deeper. "But I thought you only met at parties?"

"No," said Cathleen, caught up in too impetuous a speed, and unable to slow down. "This was in a hotel in Torquay!"

"You've never been to Torquay, dear," said Daisy steadyingly and soothingly. "That was Doreen—on their honeymoon."

"I thought it was so important that nobody knew," Magill cut in bitterly.

"Not any more!" Cathleen returned defiantly. She looked Daisy in the eye with high-keyed deliberation. "That week you thought I was at Jill Marshall's, I went to Torquay with Conrad Singer——"

"Conrad?" exclaimed Daisy involuntarily. "But he was such a *nice* young man——"

" Why else do you think I went to Torquay with him? " her daughter countered bitterly. " I thought I was in love with him. I might have been. . . . What's the difference now? The night we got there, they came to our room and banged on the door and walked in and arrested him. I had to sit in the bed while he dressed and they stood in the doorway and sucked match-sticks. He was a professional thief. He forges cheques and steals jewels from silly women. They weren't satisfied that I wasn't mixed up in it too. A woman detective came up and asked me questions, and when I wouldn't tell them who I was, she couldn't have taken a dimmer view. Then Grant appeared from somewhere. I still don't know why; and I wish to God he hadn't; but he took over and arranged things so diplomatically that they let me go with a caution. . . . Then they wanted to turn me out of the hotel, and he wouldn't let them do that either ; so I got a bottle of brandy and I got as drunk as hell and then cried all over his shirt-front, and made a flag-day of it in general : the most unsuccessful tart in Torquay."

Magill had dug his hands in his pockets and turned and gazed morosely into the fireplace. Cathleen's voice quietened, and some of the suppressed hysteria went out of it : she looked miserably at the stunned Daisy, and then sat down and took a cigarette with trembling fingers.

" Well," she said in a dull voice, " there it is. I hadn't meant to tell anyone, and I wouldn't have, if *he* hadn't appeared this morning and started everything going all over again. Now you know ! "

Magill heard her cigarette-case snap shut, and automatically felt for his lighter, came over to her and lit her cigarette, and then wandered away again.

Daisy's whirling mind began to slow down: she put her hands together in a small, aimless gesture and smiled nervously at Magill.

"How wonderfully kind you were," she said simply. "Thank you."

Magill looked at her with appreciation and sympathy, and dropped his eyes awkwardly again.

"Well?" said Cathleen. "No parental censure?"

"Oh no," said Daisy, rather hurt. "I'm glad I can understand everything so much better. How terrible it must have been for you, Cathleen, you poor darling!"

"Aren't you funny?" said Cathleen half-wonderingly. They both felt ashamed and contrite for knowing so little of each other, and a sudden, unfamiliar sense of comradeship reduced them both to awkward silence.

Cathleen rose and picked up her bag.

"I'm sorry I've spoiled the evening for everyone with all my creating," she said to Magill. "We'll find that receipt and send it straight round to you, though."

"Where do you think you're going?" asked Magill, stepping in front of her as she turned to the door.

"Upstairs to change," she said matter-of-factly.

"Oh, now, Cathleen," Daisy begged, but Magill interrupted her. "No, let her go!" he said curtly, and turned to Cathleen.

"You're quite right," he said with heavy sarcasm. "We won't get anywhere by starting everything all over again. You go on nursing your crackpot fixations to your bosom, and I'll go on evicting widows and orphans. I'll even sue you for the rent as well as evict; that ought to make you feel that all's well with the world again!"

Daisy came between them placatingly.

"I just *can't* understand why the fact that I've mislaid that silly little receipt can stop two people going out and enjoying themselves for a few hours!" she said reasonably.

"Nor can anyone else—except Cathleen!" Magill assured her.

"I won't go over all that again!" cried Cathleen passionately, suddenly near to tears. " What does it matter whether it was a receipt or a string of onions? The whole situation's so damned humiliating and futile that it isn't funny any more—and you had to make it worse by offering to hush it up with your own money!"

" Oh dear, this is all *my* fault!" said Daisy despairingly.

" Of course it isn't! You know I didn't mean that!" Cathleen said quickly in an unsteady voice.

" Then whose fault *is* it?" begged Magill.

" Nobody's!" shouted Cathleen, stamping her foot. " For goodness' sake, will you go home?"

A great wave of self-pity suddenly topped Daisy's excitement, and she flung out her hands dramatically.

" Why don't you both come out in the open and *admit* it's my fault?" she said tearfully. " It's obvious to all of us that it *is*!"

" It *isn't*!" Magill insisted hotly. " My God, Cathleen, if I'd known what a mass of silly contradictions you were, I'd have left you sitting on your suitcase in Torquay and run for the nearest train!"

" Why the hell didn't you?" she answered fiercely.

" I would have, if I hadn't been mug enough to fall in love with you!" said Magill.

" *Did* you fall in love with her?" asked Daisy, irrelevantly enchanted.

" What does it look like, for Pete's sake!" he asked in exasperation.

" She doesn't mean what you mean!" Cathleen said unfairly.

" I know what he means!" Daisy averred stoutly.

" And condone it, what's more!" Cathleen countered in the heat of the moment.

" Well, what do you expect me to do?" cried Daisy with spirit, made eloquent by the pyrotechnics. " Send you to bed without any supper? If you don't choose to tell me about things until they're all over. . . . You're not a child any more. . . ."

She suddenly stopped and took a deep breath. " I don't know

why *I'm* getting so excited," she said in a milder voice. "*Some-body* ought to keep calm!" She went very deliberately to her chair and sat down sedately, and they watched her, with rather a shamefaced air.

"One-two-three-four-five-six-seven-eight-nine-ten," she said carefully and clearly. "Now, Cathleen—both of you—may I suggest something? Let's go at this quite quietly now; no letting off bombs and firing rockets under people's feet and getting excited. That receipt can't have *vanished*. I'll get everyone to help look. We'll have found it by the time you come home. Now will you please go to the theatre and let me find it in peace and quiet? Will you, please?"

"That makes very good sense," said Magill firmly.

Cathleen wavered; then the front door bell rang and broke the high tension, and she let her shoulders relax and looked at Magill contritely. "All right," she said. "If you still want to, Grant!"

"Come along, then!" said Grant in open relief, and slipped his hand in her arm, smiling warmly at Daisy, who smiled back and nodded approvingly.

Sydney wandered into the hall, folding his gloves, and greeted them benignly as they went past him. "Hullo, Cathleen. Just off? Evening, Mr. Magill. Ah, there, Daisy. Any false starts while my back was turned?"

"Hullo, Sydney!" said Daisy, going to meet him and guiding him into the sitting-room. "Not a peep out of Doreen, but Pynegar will probably surface any minute now and torpedo everyone in sight!"

"Good night, Lady Buckering," Magill called from the hall, "and thank you for the wise counsel!"

"Good night, Daisy," Cathleen called from the door.

Daisy scattered them with benedictions until they had vanished into the night, and then wandered back disconsolately, having remembered the wayward Bicky.

149

CHAPTER FIFTEEN

This Is Expectant Fatherhood

"YOU didn't see Bicky on the way here, did you? I thought she might be walking from the tube."

"Not a sign of her," said Sydney, warming his tail at the fire.

"Isn't it too bad? You'd think she might have rung up, or something!"

"Does she *ever* ring up?"

"No; but *this* time she might have!"

"Bit of an optimist, aren't you?"

Daisy sat down in her chair, and pushed the pink lampshade towards the wall again.

"Sydney, sit down a minute, dear," she requested worriedly. "It's about Gerda. I knew I was right."

Sydney came and sat on the sofa, and helped himself to a cigarette. "Yes?" he said helpfully.

"She's upstairs asleep. I want you to pop in and just have a casual word or two when you've seen Doreen. Don't let her think we've been talking about her . . . but Sydney, Wilfred's been wickedly cruel to her. Much worse than I thought."

"What's he done?" asked Sydney, frowning.

"She only told me scraps . . . but he made her go and have an illegal operation. She was going to have a baby. And they must have gone to some really criminal quack. She said it went wrong afterwards, and that when she cried, he behaved dreadfully, and went out and left her alone, because it got on his nerves."

" Good God ! " said Sydney, shaken and angry. " Are you absolutely certain, Daisy? "

" Of *course* I'm certain ! "

" The bloody young fools ! The bloody, stupid young fools ! " he said with energy. " You're darned right. I'll have a talk to her, Daisy ! I'll get her down to my consulting-rooms first thing to-morrow and give her a thorough check-up, then I'm going to have a little talk with *him* when I've got all my facts ! "

" Will it do any good? "

Sydney stuck out his jaw with unexpected firmness. " I've talked to one or two before, on much the same lines ! " he assured her crisply. " My aunt, Daisy, we're living in eviscerated times ! I'd like to take Wilfred, and all his ilk, and skin 'em alive ! "

" Yes, I know, Sydney dear," said Daisy. " But is *talking* going to make all that difference in Wilfred? I wish I thought so ; but I'd be happier if Gerda was free of him altogether. Though it's none of my business. I mean, I can't plough in and interfere ; it'd only make her more confused. And she's confused enough at the moment, poor darling."

" Daisy," said Dougall, in a terse and resolute voice from the door. " If Doreen really wants shrimps and Burgundy, I don't think we've got any right to keep her from having them ! "

" Oh, *haven't* we? " said Sydney militantly.

Dougall, temporarily daunted by the presence of Sydney, teetered uncertainly on his toes, and then stalked bravely into the middle of the carpet. " Well, I think it's dangerous," he announced with as much defiance as he dared. " A thing like that at a time like this may give her inhibitions——"

" Inhibiddlesticks ! " said Sydney, unmoved.

151

Dougall, cut to the quick, replied in a tone of dignified rebuke, "I don't think you quite realise just what an issue it's become, Dr. Drew!"

"I bet you a bob I have," Sydney assured him impenitently.

"Well, she won't eat anything *else*! And she's just said that she won't . . . she won't answer for what happens unless she gets them!"

Sydney tucked his arm in Dougall's companionably.

"Would you like me to describe in anatomical and gastric detail," he invited sociably, "what one fried shrimp and a sniff of the cork of a bottle of Burgundy would do to your ever-loving wife's tum at this fragile hour in her digestive destiny?"

"I'm sure you wouldn't, would you, Dougall?" intercepted Daisy quickly, as Dougall turned a pale Chartreuse and sagged slightly at his threadbare knees.

"No," he agreed in a crestfallen voice, and after a mournful look of mute reproach at Sydney, loped over to the sofa and sat on the weak spring, which gave out a sepulchral *bong*!

"Cheer up, dear," said Daisy kindly. "Things aren't as black as they look."

"They couldn't be!" said Dougall with a suspicion of a snuffle, proceeding in a rather soupy voice, rife with banal sentiment, "I don't think any man's wife could have been more wonderful than Doreen has been about this business."

This unsolicited testimonial from a biased source having evoked warm approval from Daisy and Sydney, he wrinkled his forehead painstakingly, like a backward small boy reciting "Hoenlinden," and proceeded to bare stark his soul.

"When I think," he said from the very chasms of remorse, "of the casual way I've treated her sometimes, and taken her for granted, and worried her, and not really got on as fast as I ought to have at the office . . . Oh yes, I know I'm a bit slow, Daisy; it's no good not facing these things fairly and squarely.

Old Farquah called me a Droopydrawers at the Christmas party; in fun of course, but it's that sort of thing that shows which way the wind's blowing . . . and she never grumbled about having this baby. She was thrilled and happy from the first day we knew about it. And she's never complained, and never been impatient. And upstairs just now she said"—deep emotion overcame him for the moment, and he swallowed audibly—" she said if anything . . . went wrong . . . she never wanted me to reproach myself because I wouldn't let her have those shrimps and that Burgundy !"

The petrifying significance of this high-minded exoneration was apparently lost on his audience, however, for Daisy said in a cheerful voice, " I think that was very *naughty* of Doreen. You just tell her not to talk rubbish, Dougall !"

Dougall shot her a glance so pregnant with martyred forgiveness, that for a moment Daisy believed that the shrimps and Burgundy *were* a life-and-death issue, and that her remark had been callous and unfeeling.

" Don't you do anything of the sort," said Sydney, coming to the rescue. " You keep right on humouring her, Dougall. She wouldn't be a normal human being if she didn't allow herself the luxury of dramatising things a little ! After all, it's her big moment, not anybody else's. You should have heard Daisy !"

" I can't think what you mean by that, Sydney," said Daisy without humour.

" You spent the last forty-eight hours before Cathleen was born working Mike up into such an ecstasy of morbid self-recrimination that I had to sit on his head to keep him from blowing his brains out !" Sydney reminded her disrespectfully.

A nostalgic delight spread across Daisy's face.

" That's right, I did," she admitted brazenly. " I had a *wonderful* time ! *Poor* Mike. He didn't mind a bit when Doreen was born, though. He was blasé by then."

"He was on to your tricks by then!" Sydney corrected.

Dougall rose silently and began a sombre, lonely march out of the room to regions unknown; and Daisy jumped up remorsefully and caught his arm, steering him gently back to the sofa again.

"Now, now, dear," she said with motherly affection, "don't go back upstairs for a while: stay and rest a little. Have a drink. Sydney, pour the poor boy a drink. There, there, Dougall," she said, patting him understandingly. "Try and rest a little. We know how awful it is for you, dear; really we do. If we seem a big flippant, it's only to keep your spirits up; isn't it, Sydney?"

"Of course," said Sydney stoutly.

"I know," said Dougall in a wavery voice, which then teetered with unmanly anguish. "But you don't under*stand*. . . ."

"Of *course* I understand!" Daisy assured him compassionately. "Doreen doesn't really want shrimps and Burgundy any more than you or I do, dear. It's just a temporary hallucination; and your baby isn't going to be born with a shrimp on its——"

"With or without soda?" inquired Sydney graciously.

"With, thanks," said Dougall forlornly.

"It's the easiest thing in the *world* to have a baby," Daisy pattered on brightly. "Look at old Sydney over there. Do you think he'd have brought as many into the world without dropping half of them on their poor little crumpets, if it *wasn't* easy?"

"Thanks, Daisy," said Sydney courteously, handing Dougall a well-spiked Scotch.

"There; you see? So you just sit quietly on this sofa and have a nice drink, and after dinner we'll all play rummy for matches, and before you can say Bob's-your-uncle, it'll all be over bar the shouting."

"The shouting?" echoed the harrowed Dougall, panicking afresh.

"What's a little more shouting, one way or the other, in *this* house?" Sydney pointed out reasonably.

Dougall subsided apologetically again, disconsolately nursing his Scotch.

"I *am* a fathead to fuss so much," he admitted penitently; and then two large tears filled his eyes and ran leisurely down his cheeks into his frayed collar.

"Oh, gee, what did you want to be kind for?" he said, and gave a large, clumsy sob. "Now look what you've made me go and do!" He fumbled ineffectually for a handkerchief, then unwound himself from the sofa and shuffled away to the Last Resort to wash his face in cold water.

"Ah, *there* you are, Dr. Drew!" said Pynegar from the stairs, peering over the banister into the sitting-room like an Apocalyptic horse deciphering runes. "I was just coming to look for you! I can't do *anything* with the patient!"

"What's amiss this time?" asked Sydney placidly.

'She threw the arrowroot under the bed!"

"As good a place as any for the stuff," he decreed unprofessionally. "I'm just coming, Nurse."

He went into the hall to fetch his bag, winking at Daisy on the way.

"Keep up the good work," he said encouragingly. "You've certainly got a way with the men!"

This Is Intimate

SYDNEY entered the bedroom wearing his mildest and most deceptive expression, for all the world like a well-meaning old codger beaming at ducks in a park. Doreen, who sat broodingly in a chair, sneering at a magazine, looked up aggressively.

"You can take that phoney look off your face this instant," she informed him in a smouldering voice. "A fat lot you care how I feel! I bet you roar with evil laughter inside when you see your patients writhing in agony! I bet you chalk up all your failures in a little book, and write comic comments as to how they died. Everybody hates me, and I hate myself worst—and I don't care if I live. Just to spite *you*, as much as anything!"

"*What* have I done now?" he asked reproachfully.

"Giving me arrowroot!"

"Didn't you care for it?"

"Didn't I care for it! No, I didn't care for it, Dr. Jekyll! I threw it under the bed, if you must know! And how are Burke and Hare this evening? Waiting outside in the street with a box?"

"Not at all," said Sydney, sitting down beside the bed and dismissing Pynegar with a flicker of his eyebrow. "They're downstairs digging in the cellar. They have it on good authority that Dougall buried his first three common-law wives there.

Daisy's helping by holding the divining rod, and Corder's gone to find a frog's leg to stew with the wing of a bat, to do you in that way, if all else fails. We've all been bribed by Dougall. Now; how's Percy Pieface?"

"Doing his usual clog-dance."

"Ah, that's a healthy sign."

"You'd change your tune if he was doing it inside *you* !"

Sydney giggled and ran a practised hand over her middle.

"He certainly is," he agreed.

"I do not like you, Dr. Fell; the reason why I cannot tell— except that I can !—but this I know and know full well; I do not like you, Dr. Fell !" recited Doreen balefully. "Oh, Sydney, *why* did you let me in for this? The awful, *awful* degradation of it ! . . . I'm sick of being poked about and prodded. . . . It's the *indignity* of it ! I'll *never* get over it ! Anyway, I know I'm going to die," she added with surly resignation.

"You are, are you?" said Sydney.

"And would you care? . . . Ha-ha !"

"Well, I get my fee anyway," he pointed out reasonably.

"You *will* give me chloroform, won't you, Sydney?" she said, switching unexpectedly to servile cajolery. "You won't disgrace me by letting me scream my head off?"

"What'll the girl think of next?" Sydney said in tones of pained surprise. "What'll I do with my sock filled with sand, if I mess about with effete contraptions like chloroform? I dunno what the world's coming to !"

"You're a sadist. I always knew you were. We were mad to hire you. Sydney, I'm going slowly but steadily quite, quite mad. I know I'm going to die. Sydney, if I die, I forgive everybody. Except you. And Dougall. Why couldn't *he* have had half this baby? That's what's so unfair about life. Nature's down on women. They never have a chance."

"It'll be different, now we've got a Socialist government."

" Oh, *stop* being so damned flippant ! If you think you're cheering me up——"

" Nothing was further from my intention. I'm trying to goad you into another spasm. Did you ever hear the story of the little frog that died and went to Heaven?" inquired Sydney placatingly. " St. Peter asked him what he'd done all his life, and the little frog said, ' Oh, mostly just jumped in and out of puddles.' So St. Peter let him in ; and by and by along came another little frog, and St. Peter asked him what he'd done all his life, and the second little frog said, ' Oh, mostly I just jumped in and out of puddles.' So St. Peter let him in, and by and by along came a little lady frog, and St. Peter asked her what she'd done all her life, and she fluttered her eyelashes demurely and said, ' I'm Puddles.'"

" I think that's utterly disgusting."

" Go on ! You nearly laughed. I saw you !"

" I did *not* nearly laugh."

" All you Buckering girls are congenital liars."

" Dear Sydney. Always the gentleman."

" How about a nice cup of tea?"

" No thank you."

" A nasty cup of tea, then ?"

" Sydney, will you shut up and go away?"

" There's plenty of time for a cup of tea, you know."

" Sydney . . . it *is* going to be all right, isn't it?"

" Of course it is, you silly cuckoo."

" That's not the kind of tactful reassurance one expects from a doctor in good standing."

" Who said I was in good standing? I've been paying hush-money to the Medical Board for years."

" Why?"

" Because I never took any exams. I just practised on Oxford Groupers till I knew my way about."

" How is it that there're any Oxford Groupers left? "

" Oh, I didn't *kill* any. I just grafted wings on the more backward ones."

" Sydney, I'm frightened."

" Tut."

" Well ; it's no good ; I *am*. I'll be damned if I give you the satisfaction of seeing me cry."

" Pooh," said Sydney airily. " I've seen millions of women cry. Made a good few cry in my time."

" How? "

" Oh, refusing to marry them, and twisting their wrists and biting them in the leg, and that kind of thing, you know. I'm a pretty terrible customer, once I get my corsets off."

" You can go now, you insulting old man. I've no intention of saying another word to you. You just came here to mock me, and jeer at my helplessness. *Oh, oh !* " she cried irrelevantly, and clutched Sydney's hand.

" Easy, easy ! " soothed Sydney.

" I can't bear it again," said Doreen in a small frightened voice. " It's no good, Sydney. I can't go through with it ! "

" All right," he said accommodatingly. " Let's pack up and forget the whole thing. Any good movies you'd like to see? "

" Sydney, will I die? "

" Eventually," Sydney admitted fairly. " But not from having Percy Pieface ! "

" I *will* die ! "

" What ; and make a fool of me? ' There goes old Fumble-thumbs again,' they'll say. ' Too bad about Madame Pitchford. Left his umbrella in her. Cut off in the prime of life ! ' And Daisy'll skin me alive. You wouldn't want that, would you? "

" Yes, I would. Then perhaps you'd understand how *I* feel."

" If I remember rightly, you didn't treat Daisy any too considerately when *you* made your début."

" I'm sure I did ! "

" Not you. You skulked away in a far corner, and wouldn't put your nose out for days. We tried everything. We even put a bottle of Burgundy and a plate of fried shrimps on a convenient table, in the hopes that you'd pop out when you thought we weren't looking, for a quick snack."

Doreen eyed him distantly.

" You needn't think I've forgotten about those fried shrimps and Burgundy," she said revengefully.

" I didn't," said Sydney cheerfully. " Pynegar's frying 'em now—great big ticklish-looking customers with whiskers a yard long. They were so full of bounce when Corder brought 'em in that they were singing ' Asleep on the Deep ' in three-part harmony, using nothing but basso-profundo register."

" I don't want them *now*," Doreen returned stonily, unamused. " I wanted them earlier, when no one would give them to me. I won't forget that in a hurry, Sydney. When I was helpless and at a humiliating disadvantage, and about to do my duty to Dougall and give him his child, no one bothered to humour me. Oh no ! Not old Doreen, the poor old cow. Give her a handful of grass. She won't know the difference. Just a blooming old milch cow, that's all I'm good for."

" Stuff and nonsense ! " said Sydney. " You're looking as blooming as a bed of roses ! "

" Oh *yes* ! " said Doreen heavily. " Dainty as a doll's tea-set ! A lot *you* care that my figure's ruined, and my hair's like dried string ! And I *did* have good breasts, Sydney, even if all the rest of me was humdrum. *Now* look at them ! No, don't ! At least, not while I *know* you are . . . though Heaven knows, there's not a bit of me that's private any more. . . . Talk about the mystery of womanhood. . . . What a laugh ! . . . *Oh*, if I could only get my fingers on whoever invented sex ! Trapped, that's what one is : trapped like an animal ! Why did I ever go and marry? Beastly selfish brutes men are. . . . You feed them, and wash their clothes, and submit to their barnyard instincts . . . and what do you get out of it?"

"Percy, and/or, Clementina Pieface," said Sydney.

"Sydney, I really can't stand any more of your attempts at wit. I can stand a lot, because I have to; but spare me wit. Don't hit a woman when she's down. What's Dougall doing?"

"Beating his breast and wailing, ' *Eli! Eli!* ' downstairs!"

"I bet he isn't. He's probably sitting back smugly, thinking what a hell of a chap he is, while I lie here doing all the dirty work."

"Come! Come!"

"Well, he *is* smug!"

"Now, now!"

"And so are you!"

"That's different."

"And you're getting a pot."

"You said that."

"Well, I can say it again if I like. You're not God, are you, to decide how many times a person can say something? I just wish you were here instead of me. Sydney, will it be quite awful? The pain, I mean. No, tell me honestly: don't humour me, or I'll scream. It *will* be; won't it? It's the worst pain in the world, isn't it?"

"They *do* say that it's all in the mind."

"Oh, ha, ha! Oh, very good! You unctuous old hypocrite! I know I won't be able to stand it. I shall jolly well scream my head off. I hope you make Dougall stand just outside the door!"

"I'll do better than that. I'll make him stand at my elbow!"

"Oh no, you won't! And see me at my lowest common denominator? I'd never be able to look him in the eye again! I'd hate him for life!"

"He'd probably faint dead away and never remember a thing, anyway. Let's feel that pulse a moment."

"Feel your own silly pulse! As if you can tell anything from my pulse. What do you think I am—a time-bomb? . . . . *Oh God, there it goes again!* Oh, Sydney, I wish I was dead. I can't go on. I hate life, and I hate men, and I hate my stomach, and I hate me. I just want to roll over and die. . . . You *did* say you'd give me chloroform, didn't you? Yes, you did! Yes, you did! Yes, you did!"

"Of course I will."

"You swear it on your solemn oath?"

"Scout's honour."

"You're *not* to be feeble, Sydney! Swear to me seriously that you'll *soak* me in chloroform at the first *twinge*!"

"I swear I will."

"And keep about a quart for Pynegar afterwards! Not that she deserves anything so humane. I suppose you know that you've landed us with a nurse that receives surreptitious literature from Jehovah's Witnesses?"

"I never knew Jehovah *had* any witnesses."

"Well, he must have; and they're a gruesome crew, if their literature's anything to go by. Everybody's for it, except them and Pynegar—if she joins in time. Have you ever heard her eat cough lozenges? She chews them up like a horse eating gravel, and then breathes it round the room like a flame-thrower. I have to hold on to the chair with both hands to keep from screaming."

"Well, she won't be here much longer."

"Nor will I."

"You can start talking in that vein when I deliver your thirteenth or fourteenth."

"*I wouldn't go through this again! . . .*"

"That's what they all say. You get a taste for it, though."

"I'll jump in the Thames first! One, and one only! I solemnly give oath——"

"That's what Daisy said."

"Then she was a weak-minded chump."

"Not at all. She was enchanted by the ease with which she had you all; though she never let on to Mike," said Sydney.

"You were younger then. Probably a bit more nimble."

"I'm not exactly bedridden now."

"No, but you get rheumatism."

"I do *not*! When did you ever hear me say I had rheumatism?"

"You've never *said* it; you're too vain. But it *shows*."

"I consider that not only bad taste but macabre."

"You sound just like Pynegar."

"I *do* not!"

"You do."

"I do not! Nobody could sound like Pynegar unless they'd swallowed a blue-bottle and were sitting at the bottom of a hollow drum."

"She probably has a heart of gold under that unprepossessing exterior."

"She probably has a cold hot-water bottle in aspic, you mean."

"She's just a poor woman trying to earn an honest living."

"As a body-snatcher. I can just see her at night, with a sack over her head, digging up graves."

"With a cat perched on her shoulder."

"No, an owl. And she has a card to prove that she belongs to the Ghouls' Union."

"And she rides a broom."

"No, she doesn't. She rides a *huge* enema, yelling ' Tally-ho! Yoicks! Gone to Earth!'"

Doreen laughed, and then took his hand.

"I'm sorry I've behaved like such a beast, Sydney," she said contritely.

"Who said you'd behaved like a beast? You've been wonderful. You should see *some* of my cases. They bring a portable Weeping Wall with them, and let fly at the first suspicion of a twitch. You're Amazonian in comparison."

"No, I've been a beast to everybody!"

"No, you haven't."

"Yes, I have."

"All right; you have, then."

"Is everybody disgusted with me?"

"No."

"They are, *really*."

"We're all as proud as punch of you; and we all love you very much, Doreen; and everything's going to be fine. You're built just right for having children; and he's not an outsize; and everything's coming along like clockwork. I haven't had such an easy case for years. And whether you like to believe me or not, your figure'll improve after you've got Clementina Pieface off your chest: the female body works on the same principle as a ship. It has to weather a few storms and take a buffeting or two before it finds itself."

"How do you mean it'll improve? Will it really improve, Sydney? How can a baby make all that difference?"

"I don't know, but it does."

"I'll probably sag everywhere, and grow an *enormous* bunky."

"What's a bunky?"

"A derrière."

"No, you won't. Everything'll redistribute. If there was too much parcel-post on your bunky, it'll move to where you need it."

"My arms are skinny. *And* my legs."

"Well, they'll round up like one o'clock then."

"I've heard *hundreds* of women say that having a baby's ruined their figure."

164

Did they have a figure to start with? Or did they lie about all day stuffing themselves with chocolates afterwards?"

" Will I *really* look nicer, Sydney? "

" If such a thing were possible—yes."

" You're rather a pet. I know you're lying in your teeth; but I'm gullible enough to be flattered. . . . *Oooh, ooh, hoo, ooh, hoo!* "

" Here we go again," said Sydney cheerfully. " Hold onto your hat! "

CHAPTER SEVENTEEN

This Is Regrettable

AT a quarter to eight, Daisy told Corder to serve the dinner, decreeing that if Bicky chose to come in late, she could take the consequences of hotted up left-overs, and she and Sydney and Dougall dined in meditative self-preoccupation, straining their ears for any activity upstairs.

Gerda stayed in the spare room, claiming a headache, and had a bowl of soup; and Pynegar ate standing up in the kitchen with her back to Corder, reading avidly from a direful pamphlet called *God Is Watching You, Sinner.*

Everyone shared the same tension now; and a hunted look ebbed and flowed on Dougall's face: he had become maddeningly edgy, and started frantically at every creak and cough. He ate a small piece of potato and the corner of his napkin for dinner, spilt the salt, shyed like a horse when Sydney suggested that he take a sedative, and topped it with an attack of hiccoughs. The cauliflower was burnt, and the phone rang three times—the work of a female voice that laboured under the delusion that they harboured a Mr. Bandparts who had been trying to get her all day.

When dinner ended, Sydney went back upstairs, and he had hardly disappeared onto the landing when the front door banged open, and Daisy and Dougall shot to their feet and cantered out into the hall.

There they were confronted by the impressive spectacle of Bicky staring glassily before her and swaying imperceptibly, as if stirred by mystic zephyrs.

" *Bicky!* " exclaimed Daisy, in relief and exasperation. " Where *have* you been? I've telephoned all *over* the place for you—at least I was going to. I *did* call Roly, and he said you hadn't been there !"

" I hadn't," Bicky confirmed in a far-away voice, walking the distance from the hall to the sitting-room as if it were a rope over Niagara.

" Then what have you been doing since?" Daisy demanded, following her. " It's nearly half-past eight !"

Bicky eddied into the middle of the carpet and came to rest.

" I walked," she said in trance-like tones.

" Walked !" cried Daisy. " Where from?"

" I don't know," said her erring daughter vaguely. " I just walked. . . . And walked. . . . And walked."

" Bicky, you haven't walked all the way home?"

" I walked by the river," said Bicky dreamily, to no one in particular, gazing contentedly into nowhere. " It was deep, and still and soothing. It murmured, ' Come to me, little weary one. Here you will find peace and rest . . . peace and rest. . . .' "

Dougall wandered round her, eyeing her with forlorn curiosity, and was just in time to catch her as she toppled to the floor with a graceful sigh of resignation.

" Bicky !" wailed Daisy in a panic, falling on her knees beside her. " Whatever's the matter? Are you ill? Speak to me ! It's Daisy, dear ! Dougall, call Sydney ! No, don't !— Yes, call him ! Oh, Dougall, what shall we *do* ?"

" I'd better carry her up to bed," said Dougall methodically, and took a masterful hold of Bicky's supine form, which slid effortlessly through his arms as soon as he stood up. " Honestly,

Daisy, you'll have to send her to a finishing school before this magnificent obsession finishes her first!"

He finally hoisted her as far as his knee, where he gave a grunt of surprise and rested from his labours. "Blimey," he said with grudging admiration, "she must be filled with sand!"

"Shall I help?" offered Daisy, fluttering in a distrait semi-circle round him.

"Of course not!" said Dougall, on his mettle. "She's as light as a feather!" He gave a valiant heave and hoisted Bicky in the air, staggered back as his legs gave, and executed a neat sideways tango. Daisy threw her weight behind his, and he caught his balance and began wobbling slowly and precariously in the rough direction of the hall, while Bicky, limp in his clutches, inexorably slipped a few inches at every step, until her knees were practically touching her nose.

Their argosy had barely reached the sitting-room door, however, when Pynegar came legging down the stairs like an egg-bound roc and cantered into the pantry without breaking her journey to impart bulletins; and the grimness of her face was so pronounced that it struck dread in Dougall's heart, and he stopped in mid-hobble and called quaveringly, "Pynegar, what's happened?"

Pynegar by this time having vanished, he strained his neck anguishedly over the top of Bicky's head and shouted, "Has it started? . . . Oh, my God, Daisy; it's *started*!" and instantly lost his head and began running backwards and forwards looking for somewhere to dump his burden, sinking under her weight until he was bandy-legged. "Here, take her! What shall I do?" he roared piteously. "Oh, my God, Daisy, it's started!"

"Well, don't drop her!" Daisy beseeched hurriedly, trying to catch up with his zig-zag course round the sitting-room, and eventually seizing him by the baggy part of his pants and dragging him to a halt. "It's all right!—just keep *calm*, dear! Put her *down* somewhere, Dougall, she's *slipping*—you *must* try and be calm! The sofa! On the *sofa*!"

Dougall tottered to the sofa, tried to deposit Bicky head first, and failed, then feet first, and failed again; then performed a complicated parabola and ended up prone beneath her with his long legs trailing across the carpet and his face rammed into the sofa cushions.

"If only you'd keep *calm*," wailed Daisy, with poignant ineffectuality. "It'll be all *right*, Dougall dear!"

He began to wriggle furiously to free himself, whimpering gruffly, "I ought to have been with her. . . . Now it's started and I was down here when she needed me. . . . I'll never forgive myself, never. Daisy, *help* me, will you, for God's sake? I can't *move*!"

Daisy caught his leg haphazardly and pulled, and he slithered out from under Bicky and sat on the floor with a loud thud, where he floundered feverishly for a moment, disentangling himself from a knot of arms and legs, and then scrambled to his feet. Sydney, leisurely entering the room at this moment, observed the softly dreaming Bicky on the sofa, and remarked amiably, "So Bicky got home all right after all, then?"

Dougall reared up at the sound of his voice and gave a whinny of stark horror.

"*What are you doing down here?*" he ejaculated in a frenzy. "You can't leave Doreen alone *now*! *My God, she's up there alone!*"

He turned and thundered into the hall, tripping on the rug and landing on the stairs on his hands and knees, where Sydney, bewildered but swift, caught up with him and took his arm. "Hey, hey, hey!" he said steadyingly, "what's all the hurry?"

"Well, it's started, hasn't it?" the outraged Dougall trumpeted.

" No," said Sydney.

" Then what are you stopping me for? " roared Dougall, and bounded up six stairs before a delayed reaction to Sydney's answer took effect.

He stopped dead on the sixth stair, and then slowly turned and leaned over the banister, gazed injuredly and distrustfully at Sydney, and then asked in a befuddled voice, " Did you say it *hadn't* started ? "

" I did," Sydney affirmed with great positiveness.

There was a pause while this sank in, and then Dougall subsided like a deflated rubber duck. Then he rallied himself, and pointed an accusatory finger at the kitchen.

" Then why did Pynegar come rushing down here like a mad thing, scaring the daylight out of everybody? " he demanded indignantly.

" To get Doreen a glass of barley-water before she changes her mind again," explained Sydney obligingly. " If she likes the barley-water well enough, she's agreed to be weaned away from the shrimps and Burgundy."

" Why, that's quite wonderful of you, Sydney ! " Daisy applauded, and then, having caught surreptitious movement out of the corner of her eye, turned round in time to observe Bicky walking quietly and purposefully into the bookshelves. " No, Bicky ! Come back ! Where are you going? " she said rapidly ; whereupon Bicky made a half-hearted dash for the hall, and was neatly herded back by Dougall and Sydney.

" Sydney," said Daisy with misgiving, " she's behaving *most* oddly ! Bicky dear, do you know who we are? "

Bicky gazed glassily into the middle distance with a blank seraphic smile on her face.

Sydney strolled up and eyed her critically, and Bicky turned her vacant stare upon him sweetly for a moment, then gazed silently back into the great beyond.

"You see?" said Daisy nervously. "She *doesn't* know who we are! Oh, Bicky!"

"Come and sit down, Bicky," Sydney invited coaxingly, putting his hand gently under her elbow.

Bicky wafted out of his reach, raised her arms gracefully, and then spoke limpidly, from beyond the pale.

"There's fennel for you!" she said graciously, handing him an invisible sprig or two, "and columbine; there's rue for you," she added in Daisy's direction, "and here's some for me: we may call it herb of Grace o' Sundays. Oh, you must wear your rue with a difference."

"What the hell is she talking about?" asked Dougall in superstitious awe.

"It's all right," said Sydney soothingly. "It's only Shakespeare."

Daisy, nearly in tears and badly frightened, pressed her handkerchief to her nose and said, "Oh, *Bicky*!"

"There's a daisy," said Bicky blissfully to Dougall, "I would give you some violets, but they withered all when my father died. . . ."

"I'll give you daisies, my girl," said Sydney practically, and took her gently but firmly by the chin. "Say ah!"

"Ah," said Bicky meekly, between her teeth.

"No," said Sydney. "*Ah-h-h!*"

"*Ah-h-h!*" said Bicky gustily.

"I thought as much," Sydney nodded.

"Sydney!" said Daisy bravely, "you're not to be afraid to tell me!"

"I won't," said Sydney. "It's a particularly obscure brand of vermouth."

"*Vermouth!*" echoed Daisy, stunned; and then exclaimed indignantly, "Sydney!"

"Haven't you been drinking cocktails, Bicky?" Sydney demanded directly.

Bicky looked at him sheepishly, and then hung her head and nodded.

"I've got to go," she said inaudibly, making a wan attempt to withdraw.

"Oh no, you haven't!" Daisy corrected her militantly. "Bicky, I'm *surprised*. Where did you get all that to drink?"

"Wilfred gave it to me," said Bicky in a small voice.

"Wilfred? Don't talk nonsense! I thought you went to see Roly!"

"I did, and then I didn't," Bicky affirmed equitably; "and then I went to see Gerda to get my fare home, and Gerda was out but Wilfred was in, and so we had a little drinkie."

"You did indeedy," Sydney agreed, and Bicky gave him a dim but ingratiating smile.

"It's really too bad of Wilfred!" exclaimed Daisy indignantly. "No; it's no good smiling, Bicky! I mean it!"

"*Am* I smiling?" inquired Bicky, surprised, and then, noticing Dougall draped pensively over the sofa, bowed formally and said, "Dr. Livingstone, I presume?"

"Hi, Bicky," he returned, with a long face.

"I thought you were upstairs having a baby?"

"That's Doreen."

"Doreen who?"

"What ought we to do about her, Sydney?" Daisy asked harassedly. "Oh, I *am* angry with Wilfred! Fancy deliberately giving a child of that age too much to drink, and then leaving her to come home alone!"

A misty loyalty suddenly drifted across Bicky's face, and she drew herself up.

"You leave Wilfred alone," she bade Daisy with slightly top-heavy hauteur. "Wilfred's a great friend of mine. We understand each other very well indeed . . . very superior intellect." She wagged her finger and swayed gracefully off-kilter.

"Whose—yours?" inquired Sydney, deflecting her neatly into Daisy's chair.

"No, Wilfred's," she said, inclining her head graciously in recognition of his courtesy, and sitting very upright, as if enthroned. "One day Wilfred will be a great literary genius . . . greater'n Aldous Hussley or Dickens. Oh yes, he will; you mark me, Daisy," she added aggressively, as if divining silent disparagement in the attitude of her listeners, "and Gerda's a millstone round his neck!"

"Bicky!" said Daisy sharply.

"Well, he said so!" Bicky countered defensively. "And she is. He says she's suburban, and keeps her cosmetics locked up, and always undresses in the dark."

"Nice talk!" commented Dougall bitterly.

"She may not know what she's saying," said Daisy unhappily.

"Oh, I think she does," Sydney averred mildly.

Bicky nodded at him approvingly, and favoured him with an owlish wink.

"That's right, Syd, old cock," she assured him benevolently. "No flies on old Siddley-pish."

Gracefully ignoring this flattery, Sydney sat on the arm of the sofa and surveyed her with kindly interest.

"Did Wilfred have as much to drink as you did?" he inquired casually.

"I really don't watch for that sort of thing when a man is talking brilliantly," said Bicky, reverting to her former hauteur and raising an eyebrow in pained reproach.

"I'm going to speak to Wilfred, and see how brilliantly he talks to *me*!" vowed Daisy ominously.

"No; let's hear a little more about the hidden Wilfred, Wilfred the mystic," Sydney suggested diplomatically. "After all, he's never deigned to take down his back hair in front of *us*."

"You're laughing at him!" denounced Bicky indignantly.

"If you *knew* how little there was to laugh at !" exclaimed Daisy ruefully. "Why did he talk to you like that, Bicky? There must have been *some* reason," she added searchingly; her mind a prey to profound misgivings.

"Because we understand each other," Bicky replied, with quiet pride. "And he knew *all* about what was wrong with Roly and me. . . . I hardly had to tell him a thing about it."

"Ah, ah ! Not so good," said Sydney.

"Bicky !" said Daisy, thoroughly alarmed. "He didn't go filling you up with a lot of nonsense, did he ?"

"Quite the opposite," said Bicky, her dignity ruffled. "He treated me like an intelligent human being, which is more than some people do, mentioning no names. And the reason it's all wrong for Roly and me is because he's frustrated."

"Oh, he *is*, eh ?" said Sydney, enlightened at last.

Bicky nodded. "Gerda's frustrated too."

"No, really ! This is too much !" protested Daisy querulously.

"Yes, she is," Bicky insisted firmly. "Wilfred says so. Gerda's frustrated, and should be a lesson to us all."

"I presume this voice crying in the wilderness has solutions to offer ?" inquired Sydney respectfully.

"I'm not going to discuss serious matters facetiously," Bicky informed him severely, putting him back in his place.

"Bicky, you're to tell us *exactly* what he said—every *word* !" Daisy ordered with pardonable vehemence.

Bicky gazed at her analytically, pursed her lips debatively, and slowly shook her head.

"That'll be the day !" she said succinctly.

"Bicky ! You're talking to your mother ! I've a *right* to know !" cried Daisy stormily.

"No, you haven't !" replied Bicky impenitently. "*I'm* not going to be smothered ! Smother love, that's what Wilfred calls it, and he says it's what's wrong with Roly. Roly doesn't know if he's animal or vegetable or marsupial. And Wilfred says we were *mad* to want to get married, just as a sap to the social system."

"Sop," corrected Sydney helpfully.

"Sop," said Bicky unappreciatively.

Dougall raised his head from the sofa.

"Why did *he* marry then?" he asked resentfully, much incensed by these new perfidities on the part of his brother-in-law.

"Because he was too young to realise what a terrible blunder it was," Bicky supplied, too willingly. "And if he and Gerda had gone *on* being lovers, he might have been able to treat her rationally, and help her to develop, but as his wife she's a mill-stone; and if Roly weren't frustrated by a mother-complex, he and I might have become lovers and got it out of our systems; but as it is, it would really be quite hopeless."

"I couldn't agree more!" Sydney confirmed hurriedly.

Daisy sat heavily on the fender-stool and struggled to keep the tears out of her voice. "Do you mean to sit there and look me in the eye, and tell me that you accepted all that . . . all that synthetic Schopenhauer?" she demanded frantically.

Bicky lowered and raised her eyelids to denote tolerant censure. "My own sense of reason responded to it instinctively," she said primly.

"It's very interesting, very interesting," said Sydney, his poise recovered. "So you don't set much store by marriage, eh, Bicky?"

"Marriage is for the unthinking herd, that has to be given ritual to conform to, because it has no individual responsibility of its own, and lives in suburbia and becomes Morons," Bicky enlightened him.

"Well, that's all fine and good: but nobody really gets shocked by bombshells like that any more, you know, Bicky; even if Wilfred seems to think so," Sydney submitted strategically.

Momentarily checkmated, Bicky took a quick look at Daisy, and was gratified to see that consternation still reigned supreme on her face.

"Daisy's shocked! Look at her!" she said triumphantly.

"Ah, well, it's different for Daisy," Sydney conceded. "She is, after all, your mother."

Bicky nodded forgivingly. "Emotionally immature," she suggested tolerantly.

"Oh!" said Daisy dangerously. "So he analysed me too, did he?"

"Yes; but Roly's the one that there's no hope for," said Bicky, with the first sign of belated tact. "It's his money that did it."

Daisy, inadvertently reminded of the financial aspect, said suddenly, "Bicky, who paid for the taxi? Did *you*?"

"Which taxi? . . ." asked Bicky vaguely.

"What do you mean, *which* taxi? How many taxis have you used to-day, for pity's sake?"

"Only one!"

"Well. Did Roly pay for it?"

"Roly who?"

"Roly *Wayne*!"

Bicky looked faintly pained and slightly pitying.

"What about him?" she asked with ethereal disassociation.

"Did he pay for the taxi?" Daisy plodded on doggedly. "Sydney, what *are* we to do?"

"Wilfred said that—" Bicky began conversationally, and then unaccountably paused and let her voice trail slowly away to silence. Then, with a suddenness that made them all start, she leaped to her feet and gave a piercing scream.

"Bicky! What *is* it?" cried Daisy anxiously, catching her hand.

Bicky gazed about her like a trapped gazelle, stared at each of them in turn, and breathed very rapidly and unevenly.

"How did I get here?" she said at last in a voice of mortified horror.

"You walked," said Dougall.

"You *said* you walked!" Daisy amplified.

Bicky clapped her hands over her mouth and stifled a second wail.

"Daisy! Did he kill him?" she wailed in a vibrant tremolo.

"Kill who?" asked Daisy blankly.

"Roly! . . . The other man! Yes, he did! He must have!"

"Bicky, what *are* you saying?" beseeched Daisy helplessly.

". . . And then I went all the way to Gerda's to get my fare home, and she wasn't in! . . ."

"*Who's* supposed to have killed *who*?"

"*Him!*" Bicky gabbled in mounting hysteria. "Roly said I was going around with another man, and that he was going to kill him. . . ."

She suddenly swept a confounding finger at the floundering Daisy. "*You* told him! *You* told him I was going out with another man!" she denounced wildly.

"*I*? I *didn't*!——"

"Yes, you did! And now Roly's killed whoever it was, and they'll hang him! *Oh—wo—wo—wo—ho!*"

She jack-knifed under Daisy's restraining arm, feinted and dodged Sydney, and had reached the hall by the time Dougall came tacking downfield and collared her clumsily round the middle from behind. "Let me *go*!" she yelled hysterically. "My place is by his side! It's *my* fault! Daisy's my mother!"

"Don't be silly!" Dougall exhorted breathlessly, hoisting her in the air. "If Roly tried to kill anybody they'd mop the floor with him!"

"*Let me go!*" she repeated dangerously, wriggling like an eel in his grip, and drumming on his knee-caps with her heels.

"What the hell am I supposed to do with her?" he roared despairingly over his shoulder.

"Bicky, behave yourself!" cried Daisy impassionedly.

Bicky paused in her wrestling and surveyed Daisy from her exalted pose, with all the glittering concentration of the Ancient Mariner surveying his albatross. "You ruined my life! You've betrayed your own daughter! I hope it haunts you all the rest of your life!" she declaimed in ringing accents. "God may forgive you, but *I* never will!" And then to Dougall, thudding on his arms with her fists, "*Let me down or I'll bite you!*"

"Can't you give her a pill or something?" Dougall called long-sufferingly from behind her, and then split the air with a roar of agony as Bicky's teeth sank neatly into his wrist.

"Holy crumpets, she *did* bite me!" he exclaimed, outraged, and dropped her like a hot coal, his face as wrinkled with reproach as a Newfoundland retriever.

"*Bicky!*" Daisy exclaimed with such sorrow and disappointment that Bicky's senses cleared, and she stood remorsefully gazing at Dougall, aghast at her own pillage.

"I'm sorry, Dougall," she said in a sobered, apologetic voice. "Something must have come over me."

For a second she stood motionless, then slowly and wonderingly put her hands to her stomach, and said in a small, pathetic voice: "Daisy . . . I feel sick."

"Come on, Dougall," said Sydney swiftly. "You take one side and I'll take the other! Up to bed with her! Daisy, yell to Corder for a basin! This may turn into quite a squall!"

"Quite a squall!" echoed Daisy expressively, running exhaustedly towards the kitchen. "It's the fall of the house of Usher!"

This Is Interference

WHEN Bicky had been duly laid out in state, Sydney took the opportunity of popping his head round the spare-room door. Gerda sat curled up on the bed, smoking a cigarette and reading a novel. She looked up when she heard the door open, and smiled dutifully when she saw it was Sydney.

"Hullo," he said. "Are you receiving?"

"Of course, Sydney. Come on in. Are you looking for temporary sanctuary?" she said pleasantly, closing her book.

"You hit the nail on the head," he confirmed.

"Sit down for a bit . . . have a cigarette," Gerda invited hospitably. "No sign of the stork yet, I suppose?"

"Not a whisper." He sat down on the window seat and took one of her cigarettes.

"My lighter's on the blink. It may light and it mayn't," said Gerda, flicking at it industriously with her thumb. "Ah—there it goes! You're lucky!" She lit his cigarette and settled back, brushing her hair away from her forehead and shaking her head. The lights were very dim, but he could see that she had been crying.

"You're reading in a bad light," Sydney commented mildly.

"Am I? Yes, I suppose I am."

"Not so good for the eyes."

" No, Sydney."

He whistled a couple of notes, and eyed her like a plump robin.

" Daisy doesn't seem to be happy about the state of your health," he said thoughtfully.

" Oh ? I'm very well, considering."

" When did I last give you a check-up ? "

" I don't know. About a year ago, when I had that cold, wasn't it ? "

" About then. No colds since then, eh ? "

" No."

There was a pause, and then in a guarded, not too co-operative voice, she added, " How much did Daisy tell you ? "

" Not much."

" She exaggerates, you know."

" Don't I just ! "

" There's nothing terribly wrong with me."

" I wouldn't say so, either, from an offhand glance; but you never know. It never hurts to keep a check-up on things."

" Daisy told you about my . . . not having a baby, I suppose ? "

He nodded, his eye lively with sympathy and understanding.

She looked away, a little self-consciously.

" I exaggerated a bit, too. I was a bit tired. It wasn't half as grim as I made it out to be."

" Of course not."

" I suppose you're madly disapproving, Sydney ? "

" Why should I be ? If you didn't want a baby, you didn't want a baby; that's all there is to it."

" We couldn't have afforded one. And you couldn't keep a baby in that basement."

" Planning to live there the rest of your lives ? "

" Well, no. . . ."

" Personally, I'd call it a cut above having a baby on a house-boat."

" Doreen's different. She's *meant* to have babies."

" Aren't you? "

" No."

" Then I wonder what Nature thought she was at when she made you the way she did ! Silly old muddler, wasn't she? "

" My job's to help Wilfred get on. I couldn't do that and chase round after diapers and formulas."

" No, I see that."

" And he's got a tough enough problem to write what he wants to *and* look after me, without piling on the agony with a baby. Lots of brilliant writers have ruined themselves by marriage : let alone the responsibility of children."

" Yes, I'm sure they have. ' He who hath wife and child gives hostage unto Fortune,' eh? "

" Yes. How did you know that quotation, Sydney? "

" Must have read it on the back of a cigarette card. What I don't quite twig, though, is why writers and painters and musicians have to be quite so celibate."

" They're not, particularly ! "

" Oh? Well, if they're not, why don't they have children with the same ease and unselfish bravado as they knock off master-pieces? "

" They're not particularly unselfish. . . . I mean, they don't knock off masterpieces with ease and bravado."

" Just manage it by the skin of their eyebrows, eh? "

" Yes."

" Wilfred been knocking off any masterpieces lately? "

" Why do you ask that? "

" Does that mean that he hasn't? "

" He's been working hard."

" Would you have liked to have had that baby? "

She stiffened and looked away.

" No," she said distantly.

" Why not ? "

" He hates babies. "

" Oh ! So that means you do too ? "

" No. But it would have been impossible to have had one under those circumstances, wouldn't it ? It wouldn't have been fair to Wildred *or* the baby. "

" I couldn't agree more. "

She looked at him in surprise, and with a trace of relief.

" Do you mean really that, Sydney ? "

" Of course I do. It'd be a crime to start a baby off in the world in an unhappy environment. "

" Did you tell Daisy that ? "

" No. Do you want me to ? "

" Well, I think *she* thinks I should have had it. "

" I think she thinks *you* think you should have had it. "

" She misunderstood me, then. "

" Trust old Daisy. "

" She was sweet, though, Sydney. "

" Yes ; but she doesn't see further than her own nose. *She* can't realise that at the end of one's life there's a far greater sense of spiritual fulfilment in looking at a row of master-works on one's bookshelf, representing a lifetime's toil, than to have a family that's eaten you out of house and home and a bunch of grandchildren swarming all over the place. "

Gerda looked at him searchingly.

" That's sarcastic, isn't it ? " she said slowly.

" It's what Wilfred thinks, isn't it ? " he countered mildly.

" Yes. "

" Then, *ipso facto*, it's what you think. "

" That's a little cruel, Sydney. "

" Is it ? I don't think so, Gerda. I think it's Wilfred that's a little cruel. No one's got the right to dominate another person's ideas, or their likes and dislikes, for their own ends. That goes for parents as well as husbands and wives. You can't monkey with other people's freedom in public, and it should be a hundred times more true in an intimate relationship. Granted I'm only a layman, but it seems to me that if Wilfred can't write his books on his own steam, then he ought to pack up his typewriter and get some sort of job he *can* do on his own steam. Why should you or anyone else have to be a human sacrifice on the altar of his genius?"

"It's not a question of sacrifice."

"Then what *is* it a question of?"

"His career's as important to me as it is to him."

"Oh!"

"You needn't say 'Oh,' like that! Why else do you think I'd stay with him?"

"Because he's beaten your self-confidence to its knees, and you're a slave to habits . . . his habits."

"That's silly, Sydney . . . really silly!"

"I'm a silly old man. You know that."

"No, you're not . . . but you don't understand about creative people. Other people *have* to sacrifice some of their own freedom for them——"

"Pish! A certain type of person *does* sacrifice itself—but they don't *have* to. They're the Cutters-off-of-own-noses."

"You mean that I'm doing everything all wrong?"

"No. Wilfred is."

"Well, that's all right, Sydney. You're entitled to your opinions."

"You're miffed with me now?"

"Of course not! But you don't understand Wilfred, Sydney, and you never could."

"Then explain him to me."

"I can't."

"All right. Then explain him to yourself."

" You *are* being horrid, Sydney ! "

" *Can* you, though ? "

" Yes, of course I can ! "

" All right. Then why doesn't he want children ? "

" I've *told* you ! "

" Then if he's got all this integrity for his work, and puts it first, and won't endanger it by having progeny, and so forth, why hasn't he enough integrity not to go through the motions of having progeny—which is trying to tell Nature that she doesn't know her job—and yet pick her pockets at the same time ? If his work's the only thing in his life, why isn't he monastic, and dedicated to it ? Why did he drag *you* in ? To cook and bottlewash, to save the price of a char ? What does he give you in return, instead of wages ? Consideration ? Concessions of any kind ? Does he ever help you wash up or make a bed ? "

" Of course not. "

" It's enough reward for you just to sit at his feet, and share in his glory—when he gets it ? "

" Yes, it is ! " said Gerda with defiance.

" Fair enough," said Sydney. " At the end of your lives, when you're old, and all the assets are added up, you'll bask in the twilight of recognition and acclaim. But what happens if the balloon *doesn't* go up ? . . . Suppose Wilfred never quite makes it ? "

" He will, though ! "

" I just said ' suppose.' "

" I've got too much faith in him to suppose any such thing."

" It may not be his fault if he fails. Maybe the world won't recognise him. Maybe it won't want what he's taken such pains to create. Your old age'll be a horse of another colour, then, won't it ? It'll be a bit bitter, and somewhat lonely, and just a touch futile. One child might have made all the difference, then. At least there'd be someone to carry on: you wouldn't feel you'd both wasted your lifetimes, and were about to be snuffed out like a couple of candles."

"It's no *good* talking like this, Sydney!"

"I'm only putting another side to the case."

"I'm sorry, but I don't want to hear it!"

"Well, thank goodness you've got the spirit to snap my head off and not drizzle! *That's* a good sign!"

"You've been quite awful, Sydney!"

"I'm always awful."

"No, you're not, usually. You're usually a dear. But you just don't understand Wilfred."

"Not do you—yet," said Sydney gently. "But I'm half afraid that any minute now you'll begin to."

"What do you mean?"

"Never mind. But remember old Sydney. If by any chance you suddenly begin to see your Wilfred come unstuck and tumble from his pedestal, don't leap onto his burning ghat as a final gesture of self-sacrifice. Go and find yourself a nice extrovert young man who sells advertising, and raise yourself a whopping great family."

"Very well, Sydney, I'll do that little thing, just to please you."

"You may scorn me, my gal; but I'm not as green as I'm cabbage-looking, for all my sheltered existence. And come into my office to-morrow and we'll check up on the old body, just as a matter of routine."

"I will if I can."

"You will!" said Sydney serenely, rising and kissing her cheek. "And forget everything I've said. It's all nonsense. I don't understand Wilfred."

He winked, and wandered out of the room, leaving Gerda gazing inscrutably out of the window.

CHAPTER NINETEEN

This Is Sub-Plot

THE inclement night was yet young.

When, at nine o'clock, Daisy came downstairs again, the envelope marked " Pawn Shop " had vanished.

Quite obviously it had not got lost in the jumble, because no one had been to the desk since she had put it there . . . it was one of the few things that Daisy *was* clear in her mind about.

She had left it in the right-hand corner, on top of a pile of bills, which were still there; and there was no trace of it.

Keeping calm and forbidding herself to panic, she sat down and very precisely and deliberately took everything off the desk, and then put it back piece by piece.

Then she looked under the desk, and behind it, and then in all the drawers, and finally in the waste-paper basket.

Then she folded her hands in her lap and sat quite still.

" This is too much," she thought with a foundering heart. " Everything has come at once. No living creature could be expected to survive it. I have failed: I am beaten: I am done: I cannot cope. I shall just go upstairs quietly, and pack a small bag, and steal away, and go to Siam as a governess like Irene Dunne.

" That ring was in that envelope, right *there*, ten minutes ago.

" Well, half an hour ago, anyway.

" Then we all went upstairs, and I got the basin from Corder, and Bicky was ill, and Sydney gave her a triple-bromide. Then Sydney went to see Gerda, and Dougall went to powder his nose, and I came down here, and without hardly giving it a thought, I looked over at the desk just to make sure the envelope was still there. . . .

" Well, it's Corder, of course.

" Yes, but how can I be *sure*?

" All right, who else *could* it be?

" It could be Pynegar.

" Oh, don't be silly. People who believe they're going to ascend to Heaven off a mountain in Wales don't steal things. . . . . Solomon's Witnesses, or something. . . . Besides, she didn't have time. She was fiddling about with barley-water, and then went back to Doreen.

" Of course it's Corder.

" Call the police.

" You can't. Not until you're *sure* it's been stolen.

" My dear Daisy, it's obvious to a child of *five* that it's been stolen.

" Yes, but there's no *proof*.

" Pick up that telephone and dial Scotland Yard. Something one-two-one-two.

" Twelve twelves.

" Are a hundred and forty-four. . . .

" . . . *Bicky drunk, and Cathleen in hotels with forgers, and Gerda. . . .*

" *Much* better just to sneak upstairs, and pack a small bag, and not tell anyone I'm going.

" I'm sorry, Michael. I *have* tried, truly I have. It's just been too much for me, that's all. I'm just no good, I've bungled everything, and been a drag on people. I'm a dead weight. It should have been me that died, and not you. Nobody would have missed *me*. Everybody would have got on *much* better.

" One single ticket to Siam, please.

" *Certainly, Madam. That'll be wumpty seven pounds proo and pumpence free farvings.*

" Will you take it in shares?

" *No, madam. You'll have to walk.*

" Don't bother to read the book . . . the butler did it.

" Whitehall one-two-one-two.

" Go on; pick it up and *dial*, Daisy ! Don't just *sit* there !

" *There was an old woman who lived in a shoe.*

" You've been robbed, Daisy. Someone's stolen your ring. Now you can't pay the rent, and out you'll go.

" Corder did it. Corder did it. That'll teach you to hire a butler because he looks like Charles Laughton. You never really checked his references *properly*.

" Yes; but one was so jolly lucky to get a butler at *all*. *Corder was a butler, Corder was a thief ; Corder came to my house and stole a leg of beef.* Ring. Beef. Ring. Beef . . . Bovril . . . Oxo. . . . *Moo !*

" You're supposed to be deciding how to deal with this situation; not sitting wool-gathering and being sorry for yourself.

" Well, I *am* trying to decide how to deal with it !

" No, you're not; you're just wuffling; the way you always do when you're faced with a crisis.

" I'm sick to death of crisises !

" The plural is crises.

" A fine time to be academic ! All I really want to do is crawl away into the garden and die !"

Dougall came mooning aimlessly into the room, his hands in his pockets and his face disconsolate. His wrist still throbbed where Bicky had bitten him; and he had come through the seat of his only grey flannels at some time during the general fandango, and was now conscious of a small, icy draught every time he got up or sat down.

"Daisy," he said plaintively, "will you tell me what right *any* doctor has to turn a man away from his own wife's beside at a time when she needs him most?"

"She doesn't need him at all, dear," said Daisy absently. "His part of it's over. Dougall . . . what would happen if I was caught selling worthless shares?"

"Well, I suppose you could get ten years," Dougall hazarded, elongating himself on the sofa and picking lachrymosely at the fluff on a cushion.

"Even if I didn't know they were worthless?"

"That's what they all say!"

Daisy pondered this impersonally for a moment, and then said thoughtfully, "But somebody'd have to charge me before I could be arrested, wouldn't they?"

"If you sold dud shares, somebody'd charge you all right," Dougall assured her off-handedly, and then, as the first awful suspicion that she was talking about a *fait accompli* plucked wanly at the shoelace of his wandering wits, he looked up with a jerk, and said in a voice of awful foreboding, "Daisy, you haven't—? I mean , why do you want to know?" Then, jerked wholly from his torpor, "My God, Daisy!"

"There you go, jumping to conclusions!" Daisy flung back with spirit. "I only——"

"Daisy!" said Dougall, breaking out into small beads of sweat. "Did you sell somebody cheesy shares?"

"No! I *didn't*, Dougall! He gave them back—but *I* can't give *him* back the receipt because I've temporarily mislaid it, and *he* understands; but Cathleen's behaving quite strangely. And now I've gone and lost my ring. . . . but I *can't* have lost it. And I've *got* to have that receipt by the time they get back, because I promised. . . . And now the ring's gone. . . ."

"Oh, it's *Magill*, is it?" said Dougall, struggling valiantly along in the rear.

"I *told* you it was Magill!" she said with a scurry of exasperation. "And that ring couldn't have *walked* away! . . . Who *else* but Corder? . . . It *must* be Corder! I *know* it's Corder!"

Dougall furrowed his forehead, thrust out his lower lip Napoleonically, and then said very carefully and deliberately, taking infinite pains to verify each fact before locking horns with the next: "You've lost something and you think Corder has it?"

Daisy shot him an expressive look.

"I do not think Corder has it. I'm *certain*!" she said, speaking very clearly and distinctly.

"Then ring for Corder and we'll make him give it back," said Dougall, the happy strategist.

"Oh, *really*, Dougall! As if the man's going to *admit* that he's stolen a ring!"

This having made complex what he had hitherto seen as a lucidly simple problem, a baffled look crept into Dougall's eye; and while still ready and willing to co-operate, his voice took on a guarded and conservative note.

"Well, I don't see how else you're going to get it," he said dampingly, "unless I knock him down and search his pockets; and he can sue for that!"

"Not if you found the ring on him!" corrected Daisy militantly.

"Yes; but I mightn't!"

"Oh, *Dougall!* Don't always look on the *black* side of everything!"

"If *I'd* pinched a ring," he vouchsafed, self-consciously theoretical in the cause of justice, "I wouldn't keep it on me. I'd lock it up!"

"Then it's in his room!" affirmed Daisy positively.

"Yes; but there's a snag there too."

"What?"

"If he catches you searching his room, he can sue you for that as well."

"Not if you found the— Well, let him *sue*! I *know* he's got it! . . . Dougall! Go and look!" cried Daisy, *invictus*.

Dougall started like a stung drayhorse.

"Who? Me?" he inquired in a high voice. "Daisy; hell!"

Daisy clenched her hands and swung herself majestically into a histrionic pose of extreme supplication.

"Dougall," she said in a modulated Old Vic tremolo, "I'm letting you have your baby in my house at considerable inconvenience: I am now faced with financial ruin and Cathleen will make another crisis of it anyway, and all I do is to ask you to help me find that ring by looking in Corder's room. I can turn to no one else and I'm beginning to wish I was dead; *will* you help me or *won't* you?"

She finished on a rousing upper register calculated to bring any upper-circle huzzaring to its feet, and Dougall's conscience was waylaid and sandbagged by remorse.

"Well," he said shamefacedly, shuffling his shabby shoes, "of course I will, when you put it like that." She relaxed and gave a sigh of relief and admiration. "But I won't be *good* at it!" he warned her in prophetic self-depreciation.

"You'll do it *beautifully*!" she exhorted him in the ringing tones of an Arthurian damozel sending her favourite knight to the tilts without a helmet. "All you have to do is look *everywhere*!"

The stark simplicity of his task moved him not at all.

"Half a mo!" he said recalcitrantly. "I can't walk into his room while he's *sitting* in it! What am I going to tell him? That I'm looking for a taxi?"

"Oh dear," said Daisy regretfully. "You're such a defeatist sometimes, Dougall dear!"

"No, I'm not!" he said doggedly. "You've got to get him out of the house first, that's all! If he catches me rummaging about in his treasures, it'd be cheaper to let him keep the ring!"

"Well . . ." Daisy began harassedly, and was then blinded by inspiration and seized Dougall's arm triumphantly. "I can send him out for some aspirin! We'll say it's for Doreen! That's a *perfect* excuse! The chemist's *miles* away!"

"Is it still open?" asked Dougall warily.

"Who cares?"

"Well, how can he get the aspirin if it isn't?"

"Who *wants* the silly little aspirin *anyway*? All we're trying to do is get him out of the house! If I get him to go, Dougall, will you search his room? Is that a promise? Is it? You will, won't you? Yes, you will, Dougall dear!"

"Okay," said her tardy knight, without fervour.

Daisy clapped her hands delightedly, kissed him gratefully, and skipped with a light heart to the bell and pushed it.

"How much is aspirin?" she asked uncertainly.

"Half a crown will cover it."

She picked up her bag and dived into it energetically, scuffled through it, and then said with less elation, "Can we get a small one for a shilling?"

"I've got half a crown," Dougall conceded with moody resignation, digging his hand into his trouser pocket and unearthing a Boy Scout's whistle, a piece of string, two buttons and the half crown. "Exactly half a crown!"

"I'll give it you back," Daisy promised, taking the piece of string with it and tangling her fingers with his. "What *do* you do with all those things you hoard in your pockets? . . . *Now!* . . . He's coming!"

They struck poses of blissful indolence, separating conspiratorially to opposite corners of the room, and the air was so pregnant with suspense that any amateur detective could have cut it with a butter-knife when he entered.

"You rang, milady?" Corder inquired formally from the door.

"Yes, Corder. I want you to run down to Boots' and buy me a bottle of aspirin. I want you to go at once—it's for Miss Bicky—I mean Mrs. Pitchford—and hurry. . . . Well, you don't have to run *all* the way, but I want you to go at once, Corder. Here's half a crown."

"Very good, milady. Any particular brand?"

"Oh no, just aspirin," said Daisy airily.

"Well, in that case, I have a bottle in my room that I'd be happy to lend you, milady," said Corder philanthropically.

Daisy caught herself up on the verge of thanking him gratefully, and felt suddenly peaky.

"Oh," she said. "Oh, you *have*?"

"Yes, milady."

"Oh, well," she said aimlessly, looking at Dougall as if it were his fault. "*Isn't* that lucky?"

"Are they Genaspirin?" asked Dougall with a flash of unsuspected genius.

"No, sir," said Corder regretfully.

"Oh well, we *have* to have Genaspirin!" Daisy assured him gaily. "At least, we've always had to *before*, and Dr. Drew asked for them; so you'd better go to Boots!"

"Very good, milady," said Corder, and departed obediently for the front door.

They held their breaths until the door closed on him, and then ran towards each other.

"*Now*, Dougall!" hissed Daisy, pushing him towards the kitchen.

He resisted the push and turned back, struck by a new hazard.

"Daisy, if anything happens to Doreen, *swear* you'll call me!" he said fiercely.

"Yes, *yes*!"

"Whether I've found the ring or not, Daisy! Otherwise I won't go!"

"All *right*, I swear! Hurry, Dougall, *please*!"

She gave him a small push, and though still not at peace with himself, he tiptoed obediently towards the rear of the house with all the jungle stealth of a giraffe with corns.

Daisy watched him until the kitchen door closed on him, and then began to pace restlessly up and down the sitting-room, her ears cocked agitatedly for alarums from the front door, pausing every now and then to peer out of the window into the pitch blackness of the street. Sydney, having come too quietly downstairs, was misguided enough to give a playful "Boo!" from the door, and the effect on her was electric. When she had recovered her wits and identified her tormentor, she stamped her foot indignantly.

"*Really*, Sydney!—at *your* age!" she said tartly.

"A man's as young as he feels," said Sydney discordantly cheerful. "I popped my head in on Gerda and had a word or two, by the way."

"Oh?" said Daisy, mollified at once. "What did she say? Did she tell you anything? I was right, wasn't I?"

"She's coming to see me to-morrow morning."

"Oh, I *am* glad! Is she more cheerful?"

"Well, she's not exactly bubbling over with high spirits," Sydney conceded, going to the decanter and helping himself to a sherry. "But she could be worse."

Corder came in the front door and paused in the hall. "I just came back for my overcoat, milady—it's rather chilly out," he explained, and upon receiving a preoccupied nod from Daisy proceeded to the kitchen.

194

"And you're sure she *will* come and see you to-morrow, Sydney?" she pursued. "She wasn't just saying it to put you off?"

"Of course not," said Sydney. "Don't you worry, Daisy; we'll straighten everything out between us, or I'm a Dutchman."

"That *is* a weight off my. . . ."

She suddenly spun round and gave a tragic chirrup.

"Sydney! Was that Corder just then?" she asked hoarsely.

"Yes," said Sydney. "Why?"

Daisy clutched her throat and felt a dreadful atrophy creep over her and freeze her to the floor.

"Dougall . . . Dougall," she tried to shout, and heard her voice emerge in an ineffectual canary-like trill.

CHAPTER TWENTY

This Is A Proposal

SYDNEY sipped his sherry appreciatively and sighed. "Drinking before a case. Fine thing if it got before the Board," he said luxuriously, and then, glancing casually at Daisy, raised his eyebrows in amazement.

"What on earth is the matter, Daisy?" he asked in concern. "Are you going to faint?"

"I wish I was!" said Daisy wretchedly, and sank into her chair.

He came over and took her hand.

"Over-tired," he said kindly.

She shook her head violently, then drew a deep breath, and clutched his hand piteously.

"Sydney," she said tearfully. "A humiliating situation is about to arise at any moment. You must stand by me!"

"What have I been doing for years, rewarded with kicks instead of ha'pence?" he inquired.

"Yes, yes; you've been a rock . . . Oh, why doesn't Dougall come back!"

"What's he up to this time?"

"He's—in a room."

Sydney looked at her sharply and then patted her hand.

"So are we," he said reassuringly.

"Sydney . . . no matter how it may appear to you at first, I only acted for the best. I *swear* that to you, Sydney."

The kitchen door banged to, and Corder reappeared in the hall, neatly coated. "Will there be anything else while I'm out, milady?" he asked in his usual tone of voice.

Daisy, not trusting herself to turn and face him, tried to speak, failed, and shook her head instead.

"Very good, milady," said Corder equitably, and let himself out of the front door again.

As it shut, Daisy leaned forward tensely.

"Sydney," she said in a stage whisper, "did he seem strange to you?"

"Who? Corder? He's never seemed anything else," said Sydney.

"No, but *now particularly?*" she pressed.

"No."

She gave a sigh and leaned back and closed her eyes.

"Daisy, what *is* the matter?" he demanded patiently but firmly.

"If only you knew!" she returned tragically. "If only Dougall. . . . *Why* doesn't something happen? *Where* is he? . . . Oh, Sydney!"

Sydney pulled up a chair and seated himself before her in the awesome guise of his professional capacity.

"Now," he said efficiently. "Suppose we stop worrying about Dougall for a minute, and worry about you. Something else has gone wrong while my back was turned. What?"

". . . Nothing."

She tried to rise, and he pushed her gently but firmly back into her chair.

"Oh yes, it has!"

"No, it hasn't," said the tortured and cornered Daisy. "And why should I tell you if it had, if I didn't want to? You know

197

I would if it had, anyway. But it hasn't yet. At least I don't *think* so. . . . Sydney, let me go; I must find Dougall——"

"Sit still and look at yourself, Daisy," he commanded sternly. "All but a manic-depressive! A question of weeks: maybe days!"

"Sydney; at a time like this!" she protested, but without her heart in it.

"Something *has* gone wrong."

"No, it *hasn't*! . . . And then you come along trying to frighten me by saying 'Boo!' and calling me a manic-depressive."

"Well, why don't you give up?" rejoined Sydney unexpectedly.

She opened her eyes with a start.

"Give *up*?" she echoed hollowly.

Sydney nodded.

"Get rid of the house, break up the family and leave 'em to sink or swim. They've got their own way to make in the world. The sooner they start, the sooner they'll make it. As long as you're here, they'll batten off you till you fall flat on your face, never to rise again; and it's not helping *them*."

"You're out of your senses."

"No, I'm not!"

"Where would I go?"

"Come and live at my house."

"You *are* out of your senses!" said Daisy positively.

"I'm not! I'm proposing to you," Sydney began with dignity, to be cut short instantly by a clattering at the front door and Dougall's muffled voice bellowing anguishedly for Daisy.

". . . Though I should have known better to do it in *this* house!" he added bitterly, as Daisy leapt frantically to her feet and ran to the front door, catching her heel on the rug in the hall on the way.

She flung the door wide, disclosing the wretched Dougall

hopping disconsolately on the front steps, overshadowed by an enormous policeman with an unblinking, worldly-wise stare.

"Daisy!" he trumpeted feverishly. "Will you kindly tell this policeman that my name's Dougall Pitchford, and that I live here, and that I've got a perfect right to climb in or out of a window any time of the day or night I choose to?"

Daisy swayed on her heels and surged to the rescue.

"That's *quite* right, officer, he does!" she confirmed stoutly.

"See?" said Dougall in hollow triumph to the policeman.

"Well, I'm sure I beg your pardon, sir," said the policeman massively. "I hope you realise I was only doing my duty."

"Of *course* you were!" Daisy agreed, beaming. "But it's really *quite* all right— It was just a game they were playing: thank you *very* much for being so watchful. . . . I hope you're *always* on duty round here!"

She waggled her hand furiously behind her back until Sydney slipped five shillings into it, which she pressed forthwith upon the policeman with an enchanting smile. "There—buy yourself a beer when you go off duty!"

"Thank you, ma'am," said he cordially. "That's more than kind of you."

"Not at all. . . . It was kind of *you*. . . . Good-night!" said Daisy, closing the door on him and leaning against it exhaustedly.

Sydney having repaired to the sitting-room and poured a neat Scotch, held it out with a sympathetic nod as Dougall came flapping dejectedly towards him.

"How's Doreen? Is she all right?" were his first human words.

"She's fine, fine," Sydney reassured him. "Still becalmed."

Dougall gulped the whisky, wheezed hoarsely and shuddered, and straightened his shoulders, slightly revived.

"Dougall!" said Daisy catching his arm. "What happened?

. . . Did he throw you out? . . . Are you hurt? . . . You fought!"

"No, we didn't!" said Dougall harassedly. "I heard him coming, so I got out of the window." A note of resentful self-pity permeated his voice. "The street level's lower than the house. I didn't know! I never stopped falling!"

"*Poor* Dougall!"

"I damned nearly didn't come back at all! . . . That policeman kept saying, 'Tell it to the judge!' . . . I never knew what cold terror was like, till now!"

Sydney handed him another neat Scotch and he holed it in one.

"Did you—find what you went to look for?" whispered Daisy intently.

"Daisy, I never—" he began in an equally intent whisper, and then stopped irritably and proceeded in his normal boom. "I never had time to look for *anything*! . . . the man's room looked as if he shared it with a horse! Nothing's where it ought to be! I wouldn't have known where to *begin* looking. He keeps his laundry in a paper bag, and wears red flannel nightshirts with his initials on them!"

"There's still time to go back," suggested Daisy hopefully.

Dougall threw back his head.

"No-o-o-oo!" he howled, driven too far.

"Very well then, *I'll* go; you've done enough," said Daisy nobly, and began walking towards the door without undue haste.

"How *is* your window-jumping these days, Daisy?" inquired Sydney pleasantly. "Still up to form?"

She paused at the door and eyed him with the brooding intensity of a Flora Robson. "Does this look like a laughing matter, Sydney?" she asked distantly.

"It's all right," said the contrite Dougall, crawling numbly back onto his mettle. "I've got my breath back. I may as well go the whole hog!"

He slunk morosely towards the door, and Daisy brightened perceptibly.

"Oh, Dougall, *thank* you!" she said from the heart. "I'll send Corder upstairs when he comes in. That'll give me time to warn you!"

"*Warn* me!" echoed Dougall disconsolately, as he trailed towards the kitchen again. "I should have been warned before I married Doreen!"

"Now," said Sydney quietly and purposefully, when the kitchen door swung to behind him. "Suppose we all put our cards on the table, Lady B., and no more fiddle-de-dee?"

"Well, if you *must* know," said Daisy, with a last valiant clutch at her old defiance, "we think Corder's stolen something, and we're trying to find out for certain."

"Oh," said Sydney mildly. "Then why don't you call the police? They do it better."

"Because I don't choose to call the police till I have absolute proof!" said Daisy testily.

"How deep are you in?" he asked with compassion.

A kind word was too much for Daisy. She sat down and looked at him with her eyes full of tears.

"Oh, Sydney," she said pathetically. "Up to my neck. Everything came at once."

"All right, then," he said. "Let's start from the beginning and straighten it out as we go along."

She shook her head wanly.

"I don't really need your help, Sydney . . . thank you all the same: it's very sweet of you . . . but I'll manage. It's really a family matter."

"I'm as much a part of the family as Dougall!" objected Sydney stoutly.

"No, you aren't," said Daisy kindly.

"Upon my word, that's ungenerous to say the least, after all these years of tonsils and mumps!"

"Oh, dear," she said helplessly. "It's not that I don't *want* to tell you, Sydney. I just don't want to drag you into it too, that's all!"

Sydney snorted.

"If I didn't want to be dragged into it, should I have proposed just now?" he demanded warmly.

Daisy gazed at him in blank amazement.

"Proposed?" she echoed. "You? Who to? When?"

"To you. While you were sprinting for the door. A fine time to pick!" he added sulkily.

"Sydney, did you *really*?" asked Daisy, touched and moved.

"Yes, I did!"

"No, you didn't," she said, suddenly practical. "You just said you wanted me to come and live at your house. That could have meant anything."

"Have you ever known me to make Bohemian suggestions?" he demanded indignantly.

"Never," admitted Daisy apologetically.

"Well, then!"

Daisy felt herself overcome with shyness, and rolled her handkerchief into a ball. "But you're getting into your sixties, Sydney," she remarked inconsequently.

"My *what*?" he exploded, outraged. "I'm forty-nine, exactly two years older than you are! I've a *lifetime* to go before I get into my sixties! My hat; what a nerve you've got, Daisy! . . . But even so, I don't want to end up a lonely old mumblegum in a bath-chair at Skegness!"

Daisy gazed at him wraptly, her eyes bright.

"What *do* you want, then?" she asked almost timidly.

"I want to be looked after, and I want to be loved," said

202

Sydney resolutely, "and considering I've spent the best part of my life without you because I was too slow in the uptake twenty-five years ago, the least you can do is to share your Autumn with me !"

"Why, *Sydney* !" exclaimed Daisy, enchanted. "That's *beautiful* !"

He looked down at his waistcoat self-consciously.

"It *did* sound better than I thought it would," he admitted gruffly, and shot a quick glance at her. "Then will you, Daisy?"

"Yes," said Daisy simply. "I'd like to very much."

"When?"

"As soon as the family's settled down——"

Sydney gave a muffled roar and got to his feet.

"This family'll *never* settle down, damn its eyes !" he said fiercely.

"Oh, Sydney, it *will* !"

"When I'm out of my bath-chair, and pushing up buttercups !"

"Don't be so *morbid* !"

"Morbid !" he exclaimed indignantly. "What's morbid about it? I'll tell you what's a darn sight more morbid ! That young pup that comes yelping round here after Bicky when the moon's full, for one—and that book-worming, psychiatrist's Waterloo, Wilfred, for another ! If you're going to sit around waiting for *them* to make their mark in the world, I throw in the sponge !"

"Well !" exclaimed Daisy spiritedly. "I'd have thought that you, at least, could keep your temper and talk without yelling the place down ! You're no better than the rest of us, Sydney Drew !"

Sydney gazed at her combatatively for a moment, and then suddenly looked conscience-stricken and subsided apologetically.

"You're quite right, Daisy," he admitted meekly. "It's insidious, the way it creeps up on one. I'm abjectly sorry."

"Nonsense," said Daisy generously. "I'm glad you know how it feels at last!"

There was a thud at the top of the stairs, and then Pynegar came hurling down them with her feet working like pile-drivers on a pier.

"Dr. Drew!" she called, with the light of battle in her eye. "It's begun!"

"Coming!" exclaimed Sydney, bouncing out of his chair and heading for the stairs. "Daisy, turn the wireless on full, and for God's sake don't tell Dougall till you have to; and whatever you do, *keep him downstairs*! It won't be long now! Hold thumbs for us all!"

This Is Leading To The Climax

GERDA came downstairs, carefully made up to hide any traces of tears, with the air of one determined to be cheerful at all costs.

She found Daisy hovering in the hall, looking rather strained and nervous, which was understandable enough, seeing that Doreen was now well into her stride; and the wireless was blazing away at Stravinsky's "Rites of Spring" in the sitting-room, which was equally understandable, judging by the sounds she had heard as she passed Doreen's room on the way down.

"Ah, dear!" said Daisy brightly, pausing in her Turkish patrol. "There you are! Are you feeling better after your rest?"

"Fine, thanks, Daisy."

"The baby's started."

"So I heard."

"You mustn't on any account tell Dougall!"

"I won't."

"Would you like a drink? There's some whisky in there; on the little table behind the sofa."

"Thanks. Will you have one too?"

"Not just yet, thank you, darling. I have to keep my mind clear."

Gerda went into the sitting-room and poured herself a drink, and heard Dougall scamper into the hall from the kitchen.

"It's no good, Daisy!" he announced in a voice of thread-bare emotion. "I went through every solitary thing in that room, and I *swear* it isn't anywhere! He must have it on him!"

"Oh, *dear*—are you *sure*? Thank you all the same, Dougall, you've been quite magnificent. . . ."

"Has it started yet?"

"What?"

"The baby."

"Oh, *no*! Has it, Gerda?" inquired Daisy craftily.

"No. Come and have a drink, Dougall," called Gerda, dolloping a good four inches into a glass and camouflaging it lightly with a frisk of soda.

Dougall wandered into the living-room listing badly to starboard, and took the glass from her with a jittering hand.

"Thanks, Gerda," he said wanly. "Who turned the wireless on?"

"Me. Here's to the baby," said Gerda, raising her glass.

"Thanks," said Dougall. "That's a bloody awful caterwauling. Still if it's your idea of good music——"

"Oh, it is, I'm afraid," Gerda said swiftly. "Wilfred courted me to it."

Dougall gulped his drink thirstily, then lowered the glass, wheezing brokenly as his eyes swam and his Adam's apple ricocheted like a golf-ball.

"How much whisky did you put in that?" he asked in a croak.

"A couple of fingers," said Gerda innocently.

"What were they in—a boxing glove? My God, I've *had* two snorters already!"

"That's the stuff!" said Gerda encouragingly. "Have another."

206

" I guess I will," said Dougall, and did.

Daisy wafted in from the hall, her face dreamy with deep thought.

" Maybe Corder didn't steal it after all," she said tentatively.

Dougall banged down his glass and gazed at her agog.

" Holy cat-fish ! You mean I've been through what I've been through for *nothing* ? " he howled. " I thought you were *sure* ! "

" How *could* I have been sure, Dougall ? " returned Daisy defensively. " The man isn't going to *tell* me he's stolen something, is he ? "

" What didn't he steal ? " asked Gerda.

" Oh, I just lost something—" Daisy began evasively, and then gave a little shake of exasperation. " Oh dear, I can't go *on* being mysterious about it for *ever* ! It's my ring, Gerda. I've lost it. It was in an envelope. At least, I'm *certain* it was in an envelope—over on that desk there."

Dougall reclaimed his drink and climbed wearily onto the sofa, where he stretched out his legs, propping his head on one arm and draping his ankles over the other ; and Daisy wandered disconsolately round the room.

" Mr. Magill *saw* me put it in the envelope," she said wistfully. " He'd bear me out. . . ."

The phone rang at her elbow, and she jumped nervously and swung round, in time to see Corder come into the hall ; whereupon she stiffened and screamed, " *Dougall* ! "

Dougall catapulted out of the sofa in a panic.

" What ? " he asked with a leaping pulse. " It's started My God ! "

" Oh, *there* you are ! " said Daisy lamely. " For a minute I . . . Corder, answer the phone ! It's all right, Dougall, you can lie down again ; it hasn't started. I got muddled for a minute, that was all. . . ."

Corder picked up the phone and Dougall subsided back onto

the sofa in a shattered condition, eyeing Daisy with mortified reproach.

" Lady Buckering's residence," said Corder formally. " Just one moment. . . . It's for Miss Cathleen, milady."

" Miss Cathleen? Tell them she's out with Mr. Magill ! " said Daisy peremptorily.

" It's Mr. Magill calling," Corder returned smoothly.

"*Who* ? Mr. Magill ? But how could it be? Here, let me speak to him," said Daisy flusteredly, taking the phone. " Hullo ! Mr. Magill? . . . Yes, it's me. . . . No, she hasn't. . . ."

Corder put the aspirin and the change on the desk and with/drew silently. Dougall, beginning to feel the Lorelei cadences of the four double whiskies, contemplated the mysterious universe in somnolent grandeur, and Gerda wandered pensively over to the fire/stool and sat gazing into the gas/fire.

Daisy finished an incoherent peppering of unfinished sentences and bade Magill an apologetic good/bye, hung up the phone, and wandered back into the middle of the room.

" Cathleen went out at the second interval and didn't come back. She never talked to him the whole evening. I don't know what's come over people. . . . If I *didn't* put the ring in an envelope, where *could* I have put it? . . . Dougall, pretend you're me, and you're over here by this desk, and you've got your ring in your hand ; but you *didn't* put it in an envelope, like you thought you did. Where *might* you put it? "

" Back on my finger," said Dougall, sharp as a button.

" If I'd done that, it'd be on my finger *now*," said Daisy with some tartness, and then, noticing Gerda, went over to her. " Gerda, I do wish I knew what to do about you."

" You don't have to do anything, Daisy," said Gerda reassuringly. " I feel all right, now that I've had a chat and a rest."

" It's not as simple as that," said Daisy, looking at her with a troubled face, and haunted by the context of Bicky's bacchanalian confessional.

"Once," said Dougall, to no one in particular, but speaking in the sober accents of a Calvinist making his peace with his Maker, "once, when I was shaving and Doreen was having a bath, I struck her. Yes I did, Daisy, I struck her. It was over some row about my leaving the basin soapy after I'd shaved. I was always doing it. And suddenly I let out and smacked her on the seat, and she cried. I should never have struck her; least of all *there*. I felt an absolute outsider. I still do. Yet she forgave me. She never mentioned it again. But I never forgot. There are some things a man can never forgive himself for, and that's one."

"Aren't you being unnecessarily harsh with yourself?" suggested Daisy.

"No," said Dougall with impartiality and justice. "No, no. Just now I feel like the biggest rotter that ever walked. There she is, up there; waiting . . . waiting . . . waiting. Brave little Doreen."

He mixed himself a Scotch broodingly. "*I'll* never know what a woman goes through. It's all very well for me to talk, but *I* don't have to suffer."

The front door banged open, and Roly scuffled purposefully into the hall, scanned the sitting-room rapidly for Bicky, and then dived grimly for the stairs.

Daisy bounced from her chair.

"Roly!" she cried restrainingly. "Come back! You can't go up there! Bicky's in bed!"

Roly pivoted in mid-prance and leaned violently over the banister, all but diving onto his head.

"Then make her get up!" he petitioned hoarsely. "I've got to see her! I've *got* to see Bicky, Lady Buckering!"

"Hullo," interposed Dougall sociably.

"Hullo!" snapped Roly irrelevantly. "Please, Lady Buckering, will you tell her I must see her at once; *urgently*?" He came grudgingly down the stairs, hugging the banister in a grip of iron. "I won't go away till I have!" he added darkly. "I'll sit outside on the front doorstep till she sees me! I mean it! You can call the police if you want to!"

"No police!" Dougall objected instantly.

"Roly," said Daisy firmly and kindly. "Be a good boy and go home, will you? Bicky can't see you to-night."

"What'll she do if I kill myself?" parried Roly excitedly. "What'll she do then, eh?"

"Can't you two ever think of anything except killing yourselves?" demanded Daisy with pardonable exasperation.

"Bicky!" Roly roared up the stairs. "Bick-*ee*!"

Daisy flapped her handkerchief frantically. "Be *quiet*!" she hissed fiercely, darting a fearful eye in Dougall's direction. "Doreen's having . . . Doreen's asleep; and Bicky won't hear you; she's asleep too . . . and she's not *well*, Roly. Now will you *please* go home?"

Roly drooped visibly.

"I can't go home," he said in a defeated voice.

"Why ever not?" demanded Daisy briskly.

"I see too many ghosts."

"Ghosts of what?" inquired Dougall, his interest momentarily kindled.

"I don't mean *ghosts*," Roly answered with an irritable shunt of his shoulders. "I mean ghosts!"

"You don't mean anything, chum," Dougall averred, not unkindly, and rose and poured a Scotch.

Roly came to the sitting-room door, looking as noble and ill-used as Stewart Grainger in spanish whiskers.

"You despise me, don't you?" he said resonantly. "Yes, you you do. But not as much as I despise myself."

"Hooray!" applauded Dougall approvingly.

Roly turned humbly to Daisy.

"Please call Bicky," he pleaded.

"Roly, I've told you. Bicky's really ill," said Daisy with commendable patience. Dougall wandered over with the Scotch.

"Ill? Bicky?" repeated Roly, as its significance belatedly sank in, and when Dougall put the Scotch in his hand, his scalp twitched in panic, and he asked with foreboding, "What's this for?"

"You drink it," explained Dougall obligingly.

"What's happened?" asked Roly, frightened. "What's the matter with her? Is it anything I've done? If it's *my* fault——"

"You'll kill yourself. *We* know," completed Dougall, with a carefree air, pouring himself another Scotch.

The wretched Roly, now tossing dizzily in the blanket of his conscience, took a tidy gulp of the Scotch, and played his trump.

"Lady Buckering!" he cried ringingly, "I've *got* to see her! I've just given a man a thrashing because of her!"

"*You* have?" demanded Dougall incredulously. "Who was it?"

"For pity's sake!" Daisy lamented long-sufferingly. "This'll start *another* scandal! Roly, are you quite *sane*?"

Roly, abashed, stuck to his popguns nevertheless.

"*You* told me she was going out with somebody else," he countered defensively. "And when I faced her with it, she denied it and ran away——"

A wan and peaky little face appeared on the stairs, and Gerda, being the only one facing the door, saw it and called out reprovingly, "Bicky, are you supposed to be up?"

Daisy and Roly swung round, and Bicky confronted them forlornly, her dressing-gown swaddled around her and her hair askew.

" Bicky ! " exclaimed Daisy severely. " Go back to bed this *instant* ! "

" *Bicky !* " cried Roly dramatically, bounding towards her.

She drew herself up regally. " Leave me alone," she said in tones of austere rebuff, and walked past him into the sitting-room. " Why did you come here? "

" To see *you*, of course ! "

" Then you're wasting your time," she said distantly. " Go away."

Roly gazed at her, and then squared his shoulders and said emotionally. " Do you mean that? "

" Every word," said Bicky frigidly.

" Bicky, do you know what you've just said? " he inquired, more in wonder than in anger.

" Yes," said Bicky, with calm and awful detachment, adding disparagingly, " you and your puppy-love."

" Well, I'm a monkey's uncle ! " said Dougall admiringly. " Hark at *her* ! "

Roly raised and lowered his eyebrows very rapidly.

" I came here to-night——" he began imposingly.

" I'm not interested ! " retorted his quondam helpmeet crushingly.

" Well, you jolly well will be ! " he said with heat, recapturing some of his old bravura and straddling his legs in fine style. " I know about this man ! " He pointed forcefully at his own face, jutting it forward like a captive football.

" Do I look as if I've been fighting? " he demanded eloquently. " No, I don't ! But *he's* got a black eye; and you won't have any more trouble from *him*; *that* I promise you ! "

He stood back triumphantly and folded his arms, and Bicky, made uneasy by the cocksure pitch of his rhetoric, eyed him with faintly stirring alarm. " What are you talking about? " she said bleakly. " Whom did you fight? "

"I won't say in front of your family," he said grandly, and with a certain amount of commendable loyalty.

"Roly," said Daisy, profoundly aggrieved. "You've made a *dreadful* blunder! There *wasn't* any other man! I just told you that rubbish because I wasn't thinking, and I wanted to get rid of you . . . and now you've gone and blacked some utterly strange and innocent man's eye!"

"Innocent!" echoed Roly in a mixture of respect and indignant contradiction. "Innocent my eye! I followed Bicky to his flat, and watched till she came out, and then I went in and accused him to his face——"

Bicky clutched her head and gave a low and harassed moan.

"*Roly!*" she cried. "You *didn't* . . . it wasn't *him!*"

"You don't mean *Wilfred*?" Daisy ejaculated thoughtlessly.

"Yes, I do!" said Roly stoutly.

Daisy sank quietly into her chair, and Dougall eyed Roly with incredulity. "You blacked Wilfred's eye?" he inquired with dawning respect.

"Yes, I did," said Roly, less stoutly.

"Halleluja!" said Dougall contentedly.

Gerda had risen, and now all four of them eyed her awkwardly.

"I'm sorry, Gerda," said Roly with sincerity. "I wasn't going to tell in front of you."

"That's all right," said Gerda, in a still, quiet voice.

Bicky gave a sob. "Oh, I'm so *ashamed*!" she cried mournfully, and sank on her knees beside Daisy, burying her face in her lap.

"I don't quite understand how Wilfred got dragged into all this, though," Gerda said, still in a quiet voice.

"I was going to tell you later, Gerda," Daisy said worriedly, putting her arms consolingly round Bicky. "That's what comes of trying to spare people's feelings . . . it only makes things a hundred times worse——"

"But you're not trying to make out that Wilfred . . . that Bicky . . . I mean, just because Roly's imagined something ridiculous," Gerda began, her voice gaining in feeling as she spoke.

Roly interrupted without relish. "I didn't imagine anything, Gerda," he said apologetically. "Wilfred said the sooner I stopped seeing Bicky, the more trouble I'd save myself, because Bicky was through with me, and I said, how did he know? And he said, because he'd arranged it that way himself; and that fruit that was ripe for the plucking had to be plucked by experts, not inverts—meaning me; and I asked him right out if he was the expert, and he said he was, so I hit him in the eye."

Dougall wandered over admiringly and took his glass off to be refilled, beaming at him cordially on the way.

"It isn't true," said Bicky in a forlorn, scared voice. "It isn't true. . . I'm so humiliated . . . it wasn't *anything* like that, Gerda ! All I did, I went to your flat to get my bus fare home and you weren't there, and Wilfred told me how cheap I've been making myself, and how to improve. *Honestly*, Gerda, that's all that happened ! Please . . . you've *got* to believe me !"

"Of course I do, Bicky," said Gerda quietly and sympathetically.

"It wasn't *quite* all that happened," Dougall said unravelling himself on to the sofa again.

"It *was* !" said Bicky urgently.

"What about the little drinkies?" Dougall reminded her amiably.

Bicky turned her head to Gerda appealingly. "Was it any crime for me to have a drink?" she demanded piteously.

"About a gallon and a half long," her brother-in-law supplemented without gallantry. "We still don't know how she got home !"

Worried tears began coursing down Bicky's stricken face.

" That's not *fair* ! " she said anguishedly. " You're trying to make out I was drunk, and I *wasn't* ! I know every single thing that happened, even when I quoted that Shakespeare, and you carried me upstairs ! "

" Is that true? " inquired the scandalised Roly, profoundly shattered.

" *You* saw her leave the flat," Dougall reminded him.

" Yes, but she was walking straight. . . ." Roly stiffened indignantly. " Do you think I'd have left her to come home alone if I'd known she was wizzled—that she wasn't well? "

Bicky sobbed afresh, clutching Daisy's hands for moral support.

" Daisy, tell them I didn't do anything wicked ! " she begged piteously. " Tell them it's all lies about me and Wilfred ! " She snuggled deeper into Daisy's arms, sobbing as if her heart was breaking. " I'm not that sort of person . . . nor Wilfred. . . . Don't let Gerda believe what they're saying ! . . . Tell them, Daisy ! "

Daisy looked over at Gerda silently and expressively. " Do I have to tell you anything, Gerda? " she asked gently. Gerda looked back at her in a stricken silence, then shook her head and turned away.

" No," she said inaudibly.

" There you are, Bicky. Nobody's thinking anything unkind about you," Daisy said consolingly.

" Roly is ! " Bicky answered from deep in her burrow.

" No, I'm not, Bicky," said Roly, an unfamiliar note of compassion in his tone.

" It's all your fault," she returned bitterly, not raising her head. " With your jealousy, and lies and hitting people——"

" Now, now, Bicky," Daisy interposed.

" Well, it *is* ! "

"No, Bicky dear," said Daisy steadily. "Roly hasn't been lying."

Bicky's head bobbed up and she gazed at Daisy open-mouthed.

"But you just said——" she began, bewildered and reproachful.

"It's all right, Bicky," said Gerda in a quiet, unemotional voice from the fireplace. "We've both found out something about Wilfred for the first time . . . that's all."

The front door opened and Cathleen came in, closed it behind her, and began climbing the stairs.

"Cathleen!" Daisy called hesitantly.

"Hullo, everybody," said Cathleen briefly, and disappeared.

"Oh . . ." said Daisy undecidedly, then rose with a worried face and followed her up the stairs.

Dougall watched her go sympathetically, then filled himself another drink. Then he remembered Gerda, and went across to fetch her glass. As he passed the saddened Roly on the way back he winked cheeringly.

"Sing out when you're ready, chum," he said hospitably, then noticed Roly's empty glass and beamed admiringly. "Why, you *are* ready!" He refilled the glasses with a carefree air. "May as well get good and gay; what with me being a father any minute now," he said philosophically. "Any minute now! . . . they've been saying it for days! A fellow told me a very depressing thing in the pub this morning. He said that when Queen Anne was going to have a baby she went right along to the last minute, and then they found out it was wind. Your drink, champ." He dropped a small depth-charge into Roly's hand on his way over to Gerda with another, equally lavishly endowed.

Roly moved hesitantly over to Bicky, who was still sitting dejectedly on the floor beside Daisy's chair, and looked at her appealingly. "Bicky," he said meekly.

"Don't speak to me," Bicky said, in a stilly voice. "Why don't you go home?"

Roly gazed wanly at his drink.

"I suppose I *have* made a mess of everything," he said gloomily. "I didn't think it'd turn out like this."

He looked half-hopefully at Bicky, but no repentant reassurance greeted him.

He finished the drink with a gulp and put the glass down.

"I think I *will* go home," he said, and wandered to the door, then paused again with his eye wistfully on Bicky.

"This is good-bye, then," he said, underplaying it magnificently.

When she still ignored him, he turned away. (*Mr. Wayne played the farewell scene with heart-breaking sincerity. There was not a dry eye in the theatre.*)

At this moment, however, the front door opened and shut again, and Wilfred appeared in the doorway from the hall. He looked through Roly with studious contempt, and addressed himself to Dougall, who was back on the sofa again.

"Is Gerda here?" he asked coldly.

Dougall pointed across the room, and Wilfred took a step forward.

Gerda sat on the fire-stool, the drink in her hand untouched. She looked up, and then down again.

"You might have told me you were coming here," said Wilfred coldly.

"I didn't know I was till the last minute," said Gerda in a low voice.

"Where's Daisy?"

"Upstairs."

Roly moved forward. "I'm sorry I hit you," he said penitently. Wilfred ignored him.

"How long are you going to be here?" he asked Gerda.

"I don't know," said Gerda almost listlessly.

"Get your things and come home, Gerda."

An atmosphere of detachment had sprung up between them,

as if they were strangers talking in a bus. Gerda paused a moment, and still without looking at him, answered, "I'm not coming home."

Wilfred, secretly shaken, raised his eyebrows in aloof surprise.

"Why?" he asked civilly.

"You know why," Gerda replied quietly.

"I'm sorry, I don't."

Bicky looked up, frightened but sobered.

"She means because of me and the things Roly's told them!" she said with feeling.

"Keep out of this, Bicky," said Dougall advisedly.

"Keep out of it yourself!" Wilfred shot back angrily, and Dougall reared up with a cheerful light of battle in his eye. Daisy came into the room at this moment, and sensing the atmosphere swiftly, hurried forward to nip any potential forays in the bud.

"Dougall, dear, remember you're in my house. No nonsense, now. Go back to your nice sofa. Bicky, dear, please go back to bed," she said efficiently.

"Leave me alone," said Bicky fiercely. "It's *about* me!"

Gerda stirred, and stood up.

"It's not about you, Bicky," she said calmly. "You won't miss anything by going to bed."

"What *is* it about, then?" inquired Wilfred levelly.

"I don't want to talk about it here."

"Then where else is there, if you're not coming home to night?"

"I'll write to you," said Gerda.

It took him off his guard, and his voice shook a little. "Write to me? . . ."

He surveyed the room at large with unconcealed hostility. "You've obviously all been discussing me at great length," he said aggressively.

Dougall nodded and held his thumb and forefinger about an

inch apart. Wilfred glared at him, and then addressed himself to Gerda.

"What's got into you?" he asked in an injured and patient tone. "You can't tell me you've believed whatever that hysterical little pansy's said about me——"

"Too bad he gave you a black eye," Dougall commented in Roly's defence. Wilfred swung round on him.

"I thought I told you to keep out of this?" he asked with an ugly note in his voice.

"Oh, *that's* the tone, is it?" said Dougall, rising purposefully.

"I told you I won't have any silly quarrelling," said Daisy swiftly. "Keep quiet, Dougall." She turned to Wilfred. "Nobody's taken any notice of what Roly's said about you," she said firmly.

"It's what *I'm* supposed to have said about you," Bicky supplemented woefully. "And I never said *anything*, Wilfred! I just told them the things we talked about, and they've twisted them all to mean something else!"

Her outburst did little to reassure Wilfred, and he looked swiftly at Gerda.

"That's as good a way of putting it as any," Gerda said expressionlessly.

"Oh no, it isn't!" Wilfred rejoined sharply. "I didn't say a damned thing to Bicky that I wouldn't have said in front of you, or Daisy, or anyone, for that matter. You've just let them talk you into putting a convenient interpretation to it! My God, Gerda, do you think I'd try to burn my fingers on a numb-brained little fluffhead who goes broadcasting her emotions to anyone that'll listen? I'm not a *complete* fool!"

"There isn't anything more to be said, Wilfred," said Gerda, her voice growing strained.

"You might give me a chance to understand you," he said bitterly.

"You might have begun trying to understand me a little earlier," she said without reproach.

"I thought I did," Wilfred answered.

"You explained her to Bicky lucidly enough," Dougall confirmed cheerfully.

A tinge of self-pity came into Wilfred's voice.

"Why did you come *here* to discuss your troubles?" he asked Gerda bitterly. "You've known all along that they hate me, and always have! I know all my faults as well as any of you," he added defiantly, glaring at Dougall and then at Bicky. "If I'd had time, I'd have tried to better them—but I *haven't* the time! I don't take life as it comes! I'm fighting every minute I'm alive, to try and *amount* to something! . . . so that what I *do* is worthwhile, not what I *am*! . . . that's all that matters!"

Having thus unconsciously revealed the basic flaw in all his reasoning, his voice soared higher in its intensity, as if he himself needed to hear his own justification as urgently as anyone. "I come from a long line of failures. I've had plenty of time to see what failure could do to me if I ever gave in to it! I've worked my way up from nothing; and I only know one way of living my life . . . the way I'm living it now. Gerda knew all that, long before she married me. I didn't mince matters, or promise her anything I couldn't live up to. She went into it with her eyes open. I warned her just what it'd be like. She said she loved me, and that that was enough. Well, it hasn't been. Nothing's possible except between equals, and we're not equals anywhere along the line. Not when she brings her troubles here, and gets her family to gang up on her side! I told Bicky she's too ordinary, and I'll stick to it. Now that I've got nothing to lose, I'll say it right here in the open. All this bust-up started over the question of having a baby; but she's never been honest or relaxed enough to discuss it with me. Ninety per cent of our married life we've spent as strangers;

because Gerda wouldn't try and find out why I felt as I did about certain things. If she didn't feel them too, they were automatically wrong in her eyes, and *I* ought to change them. All right, maybe I should. I hate babies. I don't want one. That's something I can't do anything about. But even if I was as maudlin about seeing myself reproduced as Dougall is, I'd cut off my right hand before I brought a brat into this pig-wallow of a world, where it'll either be bombed to death or starve !''

"You ought to be up on a soap-box in Hyde Park !" said Dougall indignantly.

"*You've* a fat right to tell me where I ought to be !" Wilfred answered fiercely. "Three quid a week and no bloody future, and lucky to get that ! . . . You're not even able to pay for your brat being born. How do you plan to give it a decent start later on ? By sending it out to sponge on its betters like a parasite?"

"Stop talking like that, Wilfred !" Daisy cried sharply.

"That's how you talk about me !" Wilfred cried back, shaking with tension. "All right, Gerda ! Use what I said to Bicky any way you want to ! *Make* it your alibi ! I'll go to Brighton and give you a divorce, or whatever you want ! You never gave me a decent chance, and you've run away weeping instead of trying to make a go of straightening things out . . . but you'll never change the way I live, and I'll still be a great writer at the end of it, without anyone's help !"

He broke off and stood glaring at Gerda, and there was silence in the room. Then Gerda came over to him, slowly, looking at him almost wonderingly.

"Just now was the first time I ever listened to *what* you were saying, instead of how you were saying it," she said in a low voice. "People aren't real to you, are they? . . . They're just subjects for sentences. You wouldn't even want to reach out and touch my hand unless you could think of a good adjective to go with it. You can make it sound like an unnatural crime to want to have babies—you can even have me wondering whether you aren't right—until you say what you've just said to Dougall, and I suddenly feel so sick with shame for you that I don't know where to look. You're *afraid* to have a child . . . you're afraid of the world, and the future, and the unselfishness you'd have to show a baby; and the sacrifices you'd have to make. You're afraid of being a failure: you're afraid of having any of your ideas argued against, in case they don't stand up to argument. I believe you must be afraid of *me*. You're afraid of everything !"

"You seem to have taken a long time to find it all out," he said in a strained, unsteady voice.

"Yes, haven't I?" she admitted miserably. "Perhaps you'll find it out one day too. I know you'll never write until you do." She stopped and shook her head helplessly. "It's silly oı me to even talk about it. I should have started like this; not ended with it."

She turned and went past him towards the stairs, keeping her face averted.

"Gerda, wait," he said with sudden urgency, and she paused at the foot of the stairs, her hand on the banister. He came over to her, finding difficulty in choosing the words he needed.

"Gerda . . . I . . ." he began, forcing himself to speak. "Wouldn't it be any good . . . to go back to the beginning and start again?"

Gerda looked at him sadly.

"You couldn't change. No more could I," she said.

"At least give me the chance !" he said half-resentfully.

She shook her head.

"I'm sorry; but things'd only go back to the way they were," she said at last.

"But I . . . Gerda, I . . ." he said painfully. "Gerda, I *need* you !"

For a moment a look of indecision came into her face, but he missed it by turning despairingly to Daisy:

"Daisy—don't let her break up everything like this!" he pleaded almost humbly. "She'll listen to you. There *must* be some way of working it out! We'll be just as unhappy apart as we were together! It's too late to start again with other people —we're second-hand goods; our habits are set! She's part of my life! I won't know what to do!... I won't know what to do! I *will* try, Daisy, I swear I will! Don't let her leave me! It isn't just for my sake!... *I* don't mean anything... but if anything goes wrong with my writing——!"

Gerda turned and ran up the stairs.

He swung round and gave a cry of appeal. "*Gerda!...*" He stared after her uncomprehendingly for a moment, then sagged dispiritedly, and with a curious aimlessness crossed the hall and walked out of the front door, letting it bump-to behind him.

Daisy moved, and broke the silence.

"Bicky dear, please go back to bed now... please, dear," she said.

"I don't feel ill any more," Bicky replied in a small voice.

"You will in the morning!" Dougall assured her, rallying his own spirits by rising and wandering purposefully to the decanter. "Won't feel so good in the morning myself, but what the heck! Where's your glass, champ?"

Roly edged in from the background, much moved and sobered by what he had heard, and put his glass on the table.

"Not so strong as last time.... I've got to get back to Knightsbridge," he suggested guardedly.

"Knightsbridge s'far, and honour a name," Dougall intoned with a flourish, filling the glass, "but the voice of a schoolboy rallies the ranks: 'Play up, play up, and play the game!'"

He handed Roly the drink, and they put their heads together with one accord and continued in unison:

"This they all with a joyful cry, bear through life like a torch in flame;
And, falling, fer-*ling* to those behind,
Play up, play up, and play the game!"

"Learned it at school!" said Dougall proudly.

"Me, too!" said Roly.

"Only thing I ever *did* learn!"

"Me too!" They laughed uproariously, delighted to discover so much in common.

"Daisy, look at Roly!" said Bicky disapprovingly. "He's getting drunk!"

"Pots calling kettles black!" said Daisy.

"How does the damn thing go from there?" asked Dougall.

"It doesn't," said Roly regretfully. "That's the end."

"Then let's go back to the beginning!"

"Ri'—tiddledy—hi—toe!"

"Dougall, no!" Daisy protested long-sufferingly.

Undeterred, Roly and Dougall locked heads again.

"There's a breathless hush in the close to-night!" said Dougall with gusto.

"*An hour to play and the last man in!*" added Roly.

"A bumping pitch and a blinding light!—"

"*Anna nour to play, an' the last man in—*"

"And it's not for the sake of a ribboned coat—"

"*Or annour to play, an' the larsh man in—*"

"But the Captain's hand on his shoulder smote—"

"I wish he was doing some smiting here!" said Daisy feelingly.

Dougall and Roly beamed at her smugly and trilled:

"Play up, play up, and play the game!"

Cathleen, entering at this moment, her poise regained and her make-up repaired, eyed them with surprise.

"Well, well," she said. "Would one of you Poet Laureates give me a drink?"

Dougall bowed obligingly, and waved a hospitable hand at the decanter. "Gin, vermouth, port, sherry, Martini, side-car, dill-water?" he proffered.

"I'll have what you're having. You seem to be doing well on it," said Cathleen.

"One block-buster coming up," announced Dougall willingly. "Give us your glass while I'm at it, gruesome."

Roly obediently leaned across the sofa to proffer his empty glass and passed out gently in the process, subsiding calmly and contentedly onto his face.

Bicky gave a cry of protective anxiety and scrambled to her feet.

"Roly! Are you all right?" she beseeched, and pattered over to him.

"Too late. He'd had it," said Dougall philosophically, handing Cathleen her drink, and leaning comfortably across the table on his elbow to observe Bicky wriggle onto the sofa and pillow the dreaming Roly's head on her lap.

"I'm glad you came down, Cathleen," said Daisy with tentative relief. "You *do* feel differently now, don't you?"

"Yes, dear," said Cathleen amiably, sitting on the arm of the sofa, "and suitably ashamed of myself. It's all over."

"Oh, I *am* so glad!" said Daisy contentedly.

"I'm going up to Scotland to stay with Jean for a week or two; so you won't even have me about the house as a silent reproach."

"Scotland? *Now?*" asked Daisy, bewildered. "You're not going just when . . . Cathleen, it isn't because of? . . . But I thought you said you felt differently now? Oh, Cathleen—— !"

"I *do* feel differently, Daisy!" Cathleen assured her with

undue emphasis. "I don't care a damn about the whole thing. I still don't know whatever made me think I cared a damn about *him*."

Daisy gave a harassed sigh.

"Cathleen, it isn't any of my business, but I *do* think you're wrong about that boy, and what you feel. It *is* only the trouble about the rent, isn't it?"

"No; and anyway, it's too late now, Daisy. I'm not going to see him again. *Do* stop worrying about it!"

Daisy paused in her fluttering stride, and caught Bicky's eye.

"I asked you to go up to bed, Bicky!" she said severely.

"I can't," said Bicky swiftly. "He's on my lap. And he's *sweet* when he's asleep!"

She gazed at Roly lovingly, and stroked his hair. "I wish he was always like this!"

"Have him stuffed," suggested Dougall helpfully.

Daisy continued her pacing, and surveyed Cathleen remorsefully.

"It *is* because I lost that ring and can't pay him!" she said dejectedly. "I *knew* it was!"

"All right, then," said Dougall with sudden and unexpected activity, "let's act!"

He slapped Roly smartly on his exposed flank. "Wakie, wakie, *waaa*-kee!" he roared, and Roly sprang into a sitting position, goggling owlishly.

"Dougall, *don't*!" shrilled Bicky protectively. "He was *sleeping*!"

"I was not!" said Roly doughtily, wobbling to his feet.

"Dougall!" cried Daisy with misgiving. "What are you going to do?"

"You'll see," said Dougall masterfully, flexing Roly's bicep and nodding approvingly. "We'll get that ring, Daisy, don't you fret." He strode over and rang the bell, and Daisy gasped.

' I *knew* I shouldn't have let you drink so much ! " she wailed contritely. "Everything I do turns out for the worst ! Dougall, you're *not* to do anything quixotic with Corder ! "

Corder entered at this moment, and she subsided with a guilty blush and tried to look composed.

"You rang, milady?" Corder inquired smoothly.

"No. We tolled," said Dougall grandly. "Now, Corder, about this ring——"

"Yes, I did ring, Corder," said Daisy desperately. "I've lost a ring, Corder, and I'd like you to start looking in the rubbish for it—it may have been thrown out when my wastepaper basket was emptied. Dougall, *do* sit down, will you, dear, you fuss me ! It was the ring I usually wear, Corder, and of great sentimental value. Do your best to find it, will you? "

"Very good, milady," said Corder, unruffled, and turned to go.

"Ah ah !" cried Dougall blithely. "Just a minute, Corder ! It's only fair to tell you that when you were out just now I searched your room ! "

"I *beg* your pardon?" Corder said stiffly.

"I—he doesn't mean it—that's all—you may go—" Daisy twittered frantically, but Corder had drawn himself to his full height and was gazing ominously at Dougall.

"You were doubtless unaware, then, sir, that it constituted an illegal action? " he said pontifically.

"Was I not !" Dougall responded blithely.

"Corder, you misunderstood," Daisy struggled on valiantly. "Mr. Pitchford merely entered your room to close the window in case it rained while you were out——"

"*With* your permission, I understand perfectly, milady," Corder retorted with menacing hauteur. "Mr. Pitchford entered my room under the impression that I have that ring in my possession. I have been aware for some time that I was suspect ! "

227

"That's utterly ridiculous! How could you be?" said Daisy grandly.

"When every word spoken in this room," Corder replied frigidly, "can be heard with crystal clarity from my pantry, it is impossible not to be aware of one's facts. I regret that I am left with no alternative but to take adequate legal action. Will that be all, milady?"

"Yes," said Daisy weakly.

Corder bowed stiffly and withdrew, and Daisy sank beaten into her chair.

"*Now* what have you done, Dougall?" she asked tearfully. "He's going to *sue*!"

A great wave of self-pity surged over her, and she dabbed her eyes with her handkerchief.

"Why I ever bothered to try and . . . I don't care what *anyone* says; it isn't worth it in the end! . . . I'm defeated! You can all do what you like! . . . Bicky, go up to *bed*! . . . Why I've bothered with you all, I don't know! You're all much happier the way you are! Everything I've done to try and straighten things out has only pushed me deeper in! . . . To be taken to court by a *butler*!" Her voice trembled emotionally. "It's the end!"

Her brood stood and watched her penitently, and she gazed at them expressively and then sighed.

"It's all my fault, though," she said in profound self-condemnation.

"Oh, Daisy, it *isn't*!" said Cathleen.

"Yes, it is," Daisy insisted stubbornly. "I've been an unnatural mother!"

"No, you haven't, Daisy!" said Bicky tearfully. "It's *us* that's been unnatural! I feel a *beast*!"

"I've been an unnatural mother," said Daisy, deaf to comfort. "I had no right to be a mother at all. I only hope you can find it in your hearts to forgive me."

"You're just talking like that for the sake of hearing how well it sounds," said Cathleen uncomfortably. "You know perfectly well you've done all you could with us."

"No, no."

"Oh, *please* don't talk like that, Daisy!" Bicky begged anguishedly. "I'll try not to be bad any more! I'll improve, I promise I will! I'll never fight Roly again, or drink!"

"Roly," said Dougall purposefully, breaking up the delicate mood of the scene. "Follow me!"

"Dougall!" cried Daisy, brought to earth with a bump, and leaping to her feet, "where are you going?"

"To get that ring!" said Dougall.

"For pity's sake!" The door bell rang, and threw her off her guard, and Roly beamed and said, "Someone's atta door," helpfully. Dougall at once took two large steps towards the kitchen, and Daisy seized him by the arm. "Dougall, *don't* make things any worse than they are!" she beseeched pitifully.

"They couldn't be!" returned Dougall with point. "And anyway, he may as well sue for a sheep as a lamb! If he *hasn't* got that ring, I'll eat my hat!"

"Someone atta door," said Roly.

"Dougall, will you please leave Corder alone?" Daisy begged urgently. "I thought you didn't want to go to prison?"

"I don't, but he's made me mad," said the new Dougall. "Come on, Roly!"

"Dougall, I *forbid* you to go to that pantry! You're *drunk*!"

"Sommum atta dowa," said Roly faithfully.

"Well, *you* told me to stop worrying and have one or two drinks!"

"One or *two*! You don't know what you're *doing*!—and you're forgetting Doreen! At this very minute your baby's being——"

229

Roly, his loyalty to the unknown bell-ringer bursting all human ties, flung open the front door, and Magill hurried in with a rapid thank you.

"I'm sorry to trouble you so late at night, Lady Buckering," he said resolutely, "but I've got something urgent to tell you; it won't take a minute——"

"Really!" protested Cathleen indignantly, coming into the hall at the sound of his voice. "This is too much! You might have spared my mother any more——"

"Cathleen!" he said aggressively. "You've got to listen to what I have to say!"

"We intend to pay you the moment we can," Cathleen said in a high, clear voice. "Is there anything else to discuss? I don't think so!"

"Stop acting all over the goddam shop and listen, will you?" exhorted Magill masterfully. "My old man's at the bottom of all this schemozzle, not me!"

"I don't care! Do you hear? I don't *care*!" said Cathleen stormily.

"As long as he's here, I can't see what you lose by hearing what he has to say," Daisy interceded as excitedly as her daughter. "What can he possibly have to say that he hasn't said already? —unless it's a new ultimatum from his father!"

"Will you, for the love of Pete, let me get a word in edgeways? I'm not with the firm any more! I was sacked this evening! The reason why my father wouldn't accept those shares is because he knew you were broke and didn't *want* the rent paid . . . he wanted to evict. Does that sink in? He *wanted* to evict!"

"Then why didn't you let him?" Cathleen demanded heatedly.

"Because I didn't know anything about it till just now! He wants to sell this whole corner block. . . . There's nothing the matter with those shares—they're at par!"

"Par? Par?" echoed Daisy, her head swimming. "You mean they're *good*?"

"As sound as a bell. Sound as the Rock of Ages. Solid as the Bank of England!"

Daisy gave a wild laugh.

"Dougall, did you hear that?" she demanded exultantly. "They're good—" She turned round, and found Dougall and Roly gone.

"Oh, my *stars*!" she cried, with a heartfelt little scream. They're at Corder!"

CHAPTER TWENTY TWO

This Is The Climax

ROLY, from his perch on Corder's head, watched with warm approval and admiration while Dougall went systematically through his pockets. Corder was a poor adversary. He had gone down with an eldritch squawk and now lay quite still, his breath knocked out of him and his ears singing mournfully. Once, when Dougall dug into his waistcoat pockets he giggled lugubriously, being ticklish ; but for the most part, the bounce was out of him.

"Maybe he's swallowed it !" suggested Roly at last.

"Blimey !" said Dougall, looking up, thwarted.

"Dissembowlim," said Roly. "Kitchen knife'd do it. Left to right, under the ribs, like in hari·kari."

"Okay, roll him over," said Dougall, nothing if not thorough.

"No, no !" shrieked Corder, unmanned. "It's in the tea·caddy on the shelf over the stove ! I swear it !"

"Tea·caddy, tea·caddy !" said Roly rapidly, rolling off Corder and racing Dougall for it.

They seized it, dropped it, picked it up, dropped it again, scattered tea like confetti at a wedding, and finally unearthed the ring, wrapped in a twist of paper with a gold·tooth and a locket.

Dougall gave a war·whoop, vaulted Corder, fell over a chair, caught his foot in its rungs, brought down a column of pots, and leap-frogged vaingloriously into the hall roaring for Daisy.

"We've got it, we've got it! He did have it!" he bellowed triumphantly. "Hullo, Magill! . . . You can call off your bloodhounds; we found it! *And* this, Daisy!" he added, thrusting the locket into her hands.

"Why, that's *mine*!" cried Daisy, transported.

"*And* a gold tooth—who did he get that from?"

"It must be his," said Daisy. "Oh, Dougall, how *wonderful* of you !—*and* you, Roly !"

"Think nothin' of it," Roly assured her grandly, and submitted himself tolerantly to a feverish examination by Bicky for possible battle-scars.

Sydney, coming down the stairs, had to raise his voice to be heard above the general din.

"Hey—father !" he called perseveringly. Daisy heard him first and looked up in a transport of giddily conflicting emotions.

"Sydney !—is it *here*? Everything all right?" she peppered at him.

"Perfect," he assured her. "Doreen's fine."

"Which is it?"

"A boy !"

"A boy ! Oh, Dougall, how wonderful !"

She seized the blankly uncomprehending Dougall and kissed him warmly. "Congratulations, Dougall darling ! It's a *boy* !"

"What is?" asked Dougall mistily.

"Your *son* !"

"My . . .?" His voice suddenly went very weak and falsetto. "Yes, but . . . but I . . . it can't be . . . we weren't expecting it yet. . . ."

He laughed unsteadily and pulled at his collar. "You're not just imagining . . .?"

Sydney shook his head, and Dougall shook *his* head, to confirm it, and then the fog lifted and he looked slowly round at everyone, and then choked and said: "Daisy, it's here! . . ." and then back at Drew for further confirmation, and then louder, "It's here! . . . Jiminy! I'm a father! . . . It's a boy!"

His voice cracked and he began to laugh and cry at the same time. "Can I see her—it—him?" and then very loudly he laughed, and hiccuped it into a sob, and cried, "*Doreen!*" and flew up the stairs at a gallop.

CHAPTER TWENTY THREE

This Is The Post-Mortem

" IT'S quite extraordinary, Daisy. There's absolutely *nothing* to it ! "

" Well, there you are, you see, dear ! "

" No, but really—I mean, I'm not just *saying* it, now it's all over. There was absolutely nothing to it ! Old Sydney was a bit overdue with a whiff of chloroform now and then, but by and large, it was as easy as shelling peas ! "

" Well, now. "

" He *is* beautiful, isn't he? Such a *lovely* shade of red ! "

" He's divine, dear. My goodness, me a grandmother ! "

" And me a mother. "

" And me a father, " said Dougall, preening.

" *Dear* Dougall ! I *am* so glad I managed a boy ! I *do* love you so, Dougall ! "

" I wish I could tell you how much I love *you* ! "

" I was a pig to you. "

" No, you were not ! "

" Yes, I was. "

" You were an angel. Wasn't she, Daisy? "

" Yes, dear. "

" Poor Dougall. Did you suffer *awfully* while it was happening. "

"Yes, he did, darling," said Daisy quickly. "It was harrowing to watch! He was *much* worse than Mike!"

"I *was* scared before, you know. I was afraid of the pain. I thought Sydney would cheat at the last minute and go stoic on me, and not give me any anaesthetic."

"I'd have bust him on the nose if he had!" said Dougall fiercely.

"Dougall."

"Yes, Doreen?"

"I want another baby."

"Coo cor suffering blimey!"

"As soon as we can. So Michael won't grow up an only child, and be lonely, or spoiled."

"Well, there's plenty of time to think about *that*," Daisy said cheerfully.

"But you *would* like another, wouldn't you, Dougall?"

"Of *course* I would, Doreen! . . . but . . . I mean, can we afford one?" he said humbly.

"I don't care if we can't. I'll manage somehow. I'm sure if we try and live life the right way, things'll turn out all right. And I *know* now, that the thing to do is have as big a family as possible, and give them a nice home like Daisy's so that they get a good start in life. I don't ever want to be possessive, or stuff my own ideas down their necks, or make them think they were just born for our convenience. I want them to have minds of their own, the way Daisy's left us to work out things for ourselves. We've always got her to run to, if we get in a jam, but she's never bullied us, or terrorised us, or been possessive. I thought about you a lot while I was half-woozy, Daisy; and I kept saying over and over, I'm going to be as good a mother as Daisy, please God; because she's been wonderful."

"Oh, dear," said Daisy in a small voice, "you've made me cry!"

" What Doreen says goes for me double," asserted Dougall stoutly, shuffling his feet shyly and rubbing his nose.

" I know now," Doreen continued, " that if you *believe* in the right things, and *feel* the right things, everything else looks after itself. The ravens fly over and drop a couple of ounces of manna, and maybe *one* locust every now and then, as a bonus for being extra specially good . . . but I *do* believe in the ravens now, Daisy, and I'm not afraid of the future any more; and I'm sure of myself. And I *do* love my Dougall !' "

" I'm very proud of you, Sydney !"

" Thanks, Daisy. Did my best, you know. Easy job; no complications. Lot to be thankful for."

" Do you always talk like that after a confinement case?"

" Well, dammit, I'm tired !"

" Gerda's making some coffee. She'll be in in a moment. We haven't got a butler any more, you know."

" Oh?"

" Of course, I haven't told you the *great* news yet !"

" What's that?"

" Do you remember some shares Mike once bought?"

" I remember but too well !"

" Well, some of them are good !"

" Oh?"

" What do you mean. *Oh?* You *are* a stuffy old fussbudget sometimes, Sydney !"

" Well, it's very nice, Daisy . . . but who said they were good?"

" Mr. Magill !"

" Cathleen's boy friend?'

" Yes."

" And he knows?"

" He checked with some brokers.'

237

" Oh. Then you're rich? "

" Yes, I am. "

" How rich? "

" I'm not sure, off hand. "

" Thousands and thousands of pounds? "

" Not quite . . . but six or seven hundred. "

" My, my ! "

" Is that all you've got to say? "

" What are you going to do with it? "

" Oh . . . fix up the house, and buy clothes for Bicky, and pay all my bills. "

" Daisy. "

" Yes? "

" Remember my putting a proposition to you earlier last night? "

" Yes, Sydney. "

" Well . . .? "

" Well, what? "

" Is it still yes? "

" Did I *say* yes? "

" Yes, you jolly well *did* ! "

" Well, of course it's yes, then, Sydney dear. . . . You *are* sure we're not too old to go skipping about romantically? "

" *I* may be. *You're* not ! "

" *Nice* Sydney ! "

" Daisy ! "

" Yes? "

" I . . . I just wanted to thank you. "

" Whatever for, Sydney? "

" For everything. . . . For wanting me. After all these years. I'm an awfully boring old josser. And my jokes are terrible. I've got into the habit of them, from doing it professionally. But I love you more now than I did when I was a flap-eared young chump, and that's a fact ! "

238

" Sydney, *dear* ! "

" You're still so confoundedly pretty, Daisy. You've just turned your back on time and taken life at your own tempo. I look like your father."

" Then we'll buy you a lovely toupe. Parted at the side and done *very* swagger, in a cow's lick."

" Thanks, Daisy ! "

Gerda came in with the coffee.

" I left Cathleen and her gennlemun friend in the kitchen," she said. " They're making welsh rarebit. They said to ask you if you wanted one."

" Not for me," said Sydney.

" Nor me," said Daisy.

" How goes the enemy ? " added Sydney.

" It's half-past two."

" Past everybody's bed-time."

" Tired, Gerda dear ? "

" Yes, I am a bit, Sydney."

" Yes ? "

" Thanks for your little dissertation in the spare room. I didn't quite follow you at the time, but it's made good sense since."

" I'm glad, Gerda."

" We've . . . broken up."

" I rather felt you might."

" I got things straightened out at last. I know, now, that he needs somebody else . . . and that he'll find her, when he begins to look properly."

" And what about you ? "

Gerda made no answer, and he added, " You need somebody else, too."

" Maybe," she said quietly.

" What is it, Gerda ? " he prompted gently.

"It was what Wilfred said about us being second-hand goods, and set in our habits. . . . One *does* get used to habits. They're hard to break. Bad ones, even harder than good ones, I suppose. I can't help feeling . . . I can't help feeling *sorry* for him. . . ."

"It's a fine thing to feel; but it's a poor substitute for unquestioning trust and respect. He'll play on your sympathies as long as you let him, until he's learned to stand on his own feet again."

"There's a thing about loving people . . . it's different from being *in* love with them. It's different from trusting them or respecting them. And it's stronger. What'll I do, Sydney, if I go *on* loving him?"

"Wait and see if you do," said Sydney at last, "and *if* you do, and it *is* stronger than anything else, I know one thing. He'll always want you back. Maybe he's woken up to one or two blunt home truths with a bump. Nobody's entirely wicked, or entirely good, you know. They vary with the amount of faith they have in themselves. Maybe he'll change. Maybe you will. Just wait and see, and don't hurry anything. Don't feel that invisible chains bind you, because as long as you feel that, you won't be thinking straight. He may grow up, yet. Some people never do; and others do it late, the hard way. I honestly don't know which category he comes under. It's up to him to prove himself to you, Gerda; and up to you to judge wisely, when he does."

She nodded slowly.

"Some of him *is* grown up," she said at last. "I suppose it grew up too soon, and left the rest too far behind. Some of him is wise. But it's all jumbled up with what isn't wise. He doesn't know, himself, where the one stops and the other begins. I . . . I do hope . . . he comes out of it all right."

"So do we," said Daisy gently.